THE THEORY OF CELESTIAL INFLUENCE

The Theory of

CELESTIAL

INFLUENCE

MAN, THE UNIVERSE, AND COSMIC MYSTERY

by RODNEY COLLIN

SAMUEL WEISER
New York
1975

First Published 1954
Fourth Impression 1971
This American Edition 1973
Second Impression 1974

Diagrams by
Richard Guyatt and D. Bell Scott

© Rodney Collin

ISBN 0-87728-043-6
Library of Congress Card No. 73-76952

SAMUEL WEISER, INC.
734 Broadway
New York, N. Y. 10003

MAGISTRO MEO
QUI SOL FUIT EST ET ERIT
SYSTEMATIS NOSTRI
DICATUM

The whole world of six dimensions is filled with His bounty: where-soever thou lookest, it is making Him known.

JALLALEDIN RUMI: THE MATHNAWI, BOOK III (VERSE 3108)

> Look how the floor of heaven
> Is thick inlaid with patines of bright gold:
> There's not the smallest orb which thou behold'st
> But in his motion like an angel sings,
> Still quiring to the young-eyes Cherubins;
> Such harmony is in immortal souls.

SHAKESPEARE: THE MERCHANT OF VENICE (ACT. V, SCENE 1)

All the progress obtained by our cerebral effort consists in the ascertaining of material facts by ridiculously imperfect instruments, which make up in a certain degree however for the inefficiency of our organs. Every twenty years some unhappy enquirer, who generally dies in the attempt, discovers that the atmosphere contains a gas hitherto unknown, that an imponderable, inexplicable, unqualifiable force can be obtained by rubbing a piece of wax on cloth; that among the innumerable unknown stars, there is one that has not yet been noticed in the immediate vicinity of another which has ... Well, what about it?

Our diseases are due to microbes? Very well. But where do those microbes come from? And what about *their* diseases? And the suns, whence do they come?

We know nothing, we understand nothing, we can do nothing, we guess nothing. We are shut up, imprisoned in ourselves ...

GUY DE MAUPASSANT: NOTEBOOK, APRIL 7, 1888

CONTENTS

APPENDICES

PLATES

LINE-DRAWINGS IN THE TEXT

INTRODUCTION

IN EVERY AGE MEN HAVE TRIED TO ASSEMBLE ALL THE KNOWLEDGE and experience of their day into a single whole which would explain their relation to the universe and their possibilities in it. In the ordinary way they could never succeed. For the unity of things is not realisable by the ordinary mind, in an ordinary state of consciousness. The ordinary mind, refracted by the countless and contradictory promptings of different sides of human nature, must reflect the world as manifold and confused as is man himself. A unity, a pattern, an all-embracing meaning – if it exists – could only be discerned or experienced by a different kind of mind, in a different state of consciousness. It would only be realisable by a mind which had itself become unified.

What unity, for example, could be perceived by even the most brilliant physicist, philosopher or theologian, while he still trips absent-mindedly over a stool, becomes angry at being short-changed, fails to notice when he irritates his wife, and in general remains subject to the daily trivial blindness of the ordinary mind, working with its customary absence of awareness? Any unity he reaches in such a state can exist only in his imagination.

Thus the attempt to gather all knowledge into a whole has always been connected with the search for a new state of consciousness. And it is meaningless and futile apart from such a search.

Perhaps it may even be said that the few successful attempts that have come down to us show signs of being only the by-products of such a search, *when it has proved successful*. The only convincing 'models of the universe' in existence are those left by men who evidently achieved a completely different relation to the world and consciousness of it from that belonging to ordinary experience.

For such true 'models of the universe' must not only display the inner form and structure of this universe, but must also reveal man's relation to it and his present and possible fates within it. In this sense, certain of the Gothic cathedrals are complete models of the universe, whereas a modern planetarium, for all its beauty, knowledge and accuracy, is not. For the latter model completely omits man. The difference, of course, lies in the fact that the cathedrals, directly or indirectly, were designed by men who belonged to schools for the achievement of higher states of consciousness, and had the advantage of experience gained in such schools; whereas the designers of the planetarium are scientists and technicians, clever and qualified enough in their field, but claiming no particular knowledge of the potentialities of the human machine with which they have to work.

In fact, if we are in possession of certain keys for their interpretation, the most astonishing thing about these ancient 'models of the universe' arising in widely separated ages, continents and cultures, is precisely their similarity. So much so that a good case might be made out for the idea that *higher consciousness always reveals the same truth*, solely on the basis of a comparative study of certain existing models of the universe which seem to derive therefrom – for example, the Cathedral of Chartres, the Great Sphinx, the New Testament, the Divine Comedy, or certain cosmic diagrams left by the 17th century alchemists, the designers of the Tarot pack, and the painters of some Russian ikons and Tibetan banners.

Of course, one of the chief difficulties in the way of such comparative study lies in the fact that all these models are expressed in different languages, and that to the ordinary unprepared mind different language implies different truth. This is in fact a characteristic illusion of man's ordinary state. Even a small improvement in his perception reveals, on the contrary, that the same language, the same formulation may cover diametrically opposed understandings, whereas languages and formulations which at first sight have nothing in common may in fact refer to the same thing. For instance, while the words 'honour', 'love', 'democracy' are universally used, it is almost impossible to find two people who attach the same meaning to them. That is to say, different uses of the same word may be quite incomparable. On the other hand – strange though it may seem – the Cathedral of Chartres, a pack of Tarot cards, and certain many-armed and many-headed bronzes of Tibetan deities, are in fact *formulations of exactly the same ideas*, that is, they are directly comparable.

It thus becomes necessary at this point to consider the question of language in relation to the construction of a model of the universe, the delineation of a pattern of unity. Fundamentally, language or form of expression is divided according as it appeals to one or another of man's functions, familiar or potential. For example, a certain idea may be expressed in philosophical or in scientific language, to appeal to man's intellectual function; it may be expressed in religious or poetic language to appeal to his emotional function; it may be expressed in ritual or in dances to appeal to his motor function; it may even be expressed in scents or in physical postures to appeal to his instinctive physiology.

Of course, the more complete 'models of the universe' created by schools in the past aimed at combining formulations of what they wished to express in many languages, so as to appeal to several or all functions at once, and thus partly offset the contradiction between different sides of man's nature already referred to. In the cathedral, for example, the languages of poetry, posture, ritual, music, scent, art and architecture were successfully combined; and something similar appears to have been done in the dramatic representations of the Eleusinian mysteries. Again in certain cases, for instance in the Great Pyramid, the language of architecture seems to have been used not only for the symbolism of its form, but in order to create in a person passing through the building in a certain way a quite definite series of emotional impressions and shocks, which had a definite meaning in themselves, and which were calculated to reveal the very nature of the person exposed to them.

All this refers to objective use of language – that is, the use of a definite language to convey a definite idea with previous knowledge of the effect which will be created, the function which will be affected, and the type of person who will respond. Again we have to admit that such objective use of language is not ordinarily known – except perhaps in an elementary form in advertising – and that its higher use can only derive, directly or indirectly, from knowledge gained in higher states of consciousness.

Besides these languages recognisable by man through his ordinary functions, there are other forms of language arising from and appealing to supernormal functions, that is, functions which can be developed in man, but which he does not ordinarily enjoy. For instance, there is the language of higher emotional function, where one formulation has the power of conveying an enormous number of meanings – either simultaneously or in succession. Some of the finest poetry, which can never be exhausted, and which, though it always yields something fresh, can never be fully understood, may belong to this category. More evidently, the Gospels are written in such language, and for this reason their every verse can convey to a hundred men *a hundred different but never contradictory meanings*.

In the language of higher emotional function, and particularly of higher intellectual function, symbols play a very large part. For symbols are based on an understanding of true analogies between a greater cosmos and a smaller, a form or function or law in one cosmos being used to hint at the corresponding forms, functions and laws in other cosmoses. This understanding belongs exclusively to higher or potential functions in man, and must always produce a sense of bafflement and even frustration when approached by ordinary functions, such as that of logical thought.

Still higher degrees of emotional language need no external expression whatsoever, and therefore *cannot be misunderstood*.

This digression about language is necessary in order to explain in part the form of the present book. For this too, it must be admitted, purports to be a 'model of the universe' – that is, an assembly or outline of available knowledge, arranged in order to demonstrate a cosmic whole or unity.

It is, indeed, couched in scientific language, and is thus primarily directed to the intellectual function, and to people in whom this function predominates. Certainly, the writer is well aware that this language is the slowest, most tedious, and in some ways the most difficult to follow of all languages. The language of good poetry, of myths or fairy-tales, for example, would be much more penetrating, and might carry the ideas with much greater force and swiftness into the reader's emotional understanding. Perhaps later an attempt in this direction may be possible.

At the same time, the reader accustomed to scientific language and thought will also encounter difficulties here. The free use of analogy throughout the book will seem to him an inconsistency. And for his benefit it were better to make a fuller explanation and a frank acknowledgment of the defects of this method in advance.

One of the main characteristics of modern thought is a contradiction between the way man regards the external world, outside himself, and the way he regards the internal world, inside himself.

As regards the external world, he has never been more objective, more convinced of the universal application of *laws*, expressable by formulae and consistently measurable in their effects. In this field, any belief which throws doubt on the principle of measurability, for example, any belief in intelligence or consciousness belonging to beings greater in scale than man, is in danger of being regarded as superstition.

As regards his internal world, on the other hand, man has rarely been more subjective, more convinced of the special validity of his every whim, imagination, hope and fear, and less willing to admit that his inner world is subject to any laws whatsoever. The greater part of modern psychology, and especially of psycho-analysis, has been based on this subjectivity. And in this field, it is precisely the belief in laws and measurability – for example, belief that much of human psychology is the result of the calculable interplay of types, or belief that man's inner world is subject to laws similar to those governing the astronomical or microscopic worlds – which is called superstition.

There have been previous periods when intelligence was seen as the ruling principle in both fields, for example, in the early Middle Ages. And there have been other periods when immutable law was seen as such, for example, in 18th century rationalism. But there has perhaps never been a period when there was such a blatant contradiction between man's attitudes towards the two.

When we find this contradiction in ordinary life, that is, when we meet a man who judges the world around him by one standard, and himself and his own actions by another and quite different standard, we take it as sign of a primitive and uncultured point of view. Yet when this same contradiction is the chief characteristic of the whole thought of our age, we call it enlightenment or emancipation. We do not see that it lies at the root of as much blindnesss, unhappiness, disappointment and moral bankruptcy, as it would in an individual case.

One of the aims of this book is precisely to try to heal this contradiction – to look at man and his inner life from the same point of view as we look at the universe. And to look at the universe from the same point of view as we look at man and his inner life. If the attempt smacks of superstition, it may, at least in part, be the palate of the time which is at fault.

In our attempt to reconcile the inner and outer world, however, we do come up against a very real difficulty, which must be faced. This difficulty is connected with the problem of reconciling *different methods of knowing*.

Man has two ways of studying the universe. The first is by induction: he examines phenomena, classifies them, and attempts to infer laws and principles from them. This is the method generally used by science. The second is by deduction: having perceived or had revealed or discovered certain general laws and principles, he attempts to deduce the application of these laws in various specialised studies and in life. This is the method generally used by religion. The first method begins with 'facts' and attempts to reach 'laws'. The second method begins with 'laws' and attempts to reach 'facts'.

These two methods belong to the working of different human functions. The first is the method of the ordinary logical mind, which is permanently available to us. The second derives from a potential function in man, which is ordinarily inactive for lack of nervous energy of sufficient intensity, and which we may call higher mental function. This function, on the rare occasions of its operation, reveals to man *laws in action*, he sees the whole phenomenal world as the *product of laws*.

All true formulations of universal laws derive recently or remotely from the working of this higher function, somewhere and in some man. At the same time, for the application and understanding of the laws revealed in the long stretches of time and culture when such revelation is not available, man has to rely on the ordinay logical mind

In fact, this is recognised today in scientific thought. In his 'Nature of the Universe' (1950), Fred Hoyle writes: "The procedure in all branches of physical science, whether in Newton's theory of gravitation, Maxwell's theory of electromagnetism, Einstein's theory of relativity, or the quantum theory, is at root the same. It consists of two steps. The first is to guess *by some sort of inspiration* a set of mathematical equations. The second step is to associate the symbols used in the equations with measurable physical quantities." [1] The difference between the work of these two minds could not be better put.

But here the great quandary of human understanding arises. For these two minds can never ordinarily understand each other. There is too great a difference in speed between them. Just as communication is impossible between a peasant plodding along a road with a load of sticks and a car which flashes past him at eighty miles an hour, *because of their difference in speed*, so is communication ordinarily impossible between logical mind and higher mind, for the same reason. To logical mind, the traces left by higher mind will seem arbitrary, superstitious, illogical, unproven. To higher mind, the work of logical mind will seem ponderous, unnecessary, and beside the point. [2]

In the ordinary way, this difficulty is overcome by keeping these two methods quite separate, giving them different labels and different fields of action. Books on religion, or on higher mathematics, which deal in laws and principles, abstain from the method of induction. Books on science, which deal in accumulations of observed facts, abstain from presuming laws in advance. And since quite different people write and read the one kind and the other kind of book, or the same people read them with quite separate parts of their minds, the two methods manage to exist together without too much friction.

In the present book, however, the two methods are employed simultaneously. Certain great principles and laws of the universe, which have found expression in different countries and in all ages, and which from time to time are rediscovered by individual men through the momentary working

1. Examples of this 'scientific illumination' are given in Appendix I.

2. The irreconcilability of these two ways of looking at the universe is described in its origins by P. D. Ouspensky in 'A New Model of the Universe', chapter viii, pp. 341-2 (English edition).

of a higher function, are frankly taken for granted. From them deductions are made downwards into the world of phenomena ordinarily accessible to us, largely by the method of analogy. At the same time, an attempt is made to study and classify 'facts' and phenomena about us, and by inference to arrange these in such a way that the classifications lead upwards towards the abstract laws descending from above.

In fact – for the reason given above, that they derive from different functions with widely different speeds – the two methods never quite meet. Between the admissible deductions from general laws and the admissible inferences from facts there always remains an invisible belt, where the two *should* and *must* join, but where such joining remains always unseen and unproven.

For these reasons, the writer is prepared to admit that the plan of the present book – endeavouring to reconcile the two methods – may be an impossible one. He realises that such an attempt inevitably involves a kind of sleight-of-hand, almost chicanery. And he also realises that this sleight-of-hand will in no way deceive the professional scientist, wedded exclusively to the logical method.

At the same time he is convinced on the one hand that present-day science, *without principles*, is headed towards ever more pointless specialisation and materalism; and on the other hand that religious or philosophical principles, uncoordinated with the scientific knowledge which characterises our age, can today appeal only to a minority. This conviction persuades him to take a risk. Those who use the logical method exclusively will never be satisfied by the arguments given, which – let it be admitted – do contain logical flaws and gaps. On the other hand, for those who are willing to accept both methods, it is hoped to present sufficient evidence to enable each reader to attempt to bridge the gap between the world of everyday fact and the world of great laws – *for himself*.

This task can never be performed in any book, nor would more facts or more knowledge, ordinarily available to science either now or in the future, ever make this possible. But, with help and effort, *it can be performed by each individual to his own satisfaction*.

Meanwhile, to the ordinary man, interested in his own fate but not particularly in science, it can only be said that perhaps, on closer examination, he may find this book in fact not so 'scientific' as it at first appears. Scientific language is the fashionable language of the day, just as the language of psychology was the fashionable language thirty years ago, the language of passion the fashionable language in Elizabethan times, and the language of religion the fashionable language of the Middle Ages. When people are induced to buy toothpaste or cigarettes by pseudo-scientific arguments and explanations, evidently this in some way corresponds to the mentality of the age, and truths must also be scientifically expressed.

At the same time, this is not to suggest that the scientific language used is a disguise, a pretence or a falsification. The explanations given are, as far as it has been possible to verify, quite correct and they correspond to actual facts.[3] What is claimed is that the principles used could with equal correctness be applied to any other form of human experience, with equally or more interesting results. And that it is *these principles which are of importance*, rather than the sciences to which they are applied.

Where do these principles come from? To answer this question, it becomes necessary to acknowledge my complete indebtedness to one man, and to explain to a certain extent how this indebtedness came about.

I first met Ouspensky in London, where he was giving private lectures, in September 1936. These 'lectures' referred to an extraordinary system of knowledge, quite incomparable with anything I had encountered before, which he had received from a man whom he called 'G'. This system, however, was not new: on the contrary it was said to be a very ancient one, which had always existed in hidden form and traces of which could from time to time be seen coming to the surface of history in one guise or another. Although it explained in an extraordinary way countless things about man and the universe, which had seemed hitherto quite inexplicable, its sole purpose – as O. constantly stressed – was to help individual men *to awake to a different level of consciousness.*

Any attempts to use this knowledge for other and more ordinary purposes he discouraged or forbade altogether.

Yet despite the staggering completeness of this 'system' in itself, one could never entirely separate it from the 'being' of the man who expounded it, from O. himself. When anyone else tried to explain it, the 'system' degenerated, lost quality in some way. And although no one could entirely neutralise the great strength of the ideas in themselves, it was clear that the 'system' could not be taken apart from a man of a certain quite unusual level of consciousness and being. For only such a man could induce in

---

3. Even 'facts', however, are not sacred. Of two recognised and reputed scientists, writing in two books published in England in the same year (1950), one states as a 'fact' that the moon is moving away from the earth, the other equally categorically that it is moving towards it.

others the fundamental changes of understanding and attitude which were necessary to grasp it.

This 'system', in the pure and abstract form in which it was originally given, has been recorded once and for all by Ouspensky himself in his *In Search of the Miraculous*. Anyone who wishes to compare the original principles with the deductions which have here been made, would do well to read that book first. They will then find themselves in a position to judge whether the applications and developments of the ideas are legitimate. And in fact, from their own point of view, it will be *their duty* so to judge.

Personally, I felt myself at a crossroads at the time, and on the first occasion I saw O. in private – at his crowded little rooms in Gwyndyr Road – I told him that I was a writer by nature, and I asked his advice upon the courses which then lay open to me. He said, very simply, „Better not to get too involved. Later we may find something for you to write."

It was typical of the strange confidence that O. inspired that this seemed a complete answer to my problem – or rather, I felt that I no longer had to worry about it, it had been taken from me. In fact, as a result of this conversation, for just over ten years I wrote practically nothing at all. There was too much else to do. But in the end O. kept his promise. And the outline of the present book was written in the two months immediately before his death, in October 1947, as a direct result of what he was trying to achieve and show at that time. Later, a second book, continuing where this leaves off, was written after his death.

During the ten years' interval, O. expounded to us in countless ways – theoretical, philosophical and practical – all the different sides of the 'system'. When I arrived, many of those with him had already been studying in this way, and endeavouring to penetrate to the result he indicated, for ten or fifteen years, and they were able to help a newcomer like myself to understand very much of what was and what was not possible. O. tirelessly explained, tirelessly showed us our illusions, tirelessly pointed the way – yet so subtly that if one was not ready to understand, his lessons could pass one by, and it was only years later that one might remember the incident, and realise what he had been demonstrating. More violent methods may be possible, but these can also leave scars that are difficult to heal.

O. never worked for the moment. It might even be said that he did not work for time – he worked only for recurrence. But this needs much explanation. In any case, he quite evidently worked and planned with a completely different sense of time from the rest of us, though to those who

impatiently urged him to help them achieve quick results, he would say:
"No, time is a factor. You can't leave it out."

So the years passed. Yet although very much indeed was achieved, it
often seemed to us that O. was too far ahead of us, that he had something
which we had not, something which made certain possibilities practical
for him that remained theoretical for us, and which for all his explaining,
we did not see how to get. Some essential key seemed missing. Later, this
key was shown. But that is a different story.

O. went to America during the war. In connection with this strange
unfolding of possibilities which went by the name of O's 'lectures', I remember how in New York about 1944 he gave us a task which he said
would be interesting for us. This was to 'classify the sciences', according
to the principles which had been explained in the system; to classify them
according to the worlds which they studied. He referred to the last classification
of the sciences – by Herbert Spencer – and said that though it was interesting, it was not very satisfactory from our point of view nor from the
point of view of our time. He also wrote to his friends in England about
this task. It was only when the present book was nearing completion, some
five years later, that I realised that it was in fact one answer to O's task.

O. returned to England in January 1947. He was old, ill and very weak.
But he was also something else. He was a different man. So much of the
vigorous, whimsical, brilliant personality, which his friends had known and
enjoyed for so many years, had been left behind, that many meeting him
again were shocked, baffled, or else were given a quite new understanding
of what was possible in the way of development.

In the bitter early spring of 1947 he called several large meetings in
London of all the people who had previously listened to him, and of others
who never had. He spoke to them in a new way. He said that he abandoned
the system. He asked them what they wanted, and said that only from
that could they begin on the way of self-remembering and consciousness.

It is difficult to convey the impression created. For twenty years
in England before the war, O. had almost daily explained the system. He
had said that everything must be referred to it, that things could only be
understood in relation to it. To those who had listened to him the system
represented the explanation of all difficult things, pointed the way to all
good things. Its words and its language had become more familiar to them
than their mother tongue. How could they 'abandon the system'?

And yet, to those who listened with positive attitude to what he now
had to say, it was suddenly as though a great burden had been taken from

them. They realised that in the way of development true knowledge must first be acquired and then abandoned. That exactly what makes possible the opening of one door may make impossible the opening of the next. And some for the first time began to gain an idea where lay that missing key which might admit them to the place where O. was and where they were not.

After this O. retired to his house in the country, saw very few people, hardly spoke. Only he now demonstrated, now performed in actuality and in silence, that change of consciousness the theory of which he had explained so many years.

The story of those months can not be told here. But at dawn one September day a fortnight before his death, after a strange and long preparation, he said to a few friends who were with him: "You must start again. You must make a new beginning. You must reconstruct everything for yourselves – from the very beginning."

This then was the true meaning of 'abandoning the system'. Every system of truth must be abandoned, in order that it may grow again. He had freed them from one expression of truth which might have become dogma, but which instead may blossom into a hundred living forms, affecting every side of life.

Most important of all, 'reconstructing everything for oneself' evidently meant 'reconstructing everything in oneself', that is, actually creating in oneself the understanding which the system had made possible and achieving the aim of which it spoke – *actually and permanently overcoming the old personality and acquiring a quite new level of consciousness.*

Thus if the present book may be taken as a 'reconstruction', it is only an external reconstruction, so to speak, a representation of the body of ideas we were given, in one particular form and in one particular language. Despite its scientific appearance, it has no importance whatsoever as a compendium of scientific facts or even as a new way of presenting these facts. Any significance it may have can only lie in its being derived, though at second hand, from the actual perceptions of higher consciousness, and in its indicating a path by which such consciousness may be again approached.

R. C.

Lyne, August 1947
Tlalpam, April 1953

I THE STRUCTURE OF THE UNIVERSE

I THE ABSOLUTE

PHILOSOPHICALLY, MAN CAN SUPPOSE AN ABSOLUTE. SUCH AN Absolute would include all possible dimensions both of time and space. That is to say:

It would include not only the whole universe which man can perceive or imagine, but all other such universes which may lie beyond the power of his perception.

It would include not only the present moment of all such universes, but also their past and their future, whatever past and future may mean on their scale.

It would include not only everything actualised in all the past, present and future of all universes, but also everything that potentially could be actualised in them.

It would include not only all possibilities for all existing universes, but also all potential universes, even though they do not exist, nor ever have.

Such a conception is philosophical for us. Logically, it must be like that, but our mind is unable to come to grips with the formula or make any sense of it.

The moment we think about the Absolute, we have to think of it as modified in some way or other. We have to think of it in the form of some body, or quality, or law. For such is the limitation of our mind.

Now the effect or influence of any body upon another varies in three ways:

(a) In inverse proportion to the square of its distance [4] – this effect we measure as *radiation*, or the active effect of the greater upon the less.

(b) In direct proportion to its mass – this effect we measure as *attraction*, or the passive effect of the greater upon the less.

(c) In direct proportion to its distance – this effect we measure as *time*, or the delaying effect between the emission of the influence of the greater and its reception by the less.

These constitute in effect the first three modifications of unity, *the first three modifications of the Absolute.*

---

4. That is, at *twice* the distance only a *quarter* the amount of influence is felt.

I

Let us imagine a ball of white-hot iron, which represents unity. Its composition, weight, size, temperature and radiance constitute one thing, one being. But its effect upon all that surrounds it develops according to three factors – it *lights and warms* them in inverse proportion to the square of its distance; it *pulls* them in direct proportion to its mass; and it *affects them after a delay* in direct proportion to its distance. If its mass and radiation are constant, then this third factor, although actually present, remains invisible and immeasurable. But for all objects standing in different relations to the radiant ball the combined effect of these three factors will be different and distinct. Thus the variations in the effect of the radiant unity, through the interaction of these three factors, become infinite.

Here, however, we are already positing two things – a radiant unity and its surroundings. Let us instead imagine a single ball of which the south pole is white-hot and the north pole at absolute zero. If we suppose this ball or sphere to be fixed in shape, size and mass, the greater the heat of the south pole, the greater the rarefaction of matter in its neighbourhood, and in consequence the greater the condensation of matter in the neighbourhood of the cold pole. If this process is carried to infinity, radiation and mass become entirely separated, the south pole representing as it were pure radiation and the north pole pure mass.

Now, *actually within the sphere itself*, these three factors – radiation, attraction and time – will create an infinite number of physical conditions, an infinite number of relations to either pole. The three modifications of unity will have created infinite variety.

Any point in the sphere will receive a definite amount of radiation from the south pole, will feel a definite degree of attraction for the north pole, and will be separated from both poles (either in receiving impulses from or reflecting back impulses to them) by definite periods of time. These three factors will together make a formula which will provide a perfect definition of any particular point on the sphere, and which will exactly indicate its nature, possibilities and limitations.

If we call the south pole heaven and the north pole hell we have a figure representing the Absolute of religion. At present, however, our task is to apply this concept to the Absolute of astrophysics, to that picture of the Whole, which modern science is struggling to discern through the unfathomable distances and unimaginable durations now opening before it.

We have to imagine the whole surface of our universal sphere, with its two poles of radiation and attraction, to be speckled with galaxies in growth, as the whole surface of the sun is speckled with whirlpools of fire.

This 'growth' of galaxies implies expansion from a pole of absolute oneness in light to infinite extension of multiplicity and distance; then contraction back to a pole of absolute oneness in matter. Yet the poles of light and matter are but opposite ends of the same axis. And all this 'growth' is but *the surface of the universe in eternity.* [4a]

This universal sphere is not subject to human measurement or human logic. Attempted measurements of it made in different ways reduce each other to absurdity, and equally plausible deductions about it lead to diametrically opposite conclusions. Nor is this surprising when we remember that it is the sphere of all imaginable and unimaginable possibilities.

For instance, looking out from our infinitesimal point within a point within a point upon the surface of this sphere, men can now photograph with telescopes galaxies from which the light takes a thousand million years to reach us. That is to say, they picture these galaxies as they were a thousand million years ago. Yet at the same time modern science believes this whole infinite sphere to have been created only five thousand million years ago, in a single momentary explosion of light in a single place, which has been expanding ever since. Very well; supposing telescopes were built five times more penetrating than those that exist today. Astronomers would then see the creation of the universe. *They would see the creation of our own universe at the beginning of time, by infinite penetration into distance.*

Such anomalies are only possible in a universal sphere of the kind we have imagined, where one pole represents radiation or the point of creation the other pole attraction or the point of extinction, and where all points are both connected and separated by the endless curved surface of time.

From one point of view all galaxies, all worlds may be seen as moving slowly from the pole of radiation to the equator of maximum expansion, only to dwindle again to the final pole of mass. From another point of view, it may be the life-force, the consciousness of the Absolute itself, which is making this everlasting pilgrimage. And again, by our very definition of the Absolute, all parts, possibilities, times and conditions of this universal sphere must exist together, simultaneously and eternally, ever changing and ever remaining the same.

In such a sphere all the different concepts of ancient and modern physics may be united. The whole sphere is that closed space first postulated by Riemann. The new idea of an expanding universe, doubling its dimensions every 1300 million years, is an expression of the movement from the pole

4a. See 'Modern Cosmology' by George Gamow in *Scientific American*, March 1954.

of radiation towards the equator of maximum expansion. Those who picture the universe as beginning with dead density and growing hotter and hotter towards some final death by absolute fire have their eyes on the movement from the pole of mass to the pole of radiation. Those who picture it as created in absolute fire and growing cooler and cooler towards final death by cold and condensation, have their eyes on the reverse movement. While Einstein, attempting with his intangible and immeasurable 'cosmic repulsion' to meet the necessity of a third force, adds to this picture of two poles the mediating and connecting surface of delay or time.

All these theories are right and all are wrong – as were those of the blind men in the Eastern story who, describing an elephant from their groping touch, said one that it was like a rope, another that it was like a pillar, and a third that it was like two hard spears.

All that we can say with truth is that the Absolute is One, and that within this one, three forces, differentiating themselves as radiation, attraction and time, between them create Infinity.

II   THE MILKY WAY IN THE WORLD OF SPIRAL NEBULAE

Within the Absolute we can, however, consider the largest units recognizable by man. These are the galactic nebulae, towards the middle of one of which, known as the Milky Way, exists our Solar System. Although the existence of other nebulae beyond our own only became known with modern telescopes, many millions are now within view and several hundreds have been clearly observed. The nearest is at 800,000 light-years distance, and stands to our Milky Way as one man at twenty paces from another.

The appearance of these nebulae, each of which consists of untold millions of stars, is very different. Some appear as lines of light, others lens-shaped, yet others as spirals in which streams of suns seem to pour out from the centre like a radiant shower. This variation is partly due to the stage of growth of the nebulae themselves, partly to the angle at which we see them.

Most mature nebulae, including our Milky Way, have in fact the same basic pattern. They are, *apparently*, vast wheels of stars, each separated by an infinity of distance from the others, yet each so immense that these stars, by their very number, appear to flow and stream like a gas or a liquid under the influence of some great centrifugal force. This force imparts to them a spiral motion or form, as a whirlwind in a sandy place imparts spiral motion to the column of dust it raises.

Doubtless our Milky Way also possesses such centrifugal form, but naturally this could be seen only from outside. To us, situated within its plane, it appears as a *curved line* or *arc* of light in the heavens above us. By contrast, we see the Sun as a *curved plane*, or *disk*, and magnified planets in the same way. While coming nearer still to our own scale, what we can explore of this earth is a *curved solid*, or the surface of a *ball*.

These three forms – an arc, a disk, and a ball – are those in which three great scales of celestial entities present themselves to man's perception. They are evidently not the real forms of these entities, for we know very well that seen from elsewhere the Milky Way, for instance, might appear not as a line, but, like other galaxies, as a whirling disk.

Yet these *apparent* forms of the heavenly worlds are very interesting and important. For they can tell us a great deal, not only about the structure of the universe, but also about man's perception, and thus about his relation to these worlds, and their relation to each other.

Now the relation between a curved solid, a curved plane, and a curved line is the relation between three dimensions, two dimensions and one dimension. So we can be said to perceive the earth in three dimensions, the Solar System in two dimensions, and the Milky Way in one dimension. Other galaxies we perceive only as points. While the Absolute we cannot perceive in any dimension at all – it is absolutely invisible.

Thus the scale of celestial worlds – Earth, Solar System, Milky Way, Totality of Galaxies, and Absolute – presents to man's perception a very special progression. With each ascent in this scale, a dimension becomes invisible to him. This curious 'loss' of a dimension is even apparent on levels beyond his perception, but which he can still imagine. In relation to the Solar System the earth is no longer a solid ball but a line of movement, while in relation to the Milky Way the Solar System is no longer a plane but a point. In each ease, a lower dimension 'disappears'.

At the same time, since *each cosmos is three-dimensional for itself*, that is, it possesses *its own* height, breadth and thickness, with each expansion of scale a new 'higher' dimension is added – one which is both unattainable and invisible to the lesser entity. A brick has its own height, breadth and thickness; but a whole course of bricks makes only one dimension – the breadth – of a house, whose height and thickness will be *higher* dimensions for the brick.

Similarly man, himself solid and three-dimensional – that is, having his own height, breadth and thickness – can travel all over the surface of the earth, the configuration of this surface creating on his scale the three-dimensional world in which he lives. On the earth's scale, however, this surface is only two-dimensional, a quite *new* third dimension being added – the thickness of the earth – which is unknowable and impenetrable by man. The third dimension of the earth is thus a higher and different kind of third dimension, incommensurable with the third dimension of man.

So in this great celestial hierarchy, each superior world appears to discard the lowest dimension of the world beneath it, and to add a new dimension above or beyond the reach of that world. Every such complete world exists in three dimensions of space, yet possesses one more dimension than that below, and one less than that above. This means that each world is *partly* invisible to those worlds greater and smaller than itself. But whereas it is the *lowest* dimension of the lesser world which disappears in relation to the greater, it is the *highest* dimension of the greater which is invisible to the lower.

From our point of view, the greater the celestial world the more of it must be invisible, while those parts of such higher worlds as are visible to man must always belong to their lower or more elementary aspects.

Now we may begin to understand better the meaning of this linear appearance of the Milky Way. It must mean that the real Milky Way is largely invisible. What we see is an illusion of our limited perception. The apparent 'arc of light' must be an effect of our *not seeing it in enough dimensions*.

When we see apparent lines or circles in our ordinary surroundings, we know very well what to do in order to investigate the bodies to which they belong. Either we move in relation to them, or we move them in relation to ourselves. Sitting down to table in a dim room I see what looks like a line of light; as I rise to look closer the line turns into a circle; I put out my hand towards it and grasp an object which turns out to be a glass. Before the glass was picked up only the rim caught by the light had been visible – first at eye-level and then from above. Now, as I turn it about in my hands, my changing relation to it in space and time reveals that it is neither a line nor a disk, but a solid body containing an interesting drink.

We cannot do this in relation to the Milky Way or other galaxies. On their scale we cannot by one iota change our position, in space or time. In relation to them we are fixed points, and there is no way in which we can alter our sight of them. Even the motions of the earth and sun produce no perceptible change in man's viewpoint in thousands of years; while these thousands of years, compared with the age of galaxies, have no duration at all. It is as if we were condemned all our lives to see only the rim of the glass. And we may equally suppose that it is but a rim or cross-section of the galaxy which men see, and always will with their bodily perception.

THE STRUCTURE OF THE UNIVERSE

What could be the real nature of the Milky Way, and its relation to other galaxies? What is a nebula for itself? We would be at a loss, were it not for the fact that the relation between the celestial worlds of Earth, Solar System and Milky Way must by analogy be parallelled in the inferior worlds of electrons, molecules and cells. For this relation between interpenetrating worlds is itself a cosmic constant, which may be verified both above and below. On its own scale – revealed by the microscope – a cell is a solid three-dimensional organism, but to man it is an immeasurable point. Thus between the microcosmic worlds the same addition and subtraction of dimensions may be observed. But with this difference – that here the nature and being of the superior world, its relation to and power over the lower worlds within it, may be known and studied. For that superior world is man himself.

Now the situation of our Solar System within the Milky Way is almost exactly that of a single blood-cell within the human body. A white corpuscle is also composed of a nucleus or sun, with its cytoplasm or sphere of influence, and it too is surrounded on all sides by untold millions of similar cells or systems, the whole forming a great being whose nature it could hardly be expected to imagine.

If, however, we compare the human body to some great body of the Milky Way, and one cell of it to our Solar System, and we wish to find a viewpoint comparable to that of a human astronomer on earth, we should have to try to imagine the perception of something like a single electron of a molecule of this cell. What could such an electron know about the human body? What indeed could it know about its cell, or even its molecule? Such organisms would be so vast, subtle, eternal and omnipotent in relation to it, that their true meaning would be utterly beyond its comprehension. Yet no doubt the electron could perceive something of its surrounding universe; and though this impression would be very far from reality, it is interesting for us to imagine it.

For these electrons, by the insignificance of their size and duration, would also, like men within the Milky Way, be fixed one-dimensional points, unable to change their view of their human universe by a single hair's-breadth. It is true that their cell would be travelling along its artery – as the Sun along its track in the Milky Way – and that this cell might be expected to make many thousand circuits of the great body within the course of its existence. But to the electron this would mean nothing, for in the whole duration of his spark of life, the cell would have advanced no measurable distance at all.

7

As points then, the electrons would look out upon a stationary cross-section of the human body, at right angles to the artery in which their cell was destined to move. This cross-section would constitute their visible universe, or the *present*. Within this universe they would first and above all be aware of the blazing nucleus of their cell, the source of all light and life for them and for the whole system of worlds in which they lived. Looking beyond this system into the zenith – that is, out of their cross-section and up into the artery – they would see nothing. For that would be where their cell and its universe was going in *the future*. Equally empty space would lie below them in the nadir. For that would be where their universe had come from, or *the past*.

If, however, they looked out along the present plane of their universe, they would see blazing on all sides what appeared to be a brilliant ring formed of an infinite number of other cell-nuclei or suns, more or less distant from their own. Were they of some shrewdness, they might realise that this ringlike appearance was an illusion due to the foreshortening of distance, and instead might suppose a vast disk of cells of which theirs was but one among many millions. Further, by measuring the density of the cellular cloud to the various points of the compass, they might even calculate that their own position lay near the centre or more to one or other edge of this disk. Thus they could locate their own system within its galaxy. For this disk or ringlike cloud would be their Milky Way.

In many ways, the discoveries of the electrons might parallel the discoveries of human astronomers, and they would find themselves faced by very similar problems. As they studied the Milky Way of other cells, and applied the subtlest methods of measurements, they might for instance gain the idea – as human astronomers have done in like circumstances – that all these cells or suns were imperceptibly receding outwards. From this human astronomers conclude that the suns of the Milky Way were all created together in a densely-packed mass, and have since been spreading outward from the middle in an ever-widening and ever-rarefying disk. They speak of an 'expanding universe'. Were the electrons to reach a similar conclusion regarding their universe they would, of course, be describing what happens in a cross-section of the human body after adolescence, when most cells no longer multiply, but the already existing cells spread, stretch, and becoming laden with water and fat, produce the effect of a body expanding in circumference.

At last, when they had exhausted speculation upon their Milky Way, the

8

electrons might descry, immeasurable far beyond its limits, but still upon the same plane, faint lines and clouds which appeared to be similar universes. These we would recognise as the cross-sections of other human bodies. But to the electrons they would be extra-galactic nebulae.

Now the study of these distant nebulae or universes might introduce some curious problems to the electronic observer. Some he would see simply as lines of light, and he would realise that he was looking at the edge of just such a galactic disk as that in which he found himself. Others, however, might appear circular or spiral, as some nebulae do to us. And in this case he would guess that he was looking at them as someone *in the future* or *in the past* might look at his own universe.

How could such a thing be possible? It would mean that the electron, hitherto unable even to imagine the form of the being to which it infinitesimally belonged, was actually seeing the silhouettes of other similar beings – other men, standing, lying or sitting – far away across the plane through which its own universe was moving. These other men or universes would be seen scattered over that landscape where the electron's universe might itself later go or already have been – that is, the electron would indeed see them as someone *in the future* or *in the past* would look at its own universe. The electron would at last be looking at a human 'galaxy' from *outside the latter's time*. And in this way it might gain – perhaps for the first time – an idea of the form and nature of its own 'galaxy', that is, of a man.

In a similar way, studying extra-galactic nebulae, human astronomers have for the first time guessed the form of our own. Moreover, they have found the greatest concentration of such nebulae in the zenith and the nadir of our Milky Way, that is, in the plane through which it is moving; and finding none at right angles along the plane of its diameter, have supposed an 'obscuring layer' there. But neither of course would our electronic astronomer observe other human universes above or below the path of its own, that is, in the sky overhead or in the earth underfoot. For the nature of such human universes would be to move only over the surface of a greater sphere – the Earth.

In the first section of this chapter we similarly supposed the vast army of nebulae moving over the surface of a greater sphere – the Absolute one. Perhaps after all the 'obscuring layer' is corroboration of this idea, and if so, then it is not a mere extension of nebulae which is obscured from us, but the very nature of this Absolute.

Such, were our analogy a true one, might prove the significance of the celestial phenomena which appear to us as the Milky Way and far-distant galaxies. They would represent sections of immense bodies, inconceivable and eternal to us, and of which we could say nothing but that they must be live. But is it true? There can be no direct answer. We can only say that another scale of life, rightly studied, reveals phenomena closely comparable to those which we perceive in the heavens, and which there, on that immense scale, are beyond our comprehension. And we may add that since natural laws must be universal, and since man cannot himself *invent* a cosmic scheme, analogy, which shows the correspondence between patterns created by such laws above and below, is perhaps the only intellectual weapon strong enough for certain problems.

It can, in any case, reveal relationships. So that in studying the electron in the human body, we see well the scale of the being who strives to appraise the structure, lifetime and purpose of the many galaxies, in comparison with the phenomena he witnesses.

III THE SOLAR SYSTEM IN THE MILKY WAY

About the extra-galactic nebulae we have little knowledge save of their shape and distance. About our own galaxy, the Milky Way, we can say more. According to recent ideas it is itself a spiral nebula, perhaps 60,000 light-years in diameter and 10,000 light-years thick.

This visible part of the Milky Way, we may take as a plane or sea of stars, round the centre of which circles our Solar System – a pinpoint vessel upon that ocean. Since such a journey may take it several hundred thousand years, it appears stationary against the unchanging background of 'fixed' stars to the extreme limit of man's observation, in the same way as a ship in mid-ocean appears stationary to its passengers against the unchanging watery horizon. Yet move the ship of our Solar System does, its course presently set towards the bright star Vega, which shines ahead and a little *above* the plane of the Milky Way itself.

This means that the ship's motion is not exactly parallel to the surface of the sea, but cuts across it at an angle, as though rising with a wave. And this in turn means that the cross-section of the ship, or the plane of the Solar System in which the planets move, is not at right angles to the surface of the galactic sea, but tilted at 55° to it.

In practice, we establish both the great plane of the Milky Way and the lesser plane of the Solar System by the constellations or legendary patterns of stars which lie round the horizon of each. Those which mark the com-

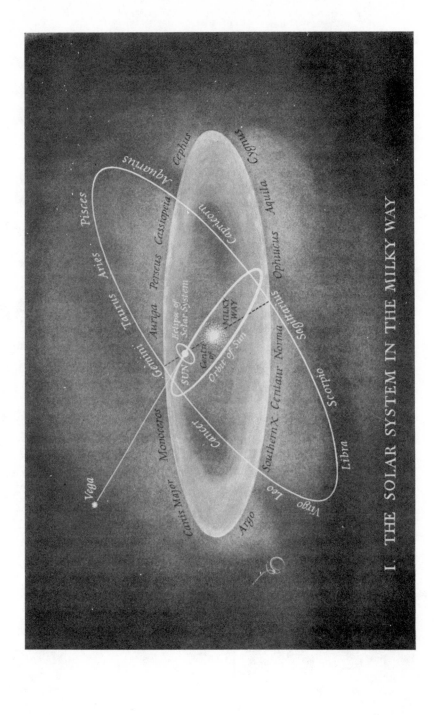

I. THE SOLAR SYSTEM IN THE MILKY WAY

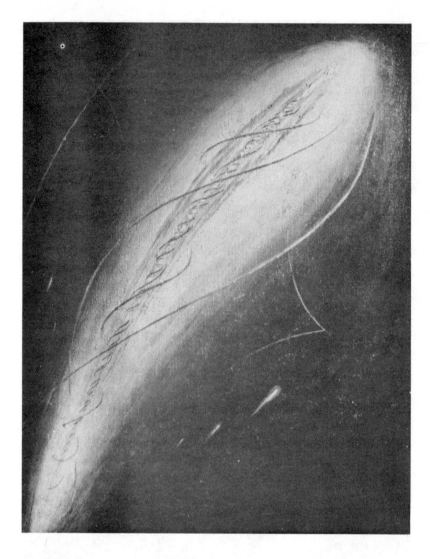

II. THE LONG BODY OF THE SOLAR SYSTEM

pass-points for the plane of the Solar System are the well-known Aries, Taurus, Gemini, Cancer, Leo, Virgo, Libra, Scorpio, Sagittarius, Capricorn, Aquarius and Pisces. At Gemini and again at Sagittarius the plane of the Solar System is cut by the greater plane of the Milky Way, or in our other figure, the cross-section of the ship intersects the surface of the sea. The constellations of Gemini and Sagittarius thus lie at right-angles to the course of the Solar System, and since the Solar System is voyaging round the centre of the Milky Way, one of them must represent the direction of this centre and the other the direction of its nearest edge. In fact the mass of stars towards Sagittarius is denser, as we should expect looking through the width of the galaxy, and it is also *broader*, seeming to divide into two layers, as though we were in fact seeing more *thickness* of the galaxy at the greater distance. Towards Sagittarius then lies the galactic centre, towards Gemini the nearest frontier of extra-galactic space.[5]

Now we must seek an explanation of this strange idea that man can see a little into the past of the galaxy, a little into the depth or thickness of the sea upon which his Solar System sails. How is this possible? The Milky Way is so vast that light takes 60,000 years to travel from one side of it to the other. This means that its nearer edge is about 10,000 light-years from us, and its distant one 50,000. In other words, the remotest stars towards Gemini appear to us in the positions they occupied ten millenia ago, while those towards Sagittarius seem to stand where in fact they stood 50,000 years ago, at a time when familiar man was perhaps first appearing upon earth.

We are literally *looking into the past of the Milky Way*. The farther we look the deeper into its past we see; and the explanation of this ability to look out of the galactic present lies in the slowness of the impulses of light which provide our only means of perception, compared with the almost unimaginable vastness which it has to cross. Later, when we discuss the speeds of diffusion of different kinds of energy, we may indeed come to the conclusion that the scale of the galactic world implies the existence of some energy *far faster than light*, with which man is not yet acquainted.

Meanwhile, if we suppose the whole Milky Way moving forward, like all other systems in the universe, then we can say that the angle of our perception out of the plane of the present must be proportional to the speed of the Milky Way divided by the speed of light. In daily life an exactly comparable phenomenon results from the time taken for the transmission

5. This supposition, which can be verified by the naked eye, was supported by the detailed star-counts of Hertzspring, Perrine and Shapley between 1912 and 1918.

of sound, which causes us to hear at a distance a cry uttered seconds before, and so enables us to listen deeper into the past the further off we stand.

Thus we do not in reality look out over that imaginary sea or disk which represents the present Milky Way at all. We look down a cone extending through the galaxy's time or fourth dimension. For while stars near to us appear from ten or twenty years *behind* this plane, others shine from their

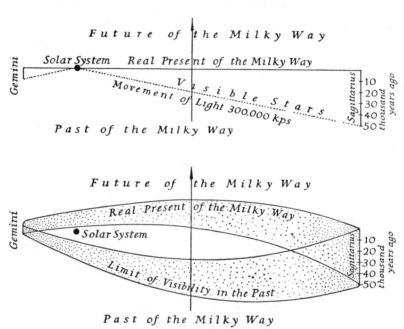

Fig. 1   Cross-section and Appearance of the Milky Way

positions of a hundred, a thousand, or ten thousand years ago, in proportion to their distance. From our position all these stars, extending from the present backwards for dozens of millennia, are seen superimposed, giving the illusion of that wide *ring* or wall or stars which in fact we see.

But, as we calculated, on the far side of the galaxy we see five times deeper into the past than we do on the near side. Precisely because of this greater distance, we see much more of its time or fourth dimension there, and it is thus only natural that the visible band of stars should be denser and thicker towards Sagittarius, where its centre and greatest extension lie.

Now because the Milky Way is a spiral nebula, when we face Sagittarius we address ourselves towards the centre or source of its creative energy; just as when we face the sun we address ourselves towards the centre or source of the creative energy of the Solar System. So also, when we face Gemini, we face away from this centre, as at midnight we look up into that part of the heavens in opposition to the sun. Here then is an objective measure for the long-believed 'characters' of the zodiacal signs. They are in fact a measure of our inclination towards the focus of our galaxy, as definite as the hours of the day are of our inclination towards the sun.

When the sun is in Sagittarius it means that the solar radiations and any unknown higher radiations from the focus of the Milky Way reach us from the same direction, or are in conjunction. When the sun is in Gemini it means that the solar and galactic radiations reach us from opposite directions. And when we face the sun in the intermediate signs of Virgo or Pisces it means that we see it against outer emptiness, or against the invisible past and future of the Milky Way, whose central radiation reaches us at right angles to the solar rays.

At present we cannot specifically state the nature of the radiations which may be given off by the galactic centre. But a general radiation of a few metres wave-length has been detected which is notably stronger in the direction of the densest star-clouds in the Milky Way, and strongest of all in the direction of Sagittarius.[6] This radiation is now regarded as a definite characteristic of our galaxy, and particularly of its centre, whose physical nature is hidden from us by star-clouds. It is distinct from but similar to what have been known as cosmic rays which, reaching the earth from all angles and directions and being of higher frequency than any known to originate in the sun, must also convey to us matter or influence from the vital centre of some even greater world.

We have posited this next greater world or cosmos above the Solar System to be the Milky Way. But there are many indications that the gap in size here is impassibly great. Later, when we come to measure the relative sizes and dimensions of the cosmoses which we have been able to identify,[7] we shall see that the factor of multiplication between the Solar System and the Milky Way is far greater than that between cell and man, between man and Nature, between Nature and Earth, or between Earth and Solar System. The Solar System seems lost in the distances of the Milky Way, as a single man would be lost on the surface of the Earth, were it not for

6. First noticed by Jansky: "A Concise History of Astronomy", Peter Doig, pp. 202-3 and 301-2.
7. See Appendix II, 'Table of Times and Cosmoses'.

the orderly world of Nature of which he forms part and which mediates, so to speak, between him and it.

The diameter of the Earth, for instance, is one-millionth that of the Solar System; but the diameter of the Solar System is only perhaps one forty-millionth that of the Milky Way. When in our own system we find such relationships, it is not between sun and planets, but between sun and *satellites* of planets. That is to say, by analogy of scale and mass, we should expect the Solar System to be revolving about some greater entity, which in its turn was revolving about the centre of the Milky Way; just as the Moon revolves about the Earth, which in turn revolves about the Sun.

What and where is this 'sun' of our Sun? Several attempts have been made to discern a 'local' system within the Milky Way, particularly by Charlier who in 1916 seemed to have established such a group 2000 light-years across and with its centre several hundred light-years away in the direction of Argo. If we study our immediate surroundings in the galaxy, we find an interesting gradation of stars, two of which are suggestive from this point of view. Within ten light-years we find one star similar in scale to our sun, and Sirius, over twenty times as bright. Between forty and seventy light-years distant, we come on five much larger stars, 100 to 250 times brighter than our Sun; between seventy and two hundred light-years, seven greater still, 250 to 700 times brighter; and between three hundred and seven hundred light-years six immense giants tens of thousands of times more brilliant. The greatest of these, Canopus, which lies 625 light-years behind in the exact wake of the Solar System, and is 100,000 times more radiant than our Sun, could indeed be the 'sun' of Charlier's local system.

But, as in so many of these problems, it is only when we abandon astronomical theory, and return to direct observation of the sky and heavenly bodies, that we find a more immediate starry influence to which the Solar System must be subject.

For the most brilliant object in the heavens, after those within the Solar System itself, is of course the double star Sirius. This consists of an immense radiant sun, 26 times more brilliant than our own, which circles in a fifty year period with a white dwarf as big as Jupiter and 5,000 times denser than lead. The mass of the light star being two and a half times that of our Sun, and that of the dark one equivalent to it, the influence upon the solar system of this starry pair, which lie at less than nine light-years remove, must certainly far exceed that of any other extra-solar body that we can think of. By physical distance as by radiance and mass a Sirian system would seem in some way to fill the excessive gap between the cosmoses of the Solar System and the Milky Way. Indeed, the distance from the Sun to Sirius – one million times the distance from the earth to the Sun – falls naturally into the scale of cosmic relationships mentioned, and provided nineteenth century astronomy with an excellent unit of celestial measurement, the siriometer, now unfortunately abandoned.

No astronomical data contradict the possibility that the Solar System circles about Sirius, in the course of the latter's circuit of the Milky Way, as Kant believed. For such a circling would only noticeably alter the position in the heavens of Sirius itself and of two or three other near stars, and in a periodicity of some hundreds of thousands of years this could easily pass unnoticed. In fact, we have definite evidence to show that such is the case. As the ancient Egyptians observed, the apparent motion of Sirius – measured by its rising with the sun – is a little less than that of the apparent motion of all the other stars, which is recognised in the precession of the equinoxes. Whereas the general star mass rises twenty minutes later on a given day each year, Sirius rises only eleven minutes later. This corresponds to the difference in apparent motion between points outside a circle and the centre of the circle itself, when observed from a moving point on its circumference – just as, in a landscape seen from a moving car, far and near objects seem to run past each other.

From such an observation we have good reason to believe that our Sun does circle about Sirius. And if we suppose the generally accepted figure of 20 kilometres a second for the sun's motion through space to be correct, then this circling would require 800,000 years – in other words, our Sun would make some 250 revolutions about its greater sun for every full circuit of the Milky Way. Later we shall see that this figure of 800,000 years is equivalent to about a third the lifetime of nature, or a month in the lifetime of earth, and that it fits in very well with the general relation between cosmoses.[8]

Meanwhile, another very striking fact appears to confirm the idea of a local star system with Sirius as centre. If we take the great familiar stars within say forty light-years of the Sun – Sirius, Procyon, Altair, Fomalhaut, Pollux, Vega and so on – we find that all but two lie within 15° of the same plane.[9] There is only one likely explanation of this – that all the

8. See Appendix II, 'Table of Times and Cosmoses'.

9. This section through the heavens cuts the celestial equator at an angle of 60° at about 7.30 and 19.30 hours right ascension and rises to 55° declination in the neighbourhood of the Plough.

near stars revolve about a common centre, and that this section is the ecliptic upon which all their orbits lie.

Supposing Sirius to be the sun of these suns, then our Sun – curiously enough – appears to occupy a similar place in that system to that occupied by the earth in the solar one. And if this is so, then the Sirian system may be regarded as almost exactly a million times greater in diameter than the solar system, as the latter is a million times greater in diameter than the earth, and the earth a million times greater in diameter than an ordinary house.

What kind of influence could reach us from the Sirian sun, with its strange combination of a radiance far greater than solar radiation and a density far more appalling than any conceivable in the darkest interior of the densest moon, we cannot know. Such super-heaven and infra-hell are unimaginable for us, nor can we know whether the cosmic rays or any other super-solar radiation is connected with it.

We can only in a general way picture each of the worlds we have considered as bathed in radiations or influences from all the worlds superior to it, as our earth is simultaneously bathed in cosmic rays and solar heat. The sum of these radiations will constitute the 'medium' in which a world exists, and their variety will introduce the possibility of choice of response as between one influence and another.

Seen from another point of view this 'medium' is composed of the sections of higher worlds. We have already compared our Solar System within a section of the Milky Way to a cell within a section of the human body. The cell to the human section, and our Sun to the Milky Way, are as points to planes. So we may say, as a law, that the medium in which any world lives and moves and has its being is to it as a plane is to a point. The cross-section of the human body is the plane in which the cell moves; the surface of the Earth is the plane of Nature in which man moves; the ecliptic of the Solar System is the plane in which the Earth moves; and the disk of the Milky Way is the plane in which the Sun moves.

Now the relation between a point and a line is infinity, and the relation between a line and a plane is again infinity. Thus the relation between a point and a plane is infinity squared. This means that they are doubly incommensurate; two new dimensions have entered. And when we compare each world not with the section of the higher world which it inhabits but with the complete body of that higher world, the comparison is between point and solid, or infinity cubed.

The squaring or cubing of infinity can best be understood by us as the introduction of plan, purpose and possibility. An infinite number of points make meaningless extension, but a point multiplied by infinity cubed can constitute a solid block on which one may sit. An infinite number of cells form only a mass of protoplasm, but cells multiplied by infinity cubed constitute a human body. An infinite number of organic bodies mean nothing but tons of flesh and sap, but organic bodies multiplied by infinity cubed constitute the harmonious world of Nature. In the same way, though we cannot understand its significance, the Milky Way must be composed not of an infinity, but of an infinity cubed, of suns.

Yet cell, human body, world of Nature, Earth, Solar System and Milky Way are at the same time complete in themselves, each containing a pattern and possibility of the whole. Such entities, connected by the sliding triad of dimensions with similar entities on larger and smaller scales, are rightly called cosmoses.

Two questions may arise in the reader's mind at this point. First, what exactly constitutes a cosmos? And second, what grounds are there for assuming that higher and lower cosmoses than man are capable of intelligence and consciousness?

The word *kosmos* in Greek means 'order', 'harmony', 'right behaviour', 'honour', 'a whole', 'the outward fashion of a whole', and finally 'the harmonious order of the whole', 'the universe in its perfection'. As used by the Pythagoreans it also meant 'a self-evolving or self-transcending whole'. As we shall see in detail later, the possibility of self-evolution or self-transcendence implies a very special plan and structure which some creatures have and others do not have. Thus man, who possesses the possibility of perfecting and transcending himself, can be called a cosmos, whereas a dog, which seems to be a finished experiment with no further possibilities, cannot. By the same token, a sex-cell, which can transcend itself into a man, is probably a complete cosmos, whereas a bone-cell is not; a planet, which can transcend itself into a sun, is a complete cosmos, whereas an asteroid is not, and so on.

The token of a true cosmos is in fact a particular kind of design, referred to in the Book of Genesis in the phrase 'God created man *in his own image*'. This 'divine image', the characteristics of which we must study in detail, can be found on all levels, and is the hallmark of a cosmos.

This in turn answers our second question. For whenever we find in nature or the heavens the repetition of this exact design, which in the case of man we know to be accompanied by the possibility of intelligence and consciousness, we may presume that it makes possible intelligence and consciousness on that other scale, just as we suppose that the blueprint of a dynamo makes possible the generation of electricity wherever we find it materialised.

Moreover, since the greater cosmoses give rise to the smaller, we may also presume that they enjoy intelligence and consciousness in a higher degree, just as we assume that the man who make a clever machine is cleverer than the machine he makes.

A book is composed of chapters, chapters of paragraphs, paragraphs of sentences, sentences of words, and words of letters. A letter and a word have significance on their own level, yet no true purpose apart from the whole book. So in the universe, despite all our disability, we strive to apprehend the higher cosmos in order to grasp the purpose of the lower.

II THE TIMES OF THE UNIVERSE

I THE RELATION BETWEEN SPACE AND TIME

WE THOUGHT OF AN ABSOLUTE: AND WITHIN THAT THE infinite heaven of spiral nebulae. In one such nebula – the Milky Way – we recognised our Solar System. We imagined the orientation of this system within its galaxy, and their relative size. And at the same time we tried to grasp the fundamental limitations of man's perception in relation to the heavens.

Now, if we are to understand these astronomical cosmoses better, it becomes clear that we must think not only of their vast extent, but also of their almost inconceivable time-scales.

Is it possible to gauge the duration of the Milky Way or the Solar System from their very vastness? Is there a relation between space and time?

In fact we already found the clue to this in the last chapter, where we came to the conclusion that the 'world' of each cosmos is a cross-section of a higher cosmos. Let us return to the blood-cell in the human body. A cross-section of this body at right angles to the cell's position in the artery constitutes the cell's 'present' world. Other cross-sections higher up the artery represent its world as it will appear at various moments in the future. Cross-sections lower down represent its world of the past. Passing upwards through the heart, for example, the cell might perhaps gain some impression of the thymus, lungs, and other organs lying across its section; but it could have no idea of the brain, or other organs above its section, until it reached them. All such organs, lying along the *length* of the human body, would exist *in time* for the cell. Thus the length or third dimension of the human body would represent time or the *fourth dimension* for the cell.

For a molecule moving within the cell, however, it would be the *cell's* third dimension which would represent time; while the cell's time or man's third dimension would be something outside the molecule's time altogether, and which would be mysteriously connected with the idea of survival after death or some possibility of repeated existence. We may say that man's third dimension would represent a *fifth dimension* for the molecule.

On the other hand, for the electron, whose time derived in turn from the third dimension of the molecule, no extension or repetition of its individual life could enable it to penetrate into man's third dimension, which

19

would be utterly inconceivable for it, and could only be represented as some completely unknown dimension – the *sixth* – where all, even unimaginable, possibilities were realised.

From all this it appears that the curious translation of dimensions from one cosmos to another applies not only to the three dimensions of space, which we studied in the last chapter, but also to the dimensions of time. We have to suppose for each cosmos a period of six dimensions – the first three constituting its space, the fourth its time, the fifth its eternity, and the sixth its absolute. And further, we have to suppose that with each change from one cosmos to another, this whole period of dimensions shifts, one being abandoned, one gained, and the rest changing, each into the next. Thus the length of one cosmos will appear as time to a lesser cosmos, as eternity to the next smaller, as absolute to the lesser still, while to the fifth cosmos it can bear no relation at all.

All this can be expressed in a much more simple way, thus:

Entry into each new dimension represents *movement in a new direction*. A *point* of no dimensions, such as the point of a pencil or a lighted cigarette in the dark, when moved, traces a *line*. A *line* – the spoke of a bicycle-wheel or a crayon, for example – when spun or moved at right angles to its length traces a *plane*. A *plane* moved at right angles to itself (or a disk spun on its axis) traces a *solid*. A *solid*, such as a man, when extended into the past and the future, traces a *lifetime*. A *lifetime*, extended at right angles to itself, brings us to the idea of parallel times, of *time-repetition* or eternity.[10] The totality of such repetitions, projected in yet another direction, implies an *absolute whole*, the realisation of all possibilities, everything existing everywhere.

Each cosmos may thus be seen in seven ways, according to the perception of the observer –

(1) as a *point*, that is, without dimension.

(2) as a *line*, that is, in one dimension.

(3) as a *plane*, that is, in two dimensions.

(4) as a *solid*, that is, in three dimensions.

(5) as a *lifetime*, that is, in four dimensions.

(6) as a *life eternally repeating*, that is, in five dimensions.

(7) as *all*, that is, in six dimensions.

Now, if we add to this idea the shift of dimensions from one cosmos

10. The word 'eternity', as used in this book, does not refer to an infinite extension of time, since all time is finite and limited by 'lifetimes'. It means, as medieval theologians assumed, a dimension 'outside time', formed of the repetition of time itself.

to another, which has just been described, we get the following table:

Cell	Man	Nature	Earth	Sun
Point	–	–	–	–
Line	Point	–	–	–
Plane	Line	Point	–	–
Solid	Plane	Line	Point	–
Lifetime	Solid	Plane	Line	Point
Repetition of lives	Lifetime	Solid	Plane	Line
All possibilities	Repetition	Lifetime	Solid	Plane
–	All	Repetition	Lifetime	Solid
–	–	All	Repetition	Lifetime
–	–	–	All	Repetition
–	–	–	–	All

Many interesting ideas arise from this table. And it is striking how far our *actual perceptions* follow its indications, though in many cases a mental correction has so long and so automatically been made, that we have forgotten what these actual perceptions are like.

For instance, man perceives a cell – if at all – as a point of no dimensions. As we can easily understand by looking down on a city from a nearby mountain, nature must perceive a single man – if at all – in the same way. And the sun the earth likewise.

Again, man perceives the lifetime of a cell, during which a red corpuscle for instance has traversed many miles of arteries, veins and capillaries running through every part of his body, as a solid, the solid of himself. The solid man is made up of the lifetimes of his cells. The solids of men, animals, fish, trees, in turn, become for Nature a film or curved plane covering the surface of the earth, while for the earth all this is but a track or line moving in space.

The lifetimes of men, animals, fish, trees are on the other hand solid for Nature, and their repetition solid for the Earth. Remembering his life as a whole, man sees himself as Nature sees him. Remembering his recurrence he sees himself as Earth sees him. Thus memory, for man, is the key to perceiving himself and his surroundings *as they are perceived by a higher cosmos.*

Indeed, we may continue and say that remembering the fulfilment of all possibilities, he would see as the Sun sees. For *all possibilities for man and for every living creature are solid for the sun, exist in the real solid of the sun.*

In this way the size of every cosmos is linked with the size of every other, and its time perfectly geared to theirs. In this way the length of its life is implied both in its own diameter and in that of the universe. In this way are the manifold and incommensurable scales and durations of that universe reconciled into the perfect whole which evidently exists.

There is another interesting aspect of this period of dimensions for each cosmos. Without dimension, as points, all cosmoses appear equal and identical. In six dimensions, as All, they again appear equal and identical. Seen in intermediate ways, in one to five dimensions, they appear at first more and more different and separate, and then again more and more similar.

For instance, suppose a living being seen as a line (that is, in one dimension) to be *ten* times longer than another. Seen as the plane built upon this line (that is, in two dimensions) it has a *hundred* times more area; and seen as the solid built upon this plane (that is, in three dimensions) a *thousand* times more volume. With the addition of each dimension up to three, it appears *more different, more separate*, more clearly distinguished from the other.

As soon as one introduces the fourth dimension of its lifetime, however, similarities reappear. All living beings are conceived, born, mature and die in time. Whereas seen in three dimensions a fly and an elephant appear to have nothing in common at all; seen in four, that is, in the pattern of their lives and the working of their functions, a mutual design again emerges. While seen in five dimensions, that is, as a repetition of life-cycles about a vital centre, the most diverse creatures and beings – from men to moons, and from blood-cells to planets – reveal an amazing resemblance.

It is thus literally true to say that when we perceive things in three dimensions, we see them at their maximum of differentiation. Living in a world of three-dimensional objects, we are experiencing creation in its most cold, separate and exclusive aspect.

This indeed is one explanation of the curious loneliness and desolation of men with their present three-dimensional perception. Animals, with two-dimensional perception, suffer far less sense of separation between themselves and other objects, between themselves and the world. And as man begins to develop four-dimensional perception, he again becomes – but this time consciously – aware of common pattern, dependence and unity. It is both his tragedy and opportunity that the perception with which he is endowed by nature places the greatest possible emphasis on *separate individuality*.

Yet in any given cosmos all six dimensions and ways of seeing – from line to All – are indivisibly and indeed mathematically connected. If we could correctly measure any one dimension of a cosmos, and know exactly what we were measuring, we could then calculate all other dimensions, speeds and times which that cosmos contained.

Let us take the Solar System. If we know the distance of any planet from the Sun (*line*), we can calculate by known laws

(1) the speed of that planet's motion in its orbit (*time*),

(2) the period of its revolution about the sun, and thus its relative number of such revolutions during the latter's whole existence (*recurrence*),

(3) the intensity with which the solar light shines upon it, and thus the amount of energy available to it in relation to the source of all energy (*absolute*).[11]

In other words, all its dimensions are interdependent and mutually implied. And this must be so for any true cosmos, since the totality of these dimensions, as we showed earlier, will in turn appear solid to some still higher being.

Now let us return to our original problem: What is the relation between diameter and duration? What is the relation between *line* and *time*? What is the relation between a cosmos seen in its first dimension and in its fourth? Our most important clue lies in the fact that all the above calculations depend on knowing the planet's *distance from the sun*, that is, knowing the radius which joins it to the vital centre about which it revolves. For this is the general key of time. *Time is created by rotation about the vital centre of a greater world.*

As regards the planetary world, Kepler both recognised and expressed this principle in his famous Third Law, in which he showed that the relation between distances from the sun (*line*) and periods of rotation about the sun (*time*) is the relation between square roots and cube roots.[11] Since all cosmoses are built on the same general plan, and since the relation between cosmoses now appears similar to the relation between dimensions within a cosmos, we will be justified in trying to use this formula to establish that

11. The laws concerned are:
(1) The orbital speeds of planets are in inverse proportion to the square root of their distance from the sun:
(2) The squares of the periods in which the planets describe their orbits are proportional to the cubes of their mean distances from the sun (Kepler's third law):
(2) The intensity of light (shining on a planet) is in inverse proportion to the square of its distance (from the sun).

Combining these laws we can further deduce:
(4) The orbital speeds of planets are in proportion to the square of the square of the intensity of light falling on them:
(5) The recurrence of planets in their orbits is in inverse proportion to the cube root of the square of their distance from the sun.

general relation between line and time, between space and duration, which we seek.

Put simply, Kepler's Third Law appears to suggest that while linear space develops by cubes, duration develops by squares only. In order to demonstrate this without complicated calculation, we will make two parallel columns – one representing space, in which each stage is a multiplication by 31.8 (approximately π^3), the other representing time, in which the equivalent stage is a multiplication by 10 (approximately π^2). The left-hand column will represent *radii*, and the right-hand column *lifetimes*. Our base will be *man*, and for convenience we will take his lifetime as 80 years and his radius (heart to fingertips) as 1 metre.

Upon this table we will now place examples of general classes of beings, wherever they appear to fit, either by size or duration.

Linear Space – Radii		*Duration – Lifetimes*
1,000 million kilometres	Planets	8000 million years
31.8 million kilometres		800 million years
1,000,000 kilometres	Moons	80 million years
31,800 kilometres		8 million years
	Whole world of Nature	
1000 kilometres	Continents	800,000 years
	Asteroids	
31.8 kilometres	Mountains and lakes	80,000 years
1 kilometre		8,000 years
	Towns	
31.8 metres	Largest trees	800 years
	Largest animals	
1 metre	Men	80 years
3.18 centimetres		8 years
	Small animals	
1 millimetre	Insects and plants	10 months
	Bacteria	
.03 millimetre	Large cells	1 month
.001 millimetre	Small cells	3 days

On the whole these results are promising – in the lower and middle stretches of the table strikingly so. Ordinary cells, with a radius of a hundredth of a millimetre, do live a few days. Large insects, a few millimetres long, do live a year or so, animals measured in decimetres tens of years, elephants, whales and oaks with girths of many metres centuries, and so on.

On the other hand, it does not seem possible to make calculations in this way about an individual creature or even species. Our formula, easily eluded by individual fate and fantasy, applies rather to general classes and statistical averages: as man enjoys a lifespan of three score years and ten, though a given individual die at 30, 60 or 90.

Meanwhile, from our ordinary point of view, there seem some strange anomalies in the higher reaches, where a radius equivalent to that of the earth appears to correspond rather with an age of Nature, and the suggested age of the Earth corresponds instead with the radius of its orbit. These anomalies we will treat in the next section, as we consider the time of each cosmos in turn.

II THE DAYS AND LIVES OF WORLDS

We have established that there exists a chain or hierarchy of cosmoses, each made in the same image, each formed by the infinite repetition of a smaller one, each an infinitesimal particle of a larger one. Man himself – a single individual man – is the midmost of these cosmoses. Within him lie electron, molecule, cell. Beyond him lie Nature, Earth, Sun, Galaxy.

We have established that each cosmos may be considered as having six dimensions, three of space and three of time. These dimensions are exactly and mathematically related to each other, and they are exactly but differently related to the six dimensions of all other cosmoses. Line, surface, space, time and eternity are thus appearances which slide one into the other according to the scale of perception of the beholder.

Our next problem is to discover the time-relation, that is, the *relative speed of living*, of the different cosmoses in this hierarchy. For this is connected with certain unrecognised speeds of perception in man, and thus with the question of man's possible development, which is our chief subject.

One way to discover this time-relation between cosmoses would be to deduce it from physical measurements, using the formula of cubes and squares discussed above. But as soon as we reach very large or very small magnitudes physical measurement tends to play us false, seeing as we do in the one case only sections and in the other only traces of the cosmos concerned.

Moreover, despite the mathematical interest of this space-time formula, it is in practice an extremely difficult and clumsy one to apply. If such a fixed universal relationship does exist between size and duration, it must manifest itself also in some simpler non-mathematical way which we can verify with our ordinary senses and observations. For mathematics is only one special way of formulating laws with the aid of one special capacity of intellectual function; all true laws can be equally well understood by other human functions, *in their own way*.

To this simpler understanding we have already found the clue. *Time, we said, is created by rotation about the vital centre of a higher world*. If we can discover the vital centres about which different cosmoses revolve, and how long they take to do so, we shall have the means of comparing their speed of living quite simply and directly, without benefit of formulae.

In trying to estimate their relative times and lifetimes, we thus have two methods which we can use to supplement each other. Sometimes one and sometimes the other will prove more convenient. With their joint aid, let us examine the cosmoses which lie nearest to us – a cell within a man, a man within the world of Nature, the world of Nature within the sphere of the Earth.

First – individual *man*, our best-known and most easily measurable standard. Each man literally revolves about the centre of the Earth, and this revolution takes *one day*, a natural period of sleep and waking, of rest and labour for him.

Turning to the next smaller cosmos, if we ask about what, for instance, a blood-cell revolves, we can answer very obviously the heart; and if we consider what corresponds to its period of revolution we find a very interesting analogy. A given blood-cell takes between 8 and 18 seconds to 'do its day's work', that is, to travel from the heart to a distant part of the body, leave its load of oxygen, and return with carbon dioxide. It then takes about six seconds to be restored, that is, to pass from the heart through the lungs and back again. This exactly corresponds with the period of work and sleep for man. If we take for convenience 12 seconds work and 6 seconds rest for the *blood-cell*, we get a 'day' of *18 seconds : and thus a 'life' of six days*.

Now if we apply the completely different method of our cube-square formula and we compare the red blood-cell's 1/2500 centimetre radius with the more exact 1.30 metres of radius from man's heart to his extremities, we get a size-factor of 325,000 times, and consequently a time-factor of 4700. One 4700th of a human lifetime again gives almost exactly six days. Our two methods have verified each other, and we may reasonably suppose this figure to be more or less correct.

We cannot study practically the question of the molecule's day, nor the speed at which it revolves upon its centre. But here common-sense comes to our rescue. We do know that when a blood-cell passes through the lungs and becomes oxygenated, this implies the destruction and re-arrangement of its constituent molecules. Each time a blood-cell is oxygenated, its molecules 'die' and are 'reborn'. Thus the 'day' of a blood-cell, or 18 seconds, must exactly correspond with the 'life' of its constituent molecules. And proportionately, a *molecule's day* will last but *1/1500th second*.

Proceeding to the next larger cosmos beyond man, Nature or all organic life on Earth, we find a very strange situation as regards its centre. For in fact, different aspects of such organic life revolve about different centres. In its totality, Nature appears to us as a sensitive skin of almost no thickness, covering the whole surface of the earth. But in fact it is composed of clearly distinguished 'kingdoms', each of which literally revolves about a particular planet which controls it, in that planet's synodic period. So that we may say that Nature as a whole completes a revolution, only when it has returned to the same relation with all its centres, that is, with all the major planets. Later we shall see that this complete cycle of planetary influences during which nature 'does a day's work', as we said of the blood-cell, is a period of about 77 years. And this in turn will connect with old ideas that the 'life' of man is but a 'day' for nature.

Without further evidence, however, this can be no more than an arbitrary flight of fancy, and again we must have recourse to our formula. Comparing man's 1.30 metre radius with the 6400 kilometre radius of the world of Nature (from the centre of the Earth to the limits of the atmosphere), we get a size factor of approximately five million times, and a subsequent time factor of 29,000 times. *Nature's day* should thus be 29,000 times longer than that of a man. And this does indeed give a period of about 75 or 80 years.

When we come to the cosmos of the Earth, it would be very tempting to take one year as its period of revolution about its centre. But this period, in relation to the Earth, is much too short, and on reflection we remember that the Earth must also be turning about the 'sun of our Sun', which we discussed in the last chapter, whether this be Sirius or Canopus or some other. There is every reason to believe that the slow shifting of the Earth's axis round a circle of fixed stars, which produces the precession of the equinoxes, is a reflection of this movement. Were the Earth to keep its magnetic pole permanently inclined towards some great centre about which the whole Solar System revolved in 25,765 years, it would have to behave in exactly this way.

Indeed, in this period the Earth passes through a full cycle of relationships to the galactic centre and the zodiac, just as in 77 years Nature passes through a full cycle of relationships to the planets, and man in one day a full cycle of relationships to Nature. Further, the proportion between this long earthly 'day' and Nature's day of 75 or 80 years, is very nearly the same as that between an ordinary year and an ordinary day, two other cycles which belong to the Earth and to Nature respectively. Thus we have a treble reason to believe Earth's time to be about 360 times longer than Nature's time, and *Earth* – in consequence – to have a day of 25,800 years.

Into the above sequence of daily cycles the Sun's motion round the centre of the Milky Way falls naturally. Such a motion, according to the latest calculations, takes about 200,000,000 years, and this period will constitute a day for the *Sun*.

We have no knowledge about what centre the Milky Way as a whole revolves, but – as mentioned before – its radius is nearly 40,000,000 times that of the Solar System. From this figure our formula gives a time-factor of over 100,000 times. On this basis a day for the *Milky Way* would be no less than 20 million million years.

In this way, working from sizes and from periods of revolution, we obtain the following sequence of 'days' for different cosmoses:

Molecule	1/1500th second	*Nature*	77 years
Blood-cell	18 seconds	*Earth*	25,765 years
Man	1 day	*Sun*	200 million years

Milky Way 20 million million years

If we now suppose what we must later proceed to substantiate – namely, that not only for man but for all cosmic creatures a life-span is composed of about 28,000 days – then our table develops further:

Cosmos	Time Relation to Larger Cosmos	Day	Life
Electron	× 28,000	?	?
Molecule	× 28,000	1/1500 sec.	18 secs.
Blood-cell	× 4,700	18 secs.	6 days
Man	× 28,000	1 day	77 years
World of Nature	× 360	77 years	$2\frac{1}{4}$ mn. yrs.
Earth	× 7,800	25,800 years	750 mn. yrs.
Sun	× 100,000	200 mn. yrs.	5.6^{12} yrs.
Milky Way		2^{13} yrs.	5.6^{17} yrs.[12]

12. Compare these periods with those of Hindu chronology, in which 4.3 million years make a Mahayuga or great age, after which Nature is destroyed; a thousand Mahayugas a Day of Brahma (4320 mn. years), after which heaven and earth are destroyed; and the proper number

How do these figures of lifetimes compare with estimates which have been arrived at in other ways? Working with cultures of unicellular organisms for more than twenty years, Metalnikov found that they produced 386 generations a year, or almost exactly one a day.[13] Cells within the human body have varying life-times. The longest-lived – the ovum, or female sex-cell – evidently has an existence of one month; the male, probably of a day or two. We shed between a sixth and a tenth of the skin every day, the corresponding amount being regenerated beneath; so that individual skin-cells must be born, live their life, and die in about a week. On this scale, the figure of six days we have obtained for the life of a blood-cell occupies a middle place and is probably correct.

Estimates of the present age of the world of Nature such as we know it, that is, since the beginning of the Quaternary Era or Era of Man, average about two million years. The duration of the previous world of Nature – for that belonging to the Pliocene period of the Tertiary Era was undoubtedly a different creation from ours and separated from it by an ice-age equivalent to death – is placed at six million years.[14] Again, our estimate is reasonable.

Passing to the lifetime of the Earth itself, deductions based on the periods of degeneration of uranium into lead place the age of the oldest rocks (Lower Pre-Cambrian) at 1,300 million years. Other arguments based on the thickness of sedimentary deposits and on astronomical data suggest that the Earth's crust was formed between two and three thousand million years ago.[15] In this case, our figure, for some reason, is less than half those obtained by other means.

One of the few plausible guesses at a possible duration for our Sun, which is based on the time that its apparent supply of hydrogen could continue to be transformed into radiant energy by the carbon cycle, gives it a life-expectation of 40 thousand million years – an eleven-figure digit as compared with the twelve-figure digit given by our calculation.

Upon the potential age of the Milky Way few authorities have ventured to express themselves, and it is difficult to obtain counter-estimates by which to check our supposition. In this case, therefore, we may perhaps be permitted to have recourse to analogy.

of such days a Life of Brahma (1.6^{14} years) after which the Solar System is destroyed. The life of the Solar System, again, is but the twinkling of an eye of Shiva. See "The Vishnu Purana", translated by H. H. Wilson (Bk. I, Ch. III) pp. 46–54.

13. S. Metalnikov: "La Lutte contre La Mort", p. 40-1.

14. Richard M. Field in "Van Nostrand's Scientific Encyclopædia".

15. H. Spencer Jones: "General Astronomy", p. 29.

Let us return to our previous conception of this galaxy as the cross-section of some unknown solid living body; and let us further suppose that the passage of light across it, as the quickest known means of communication between one point and another, corresponds to the dissemination of nervous impulses in man. We know that such impulses, travelling at 120 metres a second, take approximately 1/100th of a second to traverse the human body. Suppose this then to be analogous to the 60,000 years which are necessary for light to cross the body of the galaxy. Then by simple proportion we get for the lifetime of the Milky Way a figure in years containing seventeen digits. This, continuing our analogy, would be the scale of existence of our galactic being or god. And this is what our table proposes.

Evidently, in this table – rough as it is and based on insufficient material – there are grave inconsistencies. In some cases the figures yielded by the method of our space-time formula do not tally with those resulting from a comparison of periods of revolution. And yet, in a general way, the picture looks right, and the results fit together and synchronise one with another in a manner which would be inconceivable were the methods used to obtain them purely arbitrary. These inconsistencies are probably due to our failure to perceive in certain cases what in fact constitutes the radius of a given cosmos or what is the true centre about which it revolves. Mechanically, with more accurate means of scientific measurement, or consciously, with the achievement of a different level of perception, better results could be obtained.

Meanwhile, what does it all mean? Where do all these difficult figures lead us? They lead us to the inevitable conclusion that for each cosmic being – including man – time and form create a single pattern. No creature can be understood apart from its form: no creature can be understood apart from its time. For its form multiplied by its time yield its very self, its own unique signature, by which it differs from all other beings in the universe.

Moreover, for each individual this form and this time, which constitute his pattern, bear a certain intimate relation to each other. Each implies the other, as one face of a cube implies another exactly equal face, as a river-bed implies an exactly corresponding river. The trace of time is left in form, the root of form is revealed in time. Just as a man's whole character, capacity and fate are written in his face – could we but read it – so they are written again in his time. *His lifetime is himself*, and it sets him in a quite definite and constant relation to every other cosmos in the universe large and small.

There is, however, one further deduction from our calculations. If each cosmos has its own time, which – along with its form – constitutes an inalienable and unique property of its being, what shall we make of the fact that each cosmos either includes or forms part of every other? For instance, every single man contains within himself the cosmoses of electron, molecule and cell, and he forms part – however small – of the cosmoses of Nature, Earth, the Solar System and the Milky Way. That is to say, somehow hidden within him or pervading him, work the times of all other cosmoses in the universe.

Apart from his own time, which at first sight appears to him the only and inevitable one, he participates or can participate in the time of all cosmoses, and thus, in the being of all cosmoses. This, one of the greatest mysteries of his nature, is the clue to certain unknown and unrealised possibilities, whose significance we must first approach in an entirely different way.

III   MOMENTS OF PERCEPTION

From the example given of human breathing, we saw how the time of a man's *breath* is closely connected with the *day* of a cell, and the *life* of a molecule. In a curious way, these periods of different cosmoses depend on each other; or perhaps it were better to say that the very lives and days of smaller cosmoses are only a *result* of the breathing of a larger cosmos. In the case of blood-cells and the molecules of gas which they bear, this description is quite exact.

Life, day and breath therefore seem to be definite cosmic divisions of individual time, which link the fate and experience of each being inexorably with those of the cosmoses above and below it. And in fact there exists a strange and constant relation between these divisions.

As regards our own experience, we know very well that a lifetime is divided into days. Each day is divided from another by a period of sleep, by a break of unconsciousness which has the effect of closing one unit of time for us, and providing us with a fresh start each morning. A day is something complete in itself on a certain scale, containing a full cycle of digestion, a complete alternation of sleeping and waking, and a sequence of experience which can be mentally reviewed and thought of as a whole. There are about 28,000 days in a man's full life of 75 or 80 years.

Throughout each day of his life a man breathes. And just as one cycle of digestion of food takes 24 hours, one cycle of respiration or digestion of air takes about three seconds. This also is a definite and complete period of time for a man. If he observes closely he will find that every breath brings a new thought to his mind, or a new turn of repetition to an old thought. He may even perceive a very subtle pulsation in his awareness, almost analogous to the longer one of sleeping and waking. During the course of a day he breathes about 28,000 times.

For a man, and probably for all creatures, there are thus 28,000 breaths in a day, and 28,000 days in a life. If we turn now back to our table of times we shall see that this same figure occurs several times there also. Not only is the time of a blood-cell 28,000 times that of its constituent molecules, but the time of the world of Nature is 28,000 times that of man, and again the time of the Milky Way is 28,000 times 28,000 times that of the Earth. Many interesting connections follow from this. A molecule's *day* must be equivalent to the *breath* of a blood-cell. A man's day must be equivalent to a breath of Nature. The life of the Earth must be equivalent to a breath of the galaxy. And so similarly, will all the other time-divisions of these cosmoses be related.

Even where this key-figure of 28,000 does not occur, we begin to see that the time-factor between cosmoses may represent the relation between other temporal divisions. We saw how a year for Nature is equivalent to a day for the Earth. Similarly a year for the Earth appears to be almost an hour for the Sun. Again, a month for the Earth is a second for the Sun, a day for the Sun a second for the Milky Way, and so on. Not only breath, day, life, but also 'second', 'minute', 'hour', 'week', 'month' appear to be truly cosmic time-divisions, which link the units of experience on one level with those upon many others.[16]

We spoke of a day as the period of digestion of food, and of a breath as the period of digestion of *air*. Although it is not easy to verify, there appears to be an even shorter division of human time, connected with the period of digestion of the third kind of human nourishment, namely, perceptions. This is the time taken to receive and digest one single photographic image or impression. If the eye were a camera, this would be its fastest shutter-speed.

In fact, there are two degrees of this shortest measure. The first and briefer is the moment of perception of pure light. A man notices an electric spark or flash, which a meter tells him could not have lasted a thousandth of a second. Such minimum moment of perception of light may well be

16. See Appendix II: 'Table of Times and Cosmoses'.

1/28,000th part of a breath, just as a breath is 1/28,000th part of a day, and a day 1/28,000th part of a lifetime.

Were this so, we should have four major cosmic divisions of time for all creatures – their moment of perception, or period of digestion for light; their breathing-space, or period of digestion for air; their day, or period of digestion for food; and their lifetime, or period of digestion for all experience. Moreover, these four divisions would have a constant and cosmic relationship, which is also the standard relationship of time between one cosmos and the next – namely, 28,000.

For our present purpose, however, it is more interesting and practical to consider the rather longer period which a man requires, not to perceive formless light, but to recognise a specific form or object. In particular and more important, the time necessary for him *to recognise himself*, the time in which, standing before a mirror, he can take himself in with the feeling, "That is I, I am like that." For later we shall see that this is connected with the possibility of self-consciousness. And moreover, we shall try to establish how the Sun may see itself, and to do so we shall need such a relation.

Many clues help us to establish this minimum *moment of recognition*, as distinct from the minimum moment of perception mentioned above. For instance, we know from the cinema that successive images lasting less than a thirtieth of a second or so give the illusion of movement, and are no longer recognisable individually. This is confirmed by a certain class of rare experience – in the midst of some sudden accident or emergency, for instance – when events that happen at speed appear to last a very long time. For such experiences have definite limits. They may allow one to watch oneself falling downstairs, but they do not enable one to see an approaching bullet. In other words, they appear to slow down and expand a series of perceptions lasting a thirtieth of a second or so, but not to make possible much shorter ones.

There is an electrical pulsation of the brain which may be measured through the skull, and which is evidently connected with the digestion of perceptions, since when the eyes are closed, it very strikingly diminishes. This pulse is at the rate of about 10 per second, and the active part of its cycle probably constitutes the minimum moment of human recognition. Indeed, the Egyptian hieroglyph for this period of time, *anet*, usually called 'the twinkling of eye', combines precisely the two signs for 'eye' and for 'wave' or 'vibration'.

All this can be verified experimentally by opening the back of a camera, and looking through the aperture at various shutter-speeds. At one-thousandth of a second or less, one can know that the shutter has opened; at one-thirtieth, with great attention, an actual object may be recognised.

The time in which a man sees himself may thus be taken as perhaps a thirtieth of a second. And we find that the comparable time for the Solar System will be eighty years, or the whole life of man.

Bearing in mind that all these periods must be taken as *orders of time* rather than exact measurements, we can now have some notion of the possible duration of life, of day and night, of breathing, and of recognition for the Sun. And if our deductions are correct, we may suppose that all living organisms have similar divisions of their time. This means that between its birth and death a cell breathes as many times as does a man in his lifetime. And a man receives within his life as many perceptions as the Sun. Once rid of our accustomed belief in one time, we come to the strange conclusion that *all lives are the same length*.

III THE SOLAR SYSTEM

I THE LONG BODY OF THE SOLAR SYSTEM

AS CONCEIVED BY MAN, THE SOLAR SYSTEM CONSISTS OF A GREAT radiant sphere, round which lie at harmonically increasing intervals, like the ripples round a stone-splash, the orbits through which revolve other smaller and non-radiant spheres. Like the stone in the stone-splash, this central radiant sphere or sun appears the source of the energy by which the whole phenomenon is created. With a diameter perhaps one-ten-thousandth that of its entire system, it stands in almost exactly the same relation to its vast field of influence as does a human ovum to the body which will grow from it. And since in both cases the smaller gives rise to the larger, the concentration or intensity of energy must be of a similar order.

The concentric orbits of the dependent spheres or planets are harmonically related according to a law named after Bode. Taking the geometrical development 0, 3, 6, 12, 24, 48, 96, 192 and adding 4 to each figure, we arrive at a series which more or less represents the relative distances of the planetary orbits from the Sun.

The planets themselves vary in size – in general increasing from the smallest, Mercury, which is nearest the centre, to the largest, Jupiter, midway between centre and circumference, and then again diminishing to the outermost known planet (Pluto), which is little larger than Mercury.

The more remote the planets, the slower their apparent speeds, which diminish from Mercury's 30 miles a second to Neptune's $3\frac{1}{3}$. This again is a characteristic of the dwindling of impulses sent out from a central source as it plunges ever more deeply into distance. A very good model of the process is provided by a catherine wheel, which as it spins sends out streams of sparks that appear to curve backwards, away from the direction of the spin – that is, the sparks lose orbital speed the further out they are thrown.

It is noteworthy that the orbital speed of planets is in inverse proportion to the square root of their distance from the Sun. Since the intensity of light diminishes in inverse proportion to the square of its distance, we can add further that the orbital speed of planets is in proportion to the square of the square of the intensity of sunlight falling on them. Like cells, men, and apparently every other living creature, their speed depends upon the stimulus they receive.

In the catherine wheel the sparks of course fly out originally from the centre. Most theories agree that in the same way planets were once born

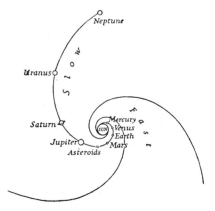

Fig. 2 : *The Solar System*

or torn from the very body of the Sun, children perhaps of the tension created by near passage of another star. In the infinitesimal flash of solar time covered by the whole recorded period of man's study of the heavens no trace of an outward motion of the planets has become apparent. But this is hardly surprising. For did the original birth of the planets take place several thousand million years ago, as is suggested, such outward movement would be no more than a mile or two a century.

We can only say that the whole structure of the solar system – like that of the spiral nebulae – suggests such expansion from the centre. This implies not only recession of the planets but also the growth and expansion of the Sun itself. For only a hotter and larger sun, that is, one whose matter had been raised to a far greater incandescence and rarefaction than ours, could sustain and vivify its satellites at a greater distance. In such a giant as Antares, a millionfold more rarefied than our sun, and whose radiant diameter would embrace the whole orbit of the earth, we may see the trace of such an older and more developed system. For there the central life and heat no longer occupies a particular astronomical point, but has already grown to *envelop* the greater part of its domain. It is the difference between human awareness on the one hand confined to a single organ, and on the other pervading the whole body and functions of a man. This latter we recognise as a more developed state.

If the outward motion of the solar system is imperceptible to man by reason of his time-scale, its circular motion is clear and calculable. The spindle of the system, that is, the Sun itself, rotates in rather less than a month. By the time it has reached the orbit of Mercury, the speed of the circular impulse has fallen to three months; at that of Venus to eight months; of the earth to twelve months; and so in diminishing ratio until at the orbit of Neptune it takes no less than 164 years to complete a revolution. Kepler's third law is the formal expression of this dwindling.

What in fact we are trying to describe in this complicated way is simply the relation between space and time. We are trying to describe the changes brought about in a section which gradually moves through the third dimension or length of a higher body, the Solar System. Just so would a cell in the bloodstream, seeing only a section of the human body, try to analyse the apparent motions of the cross-sections of arteries and nerves, whose different speeds would depend on the angle at which they passed through his plane.

As we said in the beginning, all such descriptions refer to the Solar System 'as conceived by man'. How can we imagine, not its section only, but the whole body of the Solar System?

Now the unity and pattern of a human body exists in the dimension higher than that of the cell's present, where what it regards as past and future coexist as a single human being. In the same way the unity of the Solar System, the plan or pattern of its body, must exist in the next dimension beyond man's present universe. Our problem then, is to try to visualise the past and future of the Solar System as coexisting and solid. We have to imagine the Solar System as it would see itself; just as, to comprehend the unity and pattern of a man, the cell must try to imagine how man would see himself or other men see him.

We have calculated that the 'moment of perception' of the Sun is 80 years long. When we considered our usual sectional view of it, we thought of the ripples sent across the surface of a pond by a cast stone. Now we must think of the stone sinking through the whole depth of the pond, and of the corresponding waves spreading outward through the solid body of water. Or better, we must visualize our catherine-wheel not only spinning, but at the same time projected forward fast enough for us to see the whole fiery train of it at once.

What, first of all, will be the proportion of this vortex of fire which our model has now become?

Astronomers, calculating the difference between the mean speed at

37

which the constellations directly above the ecliptic appear to be approaching us, and the mean speed at which those directly below appear to be retreating, estimate that the whole Solar System is driving towards Vega at about $12\frac{1}{2}$ miles a second. The fact is that in 80 years the sun, drawing the whole radiation of its system behind it, drives forward about 30,000 million miles into space. The diameter of Neptune's orbit is about 6,000 million miles. So that the sphere of radiation, the fiery train, or the 'body' of our Solar System in 80 years is a figure about five times longer than its width, or about the proportion of an erect human figure. This is the silhouette of our solar body.

Let us remember that the 'moment of perception' of a comparable being looking down upon the Solar System is 80 years. There will then appear to this being an extraordinarily complex and beautiful figure. The planetary paths, drawn out into manifold spirals of various tensions and diameters, have now become a series of iridescent sheaths veiling the long white-hot thread of the sun, each shimmering with its own characteristic colour and sheen, the whole meshed throughout by a gossamer-fine web woven from the eccentric paths of innumerable asteroids and comets, glowing with some sense of living warmth and ringing with an incredibly subtle and harmonious music.

This figure is not in one detail fantastic. The width of the planet's orbits will determine the size of each enveloping sheath: the diameter of the planet, the coarseness or fineness of the thread of which it is spun: the planet's relative curvature, its refractive index or colour: the number and distance of its moons, the varying texture, as of silk, wool or cotton: the density and degree of atmosphere, its sheen or luminescence: while the speeds of planetary rotation will cause the totality of sheaths to emit a magnetic or living emanation.

No material analogy can convey, indeed, the multiplicity of manifestations and impressions which one by one we can painfully calculate, but which would there be simultaneously apparent. For we know upon our own level that when such a multiplicity of impressions are generated together, we are faced by a phenomenon which defies our every effort at exact analysis, that is, the phenomenon of life. And he who continues long enough to develop this exercise in exact analogy cannot escape the conclusion that *there*, in a world where the 'moment of perception' is 80 years, the Solar System is, in some way incomprehensible to us, a *living body*.

Seeing the incredible heightening and significance which attaches to even the simplest and dullest phenomena of size and curvature when translated to that scale of time, we are utterly at a loss to imagine the possible appearance of that four-dimensional Sun, when even our three-dimensional one blinds us with its brilliance. And we can only suppose that it would in some way represent the innermost life-force of that Solar Being, as incomprehensible even to an observer upon that scale as is the consciousness of one man to another.

We spoke of other systems, like that of Antares, in which the central solar radiance has already enveloped a far greater volume than that occupied by our sun. And we spoke of the inevitable conclusion, from the idea of an expanding Solar System, that our Sun also must be growing hotter, brighter, more radiant.

In fact, this difference in the degree of radiance of their central sun may be the chief distinction between the million solar systems which compose the Milky Way. All such systems, to be capable of development, must include their full complement of elements and of planets, just as all men, to be capable of development, must include their full complement of organs and functions. The one factor which remains variable and improvable is in the one case, the intensity and penetration of its central light; and in the other the intensity and penetration of the central consciousness.

All men are similar in their pattern and their constitution: so most probably are all suns. What distinguishes men is their degree of consciousness: what distinguishes suns is their degree of radiance.

Indeed, the more we study the question the more clearly it emerges that light and consciousness obey exactly the same laws, and wax or wane in exactly the same way. We may even say that they are *the same phenomenon*, seen on different scales.

This indeed is the one variable factor in the universe, the one factor which can change in response to the individual work, effort and understanding of the individual cosmos. As regards their constitution neither man nor sun can do anything, for each being is endowed as he is by the pattern of the universe, which ensures that each shall receive in the beginning all that is necessary for self-development. But this self-development, that is, the gradual illumination and irradiation of the individual cosmos by self-generated light or consciousness, depends wholly upon the individual being himself. In this he must *do* everything.

Moreover, the whole can only become more conscious if the part becomes more conscious, and the part can only become more conscious if the whole becomes more conscious. If I suddenly make myself conscious of my foot, my foot also becomes conscious of itself, and begins to register all kinds of new sensations and motions of which neither it nor I were aware before. If a single cell of my body is galvanized into awareness by some terrible threat on its own scale, I too become conscious of the pain. In the same way, increasing radiance of the sun must be connected with increased absorption and transformation of light by the planets – that is, by their gradual acquisition of radiance also.

For a man to be fully conscious, all his parts must become fully conscious. For a sun to become fully radiant, all its planets must become radiant. For the Absolute to remember itself, all beings must remember themselves.

To those who ask, What is the purpose of the universe? we can thus reply that the task of the universe and of every being within it, from sun to cell, is *to become more conscious.*

II THE SOLAR SYSTEM AS TRANSFORMER

The figure which we have described as a network of interlacing sheaths, will no doubt suggest analogies to each specialist according to his study. To the physiologist, for example, it might recall the interpenetration in the human body of its various systems – muscular, arterial, lymphatic, nervous and so on – each built up of fibres or channels of different size and each the bearer of a different energy.

One of the most profitable analogies for our present purpose is that which will occur to the electrical technician. For stripping our figure of its sensuous manifestations and reducing it simply to a geometrical projection of spirals upon paper, he might recognize it as the diagram of a polyphase transformer. The mechanic's universe of flying balls has left as trace in time an electrician's universe of coils – designed, he would guess, for no other purpose but the transmission and transformation of solar energy.

For the layman's benefit, let us recall that electricity has two measurements – rate of flow (amperes) and pressure (volts) – and that a transformer is a device for changing the relation between these two factors. In a very general way, the heavier the machine to be operated, the greater amperage is needed. To meet such varying demands from a single source of power, the transformer increases flow at the expense of pressure, or vice versa. This is done by passing a current through a coil of a given number of turns, and allowing a sympathetic current to be induced in a neighbouring coil of a greater or lesser number. If the number of turns in the secondary coil is greater than in the primary, the amperage or flow is decreased, and the voltage or pressure increased: if less, the opposite effect is produced.

Practically, the flow or amperage is limited by the composition and thickness of the conducting wire. Thus if it be desired to carry the power available on lighter wires, it must first be transformed to higher voltage, lower amperage.

Now looking at our diagram of the tracks of the major bodies of the solar system in the light of these ideas, we clearly recognize the thick straight primary of the sun, surrounded by eight secondary coils of its planets. We also see that the thickness of these planetary 'wires' varies from one-tenth (Jupiter) to one three-hundredth (Mercury) the thickness of the solar primary. And in an 80-year diagram we count in the various coils all kinds of windings from one-half to no less than 300 turns. Here we have indeed all the factors and components of an enormous transformer for receiving current at a given tension and stepping it up for delivery at eight different voltages. The model is complete even to insulation of the wires by a thin non-conducting film of planetary atmosphere.

A transformer built in the human world from the specifications of this cosmic diagram, would deliver current at eight different tensions and

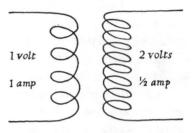

1 volt

1 amp

2 volts

½ amp

(a) Primary and Secondary Coils

Earth   Venus   Mercury

Sun

(b) Part of the Solar System in Time

Figure 3

eight different rates of flow. And from the number of turns in the planetary coils during our standard eighty years, we should even be able to calculate their relative output. Suppose, for example, the current produced by the coil of Neptune from the Sun's original power were 1 volt in pressure and 10,000 amperes in flow. Then Jupiter's output would be at 14 volts and 770 amperes, the Earth's at about 170 volts and 60 amperes, Mercury's at 700 volts and 15 amperes, and so on.[17] One effect of increased amperage in the planetary world, seen by our perception, is probably increased vibration, that is, *faster rotation of the planet on its own axis.*

If such a transformer were correctly wired with material of the same conductivity, the cross-section of wire suitable to each coil would be proportional to the amperage it carried. In fact, the cross-sections of the planets approach only within $\pm$ 10 times this requirement. But supposing the planetary coils not to be of the same conductivity. Suppose their inner cores – as is almost certainly the case – to be of different metals, each of distinct conductivity. And further suppose that those whose section is smaller than we should expect, such as Neptune, to be of metals of high conductivity, and those whose section is larger, such as Jupiter, of metals of low conductivity. Then with a judicious attribution of the metals – silver for Neptune, gold for Uranus, antimony for Saturn, bismuth for Jupiter, copper for Mars, iron for Earth, strontium for Venus, and brass for Mercury – our apparent error would be compensated, and the vast machine indeed be accurate in all its measurements. The planetary coils, it seems, are rightly constructed to play their parts as transformers of solar energy in the way described, if only we suppose them to differ in their conductivity as metals do.[17]

It may be objected and admitted that metals are arbitrarily chosen to yield such a result. Unfortunately, the planets not being themselves radiant, modern science has no means of verifying their composition. And we can only note in passing that recent theories do in fact suppose the main bulk of the earth, or barysphere, to be of compressed iron. In addition, we have the traditional attribution of metals to the planets by astrology, but this has varied at different periods, and being made from an acquaintance with few metals, is not very helpful. At present, therefore, we must place these calculations in the realm of suggestive speculation.

What is much more important, from our point of view, is the principle that an electric current, passing along a wire, produces *a magnetic field* about that wire. This magnetic field consists of concentric lines of force moving clockwise round the wire when seen from the direction towards which the current is moving. In other words the magnetic field rotates when the current moves forward, as a corkscrew has to rotate when it is driven forward into the cork.

If we now try to translate this from the world of spirals seen in the sun's time to the world of spinning balls seen in man's time, we shall understand

17. See Planetary Tables - Appendix IV (a) and (b).

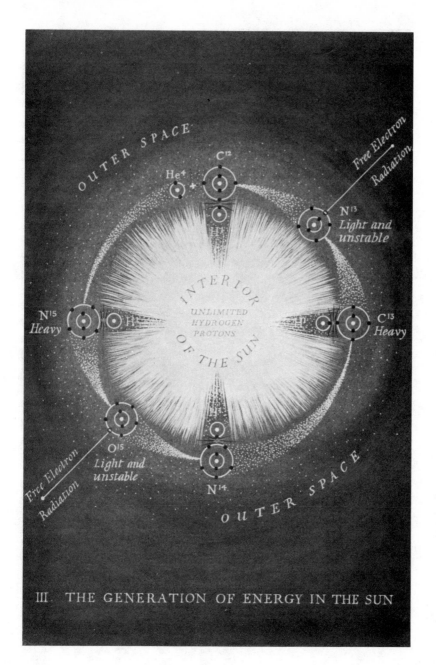

III. THE GENERATION OF ENERGY IN THE SUN

IV. THE CONJUNCTION OF VENUS

how it is that *all rotating bodies in the universe create and are surrounded by a magnetic field.* For their very rotation, as we saw just now, is an indication that they are sections of a line through which some tremendous current is passing in another dimension. We shall also understand that a planet's speed of movement along its orbit represents in a recognisable way the speed of flow of this great current. For, as we saw earlier, this orbital speed is a direct effect of the intensity of sunlight available, that is, it is induced by the central energy of the sun.

All the planets are thus individually surrounded by magnetic fields. The section of the wire round which the field of magnetic force rotates will be represented by the planet's equator, while the planet's north pole will represent the direction of movement of the planet in time, that is, the direction of the great current which informs it. Thus the attraction of the north pole of a planet may be regarded as the attraction of the future, the attraction of the direction in which the planet with all its inhabitants is going; while the repelling effect of the south pole represents the repulsion from the past, the repulsion from the direction whence the planet with all its inhabitants has come. For all beings, the future is the positive pole of time and the past the negative. They can do nothing else but be drawn towards the one, and be repelled from the other.

Now these magnetic fields of the planets all overlap and interact, the combined effect of all producing constant minor changes in the individual field of each. In practice, only the magnetic field of the Earth has been studied in much detail, together with the effects upon it of the magnetic fields of the Sun and of the moon. It is known, for example, that the Sun's magnetic influence upon the Earth is about twelve times stronger than that of the moon – a field of 60,000 amps against one of 5000.[18] The magnetic influences of the planets have not yet been individually measured or distinguished, though the existence of such influence has been recognised scientifically in connection with the effect of differing planetary configurations on short-wave radio receptivity.

In the case of the Sun, its magnetic influence is dwarfed – to our perception – by the far stronger influence of the vibrations which we feel as light and heat, and which are much more characteristic of the sun. Nevertheless this magnetic influence is quite distinct from light. For measurement of the delay between magnetic disturbances seen on the surface of the Sun, and the magnetic storms felt as effect in the Earth's atmosphere, shows that

18. Sydney Chapman, "The Earth's Magnetism", p. 76.

this influence travels at quite a different speed. Whereas light from the Sun reaches us in seven minutes, magnetic influences from the same source take between one and two days to be felt here. Whereas light travels at 186,000 miles a second, magnetic waves travel at only about 400 miles a second, or nearly 500 times more slowly.

What is the effect of this magnetic influence? Perhaps the most obvious and beautiful phenomenon which directly results from it is the aurora borealis, or Northern Lights. Now this is interesting, because in the aurora borealis we see pure light – which is invisible itself – first *endowed with form*. This form constantly changes, shifts, transforms itself, creating majestic curtains or shimmering spheres or pulsating fields of radiance in the northern sky. The aurora borealis is almost completely insubstantial and is the result of magnetism acting directly on free hydrogen ions. In it we clearly see the effect of a magnetic field as form, and changes in that field as changes in form. The same phenomenon occurs when we place a magnet under a sheet of paper covered with iron filings, and it imparts to the hitherto amorphous mass the visible form of its field. This is in fact a general principle – *magnetic influence, acting on matter, is that which gives rise to visible form.*

We said that in the Sun's case, although its magnetic influence is enormous, this is dwarfed by the far faster influence of light, which from our point of view is much more characteristic of it. But the moon and planets do not emit light of their own, so that in their case magnetic influence is in reality their characteristic emanation. The combined magnetic influence of the moon and planets must then create form on earth; just as the magnetic influence of the Earth must in turn help to create form on all the other planets.

Many interesting ideas about the role of magnetism arise from all this. If we study the different forms of energy we know, we see that each has a definite field of action depending upon its origin and its speed. Light, which travels at 186,000 miles a second, is produced by the *Sun* and for all practical purposes is limited by the field of the *Galaxy*. Sound, travelling in air at one-fifth of a mile a second, is produced by the phenomena of *Nature* and is limited by the field of the *Earth*. While between light and sound lies this third form of energy, the magnetic, which, travelling at 400 miles a second, may be regarded as arising from the *planets* and limited by the field of the *Solar System*.

Light, magnetism and sound constitute a clear hierarchy of energies, characteristic respectively of a sun, of a planet, and of nature. And they represent the means by which these cosmoses act upon us, by which the first endows us with life, the second with form and the third with sensation.

The picture of the universe which gradually emerges before the electrician is thus one of coils within coils, each transforming energy from a higher source to its own needs and capacity. The vast coil of the Sun must transform its white-hot energy from the still more primary source of power at the core of the Milky Way. By induction, the Milky Way must produce current in the Sun, the Sun in the planets, Earth in the encircling moon, and the sage wisdom in the pupil who faithfully revolves about him.

That about which other creatures revolve imparts light and life. That which revolves is in turn endowed with magnetism and form. By this magnetism it both participates in the giving of form to others, and is in turn endowed with form by them. All magnetism affects all other magnetism. All forms create all other forms. From first cosmos to last electron, the whole universe is a complex of coils within coils, spirals within spirals, magnetic fields within magnetic fields. In this aspect each creature transforms a single force to the exact tension required to drive a galaxy, a man or a mote. And when its resistance decreases with the span of age, by this very tension it is fused, the form of its magnetic field is dissipated, and it dies.

III THE INTERACTION OF SUN AND PLANETS

Certain qualifying remarks should perhaps be made here, which refer to the whole principle of analogy that we have so freely used. It is not to be deduced, from all the above evidence, that the Solar System *is* a transformer of electric current, nor that the planets *are* made of antimony, bismuth, iron and so on – though these elements may in fact play a large part in their composition. What is proposed is that the laws which on one scale permit the construction of a transformer, are the same as those which on another scale produce the Solar System. The planets may not be transforming electrical energy such as we know it to higher voltages and lower amperages, but they *are* transforming some unknown energy in a comparable way.

Similarly, though the planets are not necessarily composed of the metals mentioned, they are most probably made of substances which in some way stand in the same relation to each other as these metals – just as the notes A B C D E F G stand in the same relation whether set in a higher or a lower octave. Laws are universal; mechanisms through which they work are similar on many scales – but the materialization of the laws, and the constituents and products of the mechanisms will vary according to the elements available on the level under consideration. Thus a spring is the same mechanism obeying the same law, whether it is applied to move the hands of a wrist-watch or to propel an arrow from a bow. But it is made of different material, and used for a different purpose.

It must also be understood that every analogy, even the most exact and illuminating, is incomplete. It only explains one aspect of the phenomenon, and may leave out another side which is equally or even more important. In particular, the aptness of analogies drawn from the mechanical operation of laws in magnetism or physics must never lead us to forget that the Solar System in its every part gives indication of *life* and *intelligence*. We are dealing, not with coils or ripples, but, we have every reason to believe, with living beings of a power and nature incomprehensible to us: though we can apprehend their existence and possible aspect.

Bearing this in mind, we may try to come to a clear conception of such higher beings by proposing many different analogies, each of which may add something to our understanding. Thus, while we remember our image of the transformer and all that it has shown us about the nature and function of the planets in relation to the sun, we must not rest content with that.

We may also, for example, see the planetary sheaths around the long body of the Solar System as so many prismatic lenses, each with a different refractive index, which enables it to reflect an individual colour from the white light of the sun. Such refractive index would depend on the speed of rotation of the particular planet on its axis, in exactly the same way that the speed of vibration of electrons determines colours perceptible by man. Now between the speed of rotation of planets (once or twice a day) and the electronic frequency producing colour (10^{15} vibrations per second) there lie sixty-three octaves. If we now turn to our table of the times of cosmoses, we find that exactly the same number of octaves lie between the time of the electron and the time of a typical planet – the Earth. That is to say, the vibration of electrons giving rise to colour is exactly paralleled on planetary scale by the movement which we measure as their rotation.

If then we suppose each planet to be a coloured reflector in the sky, bathing the scene with this or that particular tint, we are in fact only imagining how the Solar System must appear to a cosmos as much greater than the planets as man is greater than the electrons. We can understand the effect of this very well from watching a theatrical stage, where the footlights may throw a white light upon the actors while coloured spots from the wings tint the shadows on one side with red, on the other with green or purple. Such is the relative effect of the Sun and the planets.

And supposing the actors to be upon the Earth or in any other part of the Solar System, then the white and coloured lights will be constantly shifting their relative position, and at every moment producing new effects. Now the white light of the Sun will be shining from the left wing, while the footlights may shine alternately red and green, which combine to fill the stage with a soft yellowish glow. The permutations will be endless and their effects constantly passing one into the other as the lights themselves revolve about the stage.

Moreover, as we all remember from childhood visits to the pantomime, each change will suggest its own emotional mood, the same scene and characters appearing in the red light terrible and bloody, in the green eerie and mysterious, in the blue spiritual or uplifting, and in the yellow warmly benevolent and matter-of-fact. Of course, the lights themselves have no emotions – indeed, they work by quite other laws. Yet the effect they create on human beings is emotional, and their influence appears to us in this guise. So with the planets.

It must be emphasized, however, that the planets are only reflectors, only transformers. They produce no light of their own, but merely lend the Sun's light a certain 'mood' or colour. They produce no current of their own, but only adapt the current provided by the Sun for this or that particular use.

An even better understanding of the role of the planets may be obtained by regarding them as *functions* of the Solar System. Just as digestion, respiration, voluntary movement, reason and so on are functions of the cosmos of man, so Mercury, Venus, Mars, Jupiter and the rest may be functions of the cosmos of the Solar System. Between them they endow the Sun with all functions, and make it a complete cosmic being possessing all possibilities.

The implications of this become more clear in the light of a very important principle governing the relation between cosmoses. Every cosmos contains six pairs of key organs, or batteries, as it were, by which it receives influences and energy from higher cosmoses. The principle in question says that *the functions of a lower cosmos derive from the organs of a higher cosmos.*

In man, for example, these organs or batteries are represented by the endocrine glands, and the secretions of these glands, penetrating the cell, create the latter's functions. Working towards higher cosmoses, on the other hand, we find that all the breathing functions of all men, animals, birds, fish, plants, together constitute a single organ for Nature; all the motor functions of all moving creatures together constitute another organ for Nature, and so on.

And finally, taking Mercury, Venus, Earth, Mars, Jupiter and Saturn as functions of the Solar System, and remembering the millions of suns and systems which compose the Milky Way, we have to think of all possible Mercurys together as constituting one organ for our galaxy, all possible Earths together as a second galactic organ, and so for the rest.

In this way, the anatomy and physiology of each cosmos is knitted into that of every other. And the actual physical organs of a greater cosmos determine the very nature of the functions enjoyed by lower ones.

Thus, while for the Solar System and all in it, the *Sun* is the only source of all energy and life, this is endowed with form, colour, expression and function by the planets. These forces interact, merge and separate in infinitely varying combinations throughout the whole field of solar influence. One factor, however, is still lacking for the creation of all the manifold and intricate phenomena of nature with which we are familiar – that is, matter or *Earth*.

IV SUN, PLANETS AND EARTH

I THE THREE FACTORS OF CAUSATION

ACCORDING TO MANY ANCIENT SYSTEMS OF PHILOSOPHY, ALL phenomena that exist, from the gods downward, arise from the interaction of three forces. One is described as of an active or creative nature; the second as passive or material; and the third as mediating or formative.

In Christian philosophy these three forces are expressed by the three persons of the Trinity – Father, Son and Holy Ghost – which create the universe. In medieval alchemy, all things were seen as varying mixtures of salt, sulphur and mercury. In Indian Sankhya a similar role was assigned to the three gunas – Rajas, Tamas and Sattva. In Hinduism the forces were again personified as Shiva, Parvati and Vishnu; and in China they acquired metaphysical cast in the interplay of Yin and Yang overseen by the Tao.

In all these systems, the nature of the three forces was universal, that is, they were regarded as entering into everything, everywhere, and on every scale – from the world of maggots to the world of stars, and from the effect of light to that of thought or aspiration. No such general idea of three forces exists in modern philosophy, though specific instances are recognised, as for example in the proton, neutron and electron of atomic physics, or in the reactant, reagent and catalyst of many chemical processes.

If we consider the three forces from the point of view of physics we have to say that active force is of the shortest wavelength, the fastest vibration; passive force is of the longest wavelength, slowest vibration; and mediating force of an intermediate wavelength and vibration. For example, the octave of colour stretches from blue (wavelength about 4000 angström units) to red (about 8000). But as we know, the possibilities of red and blue are very limited, and the whole infinite wealth of colour that we see depends on the presence of an intermediate colour, yellow, quite different from and midway between the others (about 5750 angström units). This is the basis of the three-colour process in printing. As far as the phenomena of colour are concerned, we may call blue active force, red passive force, and yellow mediating force. All possible colours derive from the combination of these three.

The same example demonstrates another aspect of this law, namely, that the characteristics of the three forces depend, not upon the phenomena through which they manifest, but upon *their relation to each other*. The wavelength of red, for example, is *passive* in relation to the phenomena of colour, but on the contrary *active* in relation to the phenomena of heat which belong to the octave below: red heat is more intense than black heat. Thus all objects and energies which exist in the world are constantly changing places from the point of view of the law of three, acting as instruments, now of active, now of passive, and now of mediating force. It is exactly this constant flux and change which makes the law of three so elusive to our perception, and makes it necessary to take each example separately, apart from all others.

A more general example may, however, explain the idea better. Think of trade, commerce. *Man* exists in the world: and there exist also all the objects which he grows or makes out of the materials that surround him – *goods*. Man is active, goods are passive. But with these two forces alone very little interchange can take place, and it was necessary for a third force to be invented which would enable the other two to work together in an infinite number of combinations. This third force is *money*. The triad, *men, goods, money*, gives rise to the general activity of trade.

This example brings us to another very interesting aspect of the law of three forces. For money is *invisible*. Certainly paper or gold is visible; but the *power* of money is invisible and with the growth of commerce and development of banking, money always tends to grow more invisible, more abstract, and to correspond less and less with any tangible reality. And this exactly echoes the explanations of the law of three given in ancient philosophies, which always emphasised that the entry of *the third principle remains invisible to man on his usual level of perception*. The third principle thus represents the unknown, unrecognised, determining factor in each situation.

In some cases it may be merely physically invisible – as many chemical processes involving the interaction of active acid and passive alkali are made possible only by the invisible presence of moisture. Or again its method of action may be invisible, as the method of action of catalysts in chemistry and enzymes in physiology remain invisible. In other cases this invisibility is more subtle. A man decides to raise himself to a higher level of consciousness. His active will, desire and effort are pitted against the passive inertia of his physical machine with all its inborn tendencies and acquired habits. These two forces struggle together without result until he can attract the intervention of a third deciding force – the aid of an esoteric school and school knowledge. This aid and this knowledge are, quite literally, invisible.

Further, money, air, catalysts, enzymes, and school – though they produce great changes in that with which they come in contact – themselves remain unaffected and undiminished. They cannot lose their virtue or be used up. Thus it is a characteristic of the third principle that it is always unchanging, invisible and unrecognised, and it can be neither commanded nor manipulated by the other two factors. In relation to them its role will always be *mysterious*.

Invisibility is as it were the cloak of this mystery, and may be of many different kinds. Some things are invisible to us because they are too far, like distant galaxies; others because they are too near, like the inside of our brain: some because they are too big, like the earth, others because they are too small, like a cell: some again because they are too rarefied, like air, others because they are too dense, like the inside of a rock; some because they are too fast, like a rifle-bullet in flight, and still others because they are too slow, like the shape of a civilisation.

Yet these different kinds of invisibility are not accidental. They place the things to which they refer in a quite special relation to man, one in which they are peculiarly liable to act as third force in his affairs. Thus to achieve what he wishes he must learn to take third force into account, and to take third force into account, he must learn *to consider the invisible*.

We touched theoretically upon the idea of three factors or three principles in the development of multiplicity from the Absolute. Any analysis we may try to make of the forces which create and maintain the galactic worlds is likely to be philosophical also. We see and understand too little on this level, and any ideas which come to us belong to the realm of metaphysical speculation rather than of physical phenomena susceptible of study and proof.

On the particular scale we are about to consider, however – that of the creation and maintenance of life on earth – three clear physical factors become apparent to the mind which has accustomed itself to think in this way.

All the phenomena of life recognisable by us upon the earth are the product of the *Sun*, the *Earth*, and the *planets*. The Sun provides the life-force, the Earth the materials, the planets form. Without these three elements, no living being can exist. Moreover, these three elements are of varying levels of energy – the Sun, as we know, is most radiant, most active; the Earth is most inert, most passive; while the planets stand between the two, refracting and reflecting, the third or mediating force.

An extraordinary diagram of this idea may be found in the façade of many French Gothic cathedrals, where the rose-window represents the sun; the five lower lights filled with archangels, the planets; and the carved wealth of figures and scenes about the porch, life upon earth, which is of course the very rock upon which the whole is built.[19] There could be no better representation of the origin of life as we know it – the offspring of triple and celestial creators.

But before going any further, let us make more clear what is meant by Sun, planets and Earth in this general sense. By the *Sun* is meant all its emanations, including those received as heat, light, ultra-violet rays and other radiations as yet unrecognised, as well as its function in sustaining the whole Earth in its proper place and orbit. By the *planets* is meant the combined effect of the movements, magnetism and reflections of the main planetary bodies, taken as a whole. By the *Earth* is meant the basic material commonly available on the surface of our world, taken devoid of life and form – that is to say, the chemical elements from hydrogen to lead, in their unorganised state.

One thing immediately strikes us about this classification. The invisibility of the third force, which we mentioned, holds very true. Although organic life is generally recognised as a product of Earth and Sun, the equally essential and deciding role of the planets has for many hundred years gone unstudied and unseen. But to this role, we now have a clue. If the Sun is the source of life and energy, and earth the quarry of raw material, we may propose as hypothesis that planets are the creators of form and function. The result is the whole world of Nature.

Such may be the general triple cause of the phenomena of life on Earth. But this alone does not explain to us the completely different quality of varying aspects of this life, all the contrasting, contradictory, complementary processes whose total result appears to us as the world in which men live.

If we return to the example of men, goods and money, we realise that these three forces can combine in quite different ways, producing quite different results. Money may serve men, and enable them to enjoy to the full the benefit of goods. On the other hand, it may happen that men begin to serve money, and even forego the goods they previously enjoyed in order to acquire it. Again, at other times, money loses its value and goods themselves rule men's lives and dictate the role of money. Each of these interactions of the three forces produces a different state of society, with different

19. Notably Chartres: the five planets then known were Mercury, Venus, Mars, Jupiter and Saturn.

possibilities and different results – some better, some worse, and some merely different in their nature, without either improvement or degeneration.

It is some such analysis of the different ways in which the Sun, planets and Earth may combine and their consequent differing effects on earthly life, which we must now attempt.

II THE SIX PROCESSES IN NATURE

In their influence upon the world of nature, the *Sun*, the *planets* and the *Earth* interact in six different combinations to create six possible categories of process:

Sun: Earth: Planets
Sun: Planets: Earth
Earth: Sun: Planets
Earth: Planets: Sun
Planets: Sun: Earth
Planets: Earth: Sun

The variable effect of the same constituents combining in different orders may be explained by taking the example of a gas-flame, water, and a kettle. The gas-flame may be applied to the water in the kettle to produce hot water. On the other hand the water may be poured out of the kettle to douse the flame. Yet again a flame may be arranged inside the closed kettle floating on the water to form a simple jet-propelled vessel; and so on and so on.

The principle that six cosmic processes, universally applicable, must result from the interaction of three forces was fully recognised by 17th century alchemy, whose theory and practice was based on the six alchemical operations – coagulation, dissolution, sublimation, putrefaction, separation and transmutation – resulting from different reactions of salt, sulphur and mercury.

Similarly, the six ways in which the Sun, the planets and the Earth combine refer to the most fundamental nature of processes; and each category may include a vast number of different phenomena which normally appear to have nothing in common. Let us take them in order.

(a) *Sun: Earth: Planets – Process of Incarnation, Growth, Multiplication.*

Here the influence of the Sun inspires Earth with life, the result being endowed with form by the planets. The life principle enters and organises the inert chemical elements, to produce a living creature which is clothed with individual shape and qualities. This is the universal process of growth, multiplication, propagation.

All men are alive: this they owe to the Sun. All men are composed of carbon, oxygen, nitrogen, hydrogen and small quantities of calcium, iodine, phosphorus, etc.: this they owe to the Earth. All men have a distinctive shape, colour, size, speed of reaction, and other outer and inner qualities: these they owe to the planets.[20] The same may be said of animals, birds, fish, insects, plants and all other living beings.

The process by which these factors combine to create the whole multiplicity of life upon the Earth is due to this first order of forces. This order can be seen most clearly in studying the conception and embryology of living beings. Of the first visible elements - the seed and the egg - we can say little more than that they represent *life:* combined, they begin to organize *matter*: last, and only gradually, the result acquires *form*.

Further, the embryo leads to the growth of the infant, the infant to the child, the child to the man, the man to another conception, and so on. This process has the characteristic of being chain-like or continuous, one phase leading inevitably into another.

(b) *Sun: Planets: Earth – Process of Decay, Disintegration, Destruction, Elimination.*

In this second order the influence of the Sun undoes the formative work of the planets, to reduce living organisms back to Earth. The life-force itself unlocks the form, enabling its constituent chemical elements to disintegrate. Pull up a living plant, and expose it to the rays of the Sun: in a comparatively short time its carbon and oxygen will have been released into the air, and its nitrogen and mineral salts into the earth. All processes of burning, rusting, rotting, decay and elimination in general proceed by the same order of forces.

This process is complementary to the first and must exactly balance it in the healthy state of any organism. On a general scale growth can only proceed at the same rate as decay: a farmer knows that the nitrogen released by the decay of this year's vegetable matter is essential for the growth of next year's crop. 'Dust to dust and ashes to ashes' – the inevitable disintegration by this second process of the matters temporarily incorporated in living form by the first.

Such ashes can not decay further. This process results in a cosmic halt – stillness and immobility.

20. The mechanism of this connection will be treated in Chapter 10, Section II.

(c) *Earth: Sun: Planets – Process of Transformation, Refinement, Purification.*

The long-term action of life on Earth is the gradual transformation and refinement of the Earth's surface. Inorganic matter is gradually transformed to organic, organic to animal, and so on. Rocks are broken down by wind, rain and frost: the lava beds of volcanoes in 300 years become fertile vineyards. Soil becomes plant-tissue, plant-tissue the motion and sensation of animals. The natural law 'Eat and be eaten' veils this upward transformation of matter, which proceeds by the third combination – Earth: Sun: Planets. Amorphous matter is worked on by the force of life and raised into form.

Analyse a specific example. Take rock as the sample of earth. Solar heat and cooling crumble it; planetarily-produced weather and meteorological cycles lay down its dust in soil-beds of particular size and disposition. These soil-beds, in the next stage of transformation, themselves may be taken as inert matter or earth; the Sun, acting by photosynthesis, transforms soil into plant-tissues; while the action of planets determines the form into which the plant-tissue grows and the colour it assumes.

This process can again be seen as complementary to the first process of growth; but in a different way. And as we see from the above example, it also is chain-like, one stage leading naturally to another stage, though within definite limits.

(d) *Planets: Sun: Earth – Process of Disease, Rebellion, Corruption, Crime.*

In this process form breaks loose from its natural subservience, and, overcoming spirit, reduces the whole to dead matter.

Responding abnormally to the stimulus of a single planet, one particular organ or group of cells in a living being outgrows its function in the general harmony and assumes a dominant role. The uncontrolled proliferation of cancer cells, the exaggerated dominance or deficiency of the thyroid gland to produce neurotics or cretins, are examples in human pathology. Gradually such dominance overwhelms the unifying force of life deriving from the Sun, and reduces first tissue and then the whole body to its inert constituents or earth.

Taking life on Earth as a whole, the comparable condition would be for one of the kingdoms of nature to step out of its role and destroy the general balance. Mankind, for example, stimulated to pathological activity by planetary influence, periodically makes war on the animal and vegetable kingdoms, and reduces this or that area of the earth to desert.

This process, initiated by unbalanced reaction to planetary influence, represents the rebellion of the part against the whole, the organ against the body, the individual against society. It represents, in this sense, crime. And, as poison begets more poison, and crime more crime, it is continuous and self-perpetuating.

(e) *Earth: Planets: Sun – Process of Adaptation, Healing, Renewal, Invention.*

The fifth process represents the rediscovery of spirit by matter, through the mediation of right form. Inert matter, assuming with planetary help new forms suitable to changed circumstances, attracts to itself the intervention of solar forces.

The working of this order is most clear in its aspect as a counter-activity to disease and crime. Healing means that the inert matters or poisons produced by the last process must be eliminated, and the tissues once more rearrange themselves in their right place and form, permitting the renewed circulation of the life-blood.

Where deserts have been made, the very sand begins in time to assume organic qualities, and discover forms suitable to the new conditions, such as those of cactus and brush. These make possible the entry of insects, the insects of birds, and so on until the solar influence is once more able to re-clothe the desert with all its fullness of life.

On the scale of human affairs, this process means the creation by man of a new form in which natural laws can operate, that is, invention or discovery. But each invention stands alone, each healing is an end in itself. Every operation of this process represents a self-contained and separate effort.

In general it is the antidote to the process of disease. It yields normality, and prepares the way for regeneration.

(f) *Planets: Earth: Sun – Process of Regeneration, Re-Creation, Change of Nature, Art.*

In this last process, form, giving order to matter, itself becomes life or spirit. The creature emulates the creator, and itself creates. Planets are but the forms or reflections of solar influence. But they too may in some way aspire to be suns, and with Jupiter and Saturn we see their transformation already far advanced. The planet, organizing the earth or matter available to it in imitation of its sun, becomes sun to its own satellites and system.

So, in the world of men, great artists, poets, or musicians strive to organize their material, whether paint, stone or words, in an order which imitates the order of cosmic creation. By creating an order similar to that created by a higher power they acquire in little the nature of that power.

Saints and great teachers, disseminating the light of truth in the darkness of ignorance, and supporting according to cosmic laws the disciples who revolve about and depend upon them, emulate the solar source of light and themselves achieve it.

But this process differs from the others in that, seen by us from the standpoint of form, it does not *happen*. For here form itself takes the initiative of creation; form alone undertakes to overcome matter or raise it to the level of spirit. This is the process of annihilating the law of gravity. By it a being changes its nature. It is the process of doing the impossible.

We may summarise the processes thus:

(a) *Sun: Earth: Planets:* or *Life: Matter: Form:*
    Incarnation, Growth, Multiplication, Elaboration.
(b) *Sun: Planets: Earth:* or *Life: Form: Matter:*
    Decay, Disintegration, Destruction, Elimination.
(c) *Earth: Sun: Planets:* or *Matter: Life: Form:*
    Transformation, Refinement, Purification, Digestion.
(d) *Planets: Sun: Earth:* or *Form: Life: Matter:*
    Disease, Rebellion, Corruption, Crime.
(e) *Earth: Planets: Sun:* or *Matter: Form: Life:*
    Adaptation, Invention, Healing, Renewal.
(f) *Planets: Earth: Sun:* or *Form: Matter: Life:*
    Regeneration, Re-Creation, Change of Nature, Art.

All phenomena on earth, known and unknown, belong to one or another of these six processes. For there are no others. And no others are possible.

III THE FOUR STATES OF MATTER

The above descriptions have been necessarily somewhat philosophical. Now we must go further to examine exactly *how* these three forces combine to produce the six aspects of natural phenomena.

The Sun is the source of life. Put in another way this means that it is the only source of electronic radiation – that is, of light, heat, ultraviolet and other rays. The Sun alone gives out *matter in electronic state*. Other objects which seem to do so only borrow that already derived from the Sun – either by reflecting it, like the planets, or by releasing some which has been temporarily stored, as does a coal-fire or oil-lamp. This is the fastest state of matter, in which it can travel at no less than 300,000 kilometres a second.

The planets of themselves neither possess nor give out matter in electronic state. Their highest part is their atmosphere, which, being gaseous, consists of *matter in molecular state*. Evidently the atmospheres of the different planets are not of the same composition or density as that with which we are familiar on earth. Yet there is reason to believe that in some degree or other nearly all the planets possess atmospheres, that of Venus consisting largely of carbon dioxide, that of Mars of water vapour, and that of Jupiter of ammonia and methane.

These atmospheres transform and reflect the light of the Sun on a molecular level, producing corresponding changes in the atmosphere of the Earth, that is, in the molecular conditions here. The planets may thus be said to control matter in molecular state. Matter in this state is much *slower* than matter in electronic state, and its order of speed may be judged from the speed of a typical molecular motion, that of sound. Sound travels in air at the rate of about 320 metres a second, or nearly a million times more slowly than light.

Lastly, the Earth, in the sense in which we took it, as quarry of raw materials, consists of *matter in mineral state*. Such matter has no natural motion of its own, and is inert.

Now we can see how the Sun, planets and Earth combine to produce Nature or organic life. It means that matter in electronic state, matter in molecular state, and matter in mineral state combine to produce *matter in cellular state*. All organic life on Earth, all cellular matter consists, from one aspect, of electrons or matter in electronic state, from another aspect of molecules or matter in molecular state, and from a third aspect of minerals, or matter in mineral state. In men, animals, plants, these three states of matter are superimposed upon each other, so to speak, to create the fourth or 'natural' state of matter.

This explains how it is that all living beings we know contain in themselves three or four incommensurable states and speeds of matter. By virtue of their electronic structure they partake of the nature of the Sun; by virtue of their molecular structure they partake of the nature of the planets; and by virtue of their mineral structure they partake of the nature of the Earth.

But the various forms of organic life contain differing proportions of matter in these four states. Evidently a tortoise with its hard heavy shell contains a far higher proportion of mineral matter – silica and calcium, for instance – than does a dog. And conversely a dog, in whose life scent plays such a large part, must contain a higher proportion of matter in molecular state than does a tortoise. While one may further deduce that man, whose whole potentialities are based on the reception and interpretation of impressions created by light, must contain a higher proportion of matter in electronic state than either.

The fact that the four possible states of matter are so closely linked with different speeds gives us a clue as to what kind of life, if any, we might expect to find in different parts of the Solar System. Apart from their orbital movement, which probably derives from some central creative impulse applying to the whole system, all the planets and all the different parts of their surface move at different speeds, depending on their speed of rotation. This speed of rotation, in turn, seems to be very closely related to the degree of 'development' of the individual planet. The smallest and densest planets, which have no moons or few, rotate most slowly; the largest and most rarified planets, which support most moons, and which are nearest to emitting their own radiation, rotate most rapidly.

In fact, rotation, as we know from a thousand human devices, is a universal method of separating matters, of separating the coarse from the fine. There are two ways of inducing this separation by rotation – one is to apply rotating force or pressure at the centre, so that the denser matters fly outward by centrifugal force. The other is to create a rotating vacuum at the centre so that the denser matters fly inward by centripetal pull. Since in practice it is extremely difficult to compete with the great centripetal or gravitational pull of the earth, nearly all man-made methods of separation – from cream separators onwards – are centrifugal.

One of the few familiar examples of centripetal separation is a whirlwind, where a temporary patch of low pressure causes leaves and twigs to fly to the centre, dust to whirl into an outer ring, while beyond the dust again is only moving air. In this second method, heavy matters are made to gravitate to the centre, while the others dispose themselves in a series of concentric layers at various distances from the centre according to their density. The higher the speed of rotation the more perfect the separation.

Exactly in this way the planets act as vacuums or pools of low pressure in the great field of solar force. And in them also rotation gives rise to the separation of matters. A planet or satellite which does not rotate at all, like Mercury or the Moon, is nothing but a solid and homogeneous sphere of rock. With the beginning of rotation, molecular matter begins to separate itself from the mineral and fly to the surface to create the beginning

of atmosphere. While between the two yet another layer of matter in cellular state may in time distinguish itself. Just as for man, the separation out of
his different sides – physical, mental, and emotional – and his consequent
recognition of them and their relation to each other, is a sign of increased
consciousness and control, so for the planets the increased separation of
matters which results from rotation must also be regarded as a criterion
of development.

It is thus quite natural that the surface-speed deriving from rotation
should be closely connected with the state of matter and form of life to be
found on the various planets. In current parlance, when we speak of 'life'
we mean matter in cellular state. The existence of this state of matter is
probably only possible within definite limits of surface-speed: in the same
way that a pipe-stem, rubbed on one's sleeve at certain speeds, will
magnetically pick up small pieces of paper and arrange them in a pattern,
but rubbed at other speeds will not.

Suppose we take the situation on Earth, which has a diameter of
12,800 kilometres and revolves on its axis in one day. At the equator, its
surface is moving about its centre at about 28 kilometres a minute, on the
tropics of Cancer and Capricorn at about 25 kilometres a minute, at the
latitude of Europe at about 23, and at the Arctic Circle at only about 11
kilometres a minute. Parts of the Earth moving more slowly than about 10
kilometres a minute, either close to the poles or within its interior, show
practically no cellular life, but only *matter in mineral state*. While that part
of the Earth moving faster than 28 kilometres a minute – that is, the higher
reaches of the atmosphere above the equator – again shows no cellular life,
but only *matter in molecular state*. Thus, in relation to the Earth, cellular
or organic life is found only in those regions where rotational speed lies
between 28 and 10 kilometres a minute. While between those limits the
faster the rotatory movement the richer, more elaborate, more dense, more
varied the forms of organic life; the slower the rotatory movement the
poorer and sparser such forms.

Certainly the angle of the sun's rays, the distribution of moisture and
warm sea-currents are also factors of great importance. At the same time
it is difficult to believe that these differences in speed of surface-movement
are not a primary cause in the enormous variation of life-forms at different
latitudes. And if we apply this principle to the other planets and parts of
planets, in search of a clue as to possible life there, the results are – to say
the least – illuminating.

On those bodies which do not rotate at all – of which Mercury and the Moon are the best examples – we see no signs either of organic life or of atmosphere. They consist only of matter in mineral state.

Mars has a rotation period very close to the earth's 24 hours, as probably has Venus. Venus, which is approximately the same size as the earth and whose surface-speeds are thus likely to be similar, has indeed a dense cloudy atmosphere, indicating much matter in molecular state, but this very fact prevents us from establishing the presence of cellular life below. On Mars, which is smaller than the earth, surface-speeds are considerably slower. At the martian equator, surface-speed is about equivalent to that on earth in latitude 60°, that is to say in Hudson Bay or North Siberia; while the speeds outside its tropics are similar to those inside the earth's Arctic Circle.

It is thus not surprising – with our general principle in mind – to find the atmosphere of Mars to be very rudimentary and rarefied, while the famous green markings which vary with the seasons and which could very well be produced by lichens or moss, are confined to its equator. Lichens and moss do indeed form the characteristic vegetation of that region on earth with similar surface-speed.

On the equator of Jupiter, on the other hand, surface-speed is about 700 kilometres a minute, that is to say, twenty-five times faster than the fastest surface-speed on earth. If there is a connection be-tween the small differences in speed on earth and the increasing diversity, richness and proliferation of life towards the equator, then obviously at such a speed as this the kaleidoscopic diversity and in-terchangeability of forms would be such that they could not be confined within cellular processes at all. They would correspond more to what we know of the speed, variety and potency of *molecular phenomena* on earth.

This indeed tallies with what we know of the surface of Jupiter, which appears to consist of one vast, constantly agitated, gaseous ocean. Such a gaseous ocean, if our theory is correct, is not too inert for organic life as we know it, but on the contrary could be the home of forms and manifestations of life far too fast to be contained within familiar cellular bodies. To find a parallel to possible forms of life on Jupiter, we should have to think of perfumes, sounds, music, essences and so on, that is, molecular phenomena, but endowed with individuality and intelligence.

The only places on Jupiter where rotational speeds could be found similar to those on the surface of the earth, and thus where cellular life is at all possible, are either close to the poles or many thousands of miles deep in its gaseous interior. And conditions on the outer planets – Saturn, Uranus and Neptune – will probably resemble those on Jupiter.

The picture which results from all this seems to be of the planets as fields of low pressure, in which matter in its four states is deposited in order – that in mineral state in the centre, that in cellular state next, that in molecular state third, and that in electronic state outermost. And further, of these four states of matter existing in and produced by definite ranges of rotational speed.

If this is so, then rotational speed indeed appears to be an index of a planet's 'development'. And we may say – in searching for organic life elsewhere in the Solar System – that certain planets appear not yet to have progressed to the point where cellular life is possible; while others on the contrary have developed to a stage where such forms of life have been transcended altogether. All are at different stages of development, yet all are equally necessary to the whole system – as bones, blood and brain may be said to be at different stages of development, while equally essential to the existence of the whole man.

This hint as to the nature of 'development' for planets gives a clue as to the nature of 'development' for the beings who live upon them. We have already seen how all living beings are literally created from the matter of the Sun, the planets and Earth. All contain electronic or solar matter – that is, matter which in old philosophies was described as divine – but this electronic matter may be more or less securely locked up. The electrons are first locked up by the influence of the planets into molecules, molecules in turn are locked up by the nature of the Earth into mineral forms.

Any process of improvement or regeneration of natural or human forms must consist in unlocking more and more of the matter of the body from mineral first into molecular and then into electronic state. Such unlocking will inevitably be accompanied by an increase in the speed of the organism – a process, taking the regeneration of nature in its largest sense, which is theoretically only limited when *all* the matter of this organism is unlocked into electronic state. In such a condition, it could supposedly travel at 300,000 kilometres a second, and thus, like light, exist in all parts of the Solar System simultaneously.

Now, however, it can be understood how such *unlocking* runs counter to all ordinary growth, and indeed to the whole process of creation, which consists exactly in the *locking up* of solar or divine energy into ever more manifold and complex forms. This is why it has been said that the process of regeneration is against nature and against creation, despite the fact that it implies a return to the fastest or divine state of matter.

V THE SUN

I THE PHYSICAL BEING OF THE SUN

IN THE EARLY PART OF THE SEVENTEENTH CENTURY, ROBERT FLUDD, an English doctor, outlined a mathematical harmony of the universe, in which the Sun stood exactly midway between the Absolute and Man. By size, energy, length of life, and responsibility, the Sun was shown to sound the middle note of a cosmic 'monochord'. So that from man's point of view, standing below, the laws and nature of the highest powers in the universe were expressed *through* the physical Sun and were best to be understood in its action. This idea will prove a useful focus to all our technical knowledge.

One of the first things we have to realise about the Sun is that we can not know anything at first hand about its interior, or its interior qualities, any more than we could know anything at first hand about the interior or interior qualities of a human body if our only means of studying it were from a distance of a hundred yards. What we study and experience about the Sun refers to its surface, and the radiations given off from its surface. All theories about the interior of the Sun, its temperature, pressure and nature, are the result of deduction only. And it is worth remembering that at least three or four mutually exclusive theories about the composition of the Sun and the generation of solar energy have in turn been accepted and abandoned by scientists during the last hundred years.[22]

This Sun, by whose energy the planets revolve and the world of Nature lives, appears to us as a great radiant ball which we calculate to be a million times larger than the Earth. To the naked eye its dazzling brilliance, shading a little from the centre to the edge, gives the impression of an incandescent cloud. Through a telescope this cloud is seen to be not only incandescent, but in a constant half-liquid, half-gaseous state of flux. Here and there in the white-hot sea huge vortices of flame and force develop which in a few hours may shoot fountains of fire half-a-million miles into space. While the molten equator, like the skirts of a dancer, whirls fastest with the great ball's spinning.

A larger telescope reveals another aspect of the solar disc. The whole blinding surface is now seen as a shimmering granulation, with still more

22. For example, Mayer's falling meteorite theory, von Helmholtz' contraction theory, Eddington's iron sun theory, Eddington's 35% hydrogen theory.

brilliant grains shifting and changing at every minute against a duller ground. These granules of light are in reality wells of hotter gases rising from below. The two or three million of them which transpire the Sun's inner heat closely correspond to the number of sweat-glands which similarly cool the human body. And these solar pores, five hundred or a thousand miles across, sweating lakes of fire as big as the Black Sea, vividly recall the relation between the cosmos of the Sun and the cosmos of man which we more intimately know.

Although the total mass of the Sun is now believed to be 90% hydrogen, the light given off by the white-hot solar surface, when examined by spectro-analysis, is found to include radiations of all elements known on earth. These elements resolve themselves into layers. The visible granulated surface, known as the *photosphere*, is composed of heavy metallic vapours which form a gaseous crust or epidermis over whatever may lie within. Above this lies a translucent and incandescent atmosphere of hydrogen and helium called the *chromosphere*. And beyond this again flames a *corona* of radiance, which at times of eclipse appears like a visible magnetic field extending many millions of miles into the void of space.

The mysterious shifting form of this corona, which at one period is like a halo, at another like a pair or double pair of wings, can be reproduced and explained by a simple experiment. If dust is sprinkled on the surface of water, and an apple transfixed upon a knitting-needle is spun half-submerged, the movement of the dust-particles will create a field similar to that of the corona, all the recorded forms of which can be reproduced by changes in the angle between the knitting needle and the surface. The corona thus seems to be the trace, in luminous particles, of the field of force set up by the Sun's rotation on its axis; akin, perhaps, to the aura of bodily warmth and magnetism which surrounds a human being.

There is one still more attenuated emanation of the Sun. This appears to us as the *zodiacal light*, a faint glow stretching from it far out across the plane of the ecliptic, and which is even visible to the

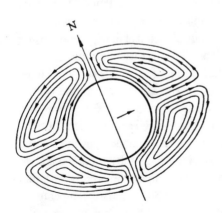

Fig. 4 : Field of Force created by a Rotating Sphere

naked eye as a luminous trail following or preceding the Sun at dusk or dawn. The zodiacal light evidently represents a lens-shaped cloud of some highly rarefied matter forming as it were a second or outer aura of the Sun, which extends in an attenuated form even as far as the orbit of the Earth. This cloud diffuses the Sun's light in some such way as do the atmospheres of the planets; and later we shall note that the one planet which does not possess any atmosphere of its own, Mercury, finds itself deep inside this cloud, and may perhaps be said to borrow or enjoy instead the atmosphere of the Sun.

The photosphere, the chromosphere, the corona and the zodiacal light thus represent four successive envelopes or emanations of the solar body.

In the chromosphere, that part most accessible to our study, the active element is hydrogen, the lightest and simplest element known to man, which forms as it were an ocean of lambs'-wool cloud (flocculi) over its entire surface. The complementary passive element appears to be calcium; and photographs of the sun by hydrogen and calcium light, that is, of the hydrogen and calcium in the Sun respectively, look like positive and negative prints of the same picture.

From a certain action which takes place in the chromosphere, where these hydrogen and calcium clouds seethe like a cauldron of boiling water, the whole immense radiation which sustains the solar system is given off. From man's point of view the most obvious characteristics of this radiation are light and heat. And it is even obvious to him that the Sun represents the source, origin, and as it were the absolute of these two qualities. At the same time, intensified to the degree in which they are found in the Sun, heat and light are evidently incomparable with anything we understand by these words on Earth, and no mere multiplication of figures representing temperature or brilliance can give us any idea of their meaning.

For instance, the temperature of the interior of the sun is supposed to be 20,000,000° Centigrade, a temperature of the same order as the central core of an atomic bomb explosion. We do not know what this figure means. Even the temperature of the solar surface, estimated at about 6000° Centigrade, is far above that required for all earthly substances, even iron and nickel, to boil and vaporize. In vaporizing, such substances expand to fifteen-hundred or two-thousand times the volume they occupy in liquid or solid state. If the Earth were raised to the Sun's surface temperature, that is, if it were to boil, it would become a radiant ball of gas 100,000 miles across, while were the Sun cooled to earthly temperature, it would solidify no bigger than the planet Saturn. Thus we may say that even the Sun's enormous size in relation to its planets is only a by-product of its intense heat. And conversely, could these planets acquire such heat they too would achieve the size and potency of suns.

Even brilliancy of radiation is directly related to temperature. Red heat of iron and rocks is about 500° Centigrade, so that if the surface of the Earth were to become hotter than that it too would begin to glow with its own light. On the other hand, were a dwarfed and solid Sun to fall below this temperature, the whole solar system would be engulfed in utter darkness, a play of lightless and lifeless balls in an empty cellar. It needs very little imagination to understand that such a system, could it be supposed at all, would be a corpse – an astronomical body in which the heart had ceased to beat, heat to flow, and the different parts to have any cohesion or common meaning.

Thus what we try to measure in degrees of Fahrenheit or Centigrade must be something akin to creative power, to life itself. It must be a state of being, quite independent of the material of which the Sun is composed, just as consciousness in man is quite independent of the elements of which the human body is composed. Indeed, the Sun and its planets appear not to differ greatly in their composition, but only in this state of being – which for lack of better measure – we attempt to calculate as heat.

Every modification of temperature and brilliance creates enormous effects. Sunspots, whirling vortices as large as planets and 1000° Centigrade cooler than the rest of the Sun's disc, act like the actual planets to create magnetic fields of their own, which as profoundly affect the atmosphere of the Earth as do the magnetic fields of these latter. Sunspots can indeed be re-garded as potential planets within the body of the Sun, the unfertilised seeds of planets, so to speak. And it is more than probable that the actual planets were in their origin projected into space and independent existence through just such vortices as these.

The separate magnetic fields of sunspots, superimposed on the great magnetic field of the sun, are reflected upon earth in northern lights, elec-tric storms, and disturbances in innumerable phases of the activity of man and productivity of nature. In fact, they may be regarded as taking effect by just the same laws as those we have established for planetary influence, and in a comparable rhythm.

Sunspot activity follows a clearly-marked eleven-year cycle, during which time the spots not only wax and wane in number, but the belt in which they appear moves steadily downwards towards the Sun's equator, only to reappear again at a higher latitude. This eleven-year pulsation, according to the time-relation already established,[23] exactly corresponds on the Sun's time-scale to magnetic frequencies on the scale of man. So that some intimate relation seems to exist between the range of vibrations felt as magnetism by different cosmoses, and we may even say that the sunspot period is our human way of registering 'the personal magnetism' of the Sun. It is thus hardly surprising that this period should so profoundly affect all life deriving from that source.

The Sun works on terrestrial man and nature in two quite different ways, by two different categories of energy transmitted at different speeds. As we have so often declared, the Sun transmits life to the Earth by means of light. But it also transmits form to the Earth by means of magnetism. Without doubt in the beginning it even ejected the very matter so to be endowed with life and form. Thus *all* things, *all* influences, *all* life, matter and form may be regarded as emanating from the Sun in the fulness and totality of time.

Only, just as the administration of a certain quantity of matter is delegated to the Earth for its lifetime, so a certain share in the formative work carried out through magnetic fields is delegated to the planets for theirs. It is in this sense that – although life, form and matter all derive from the Sun – from our point of view we must regard the planets as custodians of the second and our Earth of the third.

The radiation of light and life has, however, remained the Sun's prerogative and the Sun's alone. During all the ages covered by human history, legend and research, the Sun's radiation has remained practically constant. A change of a single magnitude in its brilliance would destroy life on Earth by boiling or freezing all water there. Yet all fossilized forms of life bear witness only to such changes of earthly temperature, as would result from an almost imperceptible pulsation of solar heat.

To our knowledge, for perhaps three-billion years the Sun has poured its immense and unvarying force into the sustenance of its planets and into the empty space between. During all that time, this field of energy has been prodigious enough to swing Neptune in its orbit three-billion miles away: and it has been delicate enough to lift the sap in the stalk of a fern. What is the source of such immense and constant energy, and what is its nature?

23. According to the time-relationships of our 'Table of Times and Cosmoses' (Appendix II), a periodicity of 11 years for the sun corresponds to a frequency of 250 vibrations a second for man.

II HYDROGEN INTO LIGHT

A very interesting answer to this question has been proposed by Bethe of Cornell. This is based on the possibility that in the conditions which exist on the Sun the *atoms* of different elements are not immutable but may break up and recombine, giving off energy in the process, just as, on earth, *molecules* can break up and recombine into new substances and organisms, radiating heat, light and magnetism as they do so. Thus on earth a molecule of wood, being burned, becomes a molecule of ash, having given off molecular heat. But on the sun, it would be an atom which was consumed, forming a different kind of atom and releasing an atomic energy.

Now atoms, as is generally known, consist of a central nucleus round which revolves a number of electrons, varying with the element concerned. The simplest atom is that of hydrogen, which has one electron; helium has 2, while carbon, nitrogen and oxygen have 6, 7, and 8, respectively.[24] But in some cases an element may vary slightly in atomic weight, that is,

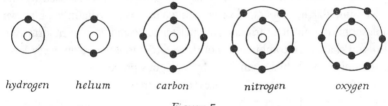

| hydrogen | helium | carbon | nitrogen | oxygen |

Figure 5

though it has the correct number of electrons for that element, it may be slightly underweight and unstable, that is, tending to slip back to the next lighter element, or it may be slightly overweight and thus be a stage nearer the next heavier one. These elemental variants are called isotopes.

We have noted that the active element in the Sun seems to consist of almost unlimited hydrogen. Bethe supposed that, in the conditions of incredible force and tension existing on the sun, hydrogen atoms with their single electron are constantly bombarding 6-electron carbon atoms with such violence that they combine to form 7-electron nitrogen atoms. But these nitrogen atoms will be light and unstable, and the odd electron will radiate into space as a free sunray, leaving a carbon atom again, but this time a heavy one. The next colliding hydrogen atom will combine with this to produce a stable nitrogen atom. In exactly the same way a new collision by a hydrogen atom will raise the nitrogen atom to a light oxygen atom,

24. For our present purpose we do not need to go into the question of electronic orbits or shells, which will be treated in Chapter 7, 'The Elements of Earth'.

from which again one free electron will escape into space as radiant energy. Now there remains a heavy nitrogen atom, which is again bombarded by hydrogen. This time, however, a different effect results – the hydrogen atom itself captures one of the nitrogen electrons to form a 2-electron atom of helium, while the 7-electron nitrogen atom is reduced to the 6-electron carbon atom with which we started.

The net result of the cycle is that four hydrogen atoms have been consumed to form one atom of helium and two sun-rays. Gamow calculated that the amount of hydrogen available in the sun is sufficient to generate by this process all solar radiation required by the Solar System for 40 thousand million years.

Physically and logically, the explanation seems sound. But as we examine it more closely we suddenly begin to recognize something familiar in the sequence described. When we were studying the different processes resulting from the combination of the three forces in the solar system, we came to the conclusion that the process of growth (a) proceeded by the order Sun, Earth, Planets, that is, active, passive, mediating; or as we philosophically put it, spirit entering matter to be endowed with form. We also said that these combinations of three forces must exist on every level of the universe, always giving rise to analogous processes.

It now occurs to us that this process of growth is exactly the one we have just described. Hydrogen, the active element, plunges into the passive element carbon, to produce an intermediate element helium and a certain radiation of life which is the very signature of this order. The production of energy by the Sun is of the nature of growth. It *is* the growth of the Solar System.

Where does it lead, this process of solar growth of which we and all we know are the product? How does this maelstrom of force congeal into the life we live and recognise? To answer this question we must go back a step.

The active element in the Sun is hydrogen. This is very interesting, because the atom of hydrogen, with its single electron revolving round a nucleus, stands on the borderline between matter in electronic and matter in molecular state. Hydrogen and all denser matter combine with other matters, atom to atom, to form molecules. But the next degree of rarefaction *above* hydrogen results in free electrons or arrangements of matter in electronic state – that is, in light, magnetic waves, and so on.

In the carbon cycle we saw how this transition from hydrogen (that is, matter in molecular state) to light rays (that is, matter in electronic state) may take place in the sun. Actually, a comparable process takes place in man when the air he breathes (molecular matter) at last becomes transformed into the nervous impulses of thought and emotion (electronic matter), and in this condition becomes sufficiently penetrating to affect others, to help or hinder them, even when transmitted over great distances. A man who has an interesting thought on a brisk walk and transmits it by phone to a friend in the next town, and in this way produces an increase in the friend's well-being and happiness, is in fact utilizing the transformation of molecular into electronic matter in much the same way as does the sun in radiating energy to the earth.

The transformation of hydrogen into light, described by Bethe, represents *change of matter into a state in which it can be transmitted at long distance*. Thus if the calcium of the sun may be said to correspond to its physical body, the chromosphere or sphere of hydrogen would be its 'life', and the solar radiation of various kinds might represent its 'thought' and 'emotion'.

According to the quantum theory developed by Max Planck this radiation is not transmitted continuously, but in a series of successive pulses or quanta, each representing a measurable packet of energy, which bears a fixed relation to the wave-length of light. A quantum is an impulse embracing a few thousand such light-waves, and separated from the succeeding quantum by some sort of interval.

In other words, if one light-wave represents a day for an electron, a quantum is almost certainly connected with the *life* of an electron. It is an attempt to measure *the amount of energy expended by a free electron during its lifetime*. And as we see from the above, the higher the frequency of the radiation, the greater the amount of energy a quantum will represent, that is, the more energy and power of penetration will the life of an electron contain. An electron transmitting blue light is actually living more intensely than an electron transmitting red light, exactly as a man transmitting the impulses of emotion is living more intensely than a man who is only transmitting the cold impulses of thought.

Moreover, this free electron, projected into space with its minute cargo of vital energy, is the product of hydrogen. For from what has been said above, it is clear that large quantities of hydrogen must be present for any body of itself to emit light of a comparable radiation. Hydrogen is, so to speak, the matter of suns, the fuel from which they create the radiations necessary to transmit life to their systems.

In this connection it is interesting to note that the two planets in the composition of which hydrogen appears to play a dominant part are Jupiter, whose atmosphere is said to be chiefly ammonia (NH^3) and methane (CH^4), and Saturn, whose atmosphere is believed to consist of hydrogen and helium. Both support complete systems of satellites and may even be faintly self-luminous, though this luminosity is rendered unnoticeable by the infinitely greater brilliance of the Sun. In any case, as we guessed when thinking of the process of regeneration, they are evidently trying to become suns.

What happens to the light created by the Sun out of hydrogen, and radiated to all quarters of space? One two-hundred-millionth of it serves to animate the earth. In six hours the rest has filled every corner of the Solar System, out to the furthest confines of Neptune's orbit. On the scale of life and perception of the Sun such a time is immeasurably small – equivalent to less than one millionth of a second on the scale of man. So that for the Sun, its light must truly exist in all parts of its system simultaneously, as can consciousness in man.

Indeed, if we remember the connection between intensity of light and orbital speed, which we established earlier, we find that in studying light we are in fact very close to the nature of that

'Amor che muove il Sol e l'altri stelli',

of which Dante spoke.

One of the most striking qualities of this light is that it is undiminishable and eternal. We are familiar with the law that the intensity of light from a given source diminishes in inverse proportion to the square of the distance. But this refers to the amount of light registered by a given receiving area. If we remember that as distance grows greater, the imaginary sphere which receives the light increases in area *in the same proportion*, then we realize that the total amount of light received from a given source is exactly the same at a distance of a million miles as at a distance of ten yards. No fraction of the light of a single candle is lost even when it reaches the outskirts of the solar system: it is only diffused around that prodigious circumference.

Moreover, this process of diffusion of light without loss goes on indefinitely. As we know from observation of the most distant galaxies, it is still going on five hundred million years after its first emission. All the light which was then radiated by such galaxies *still exists*, though now at this immense remove.

If light can diffuse and endure undiminished for half-a-billion years, it can surely do so for ever. This means that all light, from a candle or from a super-sun, sooner or later fills the entire universe. Light is *undiminishable*, *eternal and omni-present.* In every religion that existed these qualities have been recognized as divine. So that we are forced to the conclusion that light – actual sensible light – is indeed the direct vehicle of divinity: it is the consciousness of God.

When it reaches the planets, however, this light or matter in electronic state is gradually transmuted back into molecular state again. On Earth the first stages of this process take place in the upper reaches of the atmosphere, or ionosphere, where solar radiation recreates hydrogen ions. This may be seen as a kind of condensation or crystallization of free electrons into the finest form of atom. A similar process probably occurs on all the other planets, though this 'saturation' of the planet's atmosphere with hydrogen has evidently gone much further on Saturn and Jupiter than it has on Earth; and further on Earth than on Mars or Venus.

In any case, the combination of these hydrogen atoms with atoms of the various substances already existing on Earth gives rise to all forms of life known to us.

In this way, it is clear that all life on Earth is, as it were, a condensation of electronic or solar radiation, just as the drops of water on a window-pane represent the condensation of water-vapour on contact with a chilling surface. This is the sun's 'growth'.

At the same time the creation of such life does not imply a loss of the electronic nature of matter, but, as we saw earlier, its temporary locking into forms of varying shape and of greater or less density. Within these forms, the electrons, with their affinity for the Sun, still exist; and in fact, all these forms are *made* of such electrons. Further, when these forms 'die', as we say, it merely means that the magnetic field creating a certain individual shape is broken, the heavier or earthly elements composing it fall away, and the original hydrogen atoms are released. Most probably these hydrogen atoms again break up into electrons, and in this state resume their free passage throughout the Solar System which was temporarily interrupted by their incorporation into bodies.

That is to say, the energy incorporated into physical bodies, when the latter die, *becomes light again.* If we remember the conclusion we just came to about the nature of light, we can even say that, physical bodies disintegrating, their matter returns to the divine state. Only the proof of this thesis is hampered by the fact that normally we can only conceive of consciousness attached to physical bodies, or to matter in cellular state. And it could only be established satisfactorily by the actual carrying over of consciousness into matter in electronic state.

The whole question may then be put like this: Is this matter in its return to the divine state accompanied by individual consciousness? Who possesses an individual consciousness sufficiently permanent and sufficiently intense to take advantage of this infinite expansion of its vehicle? About such possibilities little is ordinarily known.

III POSSIBILITIES IN THE SUN

It is said that cosmoses are nourished by three different kinds of food, of different levels of matter. Man, for instance, eats solid organic food deriving from the World of Nature, breathes the gaseous air of his planet, the Earth, and is animated by visual perceptions of reflected sunlight. He is nourished by the free matter, so to speak, of the three cosmoses superior to himself – Nature, Earth and Sun. Seen from another point of view, he floats or swims in a sea of these higher matters, and may be said to absorb the media in which he lives, as a sponge absorbs water.

What nourishes the cosmos of the Sun? By this question we do not refer to interchanges within the Solar System itself, whereby beings or matters, long since emanated by the Sun, may return to it at last, and in this sense feed their creator. For this movement is rather an internal circulation *within* the great solar body.

What food does the Sun take in *from outside its system?* What are the free matters of still vaster cosmoses by which it is sustained? If we may be excused a rather startlingly anthropomorphic deduction from our human example, we would say that it should eat the matter of the system of Sirius, breathe the matter of the Milky Way, and perceive by virtue of the Absolute.

This last idea is clearly beyond our consideration. Of the second we have some scientific indications.

In recent years the idea has grown more and more accepted that the depths of the Milky Way, instead of lying empty between sun and sun, are filled with clouds of drifting gas – that same gas from which (it is now believed) these suns originally congealed. In the 1940's, Lyttleton and Hoyle further developed the idea that these suns, 'tunnelling' – as they described it – through this gas, pick up the medium through which they pass, leaving an empty trail behind them. Interstellar gas is sucked into our Sun, they said, and is there consumed or incorporated into the Sun's mass.

This, of course, is an exact description of a being 'breathing' the medium through which it passes. For a man could in the same way be said to be 'tunnelling' through air as he sucks it into himself while walking or running.

Hoyle further assumes, from coal deposits in Spitzbergen and the Antarctic which indicate that tropical vegetation once existed near the poles, that the Sun has at times been rather hotter than it is now. And similarly that the great ice ages may have resulted from a slight decrease in its temperature. He connects this with greater or less intake of interstellar gas, that is, with deeper or shallower 'breathing'. Such coal deposits are a hundred or two-hundred million years old. If we refer to our table of cosmic times, we find that such a period is of the order of a solar day. And combining our own line of thought with Hoyle's, we may suggest that the variations of which he speaks are connected with that fundamental change in the nature of a being's breathing which takes place between night and day, between sleeping and waking state.

The chief point of this idea of cosmic 'feeding', however, is that *the Sun stands to the Milky Way as man does to the Earth, and it stands to the Absolute as man himself does to the Sun.*

Various observations support this first relationship. We see the surface or plane of the Milky Way (which is all we can visualise of it) peopled with millions of suns, just as we see the surface of the earth peopled with millions of men. These suns revolve about the axis of the galaxy, as men revolve about the axis of the earth. And they are now said to breathe the galactic atmosphere as men breathe the terrestrial one.

Such are the material implications of the comparison. But what of the metaphysical ones? We have already seen that in relation to man the Sun possesses to the utmost the divine attributes of omnipotence, omnipresence, eternity, of creation, maintenance and destruction. What shall we say then of an Absolute which is as divine to the Sun, as the Sun is to us, which represents as it were divinity squared? If anyone fear that a physical approach to the universe may diminish his conception of God, let him meditate upon this: That the most infinite divinity to which he can pray is but a speck to the Absolute of All.

The better to do so, let us ask again: What is the Sun in relation to man? By other reasoning, we concluded that the Sun contains all possibilities for man. Now we can examine the meaning of this statement in more detail.

It is a general principle that the rarer and finer the matter the greater the number of possibilities contained in it. Philosophically, we said that the Absolute must by definition contain *all* possibilities. And as we descend the scale of worlds, on each level the number of possibilities contained in matter diminishes.

When we reach the familiar level of earthly elements, the possibilities are already clearly defined and limited. An atom of iron contains in itself the possibility of combining with other atoms to form a whole series of molecules – it contains within itself the possibility of being incorporated in steel, rust, a mordant dye, and even a raisin or human blood. But it does not naturally contain the possibility of becoming an atom of copper. This is a definite limitation of possibility belonging to the level of the earth. Similarly, atoms of carbon, oxygen, nitrogen and hydrogen between them contain the possibilities of all living matter. But they do *not* contain the possibility of becoming each other. On Earth one element does not naturally contain the possibility of another element.

If we descend another level to the world and scale of man we find molecules in turn beginning to become fixed. A molecule of wood contains in itself the possibility of becoming incorporated in a particle of table or a particle of pencil, but it does *not* contain the possibility of becoming a molecule of butter, even though its constituent elements may be the same.

Looking at conditions on our satellite, the moon, we seem to see a still lower world where to our perception nothing contains any possibilities at all. Nothing can change into anything else, but is condemned to remain eternally what it is. This is the antithesis of the Absolute, the end of creation, outer darkness.

Now, returning to the process that we seemed to detect upon the Sun, we find a much greater range of possibility existing there than we are familiar with on Earth. *There* one element *can* change into another. On Earth, one may leave an atom of iron overnight, assured that it will still be an atom of iron in the morning. Everything in our life and perception depends upon this axiom. But on the Sun this is no longer true. There what is a carbon-atom one moment is a nitrogen-atom the next, and an oxygen-atom the third. One element contains in itself the possibility of another element. We may even hazard, from a study of the principle of atomic chain-reactions, that a hydrogen atom contains within itself the possibility of all other elements.

It now becomes clear what man, in his efforts to split the atom, was trying to do. Working with uranium, he succeeded in chipping one electron off an atom of unnatural, almost pathological density. Yet even this released energy on an incomparably greater scale than any he had conceived before. Using the force so made available as starter, he then endeavoured to make hydrogen atoms combine to form helium atoms, yielding practically unlimited energy in the process, exactly as we have described.

What in fact he was attempting, was to introduce on Earth a phenomenon which does not belong to the Earth at all, but belongs to the nature of the Sun. The hydrogen bomb involved the actual creation on earth of a miniature sun. The result of this black magic could only be utter devastation and the reduction of living to inert material on a completely new scale. This process also sounds familiar. Man prostitutes solar force to produce dead earth. Form reduces spirit to matter. Such a process can only be crime.

By trying to use atomic energy, that is, by trying to discover how to change one atom into another, man was searching for entrance into the world where matter contains all possibilities. Probably there is a legitimate entrance to such a world. If man could discover how to maintain individual consciousness when his matter returns to electronic state, he would already be free of such a world. And from what we deduced earlier, it seems that this possibility is connected with the problem of death, and the mystery of death.

But evidently there is also an illegitimate way to approach such a world. This refers to the use of scientific laws *without improvement of man's consciousness and being*. Such an approach, from the nature of the forces involved, can only lead to disaster.

Yet on the scale of the Sun even this is of no importance. We must realize that there, in the Solar World, nothing that we regard as fixed is fixed. All that we see as permanent is there transient, while what we see as transient is there eternal. It means that for us the Solar World is inconceivable. In it are contained infinitely greater possibilities than exist in any world we know or can imagine. Indeed, if we remember the relation between cosmoses which we already established, we shall realize that while the world of Nature contains man's time and the world of Earth his recurrence, the Solar World must represent the sixth dimension for him, that is, *the Sun contains all possibilities for man.*

Go out and stare at the sun in the sky. Why are you blinded? Why are you unable to define or describe what you see? Why is the impression incomparable with anything else you know? It is because you are looking through a hole in our three-dimensional scenery, *out into the six-dimensional world.*

The matter of the Sun, or electronic matter, is beyond form and beyond time. It is even beyond the recurrence of form and the repetition of time. In relation to our world, it is immortal, eternal and omnipotent. And everything that its creatures can experience or conceive is but a limitation of its boundless possibilities.

77

VI THE HARMONY OF THE PLANETS

IN THE FOURTH CHAPTER THE COMBINED INFLUENCES OF ALL THE
planets was taken as a single force. Now we must see how the reflections
of individual planets, each constantly turning in its own rhythm, and
as constantly changing its relation to all the others, combine to create at
every moment a new setting and a new mood. Earlier, we tried to observe
from a place where time stood still, and the past and future of the worlds
became solid and motionless. But when we consider the influences of planets on men and nature, we are back in the world of our own perception;
and *here* the key to understanding is the sense that all moves, all shifts,
merges, separates and recombines, all is transient and changeable.

At present it is the Earth's point of view that concerns us. To a creature
on the earth's surface the familiar orbital times of the planets – though
possessing harmony and significance in relation to the Solar System – do
not have any special meaning. What is important is their relation to the
earth; just as what is important to an onlooker at a race meeting is not the
manoeuvres of the horses round the track, but their relative position when
they pass the winning-post.

Suppose each planet to reflect some influence of a constant kind and
intensity, magnetism for instance. To sensitive beings on Earth, this
influence must vary, not according to the position of that planet in its
own orbit, but according to its distance from the Earth, the speed at which
it approaches the Earth or retreats from it, and above all the angle at which
it shines upon the Earth's surface.

In terms of radiance, this variability is known to every countryman who
watches the night sky from one season to the next. Venus and Jupiter vary
a whole stellar magnitude in brilliance ($2\frac{1}{2}$ times), while Mars is fifty times
brighter at one aspect than another. The influence of magnetism varies in a
similar way.

The periodicity of a planet's influence upon the Earth must thus follow
the time necessary for it to return to the same relative position. As we saw
in an earlier chapter, all phenomena in nature are the product of three
forces – Sun, planets, Earth. Taking as point of departure the moment when
Sun, Earth and a given planet are in a straight line, that planet's cycle will
be the time that elapses before such conjunction occurs again. In other

words, it is the interval between the recurring moments when these three forces act together in the same way.

But there are greater and lesser combinations of forces in the heavens and greater and less conjunctions. While the strength of a planet's influence will in general follow the periodicity of its simple conjunction with the Sun, an exactly similar situation will only repeat when Earth, planet, and Sun all stand in the same relation to the Milky Way or zodiac. Since the Sun's position relative to the zodiac is recognized by us through the succession of the seasons, it follows that this full relation only recurs when the planetary conjunction comes again at exactly the same season as it did originally. For each planet there is therefore a double rhythm of influence – a minor cycle of its conjunction with the Sun, included within a major cycle when this condition is still further accentuated by a return to the same relation with the zodiac.

For each planet a certain and different number of minor cycles bring a major cycle. And as we shall later see, the whole combination of these cycles forms an extraordinary mathematical or musical notation.

We can make a table of minor and 'major conjunctions according to which planetary influence may be expected to wax and wane:

Planet	Conjunctions			
	Earth, Planet, Sun		Earth, Planet, Sun, Zodiac	
(Moon	$29\frac{1}{2}$ days)			
Mercury	117 days (4 lunar cycles)	$\times$ 25 =	8 years	
Venus	585 ,, (20 ,, ,,)	$\times$ 5 =	8 ,,	
Mars	780 ,,	$\times$ 7 =	15 ,,	
Asteroids [25]	468 ,,	$\times$ 7 =	9 ,,	
Jupiter	398 ,,	$\times$ 11 =	12 ,,	
Saturn	378 ,,	$\times$ 29 =	30 ,,	
Uranus	369 ,,	$\times$ 83 =	84 ,,	
Neptune	367 ,,	$\times$ 163 =	164 ,,	

Mercury and Venus thus repeat their maximum effect every 8 years, the Asteroids every 9 years, Jupiter every 12 years, Mars every 15 years, and Saturn every 30 years. If these various rhythms be superimposed, we find a very interesting series of harmonic intervals developing in time, each stage of which is marked by the major conjunction of one or more planets.

25. Theoretical conjunction, based on the average orbital time of their chief concentration.

	Jupiter × 2 / Venus & Mercury × 3	Asteroids × 3	Mars × 2 / Saturn × 1	Venus & Mercury × 4	Jupiter × 3 / Asteroids × 4	Venus & Mercury × 5	Mars × 3 / Asteroids × 5	Jupiter × 4 / Venus & Mercury × 6
Years	24	27	30	32	36	40	45	48
Notes	do	re	mi	fa	sol	la	si	do

For the inner planets, we find in addition a shorter-term series, based this time, not on their greater conjunction with the sun and zodiac, but on their lesser conjunction with the sun and moon. This second series naturally measures itself in lunar months ($29\frac{1}{2}$ days) rather than in solar years.[26]

	Mars × 3 / Venus × 4 / Asteroids × 5 / Mercury × 20	Venus × 4½	Venus × 5 / Mercury × 25	Mars × 4	Mars × 4½ / Venus × 6 / Mercury × 30	Mars × 5	Venus × 7½	Mars × 6 / Venus × 8 / Asteroids × 19 / Mercury × 40
Lunar Months	80	90	100	106⅔	120	133⅓	150	160
Days	2340	2632½	2925	3120	3510	3900	4387½	4680
Notes	do	re	mi	fa	sol	la	si	do

Now this second series is an exact repetition of the first, all the figures being simply multiplied by three and a third. These two strange and irregular progressions, though apparently independent, are the same. Further, they both belong to a harmonic series which we have met before.

For there is already one connection in which the series 24, 27, 30, 32, 36, 40, 45, 48, is familiar to us. These figures, taken as vibrations, represent the relative values of the notes of a major musical scale. And we are reminded of old stories that this same musical scale, ascribed by legend to the Pythagoreans, was invented by a special school of astronomers and physicists, *to echo the music of the spheres.*

---

26. In this second series, Jupiter and Saturn also appear to take part, but as a joint influence, working on a cycle of 390 days. Every 390 days these two planets return to a mean relation with the Earth, and make equal angles with Earth and Sun — that is, their influences balance. Such a cycle coincides with no less than five of the eight stages of this series — do (× 6), mi (× 7½), fa (× 8), sol (× 9), do (× 12). A curious corroborating fact will be touched on in Chapter 11, 'Man as Microcosm'.

THE HARMONY OF THE PLANETS

It is now clear that this is no legend, but actual fact. The octave or musical scale is a notation, adapted to man's hearing, of this harmony of the planetary cycles, which in turn is an echo of a great law which controls the development of all processes in the universe.[27]

In the interaction of what we took for so many fortuitous movements, two entirely separate and musically perfect octaves, developing eternally through the life of man and the history of his race, are now revealed. Moreover, if we recall and apply the immense factor which separates human time and perception from the time and perception of the Sun,[28] we find that this planetary harmony must effect such divine sensation exactly as audible music affects man. Between human time and solar time lie 36 octaves; exactly the same interval separates the vibrations of human music from the vibrations of planetary motions. In literal fact the motions of the planets make music for the Sun.

II THE MEANING OF THE HARMONY

What we have tried to formulate thus far is the periodic recurrence of the whole cycle of each planet's influence, and the relation of these cycles to each other. Within its cycle, however, the influence of each planet waxes and wanes in a very individual way. We have already seen that this variation can be measured in three ways. One of these ways, which we will leave for the moment, refers to its varying influence on different parts of the Earth at any given moment. The other two ways of measurement – by the changing distance of the planet from the earth, and by its changing speed in relation to the Earth – refer to its influence on the earth as a whole.

The range of its possible distance depends chiefly on the nearness of its orbit, for the closer it passes to the Earth, the greater the contrast between its conjunction and opposition. We noted one effect of this in fluctuations of brilliance, neighbouring Mars varying twenty times more than distant Jupiter. But since the inner planets do not shine in direct proportion to their distance owing to the question of phases, light alone is a doubtful measure of effect.

As we said previously, the true influence of the planets upon the Earth is almost certainly of a magnetic nature; and magnetic force varies in direct proportion to the charge of the magnet, and in inverse proportion to the square of its distance. If we suppose the charge of the planet to be propor-

27. See Appendix III, 'The Theory of Octaves'.
28. 80,000,000,000 times - see Appendix II, 'Table of Times and Cosmoses'.

tional to its mass multiplied by its orbital speed, then we can make some interesting calculations about the relative magnetic influence of the different planets upon the earth, and the variation in this influence.

If, for example, we take the magnetic influence of the moon upon the earth as an estimated 5000 amperes, then the average influence of Jupiter would be about 900 amperes, of Venus 600 amperes, of Mars 60 amperes, of Saturn 40 amperes, and of Mercury 20 amperes.[29] The influence of Uranus and Neptune on this scale would be a little more and less than one ampere.

On the other hand, the amount of variation in effect would be very different for the different planets. Mars at its strongest would be stronger than Venus, at its weakest as weak as Uranus: its influence at one extreme would be no less than 80 times greater than at the other. The influence of Saturn would double from minimum to maximum, while those of Uranus and Neptune would remain practically constant.

Now man is so constituted that he registers contrasts and changes of all kinds, while constant conditions pass him unnoticed. A man living in a city goes about his business unaware of the steady roar of traffic, but he is acutely affected by a radio down the street which alternately blares and fades. So we should expect humanity to react strongly to the disturbing variations of Mars and Venus, while remaining more or less oblivious to the influence of Saturn, Uranus and Neptune, even though the latter might be stronger and more salutary. This is not a question of *actual* effect, but of awareness of it. Later we shall see that while there is much evidence of periodicity in the violent and procreative aspects of nature, such as war, glut and famine, cycles in the sphere of thought and aspiration are much more difficult to recognise and affect much smaller numbers. Variability of distance is thus an index of *disturbance*.

The other kind of variation we spoke of lies in a planet's changing speed in relation to the Earth. This is most simply measured by the angle the planet makes with Earth and Sun. When Sun, planet and Earth are in a straight line, then the planet is moving parallel to the Earth and so is stationary in relation to it. On the other hand, if Sun, planet and Earth form a right angle, then the planet is approaching or retreating at its full orbital speed. Speeds between these two extremes will be proportional to the angle. But it is only with the inner planets that a right angle can be formed. For the outer planets the maximum angle will always be less than 90°, and decreases steadily with the remoteness of the planet's orbit.

29: See Chapter 3, II, and Planetary Tables, Appendix IV (c).

Two effects follow. The nearer a planet is to the Sun the greater its possible speed in relation to the Earth; and consequently the greater the variation in that speed. Mercury can approach the Earth at 30 miles a second, it can be stationary in relation to the Earth, or it can retreat at this same immense speed. Neptune, on the contrary, can only vary between stationary and one-tenth of a mile a second in relation to the Earth.[30]

To understand the effect of this variation, we imagine a man lying in bed and bothered by a mosquito which circles his room. He will instinctively recognise the degree of his danger by the rise and fall of the whine. For when the speed of the approaching insect is added to the vibrations of its note, they are compressed or sharpened, and when it is subtracted, they are drawn out or flattened. Just so will Mercury's fundamental note change pitch, and we may take the restless and nervous effect produced by the mosquito's song as some criterion of this planet's influence.[31]

If, then, as our electrical deductions seemed to show, each planet emits a certain note or an energy transformed for a certain purpose, this note or energy will be subject to two variations within its cycle. First, there will be a variation of *volume* depending on distance. Second, there will be a variation of *pitch* depending on relative speed. Mars and Venus have the widest range of volume; Mercury and Venus the widest range of pitch. While both in pitch and volume the outermost planets remain constant, sounding a steady groundbass to the general harmony.

Still one other variation must be taken into account. If we compare the figures of conjunctions given above with astronomical ephemeris of planetary positions, we shall find that they do not exactly coincide. Each planet runs infinitesimally fast or slow. After 8 years Venus arrives at its major conjunction $2\frac{1}{4}$ days ahead of time. Mars gains 26 days on its 15-year cycle, while Jupiter loses 5 days in 12 years, and Saturn $8\frac{1}{3}$ in 30. As watches, their accuracy would not be rated high. Mars, the least precise, would gain 7 minutes a day; Venus would gain a minute and Saturn lose one; though Uranus would keep time within 3 seconds. Thus apart from changes in pitch due to relativity, each planet of itself sounds imperceptibly flat or sharp.

This very imperfection, however, seems significant. For nothing in nature is immutably exact. And while the law of octaves takes care of the broad pattern and the vast majority, there is always a chink, a slight loop-

---

30. See Planetary Tables, Appendix IV (d).

31. Substituting light-tint for pitch, this is the method by which the approach or retreat of distant stars is measured ('Red-shift').

hole left for exception and change. Without this the cosmos would be of an appalling and iron rigidity. But because it is alive, it has a margin of resilience. The margin allowed is minute, like that between the pianist who plays with understanding of rubato and another who plays with mechanical perfection. But in that ten-thousandth of a second of difference, much may happen on another scale.[32]

Two fundamental questions arise from what we have considered. The first concerns the way in which such waxing and waning of planetary influences could be expected to affect man. The second concerns the true significance of octaves.

First then, of what consequence is it to human beings that Jupiter shines again today with the same intensity and the same relation to sun and stars as it did 12 years ago?

We know by experience the influence exercised on all living beings and even on the very tides of the sea by the periodicity of the moon, as also by the periodicity of the Earth, with its attendant seasons and their effects. It is therefore not difficult to conceive that other planets should also rule cycles in us, equivalent to their synodic periods; and also that these cycles should find corresponding rhythms in certain bodily organs – as does the lunar cycle in the female ovaries. At the moment we may consider this no more than an hypothesis. We shall find more evidence for it later.

Meanwhile, we may simply imagine these same organs as receiving-sets, each tuned in to the wavelength of one particular planet and thus varying in the intensity of its action with the periodicity of that planet's influence. The complexity of man's life then arises from the fact that all these different rhythms overlap, neutralising, accentuating or modifying each other – and yet at the same time producing a combined 'beat', which may or may not be recognised.

Much interesting work has been done recently on the cyclical character of many biological and human phenomena – a $9\frac{2}{3}$-year rhythm for the fecundity of animals, an 18-year rhythm in building activity, a 54-year cycle in man's harnessing of natural energy and in the form of this society.[33] These rhythms are recognisable individually, and also in various combinations. For instance, separate 3-year and 4-year rhythms, acting together, produce a 12-year repeating pattern. 8-year, 9-year, 12-year, 15-year and

32. The principle that harmonious tuning is not strictly mathematical is of course recognised in Western music and was enunciated by J. S. Bach in his 'Wohltemperirte Klavier' (1726-44).
33. Ellsworth Huntington: 'Mainsprings of Civilization', 1945. E. R. Dewey and E. F. Dakin, 'Cycles', 1947.

30-year cycles, superimposed one on the other, will create a pattern of behaviour recurring every 360 years, and so on.

Later we shall try to show that most established rhythms in fact tally with planetary cycles. But for the moment we may merely say that if the possibility exists that a planet may stimulate an organ in one particular man, it seems indisputable that the same conjunction could activate this organ in millions of men, producing waves of business activity or depression, cycles of wars, periodic fluctuations in the birthrate, and so on.

Two passing planets may set up a certain cosmic tension, under the influence of which unwittingly it appears to men on Earth that they must fight, kill each other and die for heroic causes for years on end. If the planets govern men at all, they are no respecters of persons, and one may perhaps ask whether, given the general state of man's being, a universal excitement of the glands of passion could have any other outcome.

But whether we attribute any significance to these cycles or not, we are still faced by the inescapable harmony produced by their combination. These perfect and everchanging octaves fill one equally with awe at the subtlety and perfection of the cosmic order, and amazement that human perception should remain unaware of it.

We said that the planets, in their quality as refractors or transformers of the life-force stand for form, colour, quality and function. But each one stands for a different form, a different function. And we now see how by this harmonic law of their succession one form must in time give way to another, one function to the next.

We have, in fact, found the archetypal pattern for the development of all progressions. Every sequence in time or density – whether the audible notes of musical scales, the visible colours of the spectrum, or the tangible growth of organic forms – follows this octave ratio. All progressions and processes on earth, brought into being by the triple forces of creation, continue and proceed under this law of successive influences.

If the sequence of planets, in their vast march through time, sound the notes of endless octaves, we may be sure that the very quanta of light, in their immeasurable journeying, do the same. Nature, man, the insect and the cell all move in time and live out their existence within this harmonious pattern. As inevitably as time moves forward, this influence succeeds to that, and now one and now another side of the man or the enterprise is galvanized into life by the rhythmic succession. As *mi* follows *re*, so yellow must follow orange, birth pregnancy, and March ploughing be succeeded by April sprouting. No power on earth can alter this inevitable sequence, nor replace this variety by the monotony of a single truth.

All variations on a theme are due to it. Life is a solar *idea*. But the scale of living beings – metals, minerals, plants, worm, animal and man – are its planetary forms. Metal in turn is an idea – but lead, quicksilver, gold, silver, zinc, copper and iron – are its planetary variations. And as we see from our octave, every variation has its hour, and every dog his day.

It is for this reason that man, intent for his own purposes on perpetuating one note or one facet of understanding, is doomed to disillusionment. For this reason the processes that he initiates change their nature under his very eyes and hands. For if one planet moves his heart today, another will move his reason tomorrow, and a third his passion the day following. The humanitarian movement he launched under Jupiter becomes scholastic under Saturn and bloody under Mars. The heavens play scales upon his keyboard, and he cannot but sound the notes they touch.

But we would be wrong if we felt the effect of this sequence to run wholly counter to man's legitimate ambition. The law of octaves is an essential part of the structure of the universe, and applies to its every part and process. To it is due that incredible profusion of colour, form, tone and function which delights man and eternally stimulates him to new endeavours and new understanding.

We should thus be mistaken if we interpreted the idea of successive influences in a moralistic way, or saw in it an iron and inflexible determinism. For the passage from one influence to another not only means that there is taken from man much that he would like to keep, but also much that he wants to be rid of. When the cold and darkness of winter becomes intolerable, it is this which brings the spring; when mediaeval doctrine grows unbearably rigid, it is this which brings the Renaissance. And when it rightly seems to man that nothing he can devise can save him from the folly of his own destructiveness, it is this which assures him that the heavens themselves must in time awaken another side of his nature, and bring him some fresh and unimaginable chance.

The everchanging harmony of planetary rhythm thus teaches us two lessons: first, that history always repeats itself, and second, that history never does. For though each cycle returns with an exactitude which makes it possible to calculate the ephemeris three years ahead, and though it may be relied upon to bring unfailingly the same urge to procreation or war, to speculation or suicide, yet always some other cycle crossing it differently brings to the scene a new shade and other possibilities. And even when, at the end of centuries, all the planetary rhythms should return again to the same united conjunction, still the infinitesimal advance of one or retarding of another forbids an exact return to that which was before. While even beyond this, the whole Solar System will stand in a different relation to the focus of the Milky Way, and receive from it some intangible new influence, which, like scarce-heard music played off-stage, may alter the watcher's whole attitude to the pantomimic play of lights.

Everything returns again, and nothing returns again. For if the great conjunctions did exactly repeat, then *all* would be the same as before. After 2147 years the same Alexander, taught by the same Artistotle, would lead just such Greeks against just such Persians, and cross the same deserts and valleys, stone by stone, to the same fabulous courts of India. The Creator of the universe is not so simple. Perhaps another Alexander, but of what race, what education? Perhaps another march to the Orient, but with what weapons and what intentions? Perhaps another apotheosis in Egypt – but who plays the role, and what is its form and meaning? 33a

The universe is simple only to the fortune-teller. Man may calculate this probability or that, and in a small and general way he may prove right. But no matter how elaborate his foresight, fate has another factor in reserve. The heavens must always leave the issue open – for the good reason that they are infinite.

III   THE CIRCULATION OF LIGHT: VISIBLE AND INVISIBLE

If we consider the moon and planets in relation to the earth (and we must never forget that this is the only point of observation from which scientific study of the solar system has ever been made), they are found to fall naturally into three groups:
  (a) Visible to the naked eye, inside the earth's orbit –
       Moon, Mercury, Venus.
  (b) Visible to the naked eye, outside the earth's orbit –
       Mars, Jupiter, Saturn.
  (c) Invisible to the naked eye, outside the earth's orbit –
       Uranus, Neptune, Pluto.

If it be objected that human perception provides a very arbitrary standard for classification, we must now reply that it is not in fact nearly as arbitrary as scientists are prone to believe. As we established in Chapter I, *a man is a cosmos*, whose times and perceptions bear a definite cosmic

33a. This period of passage through one zodiacal sign exactly separates Alexander from Napoleon.

relationship to the times and perceptions of lesser and greater cosmoses. His perception then, by its very limitations, tends to divide up phenomena in a significant and not an accidental way. It is no accident, for example, that all the movements of organic growth and all the movements of celestial bodies remain just outside the range of his perception, invisible to him. The time-relation of the human cosmos both to the cosmos of Nature and the cosmos of the Solar System mechanically ensures this.

Thus to discover his actual place and possibilities in the universe man must return to a critical study of his own unaided perception. This will show him what he is, and from where he can start. For telescopes, microscopes, spectroscopes, radio, radar, the cinema and so on, are in fact mechanical imitations of higher human faculties which he does not yet enjoy. Their danger is that they may hypnotise him into believing that he already possesses these higher functions, and thus persuade him that he is in a different position from that which is his in reality. From such imagination about himself, he can never proceed further.

Throughout this book, then, appeal will be made to the evidence of man's own perception. And such is the hold which theoretical science has upon the mind in our age, that in many cases *such recourse to direct perception may look like superstition.*

Let us see then where our division of planets into visible and invisible leads us. In the first place, the 'visibility' or 'invisibility' expresses itself in more than one way. For instance, the planets known to antiquity are not only physically visible, but their cycles repeat several or many times in the span of human life, and they can thus be studied by a single man in all their aspects. By contrast Uranus, Neptune and Pluto are not only physically beyond the range of human sight, but their temporal cycles (84, 164, 248 years respectively) are also beyond the range of human life. Uranus, however, lies only just beyond man's natural vision, and may even be detected by sharp sight, just as its cycle extends only just beyond his natural lifetime, and may in fact be compassed by longlived man.

We may therefore be correct in thinking of the traditional 'visible' planets as one octave, and the further 'invisible' planets as the beginning of a second octave; in the same way that the traditional 'visible' colours form one octave of vibrations, and further 'invisible' ultra-violet radiation the beginning of a second. We further see that even within this visible octave there are certain intervals which are 'invisibly' filled, as by the Asteroids.

This arrangement may be expressed in the form of a circle thus. Moreover, this arrangement of the planets into a visible and an invisible octave

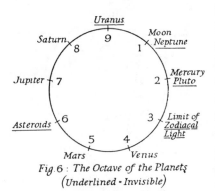

Fig. 6 : The Octave of the Planets
(Underlined - Invisible)

is found to be not peculiar to human beings on earth, but to result from the relation between creatures of human scale and the Solar System as a whole, no matter what part of it they may inhabit. For instance, to human perception on the planet Mars, Mercury would have completely disappeared into the Sun's dazzle, while in exchange Uranus would almost certainly have become visible. To the vision of a man situated on Jupiter, Venus would follow Mercury into invisibility, but Neptune in turn would enter his field of view. Thus to cosmic beings of the scale of man in any part of the universe five planets and a satellite or satellites would probably be visible, the rest invisible. So that after all our circle seems a generally applicable diagram in which, however, the individual points would have different significance from the point of view of other planets.

In the sky of each of the planets there will thus be visible seven major bodies or series of bodies, and seven only – Sun, Satellite(s), and five other planets. The seven visible from our earth are of course, Sun, Moon, Mercury, Venus, Mars, Jupiter, and Saturn. Between these there exists *one circulation of light*. For it is reflection of the same solar light which makes them all simultaneously visible, and the absence of this reflection which makes Uranus and Neptune invisible to us, and thus outside this particular circulation.

This circulation of light is a movement from the maximum brilliance we know – that of the Sun – to invisibility, and back to brilliance again. In such a pulsation between darkness and brilliance all parts of the solar system are constantly involved; as all parts of the human body are constantly involved in the pulsation between oxygen-loaded arteries and oxygen-emptied veins. But how does this circulation work? The Sun emits the light, as the heart pumps the blood. But what happens then? How does this pulsation of radiance and darkness manifest?

To the circle showing the seven visible heavenly bodies, let us add figures representing their average magnitude. Then let us join first the inner series and then the outer series in order of brilliance.

If we now further join the two more brilliant points representing the

Moon and Jupiter and the two less brilliant points representing Saturn and Mercury, and if we make the point of intersection represent on the first line the maximum brilliance we know, i.e. that of the sun (–27.6 mag.), and on the second the point of invisibility (mag. 6), we find the the whole figure (142857) has now become a complete sliding scale of brilliance.

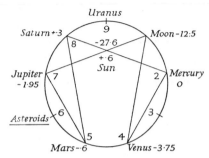

Fig. 7: *The Circulation of Light (stellar magnitudes)*

Starting from the point of invisibility and going towards Saturn we rise through the whole range of possible celestial brilliance until we reach that of the Sun; then beyond we again decline to the point of invisibility from which we started. Further, we can plot upon this line the waxing and waning of the different planets in magnitude, described in the last section, and thus show their individual *movement* backwards and forwards within the general circulation. And finally, we can see at the intersection of the two lines how maximum brilliance on one line coincides with invisibility on the other, that is, how all planets must vanish from view in their conjunction with the Sun.

The same figure also indicates, if we can read it, the *direction of development* of each of the planets. We see for instance how Mercury is emerging from an invisibility created by the brilliance of the Sun, whereas Saturn is moving into an invisibility created by distance.. We see how Jupiter is itself developing towards the radiance of a sun, while the moon is a recent offshoot of that radiance.

In fact this strange figure – 142857 – can explain to us an infinity of things, because in it we have stumbled on a mathematical enigma which in fact hides one of the fundamental laws of the universe. When *unity* is divided by *seven*, this recurring decimal – .142857 – results. And when a complete cosmos is divided into its life-principle and six functions, it is precisely the sequence of this figure which represents the relation between them.

If, for example, we regard the decimal as composed of six separate quantities, thus –

.1
.04
.002
.0008
.00005
.000007

90

– we have a series which seems to represent the relative mass of the organs which control the various functions in a cosmos. It is this sequence which explains the extraordinary variation in mass – amounting to hundreds of thousands of times – between the controlling glands of the body, *although they appear to play approximately equal roles*. In the solar system it explains the same extraordinary variation in the mass of the chief celestial bodies, from Jupiter (.001 of the Sun's mass) and Saturn (.0003) down to the major satellites, which average only .00000007. And through it we can see how the total mass of planets, asteroids, moons and comets which compose the whole is infinitely divided.

At present, however, we study this figure as symbol of the circulation of light within the solar system. And we now see that it is this circulation of light which connects all parts of this system with all other parts, which brings all possibilities everywhere. Exactly as the circulation of the blood unites all organs of the human body and makes that body a *solid* instead of an empty scaffolding; or the circulation of ideas connects different types and makes them a group instead of a number of isolated individuals, so this circulation of light makes the Solar System a *solid*, instead of a collection of remote and independent spheres. Precisely because it is such a solid, no part is separated from any other, and the whole is accessible to him who can discover the secret.

VII THE ELEMENTS OF EARTH

I ELEMENTAL OCTAVES

W E TOOK ALL THE SOLAR RADIATIONS TOGETHER AS THE active principle in our creative triad, all the planets together as the mediating principle, and all the earthly elements together as the passive principle, or raw material. Just as in the last chapter we began to analyse the total formative force of the planets into its component notes, so now we must consider more in detail the nature of this raw material.

All terrestrial material is constituted of atoms, which, as Aristotle knew, are the smallest indivisible particles of the elements. According to present theories such atoms consist of a nucleus or sun positively charged with electricity, around which revolve infinitesimal planetary electrons, negatively charged. The atomic nucleus is similar for all materials, as is also the electron, elements only differing among themselves by the number of electrons supported by the nucleus and by corresponding variations in its charge.

In spite of its minute size, much material has been collected about the structure of the atom, which appears more like our Solar System with every new discovery. Exactly as the Sun to the Solar System and the fertilized ovum to the human body, we are now told that the diameter of the atomic nucleus may be one-ten-thousandth that of the whole atom. And, as Jupiter to our Sun, we are told that its electrons may be one-tenth of the diameter of the nucleus; so that upon their own scale they circle in an immensity of space as vast as that which engulfs the Earth and its fellow planets.

This conception is indeed a tour-de-force of human reason, for upon the time-scale of man's ordinary perception, the atom does not really exist in this way at all. Only the solid trace of it exists, like the solid trace of the Solar System which we tried to visualize in an earlier chapter. For as to our perception the Solar System consists of flying spheres, and only by an effort of reason and deduction can be visualized as a solid body in its own time; so to our perception atoms produce solids, and only by an effort of reason and deduction can be visualized as systems of flying spheres. The atomic electrons, revolving round their minute nuclei at a tenth the speed of light, create units which until recently proved impenetrably rigid. If it were not so, a chair would be simply a mass of radiant energy, for it is upon the traces of atoms that we sit. The model is the same, but in one case the time-scale is immeasurably longer than man's, in the other immeasurably shorter.

Now in all our discussion of the universe, one of the chief purposes has been to discover the relative density of different worlds or phenomena. For it may be supposed that less dense means also more powerful, more penetrating, wider-ranging, more intelligent. And it is the understanding of intelligence which is our aim.

We remember that the process of growth, by which we believe the whole universe to have been created, could be described by the formula: the descent of spirit into matter, and its endowment with form. Differing densities may then be seen as differing proportions of matter and spirit in the substances or worlds under consideration. The same idea has been expressed by some writers as differing proportions of matter and motion, or of matter and energy. Or more simply still, as differing levels of energy, or again as differing scales of time. The intention is the same. It is to establish some kind of measuring-scale, which would be capable of measuring all beings and forces from the Absolute to the Abyss.

In an earlier chapter, it seemed possible to establish a scale of density, or inversely, a scale of power, for the planets. Is any such scale possible for the earthly elements?

In many ages attempts were made to classify the small handful of elements then known in order of 'nobility' or of 'virtue'. But the discovery of a whole series of rare metals between 1735 and 1755, and the isolation after 1860 of dozens of quite new elements with the aid of spectroscopy, completely changed the picture. In 1869 Mendeleev tried to arrange all this new assembly in an order based upon the relative weight of atoms of each element. An atom of lead, for instance, was found to weigh 207 times as much as an atom of hydrogen, and was given the *atomic weight* 207.

The study of atomic structure and of the role played by the planetary electrons made it possible to adapt Mendeleev's table, by simply ranging the elements according to their number of electrons. This is the method of *atomic numbers*, hydrogen with one electron having the atomic number 1, helium with two electrons 2, and so on. With two exceptions, elements have now been traced with every number of electrons from 1 to 96.

But the picture is not quite so simple. For the atom seemed to differ from the Solar System in this way: that it could have not one, but several planetary electrons (up to a certain maximum) in each orbit.[34] In the inner-most orbit it was possible to have two electrons; in the second eight more; in the third eight more again; in the fourth and fifth 18 each, and in the sixth 32. A few elements with radio-active properties were even found to have seven orbits.

Now these orbits, if we think of the atoms more realistically as solids, are in fact shells. Atoms of different elements have any number of shells from one to seven. The top shell in turn may have any number of electrons from one to its maximum complement, with resulting variations in surface rigidity; so that if a shell with a full set of electrons be regarded as made of steel, those with less might be as if made of oil, rubber or plastic.

This picture gives a good idea of the relative densities of different elements. The greater the number of shells, the more dense will the element be; while among the group of elements with the same number of shells, that will be more dense whose topmost shell is more rigid.

There are thus seven main categories of density among the elements, which are called periods. But within each period, there is again a variation in activity according to the number of electrons in the topmost shell. Each element is drawn to that with the complementary number of electrons, as sodium with one outstanding electron naturally seeks chlorine with one missing, to form salt. Here we see a parallel to Plato's analogy of human souls seeking the complementary half from which they were severed in the first creation. This is elemental male and female, electro-positive elements irresistibly impelled to combine with electro-negative ones, in exact proportion to their contrast. Every element is by nature incomplete and seeks completion, except only those whose electronic complement is entire, and who need no partner. These are the rare or so-called 'noble' gases – helium, neon, argon, krypton and xenon – whose shells are, as it were, so hard and polished that no other element can find a hold.

The general scale of density of elements now begins to clarify itself.[35] In the first category, with one shell, we find hydrogen and helium, whose rarity and range of potentiality give them some particular affinity with the sun, where, as we saw earlier, they play a special part in the generation of solar energy.

---

34. It is possible that this varying number of electrons in each orbit is in some way compara-ble to the varying number of moons supportable by the planet of each solar orbit. Thus in the Solar System the orbit of Mercury would contain only the original planet with no moons, while the orbits of Jupiter and Saturn on the other hand would each contain a full complement.

At the other end of the scale, with seven shells, we find the radioactive elements: radium, actinium, thorium, protactinium and uranium, whose density is such that they cannot exist naturally on the surface of the earth, but are only discovered by man in infinitesimal quantities in places completely remote from the life-giving influence of solar radiation, such as the rocky interiors of mountains, in lava-beds, and in deep-sea ooze. Even there these elements tend to become less dense, their very radiation being a means of raising them towards the next finer elements above. Uranium (92) tends to become radium (89), which in turn tends to split into helium (2) and the inert gas radon (86).

The phenomenon of radioactivity is indeed curiously mysterious and paradoxical. It is probably universal at a certain distance below the Earth's surface; and may in fact represent a general third or enabling principle for the geologic realm, just as air is a general third or enabling principle for the organic world and light for the planetary one.[35a] Radioactivity as third force may in turn be the unknown factor in certain subterranean transmutations which result in matters of immense latent energy – petroleum, for example.

All the radioactive elements in the last or seventh category appear over immense periods of time to be struggling upwards to the level of lead, the densest common element, which belongs to the period above. In this process, the only natural transmutation of atoms that we know on Earth, it may be possible to see the trace of some aeon-long process of terrestrial evolution or refinement.

Thus in his splitting of the uranium atom, man is in fact doing in a fraction of a second what Nature herself would do in some millions of years. What may be more serious, from the point of view of such evolution, is his gathering together of this abysmal material in quantity, and his creation, for his own destructive purpose, of several new elements – neptunium (93), plutonium (94), americium (95) and curium (96) – denser even than those which the Earth may be at such pains to raise towards life.

This splitting off of the last electron of the last orbit of the uranium atom could hardly be compared with the constant shifting of electrons in the second orbit, which appeared part of the process by which the Sun releases energy. Though it was as serious in its way, perhaps, as if some invisible moon of the planet Pluto were to be shot out of the solar system.

35. See Appendix V, 'Table of Elements'.
35a. See Norbert Casteret, 'Ten Years Under the Earth', p. 160-1.

The energy and temperature so generated, however, were used as starter for a hydrogen bomb, in which the production of solar energy would itself be simulated. Whether such divine energy can be handled or such infernal matter created by man in unregenerate state without disaster, is perhaps the chief riddle of our age.

★　★　★

When we seek for a pattern in the table of elements as usually set out, our impression is one of some extraordinarily subtle but hidden order. But when we set ourselves to unveil this order, it eludes us. Things are not as simple as they at first appear.

In the first period hydrogen stands alone. It is a unique element, which combines with half the rest but clearly has no fellow. Like solar energy, it is without peer.

The next two periods each have eight elements, and we are reminded of the octave arrangement, which, in considering the planets, we deduced must run through all creation. In the third period, there is a clue. The sequence of atomic weights from neon (20) to argon (40) are exact reciprocals of the sequence of vibrations in a descending octave – with one extra element, phosphorus, filling the half-tone between *mi* and *fa*.

The first three periods thus set themselves out as follows:

do	*si*	*la*	*sol*	*fa*	–	*mi*	*re*
I							
H							
I							
2	3	4	5	6	7	8	9
He	Li	Be	B	C	N	O	F
4	7	9	11	12	14	16	19
10	11	12	13	14	15	16	17
Ne	Na	Mg	Al	Si	P	S	Cl
20	23	24	27	28	31	32	35½

In the fourth period, we again find an almost exact octave relation in weights between the inert gases argon (40) and krypton (84). Only we have far too many elements for the intervening notes. We begin to be embarrassed by the numbers of rare elements discovered in the last century, and without the knowledge of which man managed to exist satisfactorily for many thousands of years. Can titanium or vanadium, which exist only in lodes of other ores, we ask ourselves, really have equal importance from the Earth's point of view with argon, for example, which constitutes 1% of the entire atmosphere?

And at this thought it occurs to us that in some cases the notes of our main octaves are themselves divided into lesser octaves, and that these rare elements constitute, not full notes, but only the notes of inner octaves, three or seven of them together being necessary to make one full note. Working on this principle we find it easy to discover the notes of the fourth period.

Having reached this point, further light begins to break. The seven periods of elements, that is, the categories of atoms divided according to the number of their shells, in themselves constitute a descending octave. The whole table forms an octave multiplied by an octave, or an octave squared. The physical constitution of the Earth reveals itself as a solid scale, the very notes of which form smaller harmonics. The whole atomic structure of our world is built, as it were, of crystallized and silent music.

With the fifth period, then, we have reached the note *mi* in this descending octave of periods. And we begin to discover a tendency for this octave in turn to run down. Launched with all the immense creative force of solar energy, the atomic weights quintupled in the second period and doubled in the third. In the fourth it needed the assistance of several inner octaves to achieve the requisite doubling, and in the fifth, even with this impulse, the rate of increase falls far short. The atomic weight of xenon is only 131 against krypton's 84. We have reached the half-tone or interval between *mi* and *fa*.

And now, in the sixth period, a very curious phenomenon appears. We suddenly come upon a group of fourteen rare earths, discovered in the nineteenth century, whose chief characteristic is that they are practically impossible to isolate from one another. They form as it were an intensely coherent block, which only by the most complicated methods of fractional crystallization can be torn apart. And they clearly make, not inner octaves, but an *innermost octave in one note* of an inner octave. Their very multiplicity overcomes the increasing inertia of the descending scale, and beyond them we find to our astonishment that the descent has practically regained its earlier momentum. By the time we reach the note *sol*, we find silver and gold nearly an octave apart, with atomic weights of 108 and 197 respectively. The impulse of the descending octave still lags behind a perfect doubling of density – but very little.

This role of the rare earths in overcoming the falling away of the octave

97

at the semitone helps to explain to us the cosmic method of passing this universal moment of resistance. Like a general who deploys his brigade into a mass of independent individuals to ford a river, nature at such a point breaks into multiplicity. Just as the fourteen rare earths are used to cross a single semitone in the table of elements; so the throng of asteroids fills the planetary half-tone between Mars and Jupiter. And yet again, the multiplicity of organic life bridges the interval between the Sun and the bare elemental ball of Earth, which without the latter would have no means of absorbing the solar radiance.

When we have completed the setting out of the table of elements in this way we find, as we anticipated, that it forms an octave squared. The whole of *the first horizontal octave or period* is occupied by the element hydrogen, with its special affinity for the sun and its immense potentiality. Hydrogen symbolises spirit in the assembly of elements. Upon an exact concentration of hydrogen ions in organic fluid, depends life itself.

The *second period*, from our point of view, is specially marked by the elements carbon, nitrogen and oxygen, which with hydrogen form in their union the infinite variety of the organic world. Over a quarter-million such combinations have been identified. They represent the vehicle of life.

The *third period* introduces sodium and chlorine, which as salt are the basis of all organic tension and form. It adds two light metals and the supplementary minerals, phosphorus and sulphur, which are necessary to the existence of a nervous system with all its implications.

In the *fourth period* the heavy minerals and metals begin, notably potassium, and calcium, iron and copper, which play a large part in the constitution of blood and chlorophyll and the maintenance of circulation. In minute quantities the two latter also regulate the combustion of air and the processes of respiration.

The hard metals of the *fifth period* are unassimilable by life; only iodine in this series acting as a sort of ballast to the motion of the human body. We can thus note in passing that all the matters of the human organism are comprised in the two octaves from carbon to copper with exception of hydrogen as activating principle above and iodine as balance-weight below. Later we shall return to this.

The elements of the *sixth period,* that is, below the *mi-fa* interval, appear to have no place in life. Gold, platinum and mercury, for example, are prized for their very imperviousness to chemical action and to that softening and absorption which is essential to incorporation in a living organism.

Finally, the elements of the *seventh period* have no place in Nature at all. As suggested earlier, they belong to the interior of the Earth, remote from solar influence and all its consequences. In their utter incapacity for change and participation in living processes, their affinity is with conditions such as we see them on the surface of the moon.

From these characteristics of the different periods, a curious property of the halogens – hydrogen, fluorine, chlorine, bromine and iodine – emerges. They represent the boundaries between different states of matter. We saw how hydrogen lay on the borderline between matter in electronic and matter in molecular state. In the same way fluorine stands on the borderline between matter in molecular and matter in cellular state – and it has the curious property of *dissolving* the latter into the former. Further, chlorine stands on the frontier between cellular and mineral states of matter – and by its action in salt, has a similar capacity of incorporating the lower state into the higher. Again bromine marks the border between mineral and metallic states of matter, while element 85, if we knew what it was, should stand between matters that can appear on the earth's surface and those which should not.

The table begins with the vehicle of spirit and ends with lifeless matter, begins with pure energy and ends with pure inertia, begins with the sun and ends with the moon. Between lie periods corresponding to the various functions of the Earth – the keys respectively to form and motion, to nervous sensation, to blood and breathing, and to two inorganic kingdoms. These forms between spirit and matter, as we saw earlier, are the domain of the planets. And we may tentatively assign the individual planets to them. For the moment we can regard these assignations as no more than convenient labels. Later they will prove useful to us.

Meanwhile, we do indeed begin to glimpse at last that general scale of all matters and energies in the universe, for which we have been seeking. For this table of atomic weights, extending upwards into the realm of radiant matter, is there continued by measurement of the quanta of energy which such free electrons carry. While downward it continues again through the molecular weights of all organic and inorganic substances compounded from these elements.

The table of quanta of radiant energy, the table of atomic weights of elements, and the table of molecular weights of compounds, do in fact form one single scale, extending from heaven to hell, and on the different rungs of which are to be found every substance knowable and unknowable. From this point of view everything may be regarded as physical and everything as comparable. The free motion of electrons which reaches the earth from the sun represents the highest and most rarified form of physical matter which we know; the greater the colonies of such electrons locked together by the earth, the denser the substance derived therefrom and the lower the function which employs it. All – from light to lead and from aspiration to excreta – is *measurable*.

II SPEEDS OF DIFFUSION

Different human studies deal with different matters and motions. For example, geology deals with the matters of stones, metals, pigments. Psychology deals with the motion of thought, emotion and instinct. Art may be said to deal with the matters studied by geology subjected to the motions studied by psychology.

Again physics deals with the general motion of light, sound and heat. But religion and astronomy also deal from different points of view with the first, music and acoustics with the second, dietetics and meteorology with the third.

Different human studies are thus constantly encountering the same phenomena, but approaching from different angles, give them quite different names. The result is that a well-educated man who has mastered the different series of names for things provided by religion, science, art, poetry, fashion, politics, finds himself in a world so complicated that he is constantly losing his way in it. For everything he meets has at least half-a-dozen different labels, depending whether he is looking at it as a devotee, a scientist, an artist, a poet, a man of the world, or a politician.

Can we really imagine all these matters and motions arranged on one scale? Can we really imagine all matters and motions arranged, not according to the particular human point of view with which we approach them at any given moment, but by their own innate energy, their objective density, so to speak? Can we really imagine a modern Jacob's Ladder, "set up on earth and the top of it reaching to heaven", which will be recognisable in the conditions of ordinary life?

For this purpose the system of atomic numbers is far too technical. We have to find a method of measurement which anyone anywhere can apply. Such a simple method of measuring and comparing different levels of energy and the states of matter which give rise to them does exist. It is by their *speed of diffusion*.

The limiting velocity known to man in his present state is that of light –

300,000 kilometres a second. A secondary limiting velocity, of which the significance is not yet fully known, is that of sound in air – approximately 330 metres a second, or nearly one-millionth the speed of light.

Let us then arrange a table of speeds of diffusion, from that of light downwards to and beyond the speed of sound, each category being divided from the next by a factor of one-hundred times. Such a table will take the following form:

Category I	300,000 kilometres a second
Category II	3,000 kilometres a second
Category III	30 kilometres a second
	300 metres a second or
Category IV	1,000 kilometres an hour
	3 metres a second, or
Category V	10 kilometres an hour
	3 centimetres a second or
Category VI	100 metres an hour
	1 metre an hour, or
Category VII	10 kilometres a year
	1 centimetre an hour, or
Category VIII	100 metres a year
	1 metre a year, or
Category IX	100 metres a century
	1 centimetre a year, or
Category X	1 metre a century
	1 centimetre a century

Further, to complete the table theoretically, let us make another category for motions up to a hundred times faster than light, that is, between 300,000 kilometres a second and 2 light-years a week, which we will call Category 0; and still another for speeds between 2 light-years a week and 1 light-year an hour, which we will call Category oo. Naturally, neither of these categories correspond to any phenomena at present known to man.

In this way, we have a table of twelve categories which will include all speeds of diffusion and change conceivable, the fastest being a million million million times faster than the slowest.

Now let us see what are the characteristics of these different categories.

Categories o and oo, being faster than the speed of light, if they correspond to anything at all, must represent phenomena which we may call super-solar. Only energies of such a nature could make connection between the earth and other parts of the Milky Way within the lifetime of man, while even at the topmost speed of Category oo the whole of that lifetime would be necessary for communication with the nearest extra-galactic nebula.

In Category I we find light, originating either from the Sun, from multitudes of suns (galaxies), from solar reflection (planets), or from stored accumulations of solar energy (coal, oil). Such energy, characteristic of suns, is not confined to the solar system, but judging from what we perceive of distant galaxies, can travel through the universe indefinitely. Within the same category falls the movement of individual electrons – 30,000 kilometres a second rising nearly to the speed of light for some electrons shot from exploding atoms. The continual atomic disintegration which is the nature of a sun yields free electronic motion of that kind and speed which we call *light*.

In Category II (3000–30 kilometres a second) we find movement characteristic of the solar system as a whole, and of communication between its parts. Solar magnetism, measured by the delay in sun-spot change and its effect on the magnetism of the earth's atmosphere, apparently diffuses at about 500 kilometres a second. The movement of the solar system within the Milky Way is estimated at about 250 kilometres a second.

In Category III (30 kilometres–300 metres a second) we can place movements characteristic of the planets and satellites taken individually. High up in this category comes the movement of the Earth about the Sun (28 kilometres a second), low down the movement of the moon about the Earth (1 kilometre a second). Its lower limit is indicated by the speed of sound in air (330 metres a second), which marks the beginning of Category IV and of motions definitely confined to the sphere of the earth. Thus Categories I to III refer to motions which are supersonic and in a sense celestial, Categories IV to X to motions which are subsonic and definitely terrestrial. Man himself shoots rifle bullets and rockets into Category III, and he is probably right in feeling that the crossing of the supersonic barrier is fundamentally connected with the possibility of interplanetary communication.

To Category IV (3–300 metres a second) belongs the motion of the Earth on its own axis, which at the equator is equivalent to about 250 metres a second. Here also belong the speeds of rotation of the other minor planets, and the speeds of solid bodies falling through air or planetary atmosphere. From the particular point of view of man it is noteworthy that the speed of dissemination of cortical nervous impulses, or what we may justifiably call the speed of thought (120 metres a second), also falls within this category, his function of registration having in this way some special affinity for and limitation to the planet upon which he lives.

In Category V (3 centimetres–3 metres a second) we find speeds which appear in some way characteristic of organic or animal bodies. Easy walking speed for man is one metre a second, which is also the speed at which the blood-stream courses in his veins. He cannot by his own efforts propel his body much above this category, though it is interesting that by harnessing molecular forces, such as expanding steam and exploding gas, he has been able artificially to compass the whole range of Category IV, and now, with implications which he does not yet understand, even to penetrate into Category III.

Category VI (1–100 metres an hour) includes the external motion of worms and small insects, the internal motion of food by the peristaltic action of the intestines.

Category VII (1 centimetre–1 metre an hour) includes such liquid phenomena as the rising and falling of tides, the transfer of liquids through cellular walls by osmosis. While it is significant that the speed of glacier-flow or ice-movement, that is, speed at the transition-point between liquid phenomena and solid (100 metres a year), exactly marks the limit between this category and the one below.

Category VIII (1–100 metres a year) includes all the phenomena of plant-growth, the maximum speed of growth known – that of certain tropical bamboos – lying very close to its top limit (30 centimetres a day). The spread of algae on stagnant water and other phenomena of cell propagation fall into the same range.

In Category IX (1 centimetre–1 metre a year) we find the growth or accretion of bony, horny and woody substances – the growth of hair (15 centimetres a year), the addition of tree-rings (1–3 centimetres a year), the knitting of bone-tissue.

Finally, Category X (1 centimetre–1 metre a century) represents the weathering, sedimentation and chemical change of stones and metals, the slowest speed of change ordinarily measurable by man.

At an unspecified distance below this we must place the condition of Absolute Zero, theoretically reached at –273° Centigrade, where molecular motion ceases, and matter reaches an absolute of immobility whose implications we can not even imagine.

If now we try in single words to describe the nature of the phenomena found in each category, we have a list somewhat like the following:

Category 00:	Super-Galactic.
Category 0:	Galactic.
Category I:	Solar or luminous.
Category II:	} Planetary or magnetic.
Category III:	
Category IV:	Atmospheric or nervous.
Category V:	Animal or warm-blooded.
Category VI:	Vertebrate or muscular.
Category VII:	Invertebrate or liquid.
Category VIII:	Vegetable or cellular.
Category IX:	Bony or accretive.
Category X:	Mineral or crystalline.

Is it too much to say that the physical body with which man is naturally endowed stretches from Category X to Category IV, and that he has to grow a soul of Categories II and III, to link him with that divine spirit which belongs to Category I? Perhaps.

In any case, speed of diffusion has provided us with an objective measure of phenomena, which leads to a classification remarkably similar to those which we have reached by quite different methods and arguments.

III   THE TRIPLE CREATION OF ORGANIC CHEMISTRY

We must now consider the way in which elements interact to provide suitable material for all the forms which life is able to take on earth. From our study of the interaction of Sun, planets, and Earth, we should in principle expect active to combine with passive in the presence of some third element or catalyst. This is exactly what happens in the chemistry of living matter.

In general we may say that hydrogen and the electro-positive elements of vertical notes *do, si, la,* tend to combine with the electro-negative elements of the notes *re, mi, interval, fa,* in the presence of *air,* and sometimes with the additional requirement of heat, pressure, electricity or some other form of applied energy. That is, the more active elements at the higher end of the periods tend to combine with the more passive elements at the lower end of the periods. In most cases such combinations are only made possible by the presence of atmospheric nitrogen, the catalyst or third force. For it is a principle so obvious that its significance goes unrecognised that the chemistry of life such as we know it takes place in air. And in this connection we notice from our table that nitrogen and its associated elements play the special role of filling the vertical interval between *mi* and *fa.* They form the elemental third or mediating force.

Thus in a broad way we may take the metals as active, the metalloids as passive, and air or nitrogen as mediating. The triad of creation, whose workings we strove to understand from the nature of the Solar System, finds its lesser but exact counterpart in the world of chemistry. And if we confine our inquiry to organic chemistry, we find (with the universal intervention of hydrogen) that three elements clearly and simply represent the three creative agents. Carbon is active, nitrogen mediating, and oxygen passive.

Only it must be remembered that these roles depend, not on the internal nature of these elements, but on their *relation* to higher and lower elements. Thus, in combination with hydrogen, carbon will become mediating and nitrogen passive; while in another combination oxygen, for example, will stand midway between hydrogen and sodium, and play the mediator to them.

As between themselves, however, carbon may always be taken as active, nitrogen always mediating, and oxygen always passive. And we may suppose that in this elemental world also exist six possible combinations of these forces, and six derivative processes analogous to those which, in the celestial world, held such enormous implications of growth, destruction, refinement, disease, renewal and regeneration.

This, however, is not for the moment our concern. We now have to try to study how the atoms of simple elements, representing the raw material of air and earth, of matter in molecular and matter in mineral state, are gradually built up into the complex forms of cellular life.

Earlier, in considering cosmoses in general, we established that one level of cosmos existed on the scale of a single *molecule*, and the next superior on the scale of a single *cell*. Let us now try to examine by what steps and stages are an infinite number of the smaller cosmoses built up into the intricate and self-sufficient structure of the larger. By what microscopic masonry do molecules form living matter?

First, atoms become locked together by ones, twos, threes, sixes and dozens to create molecules of different compounds. Two hydrogen atoms (atomic weight 2) and one oxygen atom (16) combine to form a molecule of water, which thus has a molecular weight of 18. Molecules of simple organic compounds – such as ether, milk, cellulose, morphine, and so on – are complicated cages or chains formed by atoms of hydrogen, carbon, oxygen and nitrogen, sometimes reinforced with sulphur and phosphorus. These organic compounds, which are essential to organic life, but can not be said to be themselves either organic or alive, have for the most part molecular weights varying from sixteen (methane) to a thousand or so.

Now if pure elements, as we have seen, are harmonically related in seven octaves by their atomic weights, we should expect these organic compounds to be similarly related by their molecular ones. And so it turns out. The individual notes – *do re mi fa sol la si do* – struck by the atoms of different elements, go echoing down the scores of octaves of organic compounds, reproducing there the same qualities in more complicated form. Nitrogen* with the atomic weight 14 is thus echoed three octaves lower by the histamine of white blood-cells (111), five octaves lower by the vitamin K of green leaves (450), and six octaves lower by chlorophyll (907). These substances enjoy a definite task in common – a specific though invisible role connected with air, blood, sap, the *media for life* upon different scales. While in the same series of descending octaves representing molecular weights, other broad classes of compounds familiar to us strike each their different and characteristic note.

Here indeed is our outline for a general scale of densities of all organic substances; though the further development of this theme must wait until we come to the action of the six different cosmic processes in the human body, and of the chemical agents through which they take effect.[36]

Meanwhile, a series of substances which fill one of these notes – the *amino-acids* – must now occupy our attention, because they act as a special stepping-stone between these molecular compounds and the proteins,

36. See Appendix VII, 'Table of Organic Compounds', and Chapter 12, III.

V. THE CIRCULATION OF LIGHT

in the Solar System as seen from the Earth

The line which joins the planets is marked in a scale of stella magnitudes. The arrows on the same line show the variation in brilliancy for each planet.

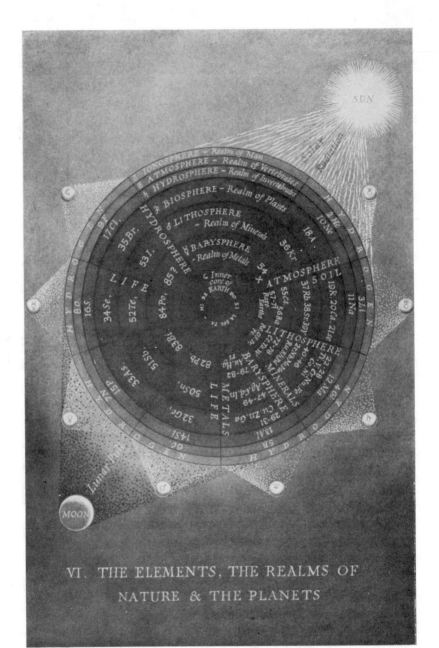

VI. THE ELEMENTS, THE REALMS OF
NATURE & THE PLANETS

which in turn serve as a direct link with life in cellular form. These amino-acids possess a curious double nature, half acid and half alkali, and are thus able to combine together in elaborate chains, the acid side of one grasping the alkaline side of the next, and so on. There are about twenty-five different amino-acids – the bricks of organic life – which combine in various ways, forming an almost infinite variety of different structures.

When these structures reach a certain degree of elaboration, we find ourselves among the natural *proteins*, and a full stage nearer to life in a recognisable sense. Are proteins themselves alive? It is difficult to say. In the sense that a house can be alive, whereas a brick cannot, yes. In the sense that a plant upon the wall can be alive, whereas a house cannot, no. Yet considering their work in a hundred different life-processes – in digesting food, in promoting growth, in making possible reproduction – we can not but think that, reaching proteins, we have already if unwittingly passed some unknown boundary between the living and the non-living.

To make even the simplest kind of protein molecule, several hundred amino-acid units must be built up into a definite form called a cyclol. Whereas the molecular weight of most amino-acids is about 130, an elementary protein – the albumen of egg-white – has a molecular weight of about 34,000. Indeed, the molecular weight of many if not most proteins seems to run in multiples of 17,000 or more probably of 16,384, which is exactly seven octaves up from the group of amino-acids mentioned, and ten from the basic element oxygen. We are, it is clear, following a quite definite line of development, that knife-edge between acid and alkali upon which the whole realm of organic life is built.

We have spoken as though these molecular structures were built up from below. But in fact, as we know, they are creatures of the cosmos above the molecule, that is, of the cell. The cell in an incredibly short time produces all the proteins and other compounds which it needs, compounds which, if they can be simulated by man at all, can only be made with enormous effort and patience. "Chemists work laboriously," says Dr. J. A. V. Butler. "They transform compounds one step at a time, using powerful chemicals, heat, and sometimes electric action, to bring about the changes they require. It may take months, in a complicated series of reactions, to build up a compound which a single cell can make in a matter of minutes or hours."[37] This indeed is very understandable, for whereas the cell is working by cellular time, the chemist is working by man's time, which as

37. 'Man is a Microcosm', p. 22.

we saw earlier is nearly 5,000 times slower. Ten minutes to the cell is actually equivalent to one month for a man, and a roughly comparable amount of work can be and is done by them in the two periods.

What is the transition from the protein molecule to the cell itself, that structure so characteristic of organic form, and which is the lowest organism to which we ordinarily accord the quality of 'life'?

Within the cell there exist minute particles called *genes*, each of which in some mysterious way bears the signature of a single feature of the greater organism of which the cell forms part. A gene probably consists of no more than ten protein molecules – it is a blue print on molecular scale of one characteristic of the complete cellular organism. A hundred or more genes form one *section* among the ten or more constituting a *chromosome*. While ten to a hundred chromosomes, a nucleus, and other minor elements too numerous to mention, enclosed within a sack or skin of cellulose, together constitute a *cell*.

We wished to establish the relation between the cosmos of a simple molecule and the cosmos of a cell. Now we see that between these two 'neighbouring' cosmoses there stretches a complete ladder of intermediate organisms. Moreover, setting out this ladder in order, and placing alongside the approximate figure of multiplication of weight from one rung to the next, we find a series highly reminiscent of an ascending octave:

do	Hydrogen atom	× 10
re	Simple compound molecule (e. g. water)	× 10
mi	Amino-acid molecule	× 1000
Life –		
fa	Protein molecule	× 10
sol	Gene	× 100
la	Section of a chromosome	× 10
si	Chromosome	× 50
do	Cell	

Now we can understand why, on reaching the protein molecule, we had the intimation if not the proof of some great transition. The sudden large factor of multiplication between the amino-acid molecule and the protein molecule indeed represents that natural interval between the notes *mi* and *fa*, which on another scale we saw filled by the whole realm of organic life on earth. Below this point the notes of our present octave belong clearly to the molecular world. Above it they already owe allegiance to the cellular one.

At this interval, to bridge the gap between two worlds, something invisible and intangible has entered. This factor we call – in our narrow human understanding of the word – *life*.

VIII THE MOON

I THE MOON AS BALANCE-WEIGHT

THE MOON IS THE CHILD OF THE EARTH. IN SCIENCE AND MYTH, IN one form or another this idea has been known and expressed from the dawn of history. The nineteenth-century theory that the moon was a fragment torn by some cosmic cataclysm from the still unformed Earth, merely echoed in new language the Greek legend that Selene was born of Theia.

But the Greek legend is in many ways more suggestive. For it goes on to add that Selene, the moon, was the daughter of Theia, the Earth, and Hyperion, the Sun; that she was beloved by Pan, the world of Nature, but enamoured of Endymion, mankind, whom Zeus had cast into an endless sleep. Here are hints of many roles, which make our purely geologic explanations curiously flat and unconvincing.

First, however, the general picture must be clear. A vitalising nucleus about which revolve a varying number of satellites, each performing a certain function for the whole – such appears to be the fundamental pattern of the universe. Thus the Sun with its planets, the planets with their moons, the atomic nucleus with its electrons. We see a further analogy in human life, where the father in the same way supports the 'satellites' of his family, the employer his workers, and the teacher his pupils. Perhaps we may go still further, and suggest that in the human body itself the various organs and their functions similarly 'revolve' about the heart, upon which the very cohesion and unity of the whole depends.

Thus on each scale, development is in a sense measured by responsibility. One man's work can support two dependents, another man's two hundred; the nucleus of a carbon atom carries six electrons, that of copper 29. Earth sustains one moon, Jupiter eleven. Such satellites can be imagined in many different ways – as offspring, as pupils, as dependents, or even as functions of their 'sun'. Studying the Solar System and the planets, it becomes clear that each of these similes contains a certain element of truth. In any case, this cosmic arrangement appears to imply in some sense a sun's 'responsibility' for its satellites, their 'service' to the sun; and again a passage of energy or knowledge from the sun to the satellites, and a reciprocal aspiration by the latter to acquire such energy and ultimately to emulate their luminary.

Now in relation to its satellite the Earth bears a responsibility which seems unique in the Solar System. It has only one moon, but the latter's size compared with that of its parent is such that not even the Sun itself seems to have shouldered such a task. The total mass of all the planets in the Solar System is but one 800th of the Sun's own mass. But the mass of the moon is no less than one 80th that of the Earth. The Earth seems to be carrying ten times more weight, size for size, than does the Sun.

Certainly it bears this weight at much closer relative range. And the importance of range will be clear if one tries holding a two-pound weight by one's side, at arm's length, or on the end of a six-foot pole. The Earth, in fact, is like a man swinging a two-pound weight at the end of a 30-foot cord. In most favourable conditions, the task would tax human endurance to the utmost.

For a planet, indeed, the distance at which the Earth supports its satellite is exceptionally great. The Moon's orbit lies no less than 30 times the Earth's diameter away. Only Saturn sustains a major moon at such relative distance, and that one, Japet, is insignificant in comparison. From one point of view, we may say that the Earth is the most hard-pressed planet in the Solar System. Conditions upon it are *less free* than elsewhere.

The effect of this burden on the Earth is like the balance-weight on a pendulum-clock, like ballast to a ship, or like the great weights on a loco-motive's driving-wheel. Whenever motor energy is applied to a mechanism, some kind of weight is necessary to smooth out and harness the animating force, and to prevent the whole from flying into space. We already saw how in the human body, constructed as it is from a narrow range of elements, the dense weight of iodine below is necessary to balance the activating principle of hydrogen above. In our example from human life, the responsibility of a child acts as weight or governor upon the motivating desires of the parents, curbing their centrifugal impulses and carrying them over moments of inertia and lassitude. In the same way, the moon acts as governor to the earth, equalizing and harnessing the solar energy.

This effect is best known in the influence of the moon upon the tides. It pulls back on the great liquid masses of the oceans, as though applying a brake to the earth's spin. Its actual effect, as the Abbé Moreux has poin ted out, is infinitesimally to reduce the weight of objects immediately below it. Lightened by one ten-thousandth of its mass, the ocean rises a yard under the moon's direct pull. The manifold phenomena of tides re-sult from this.

What, however, has been lost sight of in modern times, is that not only the oceans but all liquids are subject to this pull. The tidal effect of the moon works as well on liquids incorporated in organic matter as it does on those which are free. In fact, the effect is evidently much stronger, for the minute capillaries through which organic liquids move break them up into masses so small that they obey molecular rather than mechanical laws, and are thus infinitely more sensitive than the large bodies of water with which we are more familiar.

On this molecular scale, the pulling or lifting effect of the moon is very apparent, and no doubt provides a basis for many country traditions, such as the belief that plant-growth takes place at night and particularly on moonlit nights. In particular the moon appears to exercise this influence on sexual fluids. The Swedish scientist Svante Arrenhius has statistically shown that human ovulation follows the period of 27.3 days in which the moon makes its sidereal circuit in the sky (rather than the slightly longer period of its phases). In recent years, careful observation has established sexual rhythms of the same length in land-crabs, palolo-worms, oysters, scallops and sea-urchins, with corresponding variations in their succulence. The maximum water-content of melons, marrows and sargasso-seaweed coincides with the full of the moon, as do the heaviest catches in East Anglian and Milford Haven fisheries.[38] On the other hand, Cuban mahogany contracts have a moon-clause to ensure that the timber be cut at the moment of minimum moisture, maximum hardness.

It should be noted that most of these examples are drawn from organisms whose water-content is exceptionally high. But since all Nature is in its essence moist, the influence of the moon upon it varies only in degree. Wherever there is liquid there is lunar motion. The world of Nature, engendered by the Sun, built of the Earth, and clothed with form by the planets, is endowed with motion by the moon.

In this way the Moon takes its natural place among the heavenly bodies in their hierarchy of influence over matters upon earth. We already saw how the Sun may be said to control or influence matter in electronic or radiant state, the planets to control or influence matter in molecular or gaseous state, and how the Earth – through the force known as gravity – controls and influences matter in mineral or solid state. The influence of the Moon – half minor planet, half earthly satellite – thus naturally takes effect on matters in the state between molecular and mineral, between gaseous and solid – that it to say, upon *matter in liquid state*.

---

38. Svante Arrenhius, H. Munro Fox, Miss Semmens, Madame E. Kolisko, Messrs. Savage and Hodgson, C. P. Rickford and other authorities quoted by Robert Eisler, 'The Royal Art of Astrology', pp. 138-145.

And since the human organism is 72% water, to that extent its movements and tensions are not its own, but an unwitting result of the pull of the Earth's great balance-weight. Put in another way, we may say that the moon, balancing the pull of the Earth, holds all organic liquids in suspension. Without its support, all moist organisms would simply collapse, sucked flat by terrestrial gravity. If a man stands upright, with his column of blood and lymph raised erect from the ground, it is the moon which makes it possible. If he raises his arm, it is the moon which allows him to overcome the force of gravity, as the clockweight permits the counterweight to rise.

The two great systems of body liquids – those of blood and lymph – have one fundamental difference, however. The blood-system has a built-in pump, the heart, which keeps it in constant circulation against the terrestrial and lunar pulls. And the heart is powered by the Sun. The lymph-system has no such pump. Of itself it is a stagnant system, maintained in suspension by the Moon, and communicating with the other only by osmosis. Yet in order to cleanse the body and dispose of poisons, it has to circulate. This circulation is made possible only by the constant motion of all parts of the body, which act as innumerable vascular pumps at all stages of its network.

The moon-suspended lymph thus demands movement. And if there is no movement for an appreciable length of time, accumulation of poisons produces a muscular irritation which becomes unbearable. This irritation is relieved by movement, which renews lymph circulation. In this way, we may say that the Moon *induces* movement in man, whether he will or no.

Move he must. But he has a choice whether this movement be deliberate, intentional and useful to his aims: or involuntary, aimless and unproductive.

We have already said that the Sun controls the life-force, the vital seed of man; and the planets control his different functions. We may say that his life belongs to the Sun, his type or essence to the planets. Thus when man's movement serves to preserve or maintain life, or again when it is a natural expression of one or another function, it is – if not fully deliberate – at any rate useful. Movement of this kind is legitimate and productive movement, resulting as it were from a combination of lunar and solar, or lunar and planetary stimulus. In lives filled with the movement of physical labour, of crafts and skills, of sports and dances, the Moon's urge to movement is profitably harnessed. The itch of the lymph is used to the advantage or pleasure of the individual concerned.

But unfortunately such is not the case with large numbers of lazy and sedentary people in modern life. Since their lives contain almost no intentional movement, they are completely filled with unintentional movement, aimless movement, movement *wholly* under the Moon's sway.

Only a man who has already begun to study himself will realize what an immense part such pointless movement plays in human life. Not only all obvious kinds of fidgetting, restlessness, mechanical gestures of the hands and arms, changes of bodily position, stroking the face and chin, tapping with fingers or feet, belong to this category, but also the mechanical play of the facial muscles, which in many people incessantly produce smiles, frowns and grimaces of all kinds, *without any corresponding emotion at all*. It may literally be said of many who do not engage in intentional physical efforts which use up motor energy in a right and normal way, that *they are never still*.

This may be hard to believe. Yet it requires no more than the simple experiment of trying to remain completely motionless in any position, even the most comfortable, for five minutes, to prove that it is a literal fact. Almost all the waking and sleeping life of many city-dwellers is occupied by involuntary, unrecognized and completely aimless motion. This is what it means to be under the power of the moon. For a man or woman whose physical mechanism has been in *involuntary* motion for say twelve hours will be so exhausted, that they will have no energy whatever left for those things which from the point of view of their real nature they both should and would like to do.

We thus have the strange situation that the Moon rules that which has no conscious purpose in man, that which happens, mechanicalness. And if it be objected that power over mechanicalness is no power at all, this only attests the strange fact that mechanicalness always remains invisible to the man ruled by it – and the stronger its power over him the more invisible it remains.

For a very large part of involuntary and pointless movement takes the form of *habit*, that is, of some motion, action orreaction, originally performed for a reason, good or bad, but which goes on repeating itself *ad infinitum*, long after the original reason has been forgotten and the circumstances have changed. The lymph itches, and the body relieves itself, moving as it once was taught. Again, we may say that a very large part of human life is given over to the performance of habits; and that all this is under the influence of the Moon.

A characteristic habit, gradually spreading into all sides of a man's life, in time becomes his *chief weakness*. For instance, a man has on the one hand a tendency to be shy, and on the other a tendency to be meticulous in the performance of small tasks. While still a boy he acquires the habit of wanting to finish what he is doing rather than meet other people. Gradually, it begins to seem *right and inevitable* to him to complete even the most trivial task before fulfilling an engagement. Later still, if there is no task to delay his meeting people, he invents one. And so in the end it happens that — quite literally – he *never* keeps an engagement.

Such a chief weakness may spoil a man's life, get him into endless trouble, prevent him from accomplishing everything that he attempts. And the curious thing is that to the man himself the weakness may remain quite unknown and invisible. For to him each instance will seem separate and inevitable, and it will never occur to him that he could act in any other way.

Chief weakness is thus built on habit, habit on involuntary action, and involuntary action on pointless movement. And the primary cause of this whole sequence is the apparently innocent influence of the Moon upon liquid matter. It is for this reason that the path of conscious development is sometimes described as 'escape from the power of the Moon'.

For the whole 'lunacy' of chief weakness lies precisely in its mechanical-ness, the *automatic* nature of its manifestation. Once seen, its nature chan-ges. And with the introduction of consciousness and control, the possibility arises of using one's feature *intentionally* to serve a definite aim. Where this occurs, 'chief weakness' may be gradually transformed into 'chief strength', the 'special capacity' by which the individual is distinguished and on the basis of which he alone can achieve and serve.

In so far as he is liquid, man does what the moon dictates. He could in fact be said to be lunatic, were it not for the other rarer matters and ener-gies in him which are independent of this influence. For just as light is not subject to gravity, so the functions of reason and emotion, working with energies that are electrical rather than liquid, need not follow the moon's flux. In so far as the centre of gravity of a man's being lies in them, he is indepen-dent of the moon. In so far as he is blood and lymph he is her creature. Selene, as the Greek legend declared, is enamoured of Endymion, but unlike Pan he is only partly hers. And should he awake from the spell of sleep which Zeus cast upon him, and become conscious, he would cease to be so, wholly.

II THE MOON AS MAGNET

A quite different function of the moon now demands attention. We have seen that the weight and distance of the moon have great significance from the Earth's point of view. But several curious facts about this weight and distance can only be explained by supposing an equally intimate relation with the Sun.

THE MOON

It is well known that at certain total eclipses the disc of the moon *exactly* fits over that of the sun, obscuring its whole surface but leaving visible the fiery corona with which it is surrounded. In fact this is so well known that no one considers it extraordinary. But if the moon were a few hundred miles larger or smaller, a few thousand miles nearer or farther away, the exact coincidence could not occur. Out of all the immense range of size and distance apparently possible for a satellite, this *particular* point has been chosen. Clearly such combination of size and distance must represent some meaning, a focus in some field of unseen force.

Put in another way, if a converging beam of light be imagined emanating from the Sun and focussed on the centre point of the Earth, the moon is arranged exactly to cut out such a beam in certain recurring circumstances which we call eclipses. In terms of our electrical analogy of the Solar System as a series of transformers, it would mean that one function of the moon is in some way to change the constant influence of the Sun into an interrupted current. The principle is similar to that used in an electric buzzer, where a magnet and spring are used to make and break a steady current, and by means of an armature or reed which is pulled alternately by them, produce a mechanical oscillation which we hear as sound.

Enquiring further, we find that the sequence of such eclipses or cut-outs of solar current is quite regular, and repeats in a period lasting 18 years and 11 days, which the ancients called the Saros. In it 28 total eclipses of the sun are observed in one part of the world or another. Thus the mechanism of the moon appears to interrupt solar radiation at a frequency of about 120 cycles in the 80 years which we calculated to be a moment of perception of the Sun. Taking 80 years in the Sun's time to correspond to one thirtieth of a second in the time of man,[39] this would be equivalent to a frequency of four kilocycles.

Another little remarked fact supports this view of the moon as a make-and-break mechanism for the solar current. When allowance is made for the motion of the Earth, the speed of the moon's revolution round the latter in 27.3 days is found to be *exactly* the speed of the Sun's rotation on its own axis in 25.3 days. Whether this gearing is by some invisible mechanics or by a photo-electric influence, the effect is as if the Sun turned the moon in its orbit like two cogs of equal diameter, which always oppose and engage the same face. Again, it is impossible to believe such coincidence of speeds to be accidental, and one can only suppose that though the moon is atta-

---

39. See Chapter 2, III, 'The Times of the Universe'.

ched to the Earth's field, it is also part of a solar mechanism to produce the alternating force required.

In relation to the interrupting frequency of the moon (4 kilocycles), the Sun's radiations are undoubtedly of a much higher frequency. The moon's effect is therefore to produce pulses of high frequency current. In ordinary electrical theory this would give rise to an alternating current in any adjacent circuit tuned to the frequency at which the pulses occur. The Earth may be considered as just such a circuit.

Supposing our analysis to be correct, what is the purpose or effect of the creation of a high-frequency current in the Earth's field? The full implications of this question are far beyond us. But there is one specific effect associated with high-frequency currents which is suggestive from our point of view. This is the phenomenon known to electricians as 'skin effect'. If a direct low-frequency current be passed along a wire, it travels equally through the whole section, like water through a pipe. But the higher the frequency the more the current tends to keep near the surface of the wire, and at rapid radio frequencies it is carried on the surface almost entirely. In just the same way water passing down a rifled barrel tends to fly towards the circumference, leaving a vortex down the centre.

One of the results of the moon's creation of a high-frequency effect, then, may be to keep the transformed solar energy flowing along the *surface* of the Earth in time, that is, flowing through that part of the Earth which is covered by the world of Nature and organic life. Further, whether we think of the phenomenon electrically as 'skin effect' or mechanically as the centrifugal tendency of water in a rifled pipe, the effect will be to produce an *outward pull*, a *lifting effect* on the surface of our conductor.

Starting from quite a different point of view, we arrive again at the same conception of the moon as the sustainer of organic life, as that which holds living things erect upon the surface of the earth. It is like the invisible operator of a puppet-show, who holds the strings by which the dolls are animated. It is, as we saw before, the great *magnet* of Nature, exerting a magnetic influence upon her three times more powerful than that of all the planets put together.

Before going further, however, it were perhaps better to consider the question of magnetism in general, and in particular the curious failure of this study to keep pace with other scientific advance.

Modern magnetic science began in the sixteenth century, and was systematised in 1600 by William Gilbert who took the Earth as the great or archetypal magnet and studied all smaller magnets as 'terellas' or miniature earths. To emphasise the living quality of magnetism he subtitled his book, 'A New Physiology'. All early investigators, indeed, regarded magnetism as a universal principle, that of cosmic attraction and repulsion, which was accompanied on every scale by the phenomena of ebb and flow. In 1766 Mesmer published a thesis in Vienna, claiming that "there exists a mutual influence between the Heavenly Bodies, the Earth and Animate Bodies," by means of a "universally distributed and continuous fluid . . . of an incomparably rarified nature." The "property of the animal body, which brings it under the influence of heavenly bodies and the reciprocal action of those surrounding it," he called 'animal magnetism'.

Fifty years later Faraday realised that an electric current passing through wire produces a magnetic field of force, electro-magnetism. And about the same time this was recognised as a molecular phenomenon, depending on the smoothing out or similar polarising of all atoms within the metal concerned.

Thenceforward, two forms of magnetism – terrestrial and metallic – exclusively occupied the attention of researchers, and its other two previously recognised aspects – planetary magnetism and animal magnetism – were either rejected or ignored.

We can now press for the reconsideration of both planetary and animal magnetism as similar phenomena, precisely on the basis of Faraday's own discovery. For as we saw earlier, the tracks of the planets in time may indeed be regarded as 'wires', charged with an induced current from the Sun, and therefore surrounded by magnetic fields just as the Earth is. Again, as we now know from animal physiology, the 'wires' of the nerves carry electric impulses and must also produce magnetic fields, both small and great.

The rejection of animal and planetary magnetism is traceable to the habit – based on a misunderstanding of scientific method – of denying that which can not yet be measured by mechanical instruments. For example, the phenomena of personal attraction and repulsion between different types and different sexes is a thing which every individual daily observes and measures for himself: it is perhaps the most certainly known thing in his whole experience. This is a direct perception of animal magnetism. Every time two people's eyes meet, they can feel and study the closing of a magnetic circuit. Yet because no known instruments can measure this circuit or the degree of this attraction and repulsion, it is tacitly ignored. For the same reason planetary magnetism has also been ignored. A fresh scientific study of both of these 'forgotten phenomena' may be expected in the near future.

Meanwhile, we shall continue to treat both animal and planetary magnetism as subject to the same laws as terrestrial and metallic magnetism, even though they remain as yet unmeasurable.

The moon, then, is the great *magnet* of all Nature. It sustains the millions of separate magnetic fields which animate all individual living bodies upon Earth, and which distinguish them from dead ones. Every living organism, endowed with life by the Sun, constitutes such an individual and ephemeral magnetic field. It may indeed be said to possess *a magnetic body*, in addition to its physical one. And it is these magnetic bodies which are both produced and influenced by the magnetic action of the moon, though given form and variety by the lesser and ever-changing magnetism of the planets.

In the case of man, this magnetic field or magnetic body has many interesting aspects. It is this which, studied by Kilner and Bagnall through screens of cyanine dye, appeared as a kind of aura extending two or three inches in every direction beyond the physical body. As we should expect, it has a particular affinity for the body liquids, especially arterial blood, which – through its high iron content – is as it were the vehicle of magnetism; and it is stronger in those individuals who have a full rich flow of blood, and more tenuous in the thin and anaemic. It is thus closely connected with state of health, both of the body as a whole and of its separate parts.

It is with this magnetic body that a man is sensitive to the physical states of others, and he feels immediately sympathetic towards one and ruffled by another. It is also the medium of 'sympathy', that is, the understanding or 'feeling with' another's physical suffering or need or well-being, though this capacity must not be confused with emotional understanding, which is very much quicker and more penetrating.

The close connection between the magnetic field and the bloodstream makes it an important factor in healing. Apart from the individual himself having the power of concentrating it in a desired place by attention, some people have the natural capacity of 'smoothing out' or polarizing the magnetic fields of others. When this power is genuine, we have 'faith healers' or 'psychic healers'. In some places where very much magnetic force has been concentrated over a long time, such as certain centres of pilgrimage, it is possible that this 'smoothing out' of the magnetic body may be done impersonally, and a sense of special well-being and even physical 'miracles' produced in responsive persons. In other cases, action on the magnetic body of others may take the form of mesmerism or hypnotism.

In the normal way, the magnetic field is fluid and nebulous, embracing the whole physical body, or perhaps more concentrated about the heart.

Fixed attention has the power of focussing it, and through it of increasing the bloodflow to one particular place. But the possibility also exists that some terrible shock or violence of an emotional kind, particularly at the moment of death, may 'freeze' it permanently or semi-permanently into a given form. In this case it may retain its form or field even after the desintegration of the living body which gave rise to it. It is this possibility which is at the bottom of stories of ghosts, spectres, hauntings, and the legend of the independent existence of a doppelgänger.

As regards both abnormal and normal phenomena connected with the magnetic body, however, it is most important to remember that the latter is a purely mechanical phenomenon. Nothing connected with the magnetic body, and in general nothing subject to the influence of the moon, has any connection with psychic development or with consciousness.

III THE MOON AS EARTH'S OFFSPRING

One of the chief characteristics of the moon, it was noted earlier, is that nothing ever happens there. Modern telescopes bring man's vision as near the moon, as rockets equipped with cameras remove it from the Earth. In other words man can now study the Earth and the moon at equal distances. Indeed, lit in the brilliant glare of a Sun undiffused by atmosphere, the moon's surface is revealed almost as vividly as an earthly landscape seen from a transcontinental airplane.

But though he study it from year-end to year-end, the observer realises, with a dawning sense of horror, that nothing ever changes there. The same jagged mountain-ranges, lit dazzling white against the pitch black shadows, the same twenty-mile craters, like splashes in a milk jug frozen for all eternity, the same interminable deserts of volcanic ash, now the temperature of boiling water under a vertical sun, now 80° below zero Centigrade as they pass into the shadow – all this is identical today, tomorrow, at the time of Caesar and a thousand years hence.

Not only no growing thing exists there, but no seasons, no winds, even no frost or ice. Only a lone and soundless column of dust as a meteorite strikes, only a blinding day and a jet black night petrified by the cold of outer space; this is the extent of variation. Strangely enough, the most accurate account that could be given of conditions on the moon is to be found in certain mediaeval descriptions of hell. For only these convey the idea of *eternal* fire, *eternal* cold, the *impossibility of improvement*. We are so accustomed to the constant flux and transience of the world of Nature that it is almost impossible for us to conceive, in ordinary terms, a world where time does not bring change.

All this is characteristic of a world in which the first octaves of matters we discussed in the last chapter are lacking. If it were possible to draw up a table of lunar elements, it would perhaps begin below oxygen, where the main matters of organic life leave off. In any case, such matters can only occur 'imprisoned' in the form of metal or mineral salts.

The only kind of change which seems to occur on the moon, and which may possibly be the first preparation for life there countless ages hence, is a tendency for the dust raised by flying meteors and flaking rocks to drift towards a single region, where it seems to be filling the dead craters and creating, with immeasurable slowness, a vast plain of dusty silt.[40] This is in fact the beginning of a tide, the mass of lunar dust being dragged back by the Earth, just as the mass of terrestrial water is dragged back by the Moon.

Earlier on we studied the connection between rotation and the separation of matters into different states which can give rise to atmosphere and organic life. The moon does not rotate, and it is, as we would suppose of a body where no separative force had yet been produced, a solid and homogeneous mass of matter in mineral state.

What chance has the moon of acquiring rotation, and thus in time of generating air and life? Is it in fact growing? In answer to this we can present four facts. The moon is at present 30 times its parent's diameter away. It does not rotate. Mercury is 42 times its parent's diameter away from the sun. It does not rotate.[41] Venus is 77 times its parent's diameter away from the sun, and it *has* begun to rotate. All further planets rotate, and in general the farther removed they are the faster they do so. Meanwhile, the Moon certainly, and the planets probably, are slowly moving away from their luminary.

It thus seems extremely probable that a planet or satellite, springing originally out of the body of its parent, acquires the power of rotation and consequently of independent life of its own, only when it has emancipated itself to a certain definite distance from its source. This distance seems to be between fifty and seventy times the diameter of the parent. On this calculation the Moon will have to be twice as far away from the Earth as it is now before it can begin to rotate and generate life. It is in fact half-way between conception and *birth as an independent planet*.

40. Fred Hoyle, 'The Nature of the Universe', p. 11.

41. The so-called rotation of Mercury *once* in the course of its revolution about the sun is, of course, merely the result of its maintaining a fixed relation to the latter. It is a borrowed movement, not rotation at all in the sense of independent planetary motion.

If this then is the child of earth, what kind of a child is it? Seeking a human analogy we have to go back beyond childhood, infancy, and even birth to discover any parallel. The offspring is not only not born, but it is not even quickened. It is like the embryo or form of a future world which as yet has no life or movement of its own.

To an observer who was familiar with living human beings with their unceasing movements and moods, their never-ending play of expression, of tone, of posture and so on, and who in some way was able to watch an unquickened foetus in its mother's womb, this foetus would appear lifeless and unchanging. He would say that nothing was happening to it, and that it had no possibilities. For although its inner essential rate of change was far faster than that of the men and women he knew, it would completely lack the outer vibration of personality which he associated with them. Such may be the stage of development of the Earth's moon.

But if this is so, how is the moon nourished? Such an embryo depends for its very existence, until it shall be born as an independent organism, upon its participation in the bloodstream of the mother. It receives the nourishment necessary for its growth from her. The moon's bare ball is not yet able to transform the solar light direct. Until it acquires atmosphere and life of its own, it must receive this energy already predigested by the Earth.

We have noted the various influences of the moon upon the Earth. What is the corresponding influence of the Earth upon the moon? What passes from the parent to the offspring? Once again the phenomenon which we have variously described as the lunar *pull*, its *lifting* or *sucking* effect, its creation of a centrifugal current outward from the Earth, will help us to answer the question. For all these are simply ways of describing the effect of a certain flow from the Earth to the moon, like the flow of blood from the mother to the unborn infant.

The moon lifts or sucks the whole organic creation from the surface of the Earth. But its power of attraction does not stop there. And there is reason to suspect that at the moment when organisms die, and their elements return to the Earth's general stock, this attraction is in some way fulfilled and a magnetic circuit completed. When the puppet player releases his dolls, they fall back to the stage and become inert fragments of cardboard and cloth. Something passes from them back to him. It is their motion, their illusion of life, their puppet-soul.

All that has been deduced about the role of the moon leads us to believe that it is exactly this electric tension which constitutes the difference between living and dead matter, that provides the current necessary to the moon's existence. Every living organism, endowed with life by the Sun, constitutes an individual and ephemeral magnetic field. When it dies and its power of transforming the solar life-force is withdrawn, this magnetic tension is released. The release every hour and every moment of millions of such magnetic fields, large and small, over the whole surface of the Earth, will induce an enormous current in an adjacent conductor. Since there is no indication that this energy is used again on Earth – for the next generation of living beings always arises from *new* solar energy – we have to suppose that it is drawn off somewhere.

In fact, the magnetic current released by the death of living creatures flies to the lowest level of the ionosphere, which is now recognised as the level where lunar magnetism takes effect.[42]

There it joins the general magnetic current connecting the Earth and the moon. Calculations based on the delay between magnetic disturbances on the surface of the sun and the repercussions in the atmosphere have shown that magnetic influences travel at about 400 miles a second.[43] In ten minutes that which made the difference between a living and a dead body has flown to the moon which sustained it during life.

This magnetic current is the moon's lifeline, the umbilical cord which connects it with its mother Earth.

42. 'The Earth's Magnetism', by Sydney Chapman, p. 77.
43. ibid pp. 114-5.

IX THE WORLD OF NATURE

I THE SIX REALMS OF NATURE

THERE IS MUCH TO SUGGEST THAT THE REALMS OF NATURE SUR-round the earth with the same significance as the various key-organs serve the body. Such organs as the pancreas or thyroid, though they have their material embodiment in one place, secrete appropriate hormones which suffuse the entire organism. So the mineral kingdom, for example, though its centre of gravity lies in the geological realm of rocks and soil deposits, penetrates through every phase of nature and even into man, in whose blood and bones mineral salts play an important part. The vegetable kingdom, with its centre of gravity in trees and plants, also exists in him through the vegetative life of tissue and of flesh. But in them it is predominant, in him subordinate.

These realms of Nature, then, are not so much separate classes of creatures as levels of a particular form of life, or of a particular density. Individual creatures differ, not so much in belonging to this or that kingdom; but rather in the number of natural kingdoms which are contained in them, and to which they owe allegiance.

Thus a piece of rock belongs simply and solely to the mineral realm. The rose which grows upon it, on the other hand, belongs both to mineral and vegetable realms; while the caterpillar which eats the rose belongs to these and in addition to the realm of invertebrate animals. A dog is mineral by its bone structure, vegetable by its connective tissue, worm-like by its system of digestion, but beyond these vertebrate by its spine and the dependent nervous system which bring powers of motion, sensation, coordination of perceptions and logical action impossible for the invertebrate.

Since one of the chief causes of man's distress and confusion is that he usually regards all these different sides of himself as equally manlike and equally individual, we would do well to clarify their difference in more detail.

In a very general sense, the different realms of Nature are disposed on the globe in the way that all matters naturally settle when left to themselves – the densest at the bottom and the most rarefied above. The lowest kingdom is that of metals, which appear to have their centre of gravity in the barysphere. This is a heavy shell, 1700 miles thick, enclosing that unknown central core of the earth which transmits no vibrations and, it would seem, is more 'dead' and dense than anything we can conceive existing on the earth's surface. From the way the barysphere reacts to earthquake-waves, it has been deduced that its lowest levels may be of iron or nickel rendered immensely rigid by pressure, and that it gradually diminishes in rigidity as it approaches the surface. This is the *realm of metals*.

Enveloping the barysphere is a much thinner shell of rock and minerals, known as the lithosphere. This shell is only 50 miles thick, and consists chiefly of basalt, granite and other vitreous volcanic rocks. These rocks are crystalline forms of silica, iron, titanium and magnesium, and since they appear to be formed by the oxidation or combustion of these metals, we may imagine them as living or feeding upon the latter. They form the *realm of minerals*.

This realm includes in its topmost strata the soil of the earth's surface, and this in turn is covered with the thin green film of the *realm of plants*, which feed upon mineral salts. Two very definite changes enter at this point. The realm of plants or of living tissue is cellular in structure, and it is sensitive to light. Being cellular, it is endowed with changing form in quite a different sense from the fixed crystalline form of minerals and metals. Being sensitive to light, it is able by means of a photosynthetic mechanism based on chlorophyll, to transform the solar radiation into energy for its own use. Thus in contrast to the lower kingdoms, which in comparison seem amorphous and dead, the world of plants is particularly subject to the formative influence of the planets and to the life-giving influence of the sun.

Living and feeding upon the world of plants is the very much thinner but immensely important *realm of invertebrates*. Ten out of twelve of the main groups of animals, including the infinite army of worms and insects upon the earth, of molluscs and crustaceans in the sea, belong to this realm, which numbers hundreds of thousands or even millions of species. Most invertebrates enjoy the power of locomotion, and besides feeding on plants, they render the return service of breaking up and aerating the soil for them.

We noted that the barysphere was about 300 times as thick as the lithosphere, and in a very rough way the lithosphere is about 300 times the thickness of the realm of plants. This seems to be the general order of the relation of the successive natural realms one to another, for when we come to the *realm of vertebrates* we find a very much sparser and more tenuous layer. Every square inch of the temperate and tropical surface of the earth is alive with invertebrates, but vertebrates in comparison require square feet or even up to acres for their elbow-room.

At this point again a very definite change appears to enter, as distinct as that which separated plants from minerals. For the implications of a spinal column and its dependent nervous system and brain, however rudimentary, are enormous. It implies parallel systems of afferent and motor nerves, that is, a system for conveying impressions from the outside world to a centre where they are sorted and arranged, where certain deductions result from this arrangement, and from which an appropriate motor order is sent out by a second system to the muscles. Vertebrates, at any rate potentially, enjoy the power to see and act. They are able to transform not only solar radiation in general to their own use; but individual impressions created by such radiation. They react not only to the brightness of light, but to a certain specific pattern of light, sound and other vibrations, such as that formed by the image of man, his scent, and the crunch of his boots.

Finally, we come to the *realm of man*, a layer so rarefied and tenuous that only ten human beings are found on an average square mile of the Earth's surface. Man lives on plants, on invertebrates, and on the fleshy parts of vertebrates. When we ask in what, objectively, man differs from the other realms of Nature, we are at first at a loss for an answer. What is there in man which is not metal, mineral, vegetable, and which does not belong at least potentially to animals?

There are certain obvious traps to be avoided in trying to answer this question. For example, we must avoid using different words for things simply because they apply to the human world. We must be careful of calling 'intelligent adaptation to environment' in man what we call 'conditioning' in animals, 'cultural memory' in man what we call 'herd instinct' in animals, and so on. Thus men live in cities; but so do bees and termites. Men transmit knowledge from generation to generation; but so apparently do migrating eels. Men stand on two legs; but so do ostriches, while storks stand even on one.

After many apparent differences, due to scale or point of view, have been disposed of, we are left with a very short list of purely human characteristics. Men, for example, cook their food, use tools, wear clothes, think in concepts, are influenced by a sense of right and wrong, can develop souls.

The last idea requires a lot of explanation, the first will be touched on shortly. The other four all spring from a very special sense of *relationship*, a dawning consciousness of *oneself in relation to the universe*. We may say, for example, that the use of tools is a practical expression of this sense, the wearing of clothes an emotional or artistic one, thinking in concepts an intellectual one, the sense of right and wrong a moral one. There can be no tools, except where the craftsman feels his relation with inanimate materials. There can be no right or wrong, except where man feels his relation with other living beings. All these characteristics arise from the feeling, inherent in the race of men but very dim and confused in the individual – "Here am I, there are other creatures, around us lies the universe."

But in fact this sense is only a *possibility* for ordinary man. It is not a daily and hourly reality for him. Individual man is very proud to take credit for all that the pioneers of humanity have painfully achieved over thousands of years, and made available to him. And he often believes that because he enjoys the fruit of their work, he shares their perception and their state of consciousness. He has to be very sincere with himself indeed to admit that a great part of the time he is but an ant in his organisation, a beaver in his building, a monkey dressed in clothes, a parrot repeating words.

What is truly manlike is still only *potential* in him. We can say that it seems to depend on a higher nervous system, which gives him the possibility of being conscious of his own existence and his relation to the surrounding universe. Man can be conscious, and through consciousness he can understand. Only in this he is man. Thus he is man by the *potentiality of his organism*, rather than by its actual working; just as a vertebrate is vertebrate by the potentiality of its structure for logical action in accordance with impressions. All but one impulse and sensation which man finds in himself belong to the lower realms of Nature; his only manlike attribute is the potentiality of consciousness, of feeling both separate from and at one with all creation. If he remembers this, much will become clearer for him.

The same sequence of the realms of Nature seems also to suggest the true fate of this one manlike quality. For when we established the functions of the Earth – metals, minerals, plant-life (with no heat of its own), invertebrate flesh (with heat of its own), vertebrates and man – we seem also to have established a curious natural progression of eaters and eaten, of feeders and of food.

Plants eat metal-salts, invertebrates eat mineral matter, vertebrates eat whole plants. Man's food differs from that of other vertebrates in being cooked and hot while theirs is cold and raw. Thus man – whether by nature or artifice – may be said to eat food of the nature of warm invertebrate flesh. Only one creature we know eats whole vertebrates, the complete carcases of horses, elephants and donkeys, with spines and bones – and that is the Earth.

If the whole universe thus eats and is eaten, what then eats man? The answer appears to be, something higher than the Earth. That which is of next higher nature above the Earth and planets is the Sun. The Sun should eat man.

But we know that men's corpses, as complete vertebrate organisms, are eaten by the Earth, and as warehouses of mineral salts by invertebrates, by worms. Further, we have deduced that as magnetic fields they go to feed the moon. What then could it mean that men should be eaten by the Sun? It can only refer to that part of man which distinguishes him from all other vertebrates, that is, his consciousness. The Sun lives on the consciousness of men. Later, we may see better what this enigmatic principle may mean.

II NATURE IN SPACE: NATURE IN GEOLOGIC TIME

The arrangement of the realms of Nature which now presents itself to us makes clear something which has hitherto been uncertain. Sometimes we have taken the Earth as a cosmos, and the World of Nature as a second cosmos; at other times we have taken the two together as forming a single cosmos between them. This uncertainty has been inevitable because of the curious double role of Nature in the general scale of creation – serving as it does partly as an integral part of the planet Earth, and partly as a separate mechanism in its own right for creating vital connections between one part of the Solar System and another.

Nature (literally, 'that which is born') receives and transforms the Sun's light, creating from it a wealth of transient living forms, which at their disintegration go to feed the Earth with their bodies and the Moon with their magnetism. Nature literally links Sun, Earth and Moon.

But now having analysed the different realms of nature, we find that *the whole Earth is involved*. No part of it is left out. Nature and the Earth thus form one being, one cosmos; of which the whole variety of living forms known to us constitute but the higher functions. Nature may thus be taken as the emotional, the creative or artistic side of the cosmos Earth; just as when we say Mozart or Beethoven, it is not their bones or muscles we think of, but their creative or artistic role.

Thus in future we will take the Earth and Nature as one cosmos. But when we refer to Nature we will have especially in mind this artistic and poetical aspect of our planet, which – endlessly dressing and undressing herself in new costumes of form and colour – envelops mankind continuously in her aura of beauty and delight. For without such a concept, all our scientific knowledge can give but a dead and dreary picture of her.

Now although these different realms of Nature – the metal, mineral, plant, invertebrate, vertebrate and human – lie one over the other, like layers or strata of matter in a natural order of decreasing density, we know that in fact they are not sharply divided but interpenetrate in a very subtle way.

The law which governs their interpenetration is best known in connection with the Brownian movement of minute particles. Motes of dust in a beam of light, or particles of some dye in a glass of water, for example, do not individually obey what we call the law of gravity, but jostled by the bombardment of molecules, each performs an erratic and apparently meaningless dance in the medium in which they exist. When the whole field is seen, however, it is discovered that the totality of particles have arranged themselves in such a way that their diffusion is perfectly graded from dense to rare and diminishes in exact geometrical progression as we ascend to higher layers.

This law of diffusion, which we can very well watch as we pour milk into a glass of iced coffee, is not in fact confined to minute particles. The apparently aimless settling of mayflies upon the ceiling above a lamp is found to produce a perfect gradation of density from light to darkness. The erratic colonization of a new country by the whim of individual immigrants results in a perfectly graded diffusion of population from the centres of communication and wealth towards the wilderness. In fact the whole habitation of the Earth by man follows this law. Individual particles spread from a more favourable medium into a less favourable one in perfect geometrically decreasing gradation.

In just this way do the lower realms of Nature diffuse or penetrate into the higher, and the higher into the lower. We may even imagine the whole natural world as a vessel in which the particles of six liquids of different specific gravities interfuse according to this law. The idea becomes clearer when we see how the different natural realms have their centres of gravity in different periods of the table of elements. For it is then apparent that the elements of each particular period are to be found concentrated in their appropriate realm yet diffusing upward and downward in the manner described.

We may suppose, for example, that the true home of the unnatural radio-active elements of period 7 is in the inert core of the Earth. Minute particles of them are found, however, as high as the upper layers of the lithosphere; though not, as we noted before, in the soil or upon the actual surface of the Earth.

The centre of gravity of the dense metals and rare earths of period 6 lies probably in the barysphere. These also filter upward, occuring in lodes nearer the Earth's surface than the radio-active elements, though, like them, they find no natural place above it, except in the artifacts of man.

The affinity of the elements of period 5 is with the lithosphere. These elements still penetrate but rarely into the upper organic realms, with the exception of iodine which exists in notable quantities in the sea and marine life, and has a stabilizing role to play even in the human organism. Here, however, we begin to notice not only the diffusion of particles of the lower levels upward, but also those of the upper levels downward. For we find in the world of minerals iron, silica and magnesium from higher periods, and even oxygen in the form of oxides of these metals.

In period 4 occur potassium and calcium and the metals such as iron and copper, whose salts constitute soil, the medium of existence for the realm of plants, and which provide the key to cellular structure and the tissue and sap system characteristic of plant life. This realm is also marked by the downward penetration of carbon, nitrogen and oxygen.

The centre of gravity of the realm of invertebrates lies in period 3, where we find the sodium and chlorine of salt and the phosphorus necessary to the phosphorescence of so many insects and marine invertebrates. Sea water is particularly the medium of invertebrates and it is in the oceans that the greatest concentrations of salt and phosphorus are found. Many of the elements of this period filter upwards in small amounts into the organism of man.

The gases nitrogen and oxygen of period 2 form air, which is the medium of existence of the realm of vertebrates, and with carbon are the basis of their life as such.[44]

Finally, we deduce some special connection between the potentiality of *man* and hydrogen which fills the whole octave of period 1. The very tension, vitality and awareness of a human being depends, as we know, upon the hydrogen ion concentration of his blood. Hydrogen appears to play something the same role with regard to man's higher functions and to his power of transmuting solar radiation into the highest forms of energy, as it does in relation to the Earth. For it is the ionosphere or sphere of hydrogen sixty miles and more above the Earth's surface – the 'heaven' of the ancients – which receives and transforms the electronic energy of the sun in its purest form.

We thus find that the elements of each period constitute, as it were, the medium of life for one realm of Nature, in which that realm exists and from which it draws the characteristic materials of its structure. The realm of

44. Much detailed material on this sequence of connection may be found in 'La Biosphere', by G. Vernadsky, and 'The Cycle of Weathering', by B. B. Polynov.

metals in the barysphere, the realm of minerals in the lithosphere, the realm of plants in the soil, the realm of invertebrates in the sea, the realm of vertebrates in the air, and some affinity of the higher nature of man with the upper sun-impregnated atmosphere, are all in a general way examples of this principle.

We must remember, however, that nature is never content with octaves in one dimension. Every phenomenon participates in octaves running in all dimensions. The structure of the table of elements only became clear when it was seen as an octave squared. In the same way, although the medium of air seems characteristic of the horizontal period 2, it in fact includes in its composition all the inert gases – helium, neon, argon, krypton, and xenon – of the vertical note *do*. Although the medium of ocean seems characteristic of period 3, it includes traces of all the halogens – fluorine, chlorine, bromine, and iodine – of the vertical note *re*. Although the medium of soil seems characteristic of period 4, it comprises all the alkalis of the vertical note *si*. And similarly for the lithosphere and barysphere.

It is this squaring of octaves which produces the incredibly subtle upward and downward diffusion which we remarked on earlier. It explains certain anomalies of matter found in unexpected places, that would remain incomprehensible if we tried to understand them on the basis of horizontal octaves only. It means that every realm of Nature permeates every other, constituting the headquarters as it were of a form of life which exists everywhere. With this idea we return exactly to our starting point at the beginning of the chapter.

Every phenomenon, we said, has a place in octaves belonging to all dimensions. If an octave can be squared, it can also be cubed. So that if the octave of the realms of nature is to be discovered stretching both vertically from the centre of the Earth out to the ionosphere, and again horizontally within each of these strata, we may look for it also in the dimension of time.

And in fact, extending through the aeons of geologic time, we do find exactly such an octave. In the precambrian rocks, devoid of all fossil life and dating from more than a thousand million years ago, we see the trace of a wholly mineral world. In the primary era, despite Nature's first experiments with molluscs and trilobites, it is the hot wet forests which must have dominated the earth – those immense masses of vegetable life whose remains have come down to us as coal-beds. In the secondary, the oceans rose and fell and in them the invertebrate horde of molluscs, ammonites and corals, infinite in number and giant in size, rose to supremacy. The tertiary is the period in which the vertebrate mammals, foreshadowed in the mon-

strous dinosaurs of the secondary, suddenly develop into a thousand ingenious and delicate forms. While the quaternary includes the whole history
of that special experiment which has resulted in man as we now know him.

Each of the great geological eras represents the dominance of one of the
natural realms, each having its time of supremacy followed by its subservience to the next creation. In each era the first crude experiments are made
to prepare the type of being to which the world will next belong. The lonely
trilobites of the primary foreshadow the invertebrate world of the secondary; the unwieldly diplodocus of the secondary, doomed in his own time,
is the forerunner of the slender horse and tiger of the next age; the manlike monkey of the tertiary supposes a world of true men in the present.

This experiment of later forms in earlier times corresponds to the downward diffusion of higher elements which we noted earlier. The mollusc in
the age of tree-ferns is like silica from the period of invertebrates imbedded
in the realm of minerals. And in the reverse sense, the primitive forms of
life which still exist in the era of man play, like the element iodine in his
body, a stabilizing role in the higher world into which they have penetrated.

This geologic octave also shows very well the varying *duration* of different notes according to their density. Just as the barysphere was 1700 miles
thick, the lithosphere 50 miles, the biosphere of plants only a few hundred
feet, and the realm of animals and man a film of immeasurable delicacy, so
the sequence of geologic periods shows a logarithmic diminishment. The
era of metals and minerals must have lasted from the formation of the Earth
to the beginning of the Cambrian period, perhaps a thousand million years.
The duration of the primary era of vegetable life is sometimes put at 300
million years, of the secondary 140 million, of the tertiary sixty million, and
of our current quaternary two million.[45]

The notes of a rising octave last shorter and shorter time because their
vibrations are ever more compressed. The periods grow shorter because
more is happening in them. "Human life has changed more in the last 50
years," wrote Sir James Jeans, "than reptile life did in 50 million years in the
Jurassic and Permian Eras."[46] It is characteristic of finer energy that more
can happen in a smaller space and in a shorter time. So that, as we said
earlier about the lives of beings of different scales, all geologic eras are in
reality of the same length.

But this increasing compression of the notes as they rise carries with
it another implication. The more can happen in time, the more time be-

45. Richard M. Field in 'Van Nostrand's Scientific Encyclopædia'.
46. Sir James Jeans: 'Through Space and Time', p. 47.

comes limited, and the more jealously it is counted. The era of the tree-ferns, for the very limitation of their possibilities, lasted 300 million years, but even so came to an end at its appointed time. Sir James Jeans probably exaggerates when he says that our time-scale has accelerated a millionfold since then. At least, it is to be hoped so. For this would mean that man had but one-millionth of their time in which to realize all his possibilities.

III THE PERCEPTION OF ANIMALS

The problem of how animals think, of how they see the world has always interested man. As Ouspensky pointed out in 'Tertium Organum', the fact hat no direct means of communication has ever been devised between man and the animals with which he lives is sufficient proof that the latter definitely lack certain mental powers – such as that of evolving concepts, and of imagining a third dimension – which man takes for granted and without which the world would be unrecognisable to him. Ouspensky went on to try to deduce the nature of the perceptions which make up animal psychology, by imagining the world of creatures existing only in one or two dimensions instead of three.

We must now try to approach the same question from a different angle – from a physical rather than a philosophical point of view.

If we begin with the class of insects, for example, we realise that the chief thing which separates human perception from insect perception is *time*. Supposing, for convenience, we take an insect whose lifetime is a single day – certain summer gnats, for instance. According to the principle evolved in Chapter 2, that all lives are the same length, such a gnat will live its life nearly 30,000 times *faster* than does man. All forms of energy reaching the gnat, measured by vibrations per man's second, will be reduced 30,000 times or about 15 octaves, when measured by gnat's time.

The effect of such a transposition of course depends upon the presence and nature of the corresponding receptive organs, about which we know little in the gnat's case. But we may say theoretically and in a general way that for the gnat human 'sound' (4th to 15th octaves) will disappear altogether or become a slow rhythmic pulsation. Radio waves and the lower electrical frequencies (25th to 30th octaves) will acquire the nature of magnetism, heat and light that of electricity, and x-rays that of heat. Light in turn would be represented by gamma rays, and the fact that these rays *do not exist in nature* may have a certain cosmic meaning. It may mean that for certain reasons Nature, in relegating creatures to the scale of insects, has banished them to a region where *there is no light*, and thus no possibility of the perversion of divine energy.

We can calculate many other strange transformations of the world which will follow from the gnat's time. If the perception of radiation changes, the perception of linear space must change proportionately, since our main means of measuring space is by the distance travelled by different energies in a given time. For example, sound, travelling at 1100 feet per second for man, will cover no more than one third of an inch per second for the gnat. If a man stand at the top of his garden and shout at a gnat a hundred yards away, his 'Hullo' will reach it nearly three hours later in a series of seismic shocks lasting eight hours. In fact the man would be the equivalent of 1700 miles away and his shout could only be felt by the gnat, if at all, in the way in which human beings feel a faint earthquake or the eruption of a distant volcano. On such a scale the centre of the Earth is as far from the gnat as the Sun is from us, while the Sun itself becomes almost as remote as the nearest star.

Density too would be transposed upon the gnat's scale of time, and in relation to its size and minute weight. A rainstorm would mean that for several years large rounded blocks of water were scattered through space like icebergs in a northern sea. For water would be solid to him, and he could of course no more be hit by a raindrop than a man by a glacier; though sometimes great sheets of water such as puddles might suffer earthquakes and, the hard crust created by surface tension breaking, suck the unfortunate gnat into a bottomless bog below. Air would be liquid, in which he could swim up, down and sideways, or float at any level. While probably the scent of flowers or odour of putrefaction would in turn take the place of breathable air.

Very much of this can be verified by direct observation and by simple experiment. We readily see that gnats walk on water as though it were solid, and swim, float, and hang sideways or upside down in air as though it were liquid. We see them, too, irresistibly attracted to sources of *light*, not as light, but in the same way that bird migration follows certain invisible fields of terrestrial *magnetism*. And again, we can quickly prove that sound vibration is beyond the gnat's range of perception by the futility of any attempt to frighten it away by shouting.

Some people claim on the other hand, that certain insects and even certain small reptiles, like lizards, can be stopped and held motionless merely by *gazing at them with attention*. As long as they stare at a spider, for instance, it may remain motionless, while the moment attention wanders, it is gone in a fraction of a second. Although insects are insensible to sound, the human gaze, focussed with attention, may in some cases convey certain vibrations to which some insects mechanically react. Man stands in relation to these insects as a higher cosmos to a lower, and his attentive gaze, immeasurable to himself, can act upon them in some such way as sun or wind act upon man, completely altering his speed of movement and pattern of action.

Indeed, all this is characteristic of the world, not of animals, but of *cells*; which also have no up, down, or sideways, which also fail to react to sound, but which also (in man's body) respond directly to the intangible vibrations of his attention. The time of small insects does in fact put them in the category of a lower cosmos, and we shall understand them better if we think of them, not as creatures having individual meaning, but as *free cells*, so to speak, between which the connective tissue of animal bodies is unaccountably missing. Such beings have significance only in their repetition, that is, in the complete body of which they form part – the hive, the ant-hill, the termitary, the gyrating swarm of gnats hanging in the air on a summer evening.

In small birds and fishes, whose lifetimes of a few years places their perceptions at four not 15 octaves' removal from man, individuality still has little meaning. A flock of starlings or a shoal of mackerel weaves, turns, wheels, and migrates immense distances in the air or sea with the same unity and coordination as a hive of bees or a human body. Direct relation to the cosmos of Earth, which is characteristic of large mammals and is expressed by the sense of up, down, and sideways, is still very vague in a single bird or fish. Certain domestic birds, such as ducks, brought up alone, may develop quite individual behaviour and attachment to a human being, but as soon as they return to the flock, immediately lose all such distinctive responses and even the recognition of their friend.

For creatures of this scale of time only the four lower octaves of sound are lost. But their own sounds and songs naturally fall into or even beyond what are the highest octaves of sound of man. The cheep of bats and the chirping of small birds are often inaudible to us, and this is quite understandable when we realise that such creatures have *four more octaves of sound* beyond the highest that man can hear.

In the extraordinary phenomena of migration, in which flocks of birds travel thousands of miles year after year upon exactly repeated routes, we probably have a response to seasonal changes in the Earth's magnetic field, to which this transposition of four octaves has rendered the birds' physical organs sensitive. Again, the fact that vultures clearly distinguish carrion or dead meat from immense heights, while for other birds on the contrary only *living* animals are distinguishable and dead indistinguishable, seems to suggest that bird-sight itself may vary to include or exclude certain ultra-violet emanations to which the slower human sight is insensible.

In fact, we have to imagine the five wave-bands received by the five senses of different creatures as shifting up and down the electro-magnetic scale in accordance with their differing times; in exactly the same way as a fixed relation of five frequencies could in different radio sets be shifted to receive different groups of transmitting-stations. In this way, many if not all examples of so-called 'sixth-sense' in nature can probably be explained by such a shift bringing into range of one of the five existing senses a band of radiations which remain outside those normally receivable by man.

An interesting example of difference of time and its implications is found on the frontier between birds and insects. As Oliver Pearson puts it: "The living rate of an animal depends on its size; the smaller the animal, the faster it lives . . . Pound for pound the more diminutive animal eats more food, consumes more oxygen, produces more energy – in short, has a higher rate of metabolism . . . The humming-bird has the highest rate of metabolism of any bird or animal . . . Each gram of (its) tissue metabolises 15 times as fast as a gram of pigeon and more than 100 times as fast as a gram of elephant."[47]

In order to live at this speed the humming-bird must eat every ten or fifteen minutes, that is, about 60 times a day to man's three times. In addition, it must hibernate every night, in the same way and for the same reason that some large animals hibernate every winter, simply because it can not get the food to maintain its expenditure of energy. Watching the almost invisible buzzing of its wings, the ceaseless darting of its flight, we indeed get a vivid impression of *a creature living a hundred times faster than man*.

If in insects, and even in birds and fishes, Nature thus seems to have been experimenting upon the theme of *free cells*, when we reach the domestic animals we seem to see a play upon the idea of *free organs*. The time of the horse, cow, pig, cat or dog is removed from that of man by no more than one or two octaves, and thus their reactions and perceptions are more directly comparable with his. Upon this scale we shall get a more interesting insight into animal nature by comparing not time, but *mechanism*.

Examining the anatomy of different animals in this way, and comparing

47. 'The Metabolism of Humming-Birds', by Oliver P. Pearson, *Scientific American*, January 1953.

it with that of man, we see in each case one function or organ enormously exaggerated, while the rest are reduced to the minimum necessary to make the experiment an independent creature. Thus a horse is a walking muscular system, a cow is a walking mammary gland, a pig is a walking stomach, a hen is a walking ovary, and a dog is a walking nose. A very true understanding of animal psychology can indeed be obtained by learning to concentrate attention in a single such function in oneself, and directly 'feeling' there the nature of its particular perceptions, interests, and needs.

In a horse we exactly see and value the pleasure in movement, the skill and delicacy of coordination, the sensuous response to warmth and contact, the immense capacity for work, which we can discover in our own motor-muscular system. The dog we appreciate not only for its power of scent in hunting, but also for the quick response to change of scene or mood, and the basic attachment to one familiar master and house, which a highly developed sense of smell brings with it.

The mechanical structure of these animals also reveals very much both about themselves and the functions which they seem to symbolise. The horse can with ease and pleasure jump, buck, roll, gambol, and move and look in all three dimensions available to it. The structure of the pig, on the other hand, is such that after the first few weeks, it becomes *impossible for it to look* upwards. Its tremendously heavy neck set solid with its ponderous body, its hanging curtain of ears, permit it to raise its glance but a few inches from the earth, and never above its own eye-level. The pig lives in a plane world; the sky does not exist for it. For the stomach there can be no astronomy.

But perhaps the most important mechanical limitation upon all these animals is the fact that their eyes are set on the side of their heads. Each eye can receive a wide field of impressions, and they may even 'see' a larger arc of the horizon than human beings. But this feature also means that they can not 'focus' their gaze on specific objects as men can. And this power of focussing carries with it an immensely important psychological possibility of which animals are definitely deprived. The act of focussing the eyes creates a definite relation between the observer and the thing observed. It makes possible the sensation: "I am here, and that object is there." This sensation is the beginning of self-consciousness.

Such intelligent consciousness of oneself in one's surroundings animals can never fully achieve. And the limitation of their power of focussing the eyes is but one external sign of an inner difference in nervous structure which definitely debars them from the path leading towards individual self-consciousness and regeneration.

At the same time, certain animals seem to approach the possibility of consciousness much more nearly than others. The cat, for example, has developed to a very high degree the power of focussing, not so much its eyes as its ears. A cat watching a fly or a mouse, its ears intensely focussed on its prey, seems to express to the maximum degree possible in the animal world the sense of conscious relationship: "I, cat – you, mouse".

And in fact the cat seems to exhibit many signs of self-consciousness, lacking even in most men. On a hot day, a dog will sprawl in a passage-way, allowing its limbs to dispose themselves as they will, and regardless of the probability of being trodden on. It quite evidently *does not know where all the different parts of its body are.* Such behaviour is impossible for a cat, which is always careful *to arrange its own body*; and which equally evidently never quite loses the sense of this body as a whole. Nature appears to have played a very curious trick upon the cat. If a dog is an experiment in the function of smell, a cat is *an experiment in the function of consciousness.* But it is consciousness unrelated to mind, without meaning, and without the possibility of development. Comparing cat and man we begin to understand how consciousness can exist without intelligence, and intelligence without consciousness.

Thus it is a curious irony of Nature that man has to acquire by hard work what a cat enjoys naturally. The difference is that man has to acquire it, knowing that he is acquiring it, knowing why he is acquiring it, and knowing that it is but a necessary step to something else. To no other creature in the world of Nature is such a possibility open.

X MAN AS MICROCOSM

I THE ANATOMICAL SYSTEMS AND THEIR REGULATORS

WHEN WE TRIED TO IMAGINE THE LONG BODY OF THE SOLAR System, the interlacing sheaths or webs formed by the planet's tracks reminded us in passing of the various systems of the human body – skeletal, lymphatic, arterial, nervous and so on – which seemed to be made and put together in a similar way.

The association was not accidental. The more we study these systems, the more it appears that they are in fact analogous distributing networks for energies transformed to different tensions.

The human structure consists of seven or eight recognizable systems, supported by a skeletal framework and bound into a solid whole by connective tissue. These systems are united and harmonized by the life-maintaining action of the heart, upon which depends the very existence of the organism as an individual.

Each system covers the entire body; and over each, one of the glands of internal secretion, set in a particular place, appears to preside in the quality both of regulator and transformer. This gland transforms the general life-energy produced by the organism from food, air, light and so on, to the tension required for its own system and function.

Further, the whole of this sevenfold arrangement of human functions must be visualized as subject to three distinct but interacting nervous controls – the cerebro-spinal, which serves conscious functions; the sympathetic, which stimulates unconscious or instinctive functions; and the parasympathetic and vagus, which are explained as slowing down these instinctive functions, and thus acting as complement to the last. This suggests to us one control for relaying *active* nervous impulses, another for relaying *passive* nervous impulses, and a third for relaying the *mediating* impulses of thought, reason or consciousness.

We have indeed reason to suppose that these three nervous controls represent the law of three forces in the human body, just as the endocrine glands and their products seem to reflect the universal law of octaves. It is precisely this subjection of an ever-changing mixture of seven ingredients to a triple nervous control, itself in continuous permutation, that makes the human mechanism an image of all other cosmoses.

At the same time this combination creates a pattern so subtle that its

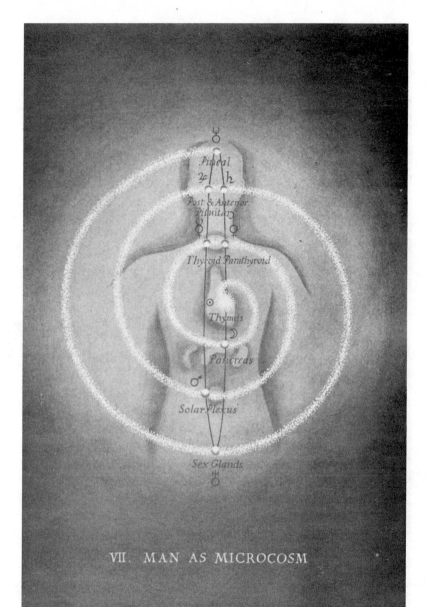

Pineal

Post & Anterior
Pituitary

Thyroid Parathyroid

Thymus

Pancreas

Solar Plexus

Sex Glands

VII. MAN AS MICROCOSM

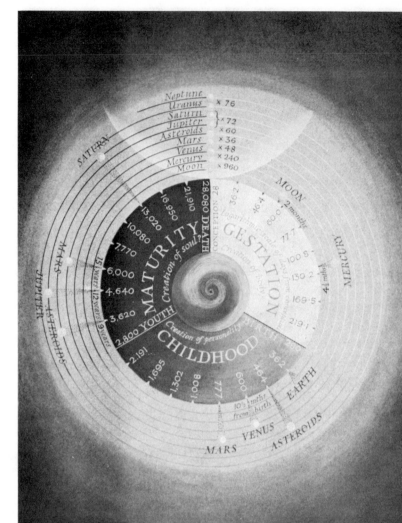

VIII. THE CLOCK OF HUMAN LIFE

working can be analysed in a hundred different ways, all true and all deceptive. For instance, it would be simple if we could say that the nerves, as agents of the law of three, control the glands as agents of the law of octaves. But besides controlling the glandular systems, the nerves themselves constitute such systems and are in turn controlled – as in the Solar System each planet acts both as mediating force by the law of three and as a single note by the law of octaves.

In other words, the three forces and the seven aspects imply different ways of looking at the same phenomenon. With our ordinary minds we are incapable of realising the two principles in operation at once, just as the human eye can not at the same moment focus on the surface of a mirror and on distant objects reflected in that mirror. Were we able to comprehend the law of three and the law of octaves simultaneously we should indeed comprehend the Solar System or the human organism in its entirety. We can not mentally simplify the interaction of these two laws, for a living cosmos is the simplest model of their union.

For the same reason, we can never really succeed in separating them. Nor can any attempt to describe in detail – say in the human body – the operation first of one law, and then of the other, ever be logically satisfying. The two explanations will always seem to overlap, and will always appear contradictory or inconsistent to the logical mind.

Nevertheless, we have to try. Let us begin from the point of view of the law of octaves. Each of the various systems and its presiding gland is now seen to endow man with a special set of qualities and capacities. By virtue of the skeletal system he is an upright and articulated creature, by virtue of the lymphatic system he can digest and assimilate, by virtue of the pulmonary he breathes, by virtue of the arterial he is self-warming, by virtue of the cerebro-spinal he sees, thinks and acts, and by yet another system he is subject to emotion and conscience. These are in fact the realms of nature within him.

Returning to our electrical analogy we find that the energies used in the different systems or circuits vary both in pressure and rate of flow. In the lymphatic system, for example, the rate of flow is very high and constant, but the pressure is extremely low. The central lymph canal of a cow, when punctured, is found to yield 95 litres of lymph a day, but this substance is itself so dilute or mild in its action that only in such huge quantities can it carry out its relatively simple work of distributing nourishment and carrying off poisons. In other words, the amperage is high but the voltage very low.

Contrast this with the energy which produces in man the emotions of religious awe, love, extreme hatred and so on. The flow here is so small that weeks, months or even years may pass without a man being aware of anything more than an occasional ineffective trickle. On the other hand, when energy transformed in this way does become available, its power is enormous. It may make him found a monastic order, or commit a murder. The amperage is low, but the voltage extraordinarily high.

Now assuming that these different glands are in fact adaptors or transformers of the general energy created by the organism, what is their relation among themselves? Do they stand in any definite order? Can we see any regular scale of tensions produced among them?

An unexpected hint comes from their disposition. If, taking the heart as centre, we lay out a schematic diagram of the human body upon which the various glands are marked, we find that they all lie upon a regular spiral similar to that which is found to represent the line of force or growth in many natural phenomena.[48] Just as a galaxy appeared to be an expanding spiral of suns, and the solar system an expanding spiral of planets, so the human body now gives the impression of an expanding spiral of functions.

The sun and source of this spiral is the heart. Thence it uncoils through the thymus, the pancreas, the thyroid and parathyroids, the solar plexus where the adrenals take effect, on to the post-pituitary and anterior pituitary, and with its final convolution through the sex-glands to the pineal body, the ultimate outpost and possibility of the organism.

If we go back to the primary differentiation of the human embryo into three germ-layers during its first fortnight of existence, we can actually see this spiral in its original form. The three germ-layers which develop from the first multiplication of cells fold round upon each other. From the germ-layer forming the inner coil (entoderm) develop the functions connected with the first three glands mentioned, namely, growth, digestion and respiration; from the germ-layer forming the middle coil (mesoderm) develop the functions connected with the next three, namely, blood-circulation and voluntary and involuntary movement; from the germ-layer forming the outer coil (ectoderm) develop the functions connected with the last three, namely, mind, emotion, and reproduction.

If we then add to this order what we know about the functions of the different glands and about the systems they control, we obtain the following table:

48. For corroborative detail concerning such spirals on many different scales, see J. Bell Pettigrew, 'Design in Narure', particularly p. 633 et seq.

Gland	Function	System
Thymus	Growth	?
Pancreas	Digestion, Assimilation of food	Lymphatic
Thyroid	Respiration, Combustion of air	Pulmonary
Parathyroids	Blood-circulation, Tissue building	Arterial and Connective Tissue
Adrenals	External Motion, Fight and Flight	Cerebro-Spinal and Voluntary Muscle
Posterior Pituitary	Inner Reflexes, Physical Sensation	Sympathetic and Involuntary muscle
Anterior Pituitary	Mind and Reason, Bone Structure	Cerebral Cortex and Skeletal
Gonads	Reproduction, Creation, Higher Emotion	Genital
Pineal	?	?

The functions controlled by the glands give, in this order, the strong impression of being graded from coarse to fine, from material towards immaterial. All the functions which we are accustomed to regard as physical lie towards the beginning, those which we regard as psychic towards the end. Translating this into our electrical terminology, we would say that on the evidence of their output the transformers appear to be arranged in order of increasing voltage, decreasing amperage.

If we recall the categories of speeds of diffusion which we worked out in Chapter 6, we find an even more striking correspondence with and confirmation of this order.

For the *thymus*, controlling growth, appears to work with the energy of Category VIII, which we called vegetable or cellular: the *pancreas*, controlling digestion and assimilation of food, with energy of Category VII, which we called invertebrate or liquid: the *thyroid*, controlling respiration and motion with energy of Category VI, which we called vertebrate or muscular: the *parathyroids*, controlling blood-circulation, with energy of Category V, which we called animal or warm-blooded.

Continuing this ascent, we would deduce that the two lobes of the *pituitary*, controlling on the one hand physical sensations and reflexes, and on the other mind and reason, work with energy of Categories III and II, which we called planetary or magnetic. The *gonads*, controlling reproduction and creation in general, must then work with energy of Category I, solar or luminous energy, communicated with the speed of light. While the *pineal*, if it functioned at all, would work with the energy of Category 0, galactic energy, energy faster than light, of which we have as yet not even a theoretical knowledge.[49]

In this way we can, at least hypothetically, calculate the speed of processes characteristic of each function, and their mathematical relation to each other. If, as we scientifically know, the blood-stream, influenced by the parathyroids, courses through man's veins at one metre a second, and cerebro-spinal impulses, influenced by the adrenals, flash through his nerves at 100 metres a second, then we have to imagine the two pituitary lobes carrying out their communication at 10 and 1000 kilometres a second, whatever this may mean. All we can corroborate by experience is that the mind, powered by the anterior pituitary, can 'be present' anywhere, in any imaginable place or time, instantaneously, that is, without measurable interval.

Yet according to this idea, true sex, its peculiar understanding and experience, should be a hundred times faster than the mind. And the perception of the unknown pineal function a hundred times faster still.

There is another remarkable aspect of this chain of transformers of energy within the human body. Their order echoes in an astonishing way the disposition of planets in the solar system – but with the sequence of tensions in *reverse*. What is nearer the centre is smaller, finer and under greater pressure in the Solar System; but larger, grosser and under less in the human one. In the first case the amperage increases towards the circumference, in the latter the voltage. This appears strange, until we remember from radio the obvious idea that the power of the receiving set is in *inverse* proportion to the power of the sending station.

And at this point the immense implications of the correspondence between these two sets of transformers begin to dawn upon us. Surely the endocrine glands *are* those very receiving sets for planetary influences whose existence we earlier supposed.

Perhaps it would be more accurate to say that the intricate antennae of the great nervous plexuses – the cervical, the cardiac, the solar, lumbar and sacral – constitute the apparatus sensitive to such planetary transmission, while the endocrine glands through which they take effect, like loudspeaker or television screen, provide the mechanism by which such invisible impulses manifest as physical motion and action.

In any case, the glands, in the order of their distance from the heart,

49. See Appendix VI, 'Table of Human Functions'.

obey the same laws as the planets in the order of their distance from the Sun. Created from the same design, the one responds to the other. And each gland is revealed as a sensitive instrument, which not only transforms human energy to the tension required for its function, but is tuned to a similar instrument on a cosmic scale and obeys its guidance.

II   TYPES: ENDOCRINE AND ASTROLOGICAL

We now have a basis for studying the possibility of planets ruling different organs, and by extension the types which these receptive organs dominate.

In other words, whether we like it or not, we find ourselves obliged to reconsider from a new and scientific point of view the general propositions of astrology, long discarded as an exact science, precisely for lack of scientific corroboration.

The tradition of Greek, Arabic and Mediaeval astrology, which was inseparable from the parallel tradition of alchemy, believed all creatures on Earth to respond in differing degrees to certain indefinable emanations of the fixed stars, the Sun, planets and moon. This response was by virtue of affinities, that is to say, different creatures contained in varying proportions substances or matters similar to those characteristic of the different celestial spheres, and whose potency waxed and waned in sympathy with the waxing and waning of their archetypes. These affinities were very complicated. All metals, for example, were supposed to have a general affinity for Saturn, while copper had a subsidiary sensitiveness to Venus, iron to Mars, and so on.

Man was believed to contain within him *all* affinities, and these separate affinities were established in different organs and parts, though their exact allocation varied considerably from one period to another. From this it followed that a man who had one organ or part highly developed, whose centre of gravity lay there, so to speak, enjoyed a special affinity or sensitiveness for the corresponding planet. He was of that *type*.

In fact, many attempts have been made in history to distinguish and cater for different types of men in this way, from mediaeval and oriental caste systems, through the different 'orders' of the Roman Catholic Church, down to the blood and endocrine classifications of the present day.

Yet never was this idea so fully developed as in the astrological teaching of the Middle Ages, and the general idea of the governance of different organs by different planets then produced some interesting attempts to describe the so-called planetary types.[50] It is a striking tribute to the astro-logical-alchemical schools of the 13th to 17th centuries that although all the rest of their system has long since been lost, the words they used in this connection have passed into general use and still convey to ordinary men probably the best idea of types that is possible without special preparation.

These words – lunatic, mercurial, venereal, martial, jovial and saturnine – derived from affinities between man and the Solar System, connect each type with its corresponding planet. Originally, of course, 'lunatic' referred to that type dominated by the function having an affinity with the Moon and only later came to refer especially to *abnormal* people of this type.

Similarly, the word 'venereal' referred in general to those with an affinity for Venus. All the other words have retained their meaning surprisingly well. Therefore, with two slight modifications, we will attempt to study human types under these, the best names available to us.

Before we do so, however, it were well to make clear the limitations and failures which astrology had to admit, even in its own field. In the first place, it was never able to suggest *how* planetary influences were communi-cated, by what medium they exercised their power over earthly creatures. This particular hiatus, if all our deductions about magnetic fields are cor-rect, we may now begin to fill. Again, the fact that the planets Uranus and Neptune were as yet undiscovered made it necessary to attribute certain baffling effects and phenomena to the then known planets, where – even by astrological standards – they clearly did not fit. Here again, modern astrono-mical discoveries seem to clarify rather than upset the main argument of astrology.

Most important of all, however, astrology was inevitably seduced from its original objective study of correspondences and tendencies, towards prognostication and fortune-telling. In this way, without necessarily be-coming untrue, it inevitably forfeited its claim to be an exact science. For the combination of influences and affinities it admitted was so elaborate, so constantly changing and so subtle, that evidently no man could deduce the correct result purely by calculation. He could never know for certain whether he had not omitted some important factor, or wrongly estimated the relative importance of those he recognised.

In this, at the same time, astrology only found itself in the same position as does diagnostic medicine today. And just as a wise general practitioner, faced by a new patient, in some inexplicable way manages to combine all

50. For example, Robert Fludd: 'De Naturae Simia', p. 627 et seq. (Book 3, "De Planetorum dispositionibus et naturibus"). Frankfurt 1618.

his theoretical study and all his practical experience of countless cases into a sudden intuitive recognition of the ill, so one may perhaps admit that the wise astrologer might indeed acquire a genuine 'feel for the future'. By recognising the factors at work in the present, he might anticipate that which was to come, as does a doctor who gives a patient with a fatal malady so long to live. Both diagnostic medicine and prognostic astrology, if they are anything at all, are arts not sciences, and thus do not immediately concern us.

If we try to review the main thesis of astrology in the light of modern ideas and free of accumulated superstition and association, however, we have the following proposition:

Each endocrine gland or its associated nerve-plexus is sensitive to the magnetism of a particular planet. This particular magnetism will naturally be strongest when the planet is in the zenith and shining vertically through the minimum thickness of atmosphere, exactly as the Sun's light and warmth are strongest at midday. The lower in the sky it sinks, and the acuter the angle at which its influence must thus pass through the blanket of air, the feebler its effect, as with the Sun at morning and evening. When below the horizon altogether this effect will be felt only in a diffused form, much modified by the peculiar magnetism of the Earth. The height of a given planet in the sky will thus be an exact measure of the degree of stimulation imparted to the corresponding gland at a given moment.

Each gland has three aspects, connected with the three nervous systems. Since some aspects become active before others, while some are not yet activated at all in ordinary man, it seems right to imagine these aspects set working at different moments, in accord with the planetary stimulus then operative. The first and most elementary aspect, which is connected with heredity in a very general way, is set working through the arrangement of chromosomes in the egg at the critical moment of conception, and determined by the disposition of the planets at that time. This arrangement decides exactly what – out of the infinite resources of the race – the man-to-be shall inherit from his parents and ancestors.

The second aspect, and that which is probably most responsible for what we ordinarily recognise as individual type, is set working at the equally critical moment of birth, when the baby, suddenly removed from the insulation of the mother's womb, is first exposed to the air and direct solar and planetary radiation. At this moment, the glands in their second aspect receive each a different and exact impetus, which both set them in operation and fix their setting for life.

If we imagine a set of seven photographic light-meters, each sensitive to the light of a different planet, and made to register once and for all the reading recorded at the moment they are brought out of the dark-room, we get some picture of this 'setting' of the human machine at birth. In another figure, we may imagine a safe with combination lock of seven rollers, all in continuous movement at different speeds. At one particular moment, the moment of birth, the lock is 'set'. The combination registered at that moment will thereafter provide the permanent key to the safe, the only one which will enable it to be opened and its contents examined.

So it seems to be with the working of the different glands, and the functions which are associated with them. By the second setting they receive from their governing planets at the moment of birth, the distinctive shape, colour, size, speed of reaction, and other inner and outer qualities of the particular person are supposedly determined.

Their third and potential aspect might then be set working at a later moment in life, the exact date of which is difficult to determine. For this third aspect must be connected with potential human functions developing from the growth of a soul.

The three aspects of the glands may thus be said to determine, the first *hereditary essence*, the second *individual essence*, and the third *quintessence* – the hidden and potential principle of unity.

At present we will ignore the first and third aspects, and concentrate on the second aspect of the glands, launched and calibrated by planetary stimuli at the moment of birth, and upon which depends the physical nature of the man as individual, that is, what we ordinarily recognise as his *type*.

It is true that most studies of type during the last century have been based on a threefold division. For example, William Sheldon, an American anthropologist who photographed 4000 college students in an endeavour to link temperament with physical measurement, seemed to find three main components in bodily form, which could combine in 76 different ways. These components were connected with the life of head, chest and gut, deriving from the ectodermal, mesodermal and entodermal embryonic layers respectively.[50a]

But as we saw in the last section, it seems ordinarily impossible to study things by the law of three and the law of octaves simultaneously, and one must choose either one or other as basis of classification. In this book,

50a William Sheldon, 'The Varieties of Human Physique' and 'The Varieties of Temperament'.

therefore, we shall concentrate on the more subtle sevenfold division of types based on endocrinology, rather than the triple division based on the three 'storeys' of the body. The two classifications do not contradict each other: they simply depend on different 'focus'.

Let us then assemble the material made available by modern psychology and physiology on the nature and function of the different endocrine types, and see how it tallies with or differs from the old astrological descriptions. At the same time, it must be remembered that there are no such things as pure types, for in every man *all* the glands must function, and he is unable to live if a single one is destroyed. Moreover, every gland affects and is affected by every other, so that in practice it is impossible to 'isolate' the effect of any.

If we study so-called 'types' it thus only means that we try to find extreme or even pathological cases of the dominance of one or another gland, in order to determine its special nature. Even so, there is something distasteful and unreal about such descriptions, as there is about the 'average man' of statistical investigation. They both remind us of those we know, and at the same time omit all that is alive and interesting about them.

Any descriptions of glandular types are unreal and repulsive because by their very nature, they carry us *away* from perfection and healthy normality. In a 'perfect' man the action of the glands would be exactly balanced, and the nearer a man approaches this balance, the less is it possible to classify him as a type. The ideal organism would be a synthesis of all types; but such men would already enjoy extraordinary powers, and they do not appear to be produced by accident. The following vignettes must thus be taken as 'glandular caricatures'.

Taking the glands in the order of our spiral and our table, we begin with the *thymus*, which forms a large spongy mass astride the windpipe in the neighbourhood of the heart. Very little is known about this gland, except that it plays some important part in the growth of the organism in childhood, and that in most cases it tends to atrophy after adolescence – apparently in proportion as the 'passionate' combination of sex and adrenals comes into play. Its cells are identical with lymph cells, and it probably helps to promote the huge supply of lymph which is required by the great speed of metabolic processes in infancy. In this aspect it is truly the most 'primitive' of all the glands.

The thymus type known to endocrinologists, with its transparent milk- and roses skin, its delicate teeth and bones, and its particular air of beautiful frailty, is simply a description of Peter Pan, the grown-up child. As far as we can see, the thymus, so closely associated with the heart and lying at the very centre of our spiral, is the gland which sets the spring of growth uncoiling. When growth is complete, its first task is done. The possibility of a further potential function, which is not normally realised, will be discussed later. This type is not usually described in astrological writings, though occasional attempts to distinguish a *solar* type are suggestive, and remind us that the place and function of the thymus indicates it to be the regulator of that original undifferentiated life-impulse which can only derive from the Sun.

The next gland, the *pancreas*, is associated with the lymphatic system, and in partnership with the liver controls the digestion of food. This represents the 'moist' nature of man, which in an earlier chapter we found to be particularly subject to the pull of the moon. One part of the pancreas secretes insulin, which promotes the storage of sugar and works against the adrenals which govern its sudden combustion on urgent and highly emotional demands. It thus tends to dampen or quench the 'fire' of the adrenal activity. Although modern endocrinology does not distinguish a pancreatic type as clearly as those produced by other glands, people with this predominance will have all their flesh-forms full and rounded ('moon-faced') from abundance of lymph. They will be passive, moody and intro-spective – all characteristics opposite to those of the passionate, vigorous and violent adrenal type. In fact, they will approximate to the descriptions of the melancholy or *lunatic* type, which was associated with the watery element and its attendant characteristics of flux and instability.

Next, in ascending order of the fineness or voltage of the energy utilized, comes the *thyroid* gland, situated in the throat below the Adam's apple. This gland controls the combustion of air in breathing, and like the damper of a locomotive furnace, regulates the heat produced and consequently the *speed* of the whole mechanism. The more intensely the thyroid works the quicker and more nervous will the appearance become. The heavy element, iodine, which is often mentioned in connection with this gland, is like the the weight hung upon the damper-door, to prevent it springing open and burning out the furnace.

In endocrinology the thyroid type is described as lean and clearcut, with thick hair, bright eyes and even teeth; rapid of perception and volition, impulsive, with a tendency to explosive crises; restless, insomniac and inexhaustible. In other words, the old airy, sanguine or *mercurial* type, to which this modern description closely corresponds.[51]

51. Most of the descriptions of glandular types are based on Louis Berman, 'The Glands of Personality'.

Concerning the effect of the next set of glands, the minute *parathyroids*, which are situated on the thyroid and act as its pair or complement, endocrinology has not much material. It is only known that they work against the thyroid (which produces movement and volatility), by promoting the metabolism of the stabilizing element lime, and the mediating element phosphorus. With parathyroids under-developed, the individual becomes pathologically nervous, jumpy and oversensitive to the mildest stimulus, even of light. The parathyroids accentuate the passive, vegetative life; they produce steadiness and tone of muscle and nerve – as it were a sensitive calm and warm passivity. Their field is that of 'flesh and blood', of tissue-building and increase in bulk. This in the old astrology, is the *venusian* type, the feminine role of growth in inactivity.

The *adrenal* glands, which use energy of the next higher power, are two small capsules saddled on the kidneys. They consist of two parts, the core or medulla which secretes an hormone producing all the phenomena connected with fear and flight; and the shell or cortex which secretes another hormone giving rise to manifestations of rage and pugnacity. Both, probably through their key-element potassium, create a general heightening of tone and sensitivity in the organism. They are the glands of 'passion', and in these different ways express the fundamental impulse of self-preservation. The adrenal type has a swarthy or freckled skin, is hairy of face and body, often with hair of an unusual colour – black among Scandinavians, yellow among Latins, red among other peoples. He has sharp teeth and a low hair-line, and is vigorous, energetic and passionate – the traditional warrior, small, fierce and *martial*.

The next two glands, like the thyroids and parathyroids, form a pair controlling complementary qualities and mutually balancing each other. Together they make the two lobes of the pituitary, a small organ the size of a cherry stone housed in a bony box behind the bridge of the nose. The first lobe, from our point of view, is that of the *posterior pituitary*. This gland, in whose action sodium plays a key role, controls the involuntary muscles of the inner instinctive part of the organism, particularly those of the intestines, bladder, and uterus. It also regulates the production of milk for suckling, and in general is the gland of maternal qualities. The type is short, rounded, stout, with large head, inclining to paunch, and little hair on the body. It tends to periodicity, rhythm appearing even in moods, activities, and in a leaning to poetry and music. Such people are cheerful, gay, and tolerant – the Falstaffs, the classic *jovial* type.

The *anterior pituitary* promotes masculine traits as clearly as the posterior does feminine ones. This gland is closely connected on the one hand with the skeletal system, and on the other with the function of abstract thought and reason. Its exaggerated secretion results in an abnormal growth of the long bones, and particularly joints and extremities, such as hands, feet and chin (acromegaly). The anterior pituitary type is long boned, with a strong frame and large firm muscles; long head, rugged face, prominent nose, square jaw, projecting cheek-bones and large teeth; with a comprehending mind, ability to learn and capacity for self-control and rule over his environment. This, in the old nomenclature, is the phlegmatic or *saturnine* type.

The first six glands thus arrange themselves in three pairs – each pair containing a masculine and feminine element, which both complement and war against each other. The adrenals and the pancreas, or Mars against Moon; the thyroid and parathyroids, or Mercury against Venus; and the anterior and posterior pituitary, or Saturn against Jupiter – between them form a complete and perfectly self-balancing hexad. As in the push-pull arrangement which keeps radio-valves in equilibrium, the unremitting tension between each pair holds the whole organism in vital balance.

When we come to the *gonads* or sex-glands, which occupy the same position on our spiral as Uranus does in the Solar System, we can now understand why their role has given rise to so much confusion. For every other gland affects sex, lends sex its colour, and tries to pass itself off as sex. In order to be understood in its purity, sex must be separated from the venusian sensuality of the parathyroids, from the martial passion of the adrenals, from the maternal affection of the posterior pituitary, and from the saturnine masterfulness of the anterior lobe. Sex must be something different from all these and more fundamental. It must be connected with the ultimate principle of two sexes, and their joint power of creation. And it will include all the deepest emotions which arise from this interaction, and which, besides children of the body, give rise to music, poetry, the arts, and the whole aspiration of man to create in emulation of his Maker.

The last gland upon our spiral, as Neptune is the last major planet in the sky, is the mysterious *pineal* body, buried at the focal point of the brain and connected with man's most delicate psychic systems. Alone among the glands, it is single rather than double in form, and from this old physiologists and psychologists, Descartes, for example, deduced that it was the place where unity or equilibrium was achieved, and that it was the ultimate seat of the soul. In Leonardo da Vinci's phrase, it was the organ of 'common sense', that is, of a sense common to all functions and beings, and which would reveal their oneness.

The pineal gland is a cone-shaped tissue, the nerve cells of which contain pigment similar to that of the retina, and which ordinarily fossilizes after adolescence through the depositing of lime-salts. As this process goes on, the muscles waste away and are replaced by fat. Practically nothing is known or even guessed about the functions of the pineal gland, and we can only say at this stage that everything points to these functions being *potential and as yet unrealized.*

This completes the series of planetary receiving sets by which the different functions of the body are sustained and regulated. And if it be objected that the descriptions of their related types border upon fortune telling, then we must admit that they are nothing but an attempt to approach the nature of different energies by an empirical study of their manifestations. This is in essence unsatisfactory; as it would be to try to express the nature of a dog by detailing its shape, colour, manner of hair-growth and so on. True understanding of the glands can only develop from direct study of their individual action *in oneself.* But in a book – by its nature – this method is debarred to us.

III THE BLOODSTREAM AS INDEX OF MAN'S BEING

The heart is the sun of the body, and the bloodstream, like the sun's radiation in the solar system, extends to its every part. No corner of the body is too remote to be warmed and vitalized by it. It suffuses the endocrine organs, as the Sun's light and heat shines upon all the planets, supplying them with life and uniting them into a single whole.

Now solar radiation has two aspects. First, it brings to the planets light, heat, ultra-violet and other vitalizing radiations from the Sun and centre of their system. Second, reflecting from them individually – according to their size, atmosphere, surface, speed of rotation and so on – it acts as a vehicle for the diffusion of their separate influences. When we see Venus or Jupiter in the sky it is, of course, the reflected light of the Sun which reaches us. There is no other light in the Solar System. But this reflected light becomes the bearer of vibrations and rhythms peculiar to the reflector. Thus the Sun's light not only reaches us direct, but it reaches us via each individual planet; and as anyone knows who has seen the old moon in the new moon's arms, it is even reflected from the Earth to the moon and then back to the earth again. Solar radiation forms as it were an immense circulation, not only uniting every part of the Solar System to the centre, but also every part to every other part. It is the means by which the Sun influences the planets, and also by which they influence each other.

The bloodstream serves the same function in the body. Bearing life and warmth, bearing hydrogen, carbon, nitrogen and oxygen, it is pumped from the heart to the scalp of the head and the tips of the toes. Free, full and ubiquitous circulation spells the health of the organism. Where circulation is constricted or cut off, illness and disease inevitably set in.

The blood-stream is the diffuser of the central energy to all organs. At the same time, passing from one organ to another, it carries the secretions of each throughout the entire organism. By it concentrated forms of energy are carried from the centres of production to storage organs such as the liver and spleen; by it also these same energies are instantly diffused, when some emergency demands their use.

Every endocrine gland secretes into the blood-stream its particular hormone in a rhythmic flow, and in greater or less volume. The proportions of these different hormones borne in suspension in the blood-stream at any moment make a man what he then is – thoughtful, sympathetic, passionate, active, lustful, and so on. In a more general way, the average composition of his blood-stream over a longer period determines his more permanent tendencies and characteristics, and moulds the different aspects of his physique accordingly. At the same time, from moment to moment, he himself affects the composition, and by lending his interest and attention to this or that manifestation in him he accentuates or restrains his natural tendencies.

Further, the *order* in which the glands pour their influence into the blood-stream follows a definite sequence, similar to that in which, as we found, the planets sound their characteristic notes in the stream of time. Thus the digested products of the *pancreas* go to serve the *parathyroids* in the building of tissue; this tissue-building demands the aeration made possible by the *thyroid*; the speed of respiration in turn affects the vigour of thought and determination arising from the *anterior pituitary*; thought and determination translate themselves into the passionate activity of the *adrenals*; such activity requires corresponding work of the inner organs from the *posterior lobe*; and this instinctive work in turn calls for more products of digestion from the *pancreas*.

It is useless to seek for cause and effect in such a sequence. The whole follows an inevitable and unbroken chain of action and reaction. Feeding produces movement, movement ambition, ambition passionate action, and the exhaustion of passionate action the hunger to feed again. This is man's life on the level of the blood-stream.

But if the arteries unite the glands regulating man's functions in one way, we must also remember that they are equally connected and united in three other ways by the three nervous systems. In fact these three nervous systems are probably connected to the three different parts or aspects of each gland to which we have referred. Some of these secondary and tertiary aspects of the glands are already in operation but not generally recognized, as the role of the thyroid in the storage of musical and word memory is not recognized. Other aspects – of the pineal gland, for example – remain unknown because they are potential and only come into operation in higher states of consciousness. In any case, if the cruder output of the glands is distributed by the bloodstream, we may be sure that much more delicate and far-reaching connections are or could be affected by these three sets of nerves.

The arterial system and the three nervous systems thus appear to bear the same relation to each other as in mediaeval philosophy did earth, water, air and fire. Water, air and fire represented the vehicles of the three creative forces, while earth represented the vehicle in which none of them yet work, or the vehicle belonging to a lower series.

Let us then change our focus, and consider the combined role of the three nervous systems as the intervention of a triple creative power from a higher level – that is, from above the level of the blood-stream.

Equally with the blood-stream the three nervous systems pervade all parts of the body and connect all glands. But they have different routes. The *cerebro-spinal system* is chiefly confined to the cortex of the brain and the spinal cord, whence branches ramify to all members within man's field of sensation and control. The *sympathetic system* consists of a large number of separate branches and plexuses directly connecting individual vertebrae with some corresponding involuntary organ. The *vagus*, on the other hand, is a single nerve, which originates in the base of the brain, and after passing through heart, gastric and sex plexuses, rejoins the bottom of the spine.

These two latter systems remind us of the electrical circuit of a car or airplane, where each instrument is individually connected to the positive source of power, though the negative side of all their circuits can be completed simultaneously through the steel frame. In this figure, the cerebro-spinal system would then represent the driver or pilot, who introduces conscious action into the mechanism – but *only at those points where controls are situated.*

What is the actual relation between these three systems, and what is their potential relation? In the first place we must suppose them working with three different energies at three different speeds. The slowest is the cerebro-spinal system, which can only work as fast as we can think. Next faster is the sympathetic system, which enables the complicated instinctive processes of digestion, tissue-building and so on, to be carried on much faster than we can follow. While fastest of all should be the parasympathetic, or vagus system, which carries the immeasurably rapid impulses of intuition, self-preservation and sex. This latter system, however, ordinarily works at only a fraction of its proper power, and from the point of view of its potentialities, we can almost regard it as unused.

According to our table of speeds of diffusion, the three energies concerned belong respectively to Category III ($\frac{1}{3}$ to 30 kilometres a second), Category II (30 to 3000 kilometres a second), and Category I (3000 to 300,000 kilometres a second).

Now we have already seen that wherever three forces interact, they can manifest in six different combinations or orders. So these three nervous systems, combining in different ways, subject the human body to the six cosmic processes which we have discussed before. Some of these processes – resulting from the dominance of thought or instinct, that is, of the cerebro-spinal or sympathetic system – are familiar to us in ordinary life. Others, produced by the dominance of the vagus system, *working with its proper energy*, are unknown to us or very rare. For they occur only when the highest kind of emotion becomes the motive force for the whole organism.

It is, however, still another possibility which concerns us now. There is in fact a seventh combination of forces, normally incomprehensible, but which is theoretically possible, and which raises the cosmos in which it occurs to direct connection with that above. In this combination, *all three forces work simultaneously at all points.*

In the ordinary way the three nervous systems operate more or less independently, in sequence, so to speak; their different energies being confined to the functions for which they are most suitable. And when small amounts of these energies do leak from one system to another – as when a man tries to think when full of instinctive excitement, or on the other hand when he tries to reason about some deep emotion – only bad results are produced.

Yet these three systems are arranged so that, *in certain circumstances and at one particular point in the brain*, a connection could be created between them. In this case all three energies would run freely through all three systems. With what result? By the general circulation of intellectual energy, a man would become *conscious in all his functions*. By the general circulation of instinctive energy, *all his functions would act to his best advantage and in harmony.* By the general circulation of emotional energy, *all his functions would work at the intensity of fear or love.*

Such a condition, in which instinctive processes were as conscious as thinking, in which thinking was as fast as attraction, and in which reason, emotion, and action combined as harmoniously as breathing and sleeping, is at present unimaginable. We can only say that the human machine is in fact designed to make it possible.

XI MAN IN TIME

I THE SLOWING DOWN OF HUMAN TIME

ONE OF OUR CHIEF MISTAKES IS THAT WE TAKE MAN'S TIME AS always the same. We regard an hour of childhood as of the same value as an hour of old age. This is quite a false view, and for a reason which we can now discuss.

Man starts his existence as a single cell, the ovum, at the moment of its fertilization by the spermatozoon. He therefore sets out upon his career by the time-scale of a large cell, which, we calculated in our study of the times of the universe,[52] is no less than a thousand times faster than that by which the grown man measures and perceives. The incredible speed of the processes of multiplication and differentiation in the days following conception fully bears out this idea.

It is only towards the latter part of his life, when he is already approaching death and can review a whole cycle of human experience, that man's perception reaches the breadth and comprehension in which it can be said to be fully characteristic of man.

Thus between conception and death man's life moves faster and faster until at the end the hours and minutes pass for him a thousand times faster than they did in the hours of his conception. This means that less and less happens to him in each hour as life progresses. His perception spreads over a longer and longer period, but in fact this longer period is only an illusion since it may contain no more than did the infinitesimal fraction of a second of his first sensation.

He thinks to tame time by measuring its passage in years, but time cheats him by putting less and less into them. So that when he looks back over his life and tries to calculate it by the scale of birthdays, he is in a strange way foreshortening his existence, like a man looking at a picture which elusively curves away from him. In another figure, we can say that man falls through time as solid objects fall through air – that is, gaining momentum, or passing faster and faster through the medium as he goes.

Now the lifetime of the ovum is, as we also recognised earlier, one lunar month; the full span of man's life about one thousand such months. To bring his life into true perspective, then, we should have to set down a

52 See Chapter 2, 'The Times of the Universe'.

scale from one to a thousand and divide it up by logarithmic rather than the familiar arithmetical progression.[53] For equal divisions of a logarithmic scale are marked 1, 10, 100, 1000; in contrast to the 1, 2, 3, 4, of an arithmetical scale, and the 1, 2, 4, 8 of a geometrical one.

These limits of one and one thousand months, indeed, remind us of the two other intermediate points. Man is born ten lunar months after his conception; and his childhood is generally accepted as coming to an end after one hundred (7 years). These are clearly key-points in his life. So that we now have our scale marked 1, 10, 100, 1000; thus dividing man's whole career into three logarithmically equal parts – gestation, childhood, and maturity.

The more we think of these three periods, the more a kind of resemblance emerges between them, as though the later ones were echoes of the first, like some tune echoed one and then two octaves lower. During the prenatal period of gestation the physical body is gradually formed, and at last launched into independent existence in a different medium, the air. During childhood, personality is formed upon the basis of the physical body, and the combination launched into independent existence in the world of men. During maturity, the psycho-physical organism so created works out its various possibilities, and when these are complete, it is launched into eternity.

The nature and possibilities of water change completely at the two points when it turns from steam to liquid and from liquid to ice. In the same way, birth and the end of childhood mark the two critical points in the life of man when, by some cosmic intervention, the whole nature and possibilities of his being are transformed. At these moments the soul comes to the surface and manifests itself in a new and more concrete form.

Let us take our logarithmic scale of man's life based on the fixed points – 1, 10, 100, 1000 months – which separate the three fundamental periods of his existence, and set it up in circular form. This circle will represent the 'long body' of man's life, measured not according to his usual calculation but according to the speed at which the vital processes actually work in him. It will be a scale of his true or organic time, as distinct from the scale of general time provided by a calendar of years. At the top of the circle conception and death will occupy the same point. Later we may understand that what appears as a circle can be more truly seen as the cross-section of a spiral.

<hr/>

53 For the general idea of logarithmic time in relation to human life I am indebted to my friend, Dr. Francis Roles, and for the lunar month as unit of such time to Miss Helen Wright. This idea, under the name of 'Biological Time', was originally worked out by Pierre Lecompte de Noüy (1883–1949) during the first World War, from studies on the speed of wound healing at different ages, and later developed in his book, 'Le Temps et la Vie'.

For convenience let us divide each of our three fundamental periods again into three. The nine main milestones in man's life so obtained will stand roughly at 2, $4\frac{1}{2}$, 10, 20, 44, 100, 200, 440, and 1000 months from conception. That is, at 2 and $4\frac{1}{2}$ months of prenatal life, at birth, and then at 10 months, $2\frac{3}{4}$ years, and 7, 15, 35 and 76 years. The periods between these milestones will be of *equal duration* on our scale of organic time.

Further reflection shows that these points do correspond to certain definite stages in human development. It is at about two months of prenatal existence that the foetus becomes fully human in *form and structure*, with the various organs and parts definitely delineated. At $4\frac{1}{2}$ months quickening occurs, and it acquires *involuntary movement* and individual blood-circulation. Birth is marked by the commencement of *breathing*. At 10 months the child begins to crawl and generally gain control over *voluntary movements*. At $2\frac{3}{4}$ years it begins to talk in complete sentences, to refer to itself as 'I', and develop simple *intellectual processes*. This is a preparation for the moment, at about 7 years, when what the Church has called 'the age of reason' is reached and with it the full mental digestion of impressions. Fifteen years marks puberty, and the beginning of the *sex function*. Thirty-five is traditionally the prime of life, marked by the momentary balance of all powers, and according to some by the possibility of appearance of quite new functions, potential but not developed in ordinary men.[54] Seventy-six years represents the normal end of man's term, death, and the beginning of any new existence which may follow it.

Now if these points are scaled accurately in days from conception, and still another finer division of the intervening periods made, some very interesting correspondences begin to emerge. The first main milestone is equivalent to one *Lunar* cycle from the beginning of our scale. The second milestone is marked by the completion of a minor cycle of *Mercury*.[55] The third milestone, or birth, occurs at ten lunar cycles; the fourth at one minor cycle of *Venus*. One hundred lunar cycles mark the sixth milestone. The seventh milestone is marked by a major cycle of *Mars*, the eighth by that of *Saturn*, while the completion of a cycle of *Uranus* more or less coincides with the ninth milestone, or death.

It seems literally as though for the new organism *time begins* at conception. More correctly still, *all times begin*; that is to say, the organism counts the time of each planet from that critical moment when time begins for it,

---

54. The possibility is developed, for example, by Dr. R. M. Bucke, 'Cosmic Consciousness'.
55. To refresh the memory of the subject of the planetary cycles, refer to Chapter 6, I, 'The Harmony of the Planets'.

the moment of conception. Here it begins, not as the individual type we discussed in the last chapter, but simply as a new representative of mankind. Where the planets then stood, how they then shone, represent its normality, the starting-point of the race of life. And as each planet in turn and according to its own cycle returns to that starting-point, it springs the mechanism of a responding function. The clock-hands after different intervals return to zero; as each does so, an alarm rings, and yet another aspect of the mechanism is set in motion.

How shall we explain this if not by the affinities of old astrology? Affinities not only of matter but of time, not only of substance but of rhythm.

Fortunately, there exists a modern idea which is almost identical with the mediaeval one of affinity, but more acceptable to the scientific mind. This is the idea of *resonance*.

According to this idea, each physical structure has a fundamental note or vibration. Other vibrations which may be imparted to it artificially are maintained in it only by force and in proportion to the energy transmitted. When the vibrations imparted begin to approach its fundamental note, however, the structure responds in a quite disproportionate way. Its inner vibration increases violently in intensity, and if the transmitted note is amplified sufficiently, it may literally disintegrate. The crumbling of the walls of Jericho before the trumpets of the Israelites is not at all beyond the theoretical possibilities of resonance. To the same principle is due the curious shuddering which goes through a car or airplane, when the pitch of its engine reaches a certain note; and the whole practice and technique of tuning-in in radio.

Disintegration, indeed, is by no means the chief phenomenon of resonance. It implies the transmission of power without visible means and with supernormal results *to that which is attuned.* One precise note of a violin makes a wine-glass 'sing'. One precise word may release in a man some inherent impulse that for years lay unsuspected. If a source of power sounds the fundamental note of an inert object, the inert object is filled with power. And conversely, if an inert object be modified to the note of that which transmits – like a glass to which water is added till it echoes a singer's voice – then the inert object suddenly becomes empowered by that to which it was previously insensible.

All this is highly suggestive in relation to the response of organs to planets. At the moment of conception the particular note sounded by a planet seems to 'set' that note as the fundamental one of an as yet dormant gland. Gradually the planet moves away from its position and, as we saw in

Chapter 6, its note grows sharper or flatter with its differing speed in relation to the earth. Only as it returns after a full cycle towards its original
position does its note grow closer and closer to that imparted to the organ
under its sway. As it repeats once more its exact relationship, its note for
a moment sounds just as it did before. An irresistible resonance possesses
the gland, the catch which held it motionless disintegrates, and a new
function is launched.

After one month the Moon repeats its fundamental note, and the digestive function is released. After four and a half, Mercury repeats his, and
involuntary motion follows. After twenty, Venus repeats hers, and within
the baby yet another aspect opens.

It grows dimly but magnificently apparent that in the term of human
life *all* the correspondences which we found in connection with the harmony of the planets and the harmony of human physiology miraculously
come together and coincide. As in man's body the different organs are
disposed in ascending order from the heart or centre, so their functions
enter in the same order in his life, one after the other dominating the
organism and ruling its destiny. Moreover, the periods of their entrance
and ascendency are determined by the astronomical cycle of the particular
planet which governs them. Man is a microcosm not only statically in his
structure, but also dynamically in time. Man is a working model of the
Solar System.

Placing the heavenly bodies and the human functions thus synchronised
in the order of their frequency round the circle, another strange parallel
emerges. As we saw, the first two functions, creation of physical form and
involuntary movement, which begin before birth, do so without the need
of air. Only at the third milestone or birth, does the shock of air enter.
Two more functions follow, voluntary movement and the power of thought.
Then, at the sixth milestone, yet another shock, the full emotional impact
of impressions based on light, leads on to the further functions of maturity
and to the potential function of consciousness.

Imagining the moon and planets as functions of the Solar System, some
very similar principle is seen at work. The heavenly bodies which rule
the first two points, the Moon and Mercury, lack atmosphere entirely.
They have only physical form and involuntary movement, that is, revolution about their luminary. But, as we saw earlier, Mercury, having no
atmosphere of its own, is nevertheless enveloped in the zodiacal light, is
embraced and protected within the aura of the mother. So similarly is the
Moon embraced within the magnetic field of the Earth. These bodies,

having as yet neither individual atmosphere nor individual movement, but only participating in the atmosphere and movement of their parents, are as it were still unborn.

On the other hand, all those planets which have become emancipated from the immediate vicinity of the Sun – from Venus onward – have, we find, acquired an atmosphere of their own. And they have also acquired something corresponding to voluntary movement, the power of rotation upon their own axis. Like the child after birth, they have begun both to breathe and to move.

Finally, only the outermost planets – particularly Jupiter and Saturn – possess a full family of satellites, as a man only can in his maturity. Moreover only they approach that physical state in which they might fully absorb solar light and begin to become radiant with their own. Whether they do in fact radiate a certain individual glow is uncertain. But what is certain is that in their present gaseous state they could do so, whereas for Mercury or the Earth such inner radiance is impossible without a complete transformation of physical state. Jupiter and Saturn may be said to enjoy ⁖he potentiality of radiance, as the adult man beyond the sixth milestone may be said to enjoy the potentiality of self-consciousness.

Thus in the cosmic cycle of functions, no matter on what scale they may be taken, three parallel lines of development may be seen, beginning in different places – the first, based on the development of solid or physical matter, which begins at point 9; the second, based on the development of air or atmosphere, which begins at point 3; and the third, based on the transmutation of light or perceptions, which begins at point 6. What the cycle of respiration and the cycle of the transmutation of light imply on the scale of the Solar System is difficult to say; but that some such cycles exist – parallel to the astronomically recognized cycle of solid or physical bodies – is clear enough.

Man lives and develops by the parallel assimilation of food, air and perceptions. The Solar System consists of a parallel development of solid spheres, atmospheric spheres, and spheres of light. And in fact this parallel development of three different levels of matter, originating at different points, is a fundamental feature of the universe and one which enables the inevitable falling away of any single line of development to be magnificently overcome.

II THE MILESTONES OF LIFE

All this is sufficiently suggestive to make us wish to study this scale of man's life and its milestones in greater detail.

Our scale begins one month from conception. Logarithmically, there will be a still faster cycle for the first month of gestation, an even faster one for the first three days (1/10th month), and theoretically others for the first seven hours (1/100th month) and the first forty minutes (1/1000th month). In 'work done', these periods will be comparable to the main divisions of gestation, childhood and maturity.[56] Little is known about such shorter scales. That of three days, however, appears to refer to the independent existence of the fertilized ovum in the Fallopian tube. And, connection once established with the circulation of the mother in the uterus, it is the first month which sees the embryo pass through the fish, reptilian and other prehuman stages that have often been adduced in support of the Darwinian theory.

At one month from conception, the 'human' development of the embryo begins, and our main scale starts. We can now take the milestones of life in order, as in the last chapter we considered the organs and their functions in order.

At the *first milestone*, sixty days from conception, we find that the embryo is a marine creature, possessing gills and fins, and dwelling in the amniotic fluid. Its whole work lies in receiving and transforming food substances received from the mother. This is the moment of dominance of the maternal liver and *pancreas*. Everything connected with this point – whether taken anatomically or in time – is essentially liquid, and being under the sway of the *Moon*, may be expected to fluctuate by the lunar cycle of about 29 days.

The *second milestone*, as we saw, coincides with the short cycle of *Mercury* (117 days). In some way the completion of a mercurial cycle springs the next mechanism in the human embryo, which is adapted to the utilization of air. Now the lung system forms, in preparation for the beginning of breathing at the third milestone; independent circulation is established; and the foetus 'quickens' or acquires its own involuntary movement. All these functions are clearly connected with the momentary dominance of the *thyroid* gland.

Birth, at the *third milestone*, is the culmination of this adaptation of the organism for transforming air. The embryo emerges into this new medium,

---

56. The idea of these faster 'life-periods' is treated in another book, 'The Theory of Eternal Life'.

breathes and lives. Henceforth it is nourished not only by *food* but also by *air*.

In the period following birth we find that the minor cycles of the Earth, the Asteroids, Venus and Mars strike upon successive points of logarithmic progression. The detailed meaning of this is not clear, though it appears to be connected with the formation of different aspects of the individual physical body.

We can, however, consider in more detail the correspondence between the *fourth milestone* and the conclusion of a cycle of *Venus*. This is connected with simple increase in bulk, the body adding more weight (17 lbs.) in the year following birth than in any other single year of existence. The peak of this process ($10\frac{1}{2}$ months) marks the predominance of the tissue-and-flesh-forming function of the parathyroids in conjunction with the thymus. In other words, the infant at this point is 'a little vegetable'.

The planetary rhythm ruling the fifth milestone is more subtle and difficult to discern than the previous examples. This period (1302 days) is very close to one quarter of a major cycle of Mars (1362 days) and one eighth of a major cycle of Saturn (1323 days). These planets, which work in harmony, appear to govern it jointly, and it is no doubt for this reason that we find a confusion between the so-called saturnine or mental characteristics which fall into place here, and the martial influence which we should expect to find from the mathematical sequence of the planets and their responding organs.

At this *fifth milestone* ($2\frac{3}{4}$ years) the speed of bodily growth by weight suddenly drops. The brain, however, continues to grow and by five years has reached 90% of its adult weight, though the body as a whole stands at no more than a quarter. The effect of this sudden dominance of brain-function is seen in the mastery of speech, as distinct from the earlier use of proper names for individual objects. Ouspensky[57] has pointed out how speech and the formation of abstract concepts – which is a main function of the human brain – are two aspects of the same thing, and that one does not exist without the other. So we may say that it is at the fifth milestone that the infant becomes capable of abstract concepts. And with these it begins to form an individual personality.

By the *sixth milestone* (7 years) the formation of personality is more or less completed. The brain is functioning fully as a receiving mechanism, and children pass through a notoriously enquiring age, when they are full of 'difficult' questions – that is, questions arising from a constant flow of new

57. P. D. Ouspensky, 'Tertium Organum', p. 82–83.

perceptions, which in the adults who are expected to answer are already familiar and taken for granted. These perceptions are busily digested into ideas, opinions, a whole pattern of experience. From this time the organism is nourished not only by *food* and *air*, but also by more fully digested *perceptions*.

The logarithmic points which follow the end of childhood are marked by the major cycles of the Asteroids, Jupiter and Mars, just as the stages immediately following birth were marked by similar minor cycles. In this case, however, the cycles appear to count from birth (that is, exposure to light and air) rather than from conception, and they no doubt influence the formation of the adult personality as the minor cycles appear to have influenced the formation of the physical body of infancy.

As we saw in the last chapter, different aspects of the glands have different starting-points, and the march of the planets is counted by one aspect from the moment of conception, by another from the moment of birth, and by yet another only from the unknown moment of regeneration. Thus rhythms counting from conception must refer to heredity, rhythms counting from birth to individuality. The only creature inescapably enslaved to heredity is the embryo in the womb, for to every human being at birth the stars bring a new and unparalleled opportunity. For this reason, it must never be forgotten that Mendelian heredity – taken as an exact system of breeding – can only apply to the fruit-flies and guinea-pigs on which his experiments were based, and in which the higher aspects of the glands are absent or incomplete. By conception or heredity a man may be haemophilitic or colour-blind. But his birth-right always accords him the chance to transmute his ill – as the English physicist Dalton used his own colour-blindness to establish once and for all its nature.

Let us return to the unfolding of man. His *seventh milestone* marks puberty. This is coincident with the cycle of Mars, and with the ascendancy of the *adrenal glands*. It is the age of passionate activity, expressed by running, jumping, climbing, and a devotion to dangerous sports and games. It marks the dawn of will, determination, grit. The adrenals also release the sex-function, hitherto held in check by the thymus. Or rather, it would perhaps be more true to say that the sex-function in the complete sense and with all the implications which we touched on in the last chapter, becomes incipient at puberty, just as the thought processes which dominated the fifth milestone became incipient with the structural completion of the brain at the fourth. With many people true sex remains only incipient all their lives, and is imitated by the adrenal passions of adolescence.

At the *eighth milestone*, 35 years, man finds himself at the prime of life, with all his powers and responsibilities at their maximum. A cycle of Saturn is complete. Holding the reins of all the other functions, and creating that unity between them which gives self-control and the power to act, the *anterior pituitary* now finds itself dominant. At this age the average man has created and must support a family; his work reaches its greatest efficiency, and his command over his surroundings is at its zenith.

In fact the continued growth of creative powers beyond this point already marks a man out as exceptional – a Rembrandt in painting, a Shakespeare in drama, a Paracelsus in medicine. And the very existence of such exceptions recalls the idea that at this milestone a new and normally unrealized function may come into action. Just as the function of breathing began at birth, and the function of thinking at the end of childhood, so at this moment of maturity there should begin a new function based on man's consciousness of his existence, and of his relation to the universe.

The awakening of this new function seems to be connected with the mid-point of man's normal life-span, which as we shall shortly see, is about 76 years. At 37 or 38 a man stands, as it were, exactly opposite the moments of his conception and his death, and as though through a crack in time, a reflection may appear to him of the universal mysteries from which he then emerged and to which he must then return. Dante, prefacing his tremendous vision of the universe – "In the *mid-point* of this mortal life, astray in a dark wood I found myself. . ." – refers to this idea.

This new function, awakening at the peak of his life, may reveal to man a sudden vision of the *whole*, of which all his other functions have given him but partial and conflicting glimpses. Sometimes in the same awakening it may also reveal to him a *new expression* of the whole, to the fulfilment of which all the rest of his life will be dedicated.

At 38 Kepler completed his 'New Astronomy' which, formulating the laws relating to planetary motion, conveyed for the first time the true unity of the Solar System. At 37 the great physicist, Clerk Maxwell, suddenly retiring from a brilliant and active life to his remote estate in Scotland, there perceived and proved the principle of electromagnetic vibration, the scientific explanation of the unity of the universe. At 37, in a sudden flash of illumination, at Sils-Maria in the Austrian Alps, Nietzsche became aware of the same vision, which, expressed in the idea of eternal recurrence, was to make accessible to human understanding the unity of time. So at the same age, Balzac conceived his 'Comedie Humaine', Tolstoy his 'War and Peace', Ibsen his 'Peer Gynt', each an attempt to express in literary form *the whole of human life.*

These were evidently cases in which this last and potential function *did* awaken, either fully or partly. And they show that its awakening enables a man to perceive directly and personally *a cosmos in its unity*.

But for this to happen it is necessary for his highest energies to be diverted into a *new channel*. And this in turn requires the most intense desire, work, knowledge, help and luck.

Only the discovery of such a new function enables man to continue to ascend after maturity. For ordinary men an ever-increasing decline leads to the *ninth and last milestone*, death. At exactly 28,080 days from conception, Mars completes 36 cycles, Venus 48, the Asteroids 60, the combination of Jupiter and Saturn 72, Uranus 76, Mercury 240 and the Moon 960. We find to our awe that the whole company of planets have returned again to that same disposition which governed at the outset.

Throughout man's life their various tempi have ruled this or that function and aspect of his existence. The quick lunar pulse of lymph, the tempo vivace of his mercurial nature, the moderato beat of flesh and blood, the andante of intellectual striving, the slow largo of instinct, and the majestic grave of man's deepest emotion – all these have risen and fallen in him according to the quicker or slower rhythms of the planets. By their perpetual harmony they have woven the intricate counterpoint of his life. In unison at last, they strike together the one great chord which sounds his death-knell.

III   THE CALENDAR: SUPERHUMAN AND SUBHUMAN TIMES

We have shown that each man has his own individual time, quite independent of the calendar and the clock, and derived from the uncoiling of the main-spring of his own individual life. This is very important to understand, for it is this hour told by *his* time which indicates his position, his outlook, his fate. It is this hour told by *his* time which alone can answer that most ominous of all questions: How long has he left?

Nevertheless, men – their own inner clocks set each at a different and personal time – have to live together, and in living together to set up a convenient common measure of time in which all can concur, however misleading that common time may be. For this purpose they quite naturally have recourse to a unit of the time of the higher cosmos which embraces them. They measure their own, each others', and their ancestors' lives by the *breathing of the Earth*, that is, by the time the Earth takes to revolve about the Sun, by *years*.

Now a year is an extremely interesting and complete unit of time, full of inner connections and relations, and which may perhaps be taken as the classical pattern of an organic time-form. For since, as we established in the second chapter, the dimensions of space and time become interchangeable as we pass from one cosmos to another, then evidently certain patterns in time must represent organic forms just as certain patterns in space do. A year is such an organic time-form, with its own functions or festivals and its own inner circulation between them. So that, although different individuals will pass through a year at different speeds according to their own personal time, that year will nevertheless bring them all comparable experiences and possibilities, and will represent a fixed common relationship for all of them.

Thus, for all men on one half of the earth, the same day of the year will be shortest, the same days will mark the waxing of the sun's power, the same day its longest light. Definite fractions of the year will separate seed-time and harvest, moisture and drought, the flower and the fruit. If a man and a woman engender a child, seven-ninths of a year will bring about its birth, no matter how different their personal times may be. The year in fact represents a great dance in which all men, animals, birds, trees and plants upon the surface of the Earth take part, no matter how quickly or how slowly they themselves pass through it.

Let us mark 360 days of the year round the 360° of a circle, leaving uncounted and 'outside time' the five days between Christmas and New Year, between the end and the beginning. In this circle of the year tradition marks three major points – the festival of the midwinter solstice or Christmas, when all life is hidden and invisible; the festival of rebirth or Easter; and the festival of harvest. These three festivals are typified by the three stages of natural growth – root, flower and fruit – and in a very general way their intermediate periods represent, not only for plants, but for all living beings an ever-repeating cycle of gestation, ripening and reaping.

Thus once again we come to the now-familiar figure of the triangle within the circle. If we make the centre of this circle to represent the Earth, and place about the triangle the twelve signs of the zodiac against which the Sun moves in the course of the year, we see also that this divine triangle represents the Sun's path. And if we further add the six intermediate points and the strange movement between them, which in the Solar System we found to represent the invisible circulation of light, we find the pattern of a year indeed to correspond with this fundamental pattern of all truly cosmic beings and forms.

Many calendar-systems – the Aztec one of eighteen twenty-day months with five 'dead' days, for example – evidently derive from this conception of the year as a nine-pointed circle. For each division thus represents forty days. In modern times these organic divisions of the year are clearly indicated by certain moveable feasts – Ash Wednesday oscillating between points 1 and 2, Easter between points 2 and 3, and Whitsunday between points 3 and 4. Forty days – Christ's sojourn in the wilderness – thus represents a definite period in which certain things can be achieved, matured or fixed. While multiples of forty days, joined together by the line of invisible inner circulation, remain connected across time by unseen processes of germination or understanding.

Winter wheat, sown at point 7 (October 6), following the mysterious motion 142857, is harvested at point 4 (June 9); spring corn, sown at point 2 (March 21), is in turn reaped at point 7. The soil, frozen or dessicated at one date, must be thawed or softened with rain at another date innerly connected with it. While to human beings, all unwitting, memories, moods and the result of long-for-

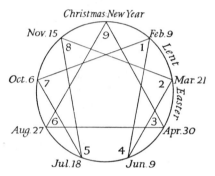

Fig. 8. The Design of the Year

gotten actions, emerge suddenly out of invisibility along this hidden circulation between one part of a year and another.

In thus passing through the years, a man, carrying his own inner time with him, nevertheless passes through an extraordinarily intricate series of repeating time-forms. A given day in a given spring must certainly be experienced at the speed appropriate to the observer's age and type. But apart from this it will also bring him echoes from the same day in all other springs, and it will be connected in yet another way with a certain day of that summer and all other summers, with a certain day of that autumn and all other autumns. In this way, a year represents for man not a line but a rippling and scintillating web of trans-temporal echoes.

A year is not at all a unit of individual time, as we often suppose, but rather the scenery through which personal time passes. For man's time moves *against the background* of the Earth's time, itself also moving, yet so relatively slowly that it seems to him motionless – as a background of moving clouds appears motionless in contrast to a swift-sailing ship in the foreground.

A similar mistake is to take historical or astronomical time as an extension of human time, of our personal time. This is quite wrong, and gives rise to all kinds of distorted views of events in the world and universe around us. As we shall see later, historical time, that is, the time of civilizations, also develops logarithmically – but on a scale of centuries rather than decades. While in the chapter on the world of Nature, we seemed to discern that terrestrial time, covering periods of millions of years, not only developed logarithmically, *but in reverse* – that is, each successive era was shorter, not longer, more compressed rather than expanded.

An approximate image of man's temporal background might then be conveyed by a clockface on which month, hour, minute and second hands were simultaneously revolving. But to make this image more correct, it would be necessary to imagine some of the hands gaining in speed, others losing, and some even revolving counter-clockwise. If the second hand now imagined that the circumference of the face was an infinite straight line, measurable only in one direction at one speed, and divided into equal parts which had one fixed meaning for all the hands, this would to a certain degree represent man's normal perception and illusion concerning the nature of time.

One very common and easily verifiable effect of this illusion is that to every man the external events of his youth – when his *own* time contained more – loom larger than those of his old age. To the octogenarian veteran the Spanish-American or the Boer War is a *bigger event* than the Second World War. And it is clear why. To him the year of war in his prime is three times as long as the year of war in his old age, and all events that year contained are three times as heightened, extended, enlarged, and filled with meaning as the later ones.

On the other hand, at certain periods of history, some externally insignificant events, such as those connected with the life of Christ, for example, may be of immense importance and go on producing effects for hundreds or thousands of years, because, unknown to the human observers, they belong to the first moments of a civilization, when its processes are developing with tremendous speed.

In this way human beings, unconsciously measuring by their own inner time, tend to make all external events longer or shorter, larger or smaller than they are in reality – that is, than they are by their own time.

Thus when we are considering questions of time, the first thing that must be asked is, Whose time, time of what? In the first two sections of this chapter we have been considering man's time. But what in fact does this mean? It appears to mean the scale of time of a very elaborate cellular organism, beginning with the first division and multiplication of its aboriginal cell, and ending with its collapse as a functioning whole and its disintegration into sub-cellular matter. It is the line of time of organic man, of man as a physical body. And usually this is the only time we know and are aware of.

When we speak about 'man', we really speak about his degree of consciousness or awareness, however rudimentary. For the rest is not human, but chemical, biological or animal. Now one of the characteristics of the ordinary consciousness of man, even the keenest level of ordinary consciousness, is that it is confined to an organic form. In the ordinary way man can not attach his consciousness to matter in electronic or molecular state, nor to superhuman forms such as continents or civilizations. He may think about this possibility and dream about it in a poetic way, but he can not actually achieve it. Therefore we are justified in regarding this organic time of his physical form as the time of ordinary man.

But is it his only possible time? Or are there other potential times for him? For we know by experience that at any moment our biological time may be split open and transcended by the entry of joy, pain or wonder. All at once and without warning, one of our ever-emptying minutes blossoms out again into an infinity of sensations and understandings. How does this happen, and what does it imply?

In the chapter on the Sun it was discussed how at the impact of creative solar energy upon the earth, electrons became locked into molecules, molecules into cells, and, we may now add, cells into organic bodies, including man's. But the electrons, molecules and cells continue to exist in these bodies, *and they continue to work by their own time.* Thus man's body, with its familiar overall time, contains the faster time of cells, the still faster time of molecules, and the almost inconceivably rapid time of electrons. And just as a civilization, with its own duration and time, not only contains the very much faster time of individual men but is also composed of their times, so every part of man's body is composed and penetrated by these three parallel times.

As we already said, we can not ordinarily imagine man's awareness attached to anything but a cellular body, or operating by any but this body's time. We do not know what new psychological and even physiological connections must be created to make it possible for human awareness to be switched, for example, to the time of its molecular counterpart. Yet records of short mystical states containing an incalculable richness of experience, of strange sensations of ample time in moments of extreme danger, of long dreams at the instant of waking which seem to refer to the inner processes of the body, all suggest that this switch of consciousness to another time does occasionally occur – under intense emotion or instinctive stress.

The conditions of *intentional* transfer of awareness to a faster time, however, are unknown to us, and evidently this power, if it exists, refers to a much higher level of consciousness than any with which we are familiar. For it does not need much imagination to realize that such power must involve not only the extremely difficult re-routing of nervous impulses between the cerebrospinal and sympathetic systems, but also a general education and strengthening of consciousness and will, to withstand the shocks and terrors arising from completely new and unforeseen sensations. It is for this reason that the work of practical penetration into other times has been confined to schools created for the purpose.

In fact, the penetration into other times, which is connected with the creation of consciousness in functions which are now unconscious or inoperative, has a double effect. As a result of the expansive and pervasive powers of matter in these faster states, awareness of their times brings with it a certain awareness of the worlds from which they derive. Penetration into the subhuman time of cells creates awareness of the superhuman rhythms of Nature, into the time of molecules awareness of terrestrial time, while further penetration into electronic time implies a similar awakening to solar time. Thus the passage of consciousness to each higher function brings man to knowledge of two new worlds – one smaller and one larger.

Still another idea arises from this multiplicity of human times. It is the cellular body whose time begins with conception and terminates at death. But the molecular matter of which the ovum is composed, and into which the corpse disintegrates, does not die, nor does its time come to an end. From man's point of view, molecular and electronic time not only exist *within* his physical body, but also *after* it and *before* it. Thus molecular and electronic time, with all they imply, must be closely connected with the problem of states after death and before birth.

It is the penalty of man's feeble awareness, which can not normally escape from the time and form of his cellular body, that this immortality of molecular and electronic matter does not concern him. But were he to create for himself a consciousness sufficiently powerful to penetrate into those other worlds and times which are contained within his own familiar body, then his whole relation to immortality might indeed be different.

XII THE SIX PROCESSES IN MAN (i)

I GROWTH

WE HAVE NOW SUFFICIENT MATERIAL TO TRY TO DISCOVER HOW the six fundamental processes, which we saw at work in the Solar System, express themselves in the microcosm of man. We will take them here in the same order as we did then, beginning with the original *process of growth*.

The process of growth is that which, on a universal scale, creates the whole sequence of worlds, producing from unity and potentiality, diversification, form and expression. The creative agents here act in the order, *life, matter, form*. An active impulse plunges into a passive material to create a living thing midway between the two.

As in every other created being, this process begins in man immediately *after* conception. It does not refer to the act of conception itself, which belongs to a different process – that of regeneration – which we will study last of all. In that mysterious act the invisible intangible signature of an individual being, acting from some unknown dimension of time, causes the passive ovum irresistibly to attract to itself the active sperm which will fertilize it and give it life. Whence this signature comes, and by what material means, are among the greatest mysteries of existence. And only later shall we see that it is borne *through time*, precisely from the death-agony of him who is about to be conceived.

But the instant conception is accomplished, *growth* begins. Where previously were two elements, male and female, is now but one – the fertilized or impregnated ovum. In this single cell two poles form, an active and a passive, and the genes becoming polarized between them, the cell splits into two, then four, eight, sixteen, thirty-two and so on. It is an exact living model of that Absolute sphere, infinitely propagating galaxies, which we imagined at the outset of this book. The radiation of *life* acting upon *matter*, yields infinite multiplicity of *form*.

At about the eighth day, the now active fertilized ovum (*life*), having multiplied its volume some hundred times, emerges from the Fallopian tube, and finds as its resting place and feeding ground the wall of the uterus (*matter*), through which it draws sustenance from the mother's organism, and begins to develop the complex embryonic structure (*form*). This stage gives rise to *differentiation*, the almost indistinguishable cellular mass of the ovum dividing into the envelopes of the amnion and the allantois, their containing fluids, and the embryo itself within. This process is already well advanced by the twenty-eighth day. Analogous on a cosmic scale is the differentiation of the parts of the Solar System with its central Sun and enveloping planetary spheres.

Of the next stage of growth we may say that it appears to be connected with the separation within the embryo itself of vegetable, invertebrate and vertebrate aspects, which now establish their headquarters in the bowels, the chest and the head respectively. At the same time, in its transient reflection of plant, fish and mammal, this stage provides an analogy with the creation of the world of nature. In fact, externally, there is nothing at all to distinguish a month-old human embryo from those of a frog, a chicken or a horse.

At the end of the second month the embryo, having passed through galactic, solar and the various organic stages, is on the threshold of humanity. This is its first milestone on the scale of life. The embryo finds itself passive and waiting. And now an active force, which for want of better understanding we may call heredity, strikes suddenly out of time to create human form. There is nothing yet of individual man in this, as there is nothing individual in the sexual urge of puberty. This is the level of mankind, or perhaps of race – the next stage of differentiation within the great category of organic life. Human heredity (*life*), inhabiting the waiting embryo (*matter*), creates the true foetus of a man (*form*).

It is not possible for us to distinguish the many successive triads of growth which gradually complete the creation of the infant in readiness for birth. No doubt each period between the main milestones of life may be taken as an octave of seven stages, such as those we have individually described. Each of these stages will involve the plunging of an active principle ever more deeply into matter and form, the resulting organism itself taking the next step downward into organized limitation. When this process, following the natural course of a descending octave, reaches an interval or pause, an active force appears to enter from without, giving the foetus the necessary impulse towards its next stage of development.

We have seen how this happened at the first milestone. At the second (130 days), another shock enters. As if by some curious anticipation of what it *will be* at maturity, when as full-grown man it will have achieved the maximum of personal power and experience, the foetus, in this fifth month of gestation, suddenly acquires the signature of an individual human being upon the general mould of humanity. At the first milestone, by some affinity with puberty, the foetus became human; at the second, by some similar affinity with maturity, it becomes individual. How such foreshadowings may connect one part of life with another *through time* may emerge later.

Now each of the fundamental processes gives rise to certain substances which are characteristic of it, as waste or inert matters are characteristic of the process of destruction, and poisons are characteristic of disease. Without yet trying to isolate them chemically or physically, we may say that those characteristic of the process we are now studying are fine matters which have the property of producing

> multiplication,
> differentiation,
> organization,
> function and form.

All of these together, seen in time, appear to us as the general phenomenon of growth.

About the orgin of these matters in the human organism we do not know very much. We know however that the thymus gland is closely connected with the cellular multiplication referred to, for when tadpoles are fed with its extract their tissue multiplies without further differentiation to create giant tadpoles. We know further that differentiation of function and perfection of form are in some way stimulated by the thyroid. Tadpoles fed on thyroid extract metamorphose into frogs as small as flies. It may thus be that all the glands of internal secretion in one of their functions, secrete the fine matters of growth, which enter in sequence to produce the whole cycle of bodily development.

In any case we may say that the activity of growth, launched with all the enormous momentum of nature at the outset of the life-circle, gradually runs down as life proceeds. At 10 the brain practically ceases to enlarge; at 12 the final proportions of the form have been achieved; at 17 height becomes almost stationary, and at 22 cellular bulk. Any further increases are the result of swelling or stretching of existing cells and the addition of fat, a process which has nothing in common with the multiplication and differentiation of growth.

Taking man's life as a whole, we may say that the running down of growth is matched, as age advances, by the steady increase of decay. Sickness and death are the inevitable counterpart and limit of growth. Disintegration defeats organisation.

But before we pass to the next process, we may touch on the process of growth from a more general point of view. How does this process express itself psychologically and emotionally, on the level of conduct and habit?

We have seen that it represents the plunge of spirit into matter, producing as result a mean between the two. So in man's psychic life it stands for eternal compromise, impulse encountering resistance, need meeting obstacle, to come to rest at the halfway solution, the point of equilibrium. It is the way everything happens in the life of mankind – the manners, customs, habits, the endless complication and diversity that spring from the adjustment of ambition to circumstance, of one desire to other desires. It is the resultant of forces.

Take a trivial example. In his youth a man feels an aspiration to become a great painter. This activating desire finds itself plunged into the general matter or resistance of life – poverty, lack of opportunity, responsibility for a family, and so on. By the time he is 40, he finds himself, as resultant of these active and passive forces, a commercial artist designing advertising layouts. Such is the final 'form' of his ambition. This process happens of itself, as growth happens, multiplying causes and karma through man's life, each resultant being the beginning of a new complication.

So the process of growth goes forward, continuously and inevitably, yet also by spurts which reveal and emphasise each facet of the organism in turn. And man watches, half-fascinated, half-horrified, before change which he can not by one wit advance or hold back. Does the baby decide to become a child, the sprig to become a tree? All *happens*; some vast clock-spring of the universe unwinds, and he and all creatures willy-nilly with it.

It is precisely when man begins to sense this fatality of growth that, being weak, he begins to deceive himself. If growth turns the body of a boy into that of a man, the body of a girl into that of a woman, will it not also put wisdom into those mature bodies and teach them to put away childish things? But it will not. It will bring accumulation of experience, but not the digestion of that experience. It will bring accumulation of knowledge but not development of being.

From man's point of view the essence of this process is that it happens *unconsciously* and *involuntarily*. An unconscious and involuntary process can not possibly bring consciousness and will. Consciousness can not be developed unconsciously, nor will involuntarily. These qualities, incomparable with the growth of muscle and organ, can only be acquired by another and quite different process, conscious and intentional from its origin.

It is precisely on this point that the idea of evolution – an idea of genius in the mind of Darwin – has become an enervating and deceptive one in its popular perversion. Darwin, describing the addition of new species and ever more elaborate forms in the course of geological ages, the predominance with each epoch of a new and higher kingdom of nature, felt and revealed the *growth* of the Earth. He showed how the physical Earth matured, just as physical man matures. And how new species were *added* to the Earth as it grew up, just as new functions are *added* to man as he grows up. This clearly has nothing whatever to do with the possibility of a given species transcending itself, any more than it has with a given function becoming conscious. Here, as Ouspensky put it, a different card has been substituted.

Applied to the moral development of mankind, the idea of general evolution can only be supported by a quite arbitrary choice of example – by comparing the methods of the Inquisition with current freedom of the press in the United States, for example, and by forgetting comparison between the mediaeval law of sanctuary and the modern institution of concentration camps.

Today, the word evolution is used indiscriminately for the process of growth, the process of refinement which we will consider next, and for the process of regeneration about which we know least of all. It is even distorted into a kind of manufacturer's guarantee that every individual octopus shall one day develop into a Buddha, and that without any effort or intention on their part all men shall inevitably become wise.

This is as fantastic as to believe that by letting his canoe drift down some river, a traveller will inevitably be carried to the summit of the highest mountain. The process of growth is indeed a vast cosmic river, flowing eternally from the Creator. Relying upon its current alone, there is only one direction in which man can go – that is, downwards. For to remount the stream needs a different understanding, a different energy and a different effort.

II DIGESTION

In this second process, passive matter is acted on by a vital force and by it raised or transformed to a higher level. All processes of purification, refinement, cooking and distillation are of this nature. In it the creative agents act in the order: *matter, life, form.*

At many points we have considered how different functions of the human machine work with energy at different tensions, with different fuels, as it were. It is possible to imagine the digestive, respiratory, arterial and various nervous systems, for example, as if stoked with coal, wood, kerosene, high octane petrol and electricity respectively. The process by which these higher energies or fuels are refined from the basic materials of food and air is exactly the one we are now considering. And the stages by which this is achieved are perfectly analogous to the distilling and 'cracking' operations carried out with the aid of pressure and catalysts in a large synthetic oil-refinery where, beginning with coal as raw-material, by-products are yielded at every specific gravity up to the finest aviation petrol, whose manufacture is the main purpose of the plant.

Let us begin with the raw material, food. As taken into the organism, this is passive *matter*. Entering the mouth it submits to the masticating action of the jaws and the kneading of the tongue, combined with the liquifying action of saliva. Enzymes in the saliva and digestive juices unlock the heavy food-molecules, and split them into finer and finer particles. All this represents the active force of *life*. The resultant *form* is a nutrient liquid known as chyme, which can already be absorbed into the lymphatic system.

One of the characteristics of the process of digestion is that it is continuous, that is, the product of one stage becomes the raw material for the next. Thus the digested food which was the product of the first operation becomes passive matter for the second, and in its turn is acted on by the bile and other active secretions of the liver (*life*). A series of intricate chemical processes yield as *form* or result a liquid which is sufficiently refined to be absorbed direct into the venous circulation.

Now we have already seen that the different systems of the body and their appropriate energies may be regarded as an ascending octave. Similarly, the successive stages of refinement of matters suitable for the use of these systems may also be seen as such an octave. Thus the passive food upon the plate may be expressed by *do*, the chyme resulting from the first stage of transformation as *re*, and the superfine nourishment which passes osmotically into the bloodstream as *mi*. Here we come to a semitone, and as we noted in the arrangement of the Solar System and of the table of elements, Nature seems always to arrange some special shock to counteract the declining tendency which such halftones represent.

Exactly such an arrangement is provided here, and we find that the now passive *matter* of the venous blood meets an activating principle not, this time, from within the body, but from without. The bloodstream, exposed over the enormous surface of the lungs to the air, is suddenly vitalized by the addition of external oxygen (*life*), and emerges as refined or arterial blood (*form*).

So far we have tried to express the products of the different stages of refinement in physiological terms. But already in the stage referring to the circulation of arterial blood such a description becomes very inadequate. For we know that blood-circulation brings with it certain subjective sensations which can not be left out of account. An ample blood flow is connected with sensations of warmth and well-being; a deficient one with sensations of chill and depression. Such sensations may colour the whole of man's emotional life and affect his general attitude to the world.

The higher we rise in the scale of human energies the more important this subjective sensation of them becomes, and the less satisfactory a purely physiological description. So in the next stage we can certainly say that arterial blood passes through the brain and is there met by a certain principle which activates it to the point where it can induce electric or nervous reactions in the cerebral cortex. But we know very well that the chief result produced at this particular stage is what appears to us subjectively as our registration of images, our association of ideas, and in general what we call our thoughts.

In the next stage, energy is refined still further to the level where it becomes the fuel of the nervous systems controlling on the one hand motor impulses and on the other the involuntary inner workings of the body. That is, the energy by which man moves and acts.

Finally, one last transformation produces the extraordinarily subtle manifestations of energy which we can describe physiologically in terms of the sex-function, or more subjectively as source of the whole gamut of higher and creative emotions of which the human being is capable. Beyond this we know of no further transformation normally carried out by the human refinery.

From these examples it is clear that at each stage a *passive* raw material, worked on or digested by an *active* principle already existing in the body, yields as result a refined or intermediate substance, which in turn feeds an appropriate function.

It is often asked at this point, 'Does not the kind of food eaten, and the manner of eating it, affect the digestion?' Certainly, it does. From this point of view the first step is to eat, not from imitation, habit or theory; but in response to the voice of instinctive intelligence. It is necessary to establish contact with this intelligence, which already knows all about the inner needs of the organism, ask its advice and listen to its promptings –

whether to seek or abstain from this or that, to eat heartily or to fast. Without this contact, all theories about diet can only serve to spoil the appetite.

At another stage of sensitivity, it is interesting to become aware of the provenance of the food one eats. Man's food is drawn from the realm of plants, like fruit and vegetables, from the realm of invertebrates, like crabs and oysters, from the realm of cold-blooded vertebrates, like fish, and from the realm of warm-blooded vertebrates, like game or meat. It may consist of the natural by-products of other forms of life, such as eggs, milk or honey; or it may require the sacrifice of those very lives in themselves. All this implies a variable factor of violence in the taking of human food, which may have considerable importance for the race or nation, and even in some cases for the individual.

Again, food may be transmuted and this factor of violence in part offset, both by the skill, attention and art of the cook, and the awareness and gratitude of the eater. A combination of the devotee's pious grace before meals and the gourmet's conscious 'physiologie du goût' would perhaps be necessary to reveal in full this strange mystery of man swallowing and transmuting the whole realm of nature within him. For the dietician and the vegetarian are concerned but with the cellular nature of food, and its effect on the cellular nature of man: only a hermit or a Brillat-Savarin begins to release its molecular nature and utilise that to enhance his own.

Yet in spite of this, no man can acquire the enormous supply of new energy necessary for self-transformation either by eating more or better. For this he must turn to the other two forms of human nourishment – air and perceptions – which pass through a similar series of refinements, giving rise to new manifestations at every stage. For whereas solid food is almost automatically refined to its final possibility, the digestion of these two finer forms of food depends largely on the attention, understanding and choice of the person concerned.

In the case of perceptions, particularly, digestion is not automatic, is not assured by nature at all. *It depends entirely on the degree of consciousness of the receiver.* And with increase in this consciousness, perceptions may be refined to a point where they give rise to degrees of ecstasy ordinarily unimaginable by us.

For example, every day one passes a certain beggar in the street. Sometimes one perceives the beggar's face, if at all, as a vague blur in the general scene, which has no more meaning or significance than an old piece of newspaper. The perception reaches one's eye; but it goes no further, gives rise to no processes within the organism at all. On another day, exactly the same photographic image will impress itself most vividly on one's consciousness. One will suddenly *see* the beggar as he is, *see* the poverty, illness, craftiness, amusement or hopelessness written on his face, and will suddenly become aware of what has brought him to this point, and of what inevitably awaits him.

This simple perception will give rise to a hundred thoughts, speculations and emotions. It will be refined into food for mind, feelings and even for the highest healing or creative activity. And this digestion of the perception will be the result of a momentary increase of consciousness on the part of the perceiver, *perhaps of his having remembered himself.*

This, however, already begins to border on another process altogether. For the chief characteristic of the process of digestion is that in it all proceeds by Nature. Every man, by his very birthright of a human body, enjoys the use of the energies so produced. And though he can in many ways interfere with and hinder their normal output, the whole miraculous series of transformations goes on quite independently of his will, intention or desire.

Thus this natural refinement, which begins, as we saw, with inert matter and ends with form, must not be confused with intentional refinement, induced by man's own will and aspiration, which begins with form and ends with life. This latter involves a different and most difficult process. Later we will see the point at which it could begin.

III ELIMINATION, AND THE ROLE OF ORGANIC COMPOUNDS

Simultaneously with the process of digestion and transformation of foods, a process of destruction and elimination is proceeding in the body. This process works in the order: *life, form, matter.* It is, as we saw earlier, the process in which the life force breaks form down again into inert matter. Here each stage is complete in itself, and results in one particular waste product which is of no further use to the organism concerned. The typical matters of physiological destruction are excretions.

The chief characteristic of excretions is that they have no further possibility of transformation, and are therefore exuded through the pores and orifices of the body. Some excretions are obvious and tangible, but there are undoubtedly many others, less recognized but equally important, which may even assume the appearance of constructive functions.

Let us try to study the process of elimination at each of the functional

levels we previously classified. Thus digestion, respiration, blood-circulation, brain activity, the work of voluntary and involuntary muscles, and
finally the sexual and emotional functions, should all have their own individual excretions. For only by so ridding themselves of their waste products
can these functions be maintained in a healthy and efficient state.

Recall how in the process of digestion, incoming food (matter) met
with active digestive juices in the body (life), and was transformed into
chyme, a form in which it could be assimilated into the lymphatic system.
In the present process, the same active principle (still *life*) enters first, and
attacking the food (now *form*), by the same splitting separates off its indi-
gestible part (*matter*), which is eliminated into the intestines. The product
of this triad, excreta, stands midway between its original form as food and
completely fossilized organic matter, such as wood, and while no longer of
any use to the human organism, may nevertheless serve as nourishment
for a different level of creation represented by the vegetable realm.

• What is interesting here, however, is to see how the two processes of
digestion and elimination are indissolubly locked at every stage, and that
the same active element acts in both, but in a different place, a different role.
Thus:

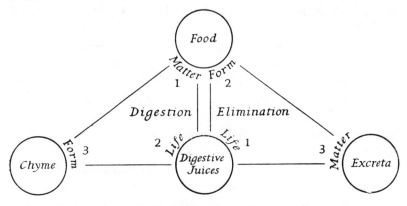

Fig. 9: *Triads of Digestion & Elimination*

Similarly, a filtering principle in the kidneys, while it purifies and refines
the blood passing through it, at the same time separates off and eliminates
urine. As faeces were the inert and final product of the food, so urine may
be said to be the inert product of water, which it exceeds in density by the
presence of urea, sodium phosphate and various other waste matters and
pigments. This too may be of value to the plant world.

At the next stage, the same inhaled oxygen which recharged venous blood to a higher state, also acts as the mechanical shock by which its pressure of carbon dioxide is released into the lungs, and thence borne off as exhaled air. This differs from inhaled air by the loss of much of its oxygen and other fine matters, by being carbonized, and particularly by being loaded with water vapour, all of which factors tend to render it inert and useless in relation to man.

Again we reach a point where physiological explanations are insufficient. At the following stage, active force is most clearly seen as exercise and heat, which, increasing metabolism, tend to break down the waste matters in cell and tissue, giving off the excretion sweat.

While further still, reaching the level of brain-activity, we find mental excretion represented by 'imagination', that is, a continuous production of waste images, the by-product of past perceptions, which flow through and out of the brain in a meaningless and unbroken stream. Just as eating is intermittent, so is the excretion of faeces: but since the inflow of perceptions is continuous, so also is this off-scouring of imagination continuous. When the direct impact of the outside world is quietened by sleep, it even becomes visible to us as dreaming. In fact, dreaming goes on night and day, without a break, as anyone who has acquired the power of arresting the more active thinking process of the mind for a few moments, can readily establish.

It is true that the current of imagination can be harnessed by will and skill for a specific end, just as a waterfall can be harnessed to drive a turbine. This is another story, which will be treated in the next chapter. It does not affect the basic nature of the flow, which is as though all the waste clippings of a great cinema-studio were stuck together at random and the result run continuously day and night through some forgotten projector in a back-room.

The waste matter of the brain reaches a further stage towards elimination in talk. And in a certain kind of talk, familiar to everyone, which proceeds without rhyme, reason, purpose or awareness, and which follows as automatically after cerebration as sweat after exercise, we do recognize quite literally 'the excretion of the mind' discussed by the early rationalists.

Certainly some talk is necessary for mental health: without some giving out of the by-products of perception, thought itself becomes clogged and stagnant, overcome by the fumes of fantasy which it generates. The problem, however, is that very many people eliminate through talk not only the waste matter of the mind, but a great deal of perception and thought which has not been digested at all. Images, which could be the food of understanding, flow in at their eyes and out at their mouths without any goodness being derived from them whatsoever. And in this case the vulgar phrase 'verbal diarrhoea' provides not only a picturesque but also an exact description of their malady.

Thus for some types, particularly the silent and saturnine, *more* talk may be necessary to aerate and cleanse their constipated minds. While for others, the garrulous and jovial, mental health may be a question of talking less, of retaining within themselves perceptions and thoughts until these are much more fully digested and understood. In both cases, the role of talk may rightly be seen as that of an excretion.

The excretions of the inner instinctive functions which depend on the sympathetic system are many and subtle. Tears of physiological relief, for example, can perhaps be classified in this category. On this level, however, 'excretions' tend to become more and more tenuous and psychological, and are indeed 'expressed' through the ever-changing play of the human face, eyes, gestures, postures and tone of voice. Such activities as singing or dancing may also be seen as a kind of intentional psycho-emotional excretion, with its consequent sense of cleansing and well-being on this particular level.

Finally, in connection with the sexual and emotional function, we are reminded, not so much of physiological excretions, as of the indefinable communication of pathos, anguish or joy, and the whole play of higher human expression. It is misleading to try to associate the waste-products of this level with tangible substances, for they evidently take the form of emanations too subtle for physical measurement and analysis. Certain kinds of laughter which are a means of rejecting impressions too contradictory or difficult for the recipient to understand may also belong here. But in general we can say that what is 'given off' as 'waste', that is, what is passed out into the world, must be proportional to what is refined within. A man can only give out the by-product of what he has digested, refined and understood – but this he must do.

For the process of destruction, working as described, is an entirely natural and necessary one, which results in the successful elimination of inert and unassimilated matters, and thus maintains the body in vitality and health. Further, what applies to the whole body also applies to every separate function, from highest to lowest. Each function must be rid of its waste matters if it is to work to its full capacity, and the penalty for not doing so belongs to the next process, disease.

From these three processes which we have examined in some detail it is already clear that certain characteristic matters are associated with each. Now if we refer back to the table in which we arranged a selection of organic compounds in descending octaves of molecular weights, we find an interesting confirmation of this.[58]

Taking carbon, nitrogen and oxygen – the basis of all organic life – as among the first notes of our first octave, and its completion as a doubling of molecular weight from carbon's initial 12, we get something like this:

do	12	carbon
—	13	
si	14	nitrogen
la	15	acetone
sol	16	oxygen
fa	18	water
—	19	
mi	20	
re	$22\frac{1}{2}$	
do	24	

In a descending octave there will be, as shown, intervals between *do* and *si*, or between carbon and nitrogen, and between *fa* and *mi*, or just below water. Later we shall find that these intervals have a quite special significance.

Meanwhile, if we continue with further octaves in the same proportion, the whole arrangement is better expressed in the form of a spiral, where each note can be clearly seen echoing down into ever more complicated forms of matter, thus:

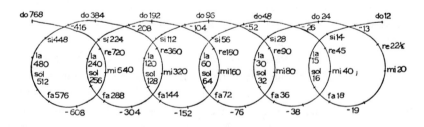

Fig. 10: The Octaves of Molecular Compounds

See Appendix VII, 'Table of Organic Compounds'.

In fact, this idea of repeating patterns of molecular structure connected with specific characteristics was already recognised in synthetic chemistry in the 1930's. It led to the 'tailoring' of artificial molecules to special requirements, the first enormously successful example being nylon. Later, the manipulation of molecules to combine known qualities produced the silicones, for example, a series of special finishes where the properties of glass and of organic lubricants were united by ingeniously replacing the latter's carbon atoms with atoms of silica, the element which lies an exact octave lower. Yet despite much brilliant improvisation, the general principle of molecular octaves does not seem to have been recognised, and it were perhaps well to treat each note in greater detail.

Suppose we begin with the note *sol*, represented originally by oxygen, and see where its harmonics sound. One octave down we find methyl alcohol, and two down nitric acid. At the fourth octave, however, the trail grows more interesting. Here are leucine (130) and lysine (132), two amino-acids which are found to be so essential for growth that proteins like maize-flour which do not include them are inadequate for the nourishment of children, and as staple diet give rise to pellagra and other diseases of arrested physical development. Young animals fail to grow when their sole protein is the gliadin of bread, though the same protein can maintain the fully-grown adult in health. Further, at *sol* in the fifth octave, we find the meconic acid (254), which newborn babies take in before their mother's milk, estrone the maternal hormone, the lactose of milk itself, and the famous vitamin A of cod-liver oil, which is especially necessary during childhood and pregnancy. All these substances are clearly associated with the *process of growth*.

Passing to the note *re*, we again find nothing revealing in the first three octaves, but in the fourth a striking group formed by the butyric acid of butter (88), the alinine of egg (89), and the lactic acid of milk (90). Yet another octave and we come on ascorbic acid (176), carbohydrate, and the fruit and milk sugars – fructose and galactose (all 180). Finally, the sixth *re* yields malt-sugar and riboflavin or vitamin B² (360), which is found all through the digestive system and seems closely connected with production of the enzymes, whose business it is to split food molecules. The fats, sugars and vitamins of this note all evidently refer to the *process of digestion*.

Fa, the note originally represented by water (18), continuing through salicylic acid (138), a basis of violet dye, and para-aminobenzoic acid (137), which tends to restore colour to grey hair, has a strange meaning. *Fa* of the fifth octave gives the brilliant dyes, alizarin orange and yellow and malachite green, and vitamin A from which the visual purple of the eye, giving sensitivity to colour, is formed. *Fa* of the sixth includes the pigments xanthophyll, bilirubin, and haematin, which colour plasma, bile and blood, yellow, brown and red respectively. Not only do the substances on this note all seem to be connected with colour and dyes, but as we pass down the octaves the very colours represented drop down the spectrum from colourlessness to violet, blue, green, yellow, orange, brown and red. Not at first do we realize that this special feature of *fa* – colouring, or the breaking up of white light – is a curiously hidden aspect of disintegration in general, that is, of the cosmic *process of destruction*.

Turning to the note *mi*, we seem to find the agents of a process which we have not yet dealt with in detail. At *mi* in the fourth, fifth, and sixth octaves we find a whole series of herbal alkaloids like eucalyptol, menthol, nicotine, thymol, tannine, quinine, strychnine, laudanine, and aconite, which from time immemorial have been used as drugs or natural agents of the *process of healing*.

La also represents a process we shall have to deal with in more detail in the next chapter. The original *la* is filled by acetone (15). Next comes formaldehyde (30), a pungent irritating liquid which callouses or produces sores on the surface of the skin, and which is used for hardening, preserving or embalming organic substances. Further, we find the urea (60) which makes rheumatic crystals, and the acetic acid (60) which degenerates wine and sugar into vinegar. While in the fourth octave comes the anaesthetic chloroform (119), whose particular function is to remove consciousness. This general power of rendering living things harder, more crystalline, less sensitive and less conscious, we recognize as belonging to the *process of degeneration* or corruption.

The first *si* is nitrogen 14. Its octave counterpart ethylene (28) is a strange gas which, it has been found, is given off by and instrumental in the ripening and rotting of fruit. Two octaves on we encounter the histamine (111) of the bone-marrow, where blood-cells are generated, and creatinine (111), a substance which is particularly found in the human testes and in the gravid uterus, and the production of which is greatly increased in pregnancy. While at *si* in the sixth octave comes vitamin E (450), the absence of which produces sterility and its abundance fertility, both in male and female. All these substances are closely connected with sex and the possibility of reproduction, either on animal or on cellular level. We may thus provisionally assign this note to that which, in other connections, we have called the *process of regeneration*.

At the same time, it must be added that many of the organic substances essential for the begetting of offspring, such as the male testosterone and the female estrone, are found in or near the note *sol*, which we assigned to the process of growth. And in general the substances of these two notes, *si* and *sol*, representing between them the joint possibilities of reproduction and growth, interact, combine and depend on each other in a very extraordinary way, just as their primal representatives, nitrogen and oxygen, combine and interact to form the air which is the basis of all organic growth and generation.[59]

With this reservation, it now appears that six of the seven notes of our descending octaves of organic compounds can with justification be assigned to the six cosmic processes, of which these compounds are as it were the molecular agents. We can summarise our findings thus:

do ?

---

si	certain vitamins:	agents of reproduction (regeneration)
la	certain poisons:	anaesthetic agents (degeneration)
sol	amino-acids, etc:	agents of growth
fa	dyes:	agents of colour (destruction)

| mi | natural drugs: | agents of healing |
| re | fats and sugars: | agents of digestion |

We will not here touch upon the note *do*, which completes each old octave and begins each new one, which resumes in itself all that which has gone before and all that which will come after.

But there do remain to consider the natural intervals, between *do* and *si* and between *fa* and *mi*, where, as we have seen, any original impulse tends to fall away or diminish, and which in cosmic arrangements are compensated by the entry of some extra impulse from another scale and another level.

The *do-si* interval in the first octave would be represented by the molecular weight 13, though no such substance is known. At the next octave we find acetylene (26), source of intense light. The element of similar molecular weight, magnesium, also has this property. At the same interval in other octaves come the strange narcotics, derived from mezcal, poppy

---

59. Note also the interaction and inseparability of the notes *sol* and *si* in the octave of planetary times, already referred to in the section on the milestones of human life (see Chapter 11, II).

and hemp, which have the effect of putting man into temporary communication with higher functions that are normally dormant, which – in mystical language – 'release inner light'.

The substances of the *mi-fa* interval – benzene, cocaine, morphine, hyoscine – seem to have very similar properties, either of giving light, or in some cases of making man impervious to physical pain by lifting his consciousness into another realm. The first *mi-fa* interval, represented by something just heavier than water, was indeed artificially filled by the 'heavy water', invented by man as a stepping stone to the splitting of the atom and the release of atomic or more accurately, electronic energy.

All this has a strong element of 'magic' in it, a sense that the laws of the world we are considering are being suddenly abrogated in favour of those of the higher world. The action of the substances found at these intervals is in some way incomparable with the action of substances belonging to the notes between, in the same way that birth and death are incomparable with life. The light-producing property of acetylene and benzene gives us a clue to the understanding of this incommensurability.

We have called this table a table of molecular compounds, and the action of the greater part of the substances referred to is molecular, that is, on the scale and time of molecules and by the combination and interaction of molecules. But with acetylene and benzene and in a different way with the narcotics, we suddenly find the intervention of *light*. Light does not refer to molecules or matter in molecular state at all: it refers to the world of electrons and to matter in electronic state. In other words, the intervals represent the intervention of matter in a higher state, from a higher world. This is the secret of cosmic intervals on all scales. They represent the door from one world to another.

In the next chapter we shall see that the process of regeneration, which we must then consider, is exactly connected with the *legitimate forcing of such a door*.

XIII THE SIX PROCESSES IN MAN (ii)

I CORRUPTION

THE PROCESS OF CORRUPTION OR DISEASE ARISES WHEN FORM, breaking loose from its proper function, overcomes life, and reduces the whole to inertia and dead matter. The order of the creative agents in this fourth process is, *form, life, matter*.

The clearest origin of disease in the human organism lies in the failure of the process of destruction. We saw that this latter process yielded certain inert or waste matters, incapable of refinement, which were properly eliminated in one way or another. But such inert matters may also be retained in the body, where they degenerate into poisons. And in this case they give rise to an entirely new process, which in relation to human affairs was referred to as rebellion or crime.

What can correspond to crime in the human body? Surely the wrong functioning or rebellion of the various parts of the organism. And these wrong functions in turn are started by the retention of inert matters in the body.

Beginning at the lowest level, the elimination of the waste matter of food, instead of taking place at once, may be delayed so that the faeces begin to decay within the organism. This is usually caused by *an active poison from a higher function* – cellular waste which, lying in the tissues instead of being sweated out, induces spasms and tensions of the peristaltic muscles.

Here we have a very good example of the principle that active, passive and mediating, or life, matter and form, are relative terms. For in the process of disease the active agent is nearly always such waste matter of a higher function, which, although inert on its own level, has nevertheless the power of starting a train of sickness in lower functions. It is in this way that the process of corruption, unlike that of destruction, is continuous, each downward stage developing automatically out of the one above.

The above example is, of course, simply a technical description of constipation. At the next level, normal urine, retained by a higher waste matter, produces the uric acid crystals of rheumatism and similar diseases, which – as we saw at the end of the last chapter – form one of the poisons of the note *la* in our table of organic compounds. In the same way unexhaled carbon dioxide produces in the body poisons which make themselves felt as headaches, bodily sluggishness, and so on.

On the level of cellular tissue, we saw how the proper working of the process of destruction, stimulated by work and exercise, led to the casting off of waste products by perspiration. It is a matter of common experience that sweating and exercise relax physical tensions, and induce that sense of calm and tone which we associate with right activity of the parathyroids and correct balance of limb-control. Absence of sweating and consequent elimination of waste cellular matters, on the other hand, will cause all kinds of physical tensions which impede the flow of blood and proper heat production. The poison formed by the process of disease at this stage is the lactic acid deposited in the muscles in a state of tension and lethargy.

Passing to the next function, we took a certain degree of talking and outward expression to be the legitimate excretion of mental activity. To remain healthy on this level, a man must speak and act as he thinks. He must be sincere. Pathologically, however, the waste matter of thought remains unexcreted, unexpressed, and turns in his mind, giving rise to morbid imaginings, fixed ideas, and recurring thoughts and dreams from which he can not escape. These are, quite literally, mental poisons, of a quite definite level of density, which in time and in quantity, can make terrible inroads on the whole physical and moral well-being of a man.

In the sympathetic nervous function, where the process of elimination yielded tears, laughter, singing or other outward physico-emotional expression, the process of disease will corrupt these waste matters into baseless fears and regrets, negative daydreams and so on. These wrong functions, also poisonous on their own level, are noticeable by the unpleasant and suspicious cast which they give to thought. For it is exactly in this way that the poisons of the higher function intrude as active force into the functions below, which in turn become infected.

Finally, in regard to the sex and emotional function, where waste was represented by the deepest and subtlest forms of human expression, the retention of this matter in the body and its pathological corruption will give rise to sexual imagining in its most feverish form, and to the whole range of violent, morbid, despairing and criminal emotions. What, however, could serve as activating agent at this stage, since it must be a poison arising from a function higher than those normal to man? Trying to answer this question, we find ourselves face to face with the devil.

From all the above, the processes of destruction and crime, or elimination and disease, begin to appear as in some sense alternatives – the one natural and healthy, the other abnormal and degenerative.

But whereas destruction, in normal cases, limits itself to the proper

THE SIX PROCESSES IN MAN (II)

elimination of waste matters proportional to those refined by digestion, the corruptive process suffers no such limitation. We have noted how in this process inert matters on a higher level serve as infectors or poisoners of inert matters on a lower level; and conversely how inert matters on a lower level serve as passive material for the infection of those above. As we can soon see by observation, physical tensions lead to morbid thoughts, which lead to groundless fears and apprehensions, which lead in turn to violent or self-destructive emotions. And similarly in reverse. The process of disease has the particular characteristic of 'spreading' or infecting all the raw material, both higher and lower, with which it comes in contact and which it immediately corrupts.

It has indeed the power of working backwards and consuming, if not restrained, endless supplies of good material, which may even represent the result of very long work and accumulation. In the molecular realm we have an analogy in the curdling, from one spoon of sour milk, of a whole jug of sweet, or the degeneration, through careless exposure, of wine to vinegar. While in the cellular world we have the almost unarrestable pro-liferation of cancer cells at the expense of healthy tissue.

To understand the corruptive process, we have to understand the idea of *poison* in a much wider sense than we are accustomed. There are physical poisons, intellectual poisons, emotional poisons. There are poisonous drugs, poisonous insects and poisonous men. One may suffer from a poisoned finger, a poisoned mind or a poisoned society. And in every case the nature of the poison is that it *undermines the unity of the organism*, cuts off the part from the life-flow of the whole and leaves it to fester helplessly on its own.

There is much talk today about bacteria as agents of disease. But almost all kinds of bacteria exist everywhere. The healthy body, with its own strong magnetic field, has a natural immunity to inimical micro-organisms. They can take no hold on it, *unless its vitality and unity are already undermined by inner poisons*. Once corruption sets in, bacteria certainly help to break up and dispose of an ill organism, just as worms help to break up and dispose of a corpse. They are the demolition men of nature, whose function is to get unsafe structures out of the way as quickly as possible. The really healthy body is in little more danger from an attack by them, than it is from an attack by maggots.

In the world of men the process of corruption appears as crime. And its understanding provides a test by which different social conceptions of crime may be objectively judged.

Real crime will be that in which knowledge, skill, understanding or forethought (*form*) are used to destroy higher possibilities (*life*), leaving the situation of the victim at a lower level than before (*matter*). By this criterion society is right in regarding murder – in which man takes *thought* to deprive another of *life*, leaving only the inert *matter* of his corpse, as the classical crime. Intentional stealing, by which the victim is stripped of goods, savings, or possibilities, is also crime. But so too is wilful lying which leaves a situation corrupted, and others – previously open-hearted – now full of malice, suspicion, envy or distrust.

Sometimes it is objected that stealing depends on the nature of our society, that if there were ample goods freely distributed there would be no stealing. This argument misses the chief characteristic of stealing, which is an attempt to get something for nothing. Since it is a universal law that nothing can be had for nothing, that everything must sooner or later be paid for in one way or another, such an attempt must always be at someone else's expense. In this sense robbery of money or goods, plagiarism of ideas, even the stealing of souls, are all of the same nature. Whether it takes place in a back-street or in paradise, *stealing is not innocent*.

On the other hand we see that failure to obey some quite arbitrary restriction, or failure to possess some document or obligatory piece of paper, when no one else is harmed thereby, can in no way be said to belong to the cosmic process of crime.

In this way, much that society regards as criminal is not really criminal at all, but at worst inadvisable or merely foolish. While on the other hand many things which society itself supports and justifies as 'patriotism', 'loyalty', 'freedom', 'duty', 'responsibility' and so on, may contain a strong criminal tendency. To what other process, for example, can belong propaganda, which – ingeniously using the skill of the artist, the experience of the psychologist, and the technique of the scientist – endeavours to put to sleep or destroy natural living judgment and replace it with a single standardised attitude, temporarily expedient from the point of view of a single policy, a single government or a single advertiser? In the modern world, the deliberate and often official killing of individual judgment and conscience constitutes crime on such a large scale that it becomes invisible, and men can not even imagine living under any other conditions.

For in this way, the chief possibility of all – that of conscious development – may be destroyed for thousands and even millions of people. Such people, who no longer possess individual judgment, individual conscience, individual remorse, or the power of reacting as living individuals to the circumstances and demands of life, may continue to the end of their days to serve as efficient and obedient citizens. But their essence has died. They are the walking dead, the zombies, of our modern civilization. And like other murdered corpses they are the product of the process of crime, both their own and others'.

At the same time, there seems to be some cosmic requirement that large-scale criminality shall declare its intentions openly at the outset. Hitler published 'Mein Kampf' many years before he began to be dangerous. "You can no more expect sincere diplomacy than wooden iron or dry water," said Stalin in his early days. The King of the Dovre Mountains gives Ibsen's Peer fair warning – "And so, my son, I must do what I can to cure your peculiar human traits." "I don't create evil," begins Ouspensky's Well-Meaning Devil, "I just collect it in an amateur way."[60]

Certainly these declarations may be put in such a winning manner that their significance is missed, and later they may be covered up by ingenious lying to prove that the devil has mended his ways. But at bottom, it is human sleep and sleep only – *the wish not to see things as they are* – which makes men ignore the clear warnings of corruption before its work begins. A man who is fully awake will not be so deceived, and he will take his own precautions accordingly.

Thus while the process of destruction results in the separation of the inert from the living, and the consequent preservation of the latter; the process of corruption on the contrary results in the reduction of the living itself to inertia and to death.

II HEALING

If the process of corruption had no check, then by the very contagion of its nature, the universe would be doomed. But we know that the sick do sometimes recover, that epidemics abate, that deserts reseed themselves, and that even wars come to an end. There is a healing process, in which the sick matter, rediscovering the original form of nature, again becomes a channel for life; and is restored to health. Its order: *matter, form, life*.

Implied here is the rediscovery of an original principle, and its adaptation to the new or abnormal circumstance. For example, certain poisonous matters begin to accumulate in the fleshy layers of the body. After a time the condition becomes too acute to be relieved by the normal methods of excretion. The white corpuscles of the blood, however, are perfectly en-

60. "The Well-Meaning Devil", short story by P. D. Ouspensky, unpublished in English.

dowed with the power and duty of eliminating poisons. Surrounding and isolating the poison with pus, they *invent* a form of excretion. A boil develops, comes to head, and bursts. The poisons are expelled, and if the condition is not too general, the tissue heals.

There are in the body healing agents of all kinds. But in some cases their work can be helped by the assistance of drugs and medicines of a similar nature – exactly those healing matters which in the last chapter we found associated with the note *mi*. These are matters containing in concentrated essence that natural principle, which is necessary to correct the abnormality and restore the healthy form. In the case of the boil, the doctor applies certain salts which contain the natural tendency to draw out or suck the poisons from the flesh. He utilizes the same principle on a molecular level by applying heat in the form of a hot compress. In other words, he remembers and uses natural laws, to *invent* a way of returning the organism to a form through which life and blood can again flow freely.

Already in this example we see the process of healing working on two levels. First, there is the natural physiological healing in the body itself. Secondly, this process is supported by human ingenuity, expressed in the art of medicine. The two processes are the same: the scale and medium of their operation is different. In the first case we see the process operating in the cellular world, in the second in the world of man. In the first it appears to us as healing proper, in the second as invention, skill, or applied science, that is, the intentional use of natural laws.

Healing, fundamentally, is that which restores to health things touched by the corruptive or criminal process. We saw how this latter process sours milk, turns wine to vinegar, and infects the blood with sepsis. In the case of free products so corrupted, man can either abandon them, like rotten food, or turn them to other but lower uses. When corruption begins to degenerate the matters of his own body, however, he can not remain so indifferent, and must strive to stop the rot and make them whole again. Vinegar can be used for its very 'sourness'; but blood-poisoning must be healed, or the man himself will succumb. Thus medicine is born.

In the Middle Ages a very elaborate and interesting system of medicine was developed on the basis of classifying organs and organisms according to the four 'humours' – hot, cold, wet and dry – and after diagnosing an excess of one or deficiency of another, trying to restore the balance by supplying the opposite 'humour' through treatments and medicaments classified in a similar way. The method of healing by balancing the four humours is still used, for example, in applying *cold* compresses to a *hot* fever, or in prescribing a *dry* climate for a *moist* condition like tuberculosis. And if this system as a whole is now discredited, it is not because it was mistaken or superstitious in itself, but only because the underlying principle has since been lost, and a completely different system of medicine constructed on another basis.

Old medicine was almost entirely based on treating the body as a whole, or on treating individual organs. Besides being studied from the point of view of the humours, these organs were classified according to their affinity with the planets, and herbal medicines – classified in the same way – used to stimulate the response to one or other planetary influence. Again, the principle used in healing was the restoration of harmony – *in the world of organs*.

It was the study of the cellular structure of plants and animals in the 1830's, the discovery of the dance of 'active molecules' by Brown about the same time, and the subsequent synthesis of organic compounds, which really led to the overthrow of mediaeval medicine. For with this knowledge came the possibility of a medicine which should restore harmony not only in the world of organs, but in the world of cells and even of molecules. Such treatment applied directly to lower cosmoses, and *utilizing the times of those cosmoses*, could of course yield results very much faster than the old-fashioned treatment of organs. And its speed and exactness seemed literally miraculous in comparison, as intervention of the laws of another cosmos must always seem miraculous from the point of view of our own.

Study of the life of cells brought to light the role of bacteria, the accomplices of corruption on a cellular level. And very much of the enormous progress of medicine under Pasteur and Lister in the second half of the nineteenth century was based on asepsis or antisepsis, that is, the elimination or destruction of these agents of disease *in the cellular world*.

Later, with the work of Ehrlich, who combined germicides with dyes which were known to stain only specific tissues, chemists began to work in a still smaller, a still faster world. Ehrlich created nearly a thousand different molecular combinations in an attempt to produce chemical messengers which, introduced into the body, would perform one specific task, *in the molecular world*.

This technique led to the discovery of the various 'sulpha' drugs, with their amazing power of penetration and speed of action. Acting thus directly to restore balance in the world of molecules modern doctors can, in some cases, effect cures in the course of hours, which old-fashioned medicine working in the world of organs, might take weeks or even months to achieve. From the point of view of speed and accuracy, this is an immense improvement.

What has not yet been taken into account, however, is the fact that by working directly in the world of molecules, modern medicine often bypasses and undermines the *intelligence of organs*. Fundamentally, old medicine recognized that each organ has its own intelligence, capable – with help – of diagnosing its own malady and producing its own antidote. These intelligences of different organs are in fact linked together in a general intelligence for the whole instinctive function, which, if trusted and not thwarted, can save the human organism from almost any ill which may befall it.

Modern medicine, working on a molecular level, for the most part ignores this instinctive intelligence altogether, and by going below it, so to speak, often undermines its authority and power. It is as if a patient, instead of entrusting himself to the responsibility of a large hospital, with its wise director and many subservient specialists and departments, went straight to the research laboratory and persuaded the assistant there to prescribe his latest drug. Although an occasional cure might prove startling, such a practice would soon make the healing work of the hospital as a whole completely impossible. In the same way, over-indulgence in molecular drugs working with startling power and speed, may undermine the organism's power of self-healing and recuperation in the future.

At the same time, it is quite clear that medicine can not go back on its own discoveries, can not retreat from the world of molecules into which its healing has now penetrated. In fact, there is only one way out. For healing to be complete, that is, for it to achieve the real benefit of the whole man, rather than the killing of a particular germ or the stimulation of a particular hormone, the patient must himself make acquaintance with the intelligence of his own instinctive function. He must first listen within himself for its voice, and when he recognizes and distinguishes this voice, he must trust in its wishes and obey its commands. If he does this, the process of healing will begin in him on a scale which may in time make the intervention of external medicine unnecessary altogether.

In fact, the possibility exists that he may acquire the power of acting directly on instinctive intelligence with the mind; that is, he may place in the cellular organ an exact electronic image of health to which it must inevitably conform. This possibility lies behind true faith-healing, the methods of Christian Science and so on. The problem is that it requires very great mental control, a completely positive attitude, and the knack of communicating with the organs in their own language. Moreover, it is often simulated by a kind of self-hypnosis, when the process of disease continues as before, but the patient persuades himself that he feels no symptoms. This is exactly putting instinctive intelligence to sleep.

It is instinctive intelligence, indeed, which provides the link between physiological healing and intellectual invention – those two main aspects of the process which we are studying. For above the level of cells and organs, what is invented by man's mind, and what is invented by his other functions, working through the instinctive intelligence, becomes increasingly mingled. We may even suppose that all the inventions of man's mind are the result of some subtle realization of the natural principles, laws or devices which are all the time operating in the mechanics of his skeletal movements, the chemistry of his digestion, the electric phenomena of his nervous system, and so on.

Suppose, for example, a woman has a very intricate piece of knitting to do. If she is skilled, something in her motor centre very quickly discovers a way of manipulating the multiple levers of the hands and combining them with extraordinary ingenuity and subtlety to produce the desired result. Later some keen observer may invent a machine which imitates the movements that her motor centre has already invented. By multiplying this machine or driving it at high speed he may even produce far more knitting per hour than the woman's single pair of hands could do. But in essence the inventor has only *rediscovered* a device which already exists in nature. In this way the crane is a rediscovery of the principle of the arm, the camera a rediscovery of the principle of the eye, and a telephone-exchange a rediscovery of the principle of the cerebral cortex. In order to achieve a desired end, *matter* is arranged in a special *form*, in which the appropriate natural law (*life*) can operate through it.

The aberrations of human ingenuity, however, should never make us overlook the fact that the true end-product of this process is indeed *life* – increased vitality, power, opportunity and so on. This is most clear in physiological and even psychological healing, where this process really means the correction of an abnormality, that is, it counters a tendency or secretion which has exceeded its function, or stimulates one which is deficient. Thus the goal of the healing process is to produce a *normal* or harmonious organism, for it is only in such an organism that life flows most abundantly.

Exactly the same process and the same agents in the body reorganize matter in a form to preserve life in changed circumstances. By it, the human organism miraculously adapts itself to extreme heat, extreme cold, long fasting or lack of sleep. By it the blind man begins to 'see' with the skin of his face, the deaf man to 'hear' with the bone of his skull.

This is the process by which errors and disasters can be repaired, a damaged organ return to health, and man approach normality by right understanding of natural law.

III REGENERATION

We are left with one final process as yet unconsidered. This refers to the order: *form, matter, life*. That which, on the cosmic level, we characterized as form organizing matter in imitation of the life principle; the creature emulating the creator.

Such process we called regeneration. The word implies a re-engendering, a re-creation. It implies that something was first created naturally, and is now to be re-created a second time by will, intention and purpose. It implies *a second birth*.

Among simple organisms we can see frequent examples of this process at work. A worm which has been cut in half does not simply heal, as a man whose leg has been amputated may heal, if he is lucky. The worm *regenerates* itself; that is, it grows a completely new half, complete with all the organs and functions which the lost half contained. Even the smallest morsel of some sea-worms contains this power of regenerating the whole organism. The very form, in some mysterious way, re-creates itself.

In the same way the lizard can regenerate its tail, the lobster its claw, and the human organism its skin and to a certain extent its liver. But for the higher human organs, the process does not work in this way. No man can grow a new head if it is cut off, nor even a new hand. If we want to find the significance of the process of regeneration for man, we must look at it differently – from the point of view of inner or psychological regeneration. Man has the possibility of re-creating himself, or more correctly, the human being has the possibility of making itself into a man. As we saw earlier, what distinguishes man from animals is his possibility of becoming conscious of his own existence and of his place in the universe. Only a being who is so conscious can be truly called a man. Thus regeneration, for a human being, is to re-create himself as a conscious man.

How can such a process work? The order of the process of regeneration is that *form* organizes *matter* in imitation of *life*. Man himself is this form: in this process everything depends upon his initiative, his will, his persistence. For this reason, this process does not happen by itself. It is, as it were, a freak of being, of which only very few men are capable and then only in connection with a certain very definite aim and concerted efforts.

What is the *matter* with which man works to recreate himself? In order to understand this more clearly we had better study one function at a time. When we came to man's mental activity, we were clearly able to distinguish the registration, storage and ordered comparison of perceptions, from idly turning thoughts and pointless imaginings. The latter we called excreta of the mind. Every man's mind turns out an endless stream of such mental waste, which in the ordinary way passes entirely unrecognized. But by the process of regeneration the *form* or function works on its own waste matter. This means that the 'fresh' part of the mind, the power of registration, observes its own end-product, that is, the wandering stream of associative thought which is its excretion. The mind is, as it were, divided into two, one part watching the other part.

Anyone who has consistently tried this experiment will bear witness to its extreme difficulty, and the great effort of sustained attention which is necessary to hold it even for a minute. They will also find it quite impossible if the excretion of the mind, that is, the ordinary associative flow, has become poisoned by the process of corruption and taken on a morbid, bitter, violent or resentful cast. At this stage the matter of the mind passes temporarily beyond the possibility of regeneration altogether. If, however, the effort can be successfully sustained, a very surprising energy is generated, and man has already taken the first step towards self-knowledge.

A further application of this process to the mental function lies in *intentional* imagination. This is quite different from *mechanical* imagination which, we saw, may be regarded as a natural excretion of the brain. In this case, the registering part of the mind organises the flow of images into a certain channel, and controls their nature with a particular end in view. For example, a man deliberately imagines how it would be if his body were as big as a house. Images are summoned from memory of scenes and people seen from above, of superhuman forces at work uprooting trees and smoothing hills, of giants on the one hand and dolls on the other: all these combining with actual sensations of his own body and its powers may, with attention, produce an extraordinarily vivid sensation of what it would be like to be as big as a house. Such purposeful imagination or 'faith' is an essential factor in the reconstruction of oneself.

When images and memories from several functions, fused together by such intentional 'imagination', find expression through some manual or mental skill, *art* results. Such art at its best is a planned recreation or reconstruction of the artist's experience of the world. It involves the regeneration of past experience. And it shares the nature of this general process.

Passing to the functions of movement and sensation, the same possibility again expresses itself in a division. The higher part of the sensational function knowingly registers the physico-emotional 'weather' of the organism. One has the sensation of one's movements, the sensation of one's sensations, physical awareness of the body and of more or fewer of the processes passing in it. This is the 'feeling of oneself', of one's physical existence in certain surroundings at a certain time, which, if seriously cultivated, observably produces a very strong and valuable emotion.

But again, except in rare and accidental moments, it requires the greatest possible attention to maintain the 'separation' between the registering sensation and the manifold feelings and impulses registered, which all the time tend to rush together into one vague and unobserved sensation of 'I'.

From these two examples, we can come to an understanding of the idea of attention, in relation to the possibility of different processes *within each function*. When attention is deliberately sustained at its most intense, as when the power of mental registration or of physical sensation is being deliberately focussed – we may hope that the process of regeneration is at work. When attention is attracted, that is, when the waste products of thought or of sensations are being 'drawn out' into uncontrolled talk, action or other automatic forms of expression, we may say that the process of elimination is at work. And finally, when there is no attention or distracted attention, that is, when these waste matters are not drawn out but degenerate within the organism into irritations, morbid imaginings and passionate hates or fears, then we may suppose that it is the corruptive process which is in question. Thus sustained, attracted and distracted attention are in one aspect the psychological keys to the process of regeneration, elimination and corruption respectively.

We now come to the last and most difficult stage of this process: that which refers to the sexual-emotional function. From the analogy of the two previous examples, we see that this must imply a higher or 'pure' emotion observing or working upon lower emotional 'waste'. The latter will be the ordinary flow of emotional desires, longings, attractions and repulsions of a more feverish kind. What is the 'pure' emotion which could observe or struggle with this torrent, despite its speed and force? Only, it would seem, some overpowering emotional aim, some constant and intense aspiration towards God or consciousness, or on the other hand some per-

manent revulsion from man's ordinary level and intense fear of its consequences. It is very clear that such an aim must be *permanent* for the process
of regeneration to work, since owing to the great speed of ordinary emotional reactions, anything which is not permanently present will not have
time to catch and wrestle with them. It will always be too late, or like them,
too fleeting to produce a sufficiently deep and lasting impression.

Should a permanent emotional aim become created, however, there becomes possible an intense struggle between the constructive and destructive
sides of man. This inner division – which may be felt as conscience –
produces *friction*. And inner friction is precisely that by which consciousness may be generated, just as physical friction is that by which heat and
light may be generated. Thus the process of regeneration always begins by
a division, a separation.

The more a man separates his aim from the habits and failings of his body
and personality, and the more he forces the latter, however unwillingly,
to serve that aim, the more intensely will he become conscious of himself.
Gradually, his most hidden weaknesses, self-indulgences, excuses, and on
the other hand his longings, capacities and aspirations will be drawn into
the light of consciousness; just as in the regeneration of heavenly bodies,
more and more of their hard hidden interior must be converted into an
atmospheric envelope capable of being irradiated and vitalised by the Sun.

In fact, the process of regeneration exactly implies the transmutation
of matter from opacity to radiance. This transformation involves two stages.
Physically, an opaque body must first become translucent, that is, it must
acquire the capacity of being penetrated by the light of another body.
Only after a long period in this state can the possibility of radiance, or of
shining with its own light, arise. In the same way, a man wishing to develop must first become translucent, that is, he must expose all sides of himself without reserve to the penetration of another man's consciousness, that
of his teacher. He must lose his solidity, become invisible and unrecognised,
be seen only by another's light. This very exposure and penetration may
then prove the means enabling him to know himself and in the end to
acquire permanent consciousness of his own.

These three stages – opacity, translucence, radiance – correspond to the
three states of matter, mineral or cellular, molecular and electronic, of which
we have spoken before. In the planetary world, the second stage is connected with the development of atmosphere, and the third with the generation
of light. In man, the second stage is connected with the development of a
new *molecular* body, capable of assimilating the consciousness of another,

and the third with the creation of a further *electronic* body, capable of generating its own consciousness and embracing others within it. Elsewhere we shall speak of these potential new bodies as the *soul* and the *spirit*.

Very much can be understood about our present state of consciousness and the next potential ones, by considering the question of invisibility. For the development of these new bodies involves the creation of vehicles with which to penetrate into the invisible worlds.

As we saw in Chapter 4, there are many different kinds of invisibility for us. Things may be invisible because they are too far, like some distant star; or because they are too near, like the glands within one's brain. They may be invisible because they are too large, like the earth; or too small, like a cell. They may be invisible because they are too rarefied, like air or thought; or too dense, like the inside of a mountain. They may be invisible because they are too fast, like a flying bullet; or too slow, like the form of a civilisation.

All these different kinds of invisibility arise because in its ordinary state our consciousness only functions freely in relation to the mineral and cellular worlds. Confined to a cellular body, it is aware only of mineral or cellular *objects*.

If this consciousness could be raised to a degree of penetration where it could function equally freely in relation to the molecular world, many of these kinds of invisibility would no longer exist for it. A consciousness which had the same powers in relation to the molecular world as ours has in relation to the cellular, could actually 'perceive' molecular matter like air or emotion; could actually penetrate into the interior of dense objects, like mountains; and would enjoy such speed of movement that the whole scale of 'far' and 'near' would be completely transformed.

Above all, a consciousness at liberty in the molecular world, that is, in the next state beyond ours, would no longer be aware only of *objects*, but also of the *relation between objects*. Because in most cases the field of force representing the relation between objects is composed of matter in molecular state. It would then be aware of the *relation* between a cat and a chair, a man and a woman, its possessor and his surroundings. In comparison with this awareness of living and ever-changing relationships, the perception of separate objects would seem to refer to a dead and unbelievably dull world.

Now for practical purposes, the first step towards this penetration of consciousness into the molecular world or world of relationships, lies in the practice of divided attention. The man who begins to learn how to divide his attention deliberately between his own body and the object or person he is dealing with, that is, who is *simultaneously aware of himself and his surroundings*, does in fact begin to live in a world of relationships, in the molecular world. He has begun to be self-conscious. *He has begun to grow a soul.*

Certainly, his first efforts to accomplish this will show him very clearly the extreme difficulty of holding this state, and will prove to him beyond question that command of it is not natural to man, but has to be laboriously acquired. At the same time these same efforts will open up before him quite a new world, the world of relationships, and will demonstrate to him that this world is actually attainable by his own consciousness, *through divided attention.* Moreover, with this progress of his consciousness towards the next state, *the sphere of the invisible will diminish for him.*

About the creation of yet another body beyond the soul, that is, the spirit, we can not speak here. This is too far from us. But now we begin to understand the literal meaning of the word 'regeneration'. By this process creatures of cellular body are literally reborn, first into molecular bodies, and second into electronic bodies. Each rebirth means entry into a new world, new perceptions, a completely new relation to the universe. In fact, all the new possibilities we have hitherto touched upon – conscience, consciousness, fusing of the nervous systems, penetration into other times, awareness of other worlds, immortality – all refer to nothing else but different aspects or different stages of such *regeneration.*

XIV HUMAN PSYCHOLOGY

I PERSONALITY, ESSENCE AND SOUL

THE WHOLE OF THE RHYTHMIC SCHEME AND TIME-PATTERN DIS-cussed in the earlier chapters on man refers, of course, to normal or rather to archetypal man. It presumes the different organs all set to an equal sensitivity, so that the various planetary influences will be received and take effect in their just harmony and proportion. In fact no individual man will perfectly reflect such a harmony, for in the men we know some glands are of a supernormal and others of a subnormal sensitivity. The descriptions of endocrine or planetary types which were given were an attempt to describe the effect of a supernormal sensitivity of one gland or receiving apparatus. A perfectly harmonized man, in whom all the planetary influences were balanced, and none absent or exaggerated, can hardly be conceived except as the result of a great work of self-perfection.

Accepting the principle of varying sensitivity in the different glands or receiving apparatus, we see how all the complexities and abnormalities of human form and age can arise. Suppose Mars to emanate certain influences which stimulate the adrenal and sex functions, while Venus, influencing the parathyroids and thymus, tends to promote physical growth and hold back sexual differentiation. If the two receiving-organs are equally sensitive the planetary motions themselves ensure that the martial influence eclipses the other at the age of 15, producing puberty. But suppose the receiving-organ for martial influence to be exceptionally sensitive, and that tuned to the Venusian radiation insensitive, then the first will naturally eclipse the second much earlier, and puberty may not occur at 15 but at 13 or even 12.

Whole races indeed, are no doubt structurally more attuned to one planet than others, and thus have their own 'normality' of time, deviating more or less from the prescribed 'normality' for humanity. Further, such people or races will be most acutely aware of the rhythm of 'their' planet, and will find it difficult to understand manifestations arising from other people's awareness of quite different rhythms.

Further light is shed on the problem by certain pathological cases, such for example as those in which a tumour on the pineal gland produces premature senility, a boy of eight acquiring the wizened appearance of an old man of eighty.

In the cases mentioned above we considered the effect of the various glands 'set' at differing degrees of sensitivity. Here on the other hand, we seem to see the gland itself, owing to pathological stimulus, increase fantastically in receptivity. Imagine a radio-set of fixed sensitivity tuned to a single wave-length; its volume will vary with the output and distance of the transmitting station. This is the normal case. But suppose the radio-set to become suddenly more responsive; it will begin to 'blare' and drown out the other sets in the neighbourhood, though the power of the transmitting station remain constant or even diminish. If the pineal gland is sensitive to the influence of a certain planet, which, working in its long slow cycle, controls the gradual aging of the human organism, then a sudden abnormal stimulus to this gland may make it unnaturally responsive to this aging influence until the latter, by sheer volume, drowns out all moderating influences from elsewhere.

In their extreme forms these two kinds of aberration – a pathological responsiveness or unresponsiveness of some gland, and a pathological variation in its working – account for all the congenital and organic abnormalities which we may meet. In these cases the very mechanism of the man is badly damaged, perhaps beyond repair. And it can not be avoided that all the psychic life arising from such a mechanism will also be warped and unbalanced.

There is, however, a different kind of abnormality, very much more common, which is found in more or less healthy mechanisms. This abnormality, which gives rise to the whole gamut of human psychiatry and to a very large proportion of the thoughts and feelings of all ordinary people, must now be dealt with.

Earlier on we came to the conclusion that the proportion of the different endocrine secretions borne in suspension in the blood at any moment make a man what he then is. His state is the resultant of all the impulses which these energies separately dictate. Impulses to study, to seek company, to restless movement, to make love, mixing in him in different intensities, produce the colour and mood of the present. This is what is called his psychology.

But let us go further, and try to imagine as a single entity a man's bloodstream throughout his whole life, all the blood that has passed through him from conception to death. Blood begins to flow through him at the very moment when the impregnated ovum attaches itself to the maternal uterus: it does not cease to do so until his heart stops beating. This 'long' bloodstream is a web joining every part of the circle of his life which we drew out in Chapter 11. In every moment, the composition of the blood-stream dictates his mood; the totality of his life-blood, bearing the final sum of the influences that have contributed to his being, *is* the man. It represents his true nature, what he objectively is, his essence.

The trouble is that no one knows what this sum is. No one knows himself objectively. No one can analyse the higher chemistry of his blood and honestly assess himself accordingly. This would already be a tremendous achievement: and the man who knew his essence would be at an enormous advantage in the world.

In fact, what a man thinks about himself and his possibilities has very little to do with his actual physical chemistry. The man who by his natural structure and capacities would be a good and successful labourer feels that he is an unrecognized poet, even though he has never written a line of poetry. The born poet, on the other hand, feels that he would be really happy on a farm, though he has never spent more than a week-end out of the city. The studious bookworm sees himself as a potential Casanova, and so on. These are their dreams, and they see everything that happens to them and everybody they meet, partly in the light of their own essential nature, and partly through their dreams.

In order to support these dreams they have to take up a certain invented attitude to everything, different from that dictated by their blood, their essence, what they actually are. This invented attitude is taken by other people as their personality, and may even be much admired and sought after.

This, however, brings us to the idea of personality in a right and useful sense, from the latin 'persona', a player's mask, that through which the actor speaks. Right personality stands between the essence of man and the outside world. It is his psychological 'skin', his protection from life and means of adjusting to it. It includes all that he has learned about orientating his organism among his surroundings, the way he has learned to speak, think, walk, behave and so on, all his acquired habits and idiosyncracies. Only in ordinary man this adaptation to life, this savoir faire which enables him to protect his inner life from unnecessary shocks and distractions, is so inextricably mixed with pretence and invented attitudes, that the two are quite inseparable. We have to take them as one phenomenon, as personality, which even at its best is something unreal, without material substance.

If we think of the circle of man's life as a sphere, his essence is as it were the physical nature of the interior of the sphere, its consistency, density, chemical composition and so on. His personality then is something imaginary, which does not exist *in* the sphere at all. It has no thickness and no dimension. It comes solely from outside. It is like light from the surrounding world reflected off the sphere's surface. We can even say that it is reflected only from one half of his life, one hemisphere, for before the age of two or three a child has no imagination about himself, no pretence, and is in fact nothing but essence.

We can gain further understanding of the nature of personality, when we realize that this light which he reflects is exactly *what he does not absorb.* What is most obvious about a man is what he rejects and the particular manner in which he rejects it. He is recognised by what he does not yet understand, by that which separates him from the rest. This is his personality. When he really understands and absorbs something, it enters into him and becomes part of his essence. It is then no longer apparent to others as his personality – *it is he, and he is it.* The separateness characteristic of personality has disappeared.

The same idea can be put in a different way. A man takes in food. But a long digestive process goes on before this food is sufficiently refined to enter his bloodstream and thus become inseparably absorbed into his organism. Until this happens the food is not part of him; he may even be sick and lose it altogether.

Similarly a man takes in experience. But a long digestive process goes on before this experience is understood and mastered to the point where it actually modifies his physical essence. This digestion of experience takes place in and through personality. And like food in process of digestion, experience or understanding which is only in personality may at any time be lost. Only when, by insistence and repetition, has it entered into essence does it become inalienably his. *Personality is the organ of digestion for experience.*

Now the fundamental abnormality or madness of men lies in the divergence between essence and personality. The more nearly a man knows himself for what he is, the nearer he approaches wisdom. The more his imagination about himself diverges from what he actually is, the madder he becomes. In the earlier part of this chapter we studied organic abnormalities. At that time we spoke, as it were, of sick donkeys and sick horses. Now we are considering the problem of perfectly healthy donkeys who think themselves horses, and perfectly healthy horses who think themselves donkeys. This is the subject of modern psychology.

There is, however, one possibility of healing this delusion. This is the potentiality which exists in man, of becoming conscious of his own existence and of his relation to the surrounding universe. For in the moment in which he is conscious of his existence, he knows *what he is* and *what he is not* – that is, he knows the difference between his essence and personality. In the same moment he also knows *what is in him and what is outside of him* – that is, he knows himself and his relation to the world.

Self-remembering, and self-remembering only, thus enables a man to shed the outer skin of personality, and to feel and act freely from his essence, that is, *to be himself*. In this way he may separate himself from the pretences and imitations which have enslaved him since childhood, and return to what he actually is, return to his own essential nature. Such return to essence is accompanied by a sense of freedom and liberation, unlike any other, and which may exactly supply the motive force required to attempt the quite new tasks which the freed man now sees to be necessary.

This famous theme of Ibsen's 'Peer Gynt' – "Man, to thyself be true" – is indeed the first and obligatory commandment on the way of consciousness and self-development. For unless a man first finds *himself*, finds his own essential nature and destiny, and begins from them, all his efforts and achievements will be built only on the sand of personality, and at the first serious shock the whole structure will crumble, perhaps destroying him in its fall.

In a man who is still developing, personality is the servant of essence. As soon as essence becomes the servant of personality, that is, as soon as a man's natural strength and skill is made to serve *his false picture of himself*, inner growth ceases and in due course essence withers and becomes incapable of further growth. The only way in which this withering can be arrested and life restored to essence is by self-remembering, that is, by the deliberate cultivation of self-knowledge and self-consciousness.

What does this imply?

In the chapter on the functions of the different glands, we saw that they were connected and unified not only by the bloodstream, but potentially in a different way. They were connected in a different order by an unused part of the nervous system. The functioning of this new connection would bring with it the possibility of a man being aware of himself. Just as his subjective sensation of the bloodstream is a feeling of bodily warmth, so the subjective sensation of this nervous system, should it work fully, would be *self-consciousness*. This is the new function which, we hazarded, should enter into operation at the prime of life.

We said that man's *essence* is the totality of his blood-stream, all the blood which flows through him from conception to death. We can now say that man's *soul* is the totality of the moments of self-consciousness during his life, or all the superfine energy which has flowed through his unused nervous system.

But here we are in a difficulty because we have already admitted that such moments are excessively rare, a few in a year or maybe even in a lifetime. In the ordinary way a man is *not* conscious of his existence. Energy does not flow through this system at all. Further, the moments of self-consciousness which a man may experience in circumstances of great stress, great joy, pain, suffering, endurance or hardship, are in fact but moments, and are gone as soon as they come. So that even if we do add them up, they come to nothing, just as a score of points still have no measurable dimension.

What then has happened to man's soul? We have no choice but to admit that *ordinary man has not yet found a soul. It has to be created.*

Psychology, by derivation, is the knowledge or wisdom of the soul. But if man has no soul, then nothing which today passes for psychology is psychology at all. Everything which goes by this name is really psychiatry, that is, the study of the illness of the soul or the conditions of the soul's absence. True psychology is therefore the study of what does not yet exist; it is the study of the art of creating a soul.

We have spoken of essence, personality and soul. It is now possible to think of the relation of these different parts of man. The 'world' of an individual man finds itself surrounded by other worlds of similar scale, permeated by the smaller worlds of cells and molecules, and included within the greater worlds of Nature, the Earth, the Solar System, and so on. From these other worlds he receives nourishment in the form of food, air and perceptions of all kinds. We have already seen how the different periods of life, with their different media and different dominating functions, utilize nourishment which specially caters for one aspect of man or another. This referred especially to different aspects of his physical organism. Now the question arises of the growth of other parts of man than his body, that is, of his essence and his soul.

We just now said that when man really absorbs something and understands it, it enters into him and becomes part of him. Certainly a man may acquire a taste for brutal or perverse impressions which, gradually penetrating essence, may in due course corrupt it. On the other hand, perceptions of greater worlds, greater forces, higher ideals, higher possibilities, or conversely terrible and painful perceptions, *taken in a certain way*, will nourish and enrich essence. If such perceptions constantly penetrate into a man and are digested by him, essence begins to grow.

At the same time, each type of essence must be fed in its own way.

For the different physical types which we outlined in Chapter 10 were exactly *types of essence*. What is true food for saturnine essence is useless for martial and vice versa. Feats of endurance which will enrich one man's essence may blunt another's, while subtleties by which this other's grows sensitive are merely enervating to the first. Thus each man must begin to feel for himself *what feeds his essence, what makes him more himself.*

Unabsorbed perceptions which do not go to feed essence will be reflected back from his surface as personality, just as the solar rays which are not absorbed by the moon are reflected back to us as its borrowed 'light'.

Further, as perceptions properly received through the bodily senses can feed essence and alter its nature; so these finer matters accumulating in essence can feed the embryo soul. These very perceptions of greater worlds and possibilities, or these perceptions of pain, suffering and great danger, deeply absorbed into his essence, can awaken in man a desire to become conscious of his existence and his relation to the universe. If this kind of nourishment is received long enough and consistently enough, it may even lead him to make direct efforts to become conscious. And these in turn, with luck and in right conditions, may in time actually bring an increasing recurrence of moments of self-consciousness and their longer duration. In this way a soul is born.

Such growth in essence and birth of a soul will imply a change of the whole being of man, an inner accumulation of energy and force. And as the reflection of perceptions as personality was found analogous to the reflected light given off by the moon, so the inner transformation of impressions to create a soul will resemble the process by which a body glows by its own light. It will be analogous to the Sun.

II   SELF-REMEMBERING, CONSCIOUSNESS, MEMORY

If self-remembering is so desirable, why is it so difficult of attainment?

To answer this we must return again in more detail to the question of attention. For the possibility of higher states of consciousness in man precisely depends upon certain fine matters produced by the body being subject to his *attention*.

The process of digestion in man consists of the progressive rarefaction of the food, air and perceptions which he takes in; and the fine matter of which we speak may be taken as the final product of this rarefaction in ordinary conditions. Unlike flesh or blood, which consist of cells, this matter may be visualised as in molecular state – that is, as in a similar state to gases or scents. It is thus extraordinary volatile, unstable and difficult to contain.

In man's case, however, it is subject to psychological control, and this psychological control is *attention*. Controlled by attention this matter becomes the potential vehicle of *self-consciousness*.

In man's ordinary state – that is, acting as a machine, when his inner processes proceed quite independently of his will or desire – this fine matter follows the laws governing all free matter in molecular state. It diffuses from him in all directions, or in the directions which 'catch his attention'. As soon as manufactured, or with very brief delay, this fine matter passes out of him in one form or another. For to contain it or accumulate it requires *will* which he does not normally possess, and produces an inner tension which can only be maintained with great self-knowledge and self-control.

This diffusing of man's finest energy from him takes many forms. It may pass from him healthily as sex energy; explode from him unhealthily as rancour or irritation; leak from him as envy or self-pity. Most commonly of all it simply diffuses from him, to create the curious psychological state of 'fascination', in which a man completely loses his identity in a conversation, a task, a friend, an enemy, a book, an object, a thought or a sensation. This 'fascination' is simply the effect of fine matter flowing out of a man in a direction determined by his type and personality, and dragging his attention with it. In extreme cases this sucking out of attention may be so complete that the man's body is left for the time being vacant of even the rudiments of psychic individuality. This fascination is the most usual of all ways of expending the fine matter of man's creative energy. It constitutes in fact man's usual state, and for this very reason is completely unrecognised and ordinarily invisible.

For the finer and more productive kinds of human work, a man learns by the use of attention to keep this 'fascination' in a certain direction. For example, a good shoemaker remains for an hour 'fascinated' by the making of a pair of shoes, a politician remains 'fascinated' by the delivery of his speech, a woman remains 'fascinated' by the letter she is writing to a friend. Without this most elementary holding of attention in one direction, no good work of any kind, even the most simple, can be produced.

There are thus three categories in this ordinary expenditure or diffusion of fine matter. The outward flow may simply drift from object to object, from sight to sound to thought, as one or another phenomenon catches the attention. Again, the outward flow may be attracted by something which exercises a strong hold on the attention – a person one is fond of, a person who irritates one, an interesting book, a grating sound, and so on. Or finally, by a simple effort of attention, the flow may be held for a certain time in one desired direction.

As we have said, these different ways in which fine matter is normally expended represent different aspects of the particular function at work – a purely automatic aspect, an emotional aspect, or an intentional aspect. Moreover, they are characteristic of three distinct processes, and give three quite different sets of results.

At the same time, they are all mechanical, and the chief characteristic of them all is that attention is only sufficient to enable the fine matter which brings awareness to attach itself to one thing at a time. This is the ordinary state of man. He can only be aware of one thing at a time. He can be aware *either* of the person to whom he is speaking, *or* of his own words; he can be aware of someone else's distress, or of a pain in his own body; he can be aware of a scene or of his own thoughts. But except on very rare occasions he is not aware simultaneously of his own words *and* the person to whom he is addressing them; of his own pain *and* someone else's; of a scene *and* his thoughts about it. Thus *all* man's awareness in his ordinary state may be classed as 'fascination'. For either becoming aware of some outside phenomenon he loses awareness of himself; or becoming aware of something in himself he loses awareness of the outside world – that is, he becomes 'fascinated' by one thing, inner or outer, to the exclusion of everything else.

Certainly, every man's experience contains instances of divided attention, and were it not so we should have no indication at all how to proceed. For example, one of the reasons for the extraordinary power which the sensations of love and sex have over men, is that in certain circumstances they bring *an intense awareness of oneself and of another at the same time*. This is a true foretaste of the next stage of consciousness. But if this sensation comes to unprepared men at all it is accidental, and beyond their control.

One of the chief things which is taught in schools of the fourth way is *intentional division of attention between oneself and the outside world*. By long practice and constant exercise of will, the fine matter of awareness is not allowed to flow uninterruptedly in one direction, but is divided, one part being retained in oneself, while the other is directed outward towards whatever one may be studying or doing. By dividing attention, the student learns to be aware of himself speaking to another, of himself standing in a certain scene, of *himself acting, feeling or thinking in relation to the outside world*.

In this way he learns to *remember himself*, by moments at first, and then with increasing frequency. And in proportion as he learns to remember himself, so his actions acquire a meaning and consistency, which were impossible to them as long as his awareness moved only from one fascination to another.

The characteristic of this second state, of self-remembering, is *divided attention*. There are several strange things about this state. First, for certain cosmic reasons, no one can attempt it or practise it until he is first told about it and it is explained to him. Second, when it is explained to him, every normal person has enough will and energy to catch a momentary glimpse of what it means. *If he wishes, he can in the moment that he hears about it, become aware of himself in his surroundings* – of himself, sitting in a chair, reading about a new idea.

But this self-remembering can not be repeated or maintained except by his conscious effort. It can not happen of itself. It can never become a habit. And the moment the idea of *self-remembering* or *divided attention* is forgotten, all efforts, no matter how sincere, degenerate once again into 'fascination', that is, into awareness of one thing at a time.

Thus it is necessary to point out that close attention put into a task, into physical awareness of one's body, into mental exercises of one sort or another, into visions or visualisations, even into deep emotions, does not of itself constitute *self-remembering*. For all this may be done with undivided attention, that is, one may become 'fascinated' by a task, by physical awareness, by a mental exercise, or by an emotion; and one will inevitably become so fascinated the moment attention ceases to be divided between an actor or observer in oneself and that which he observes or upon which he acts.

Another curious psychological trick must be mentioned in connection with the moment when a man first hears about self-remembering. If he connects it with something he has heard or read before, with some religious or philosophical or oriental term with which he is already familiar, the idea immediately disappears for him, loses its power. For it can only open new possibilities to him *as a completely new idea*. If it connects with some familiar association it means that it has entered the wrong part of his mind, where it will become pigeonholed like any other piece of knowledge. A shock has been wasted, and only with great difficulty may the man return again to the same opportunity.[61]

---

61. The extraordinary elusiveness of this new psychological state, the next open to man beyond his usual one, is very well treated in Chapter 7 of P. D. Ouspensky's 'In Search of the Miraculous', where the author describes with great accuracy his own experiments and experiences when first told about the idea of self-remembering.

When a man first hears about self-remembering, if he takes it seriously, all kinds of new possibilities immediately seem open to him. He can not understand why he never thought of it before. He feels that he has only to do this, and all his doubts, artificialities and difficulties will disappear, and all kinds of things will become possible and easy for him, which before he regarded as completely beyond his reach. His whole life will be transformed.

In this feeling he is both right and wrong. He is quite right in the belief that *if* he could remember himself all would be as different as he imagines. Only he does not at first see the enormous resistance in himself to mastering this new state. He does not realise that to achieve self-remembering as a permanent state, or even to achieve frequently recurring moments of it, he must completely reconstruct his life. For this task will require most of the fine matter that his machine can save or make, all the will and attention he can develop by the most constant exercise. He will have to struggle against and eventually give up all the psychopathic ways of burning up this fine matter, which now form such a familiar and apparently necessary part of his life – rancour, irritation, indignation, self-pity, all kinds of fears, all kinds of dreams, all the ways in which he hypnotizes himself into satisfaction with things as they are. Above all, he must *want* to remember himself, constantly and permanently, no matter how painful and uncomfortable it may be to do so, nor how unpleasant the things which he thus sees in himself and other people. For the moment he ceases to *want* to remember himself, he loses – at any rate for some time – the possibility of doing so.

Thus *self-remembering*, or the practice of *divided attention* – though the first glimpse of it may seem extraordinarily simple, easy and obvious – in reality requires a complete reconstruction of one's whole life and point of view, both towards oneself and other people. As long as one believes that one can alter oneself, or alter other people; as long as one believes that one has the power to *do*, that is, to make things other than they are, either internally or externally, the state of self-remembering seems to retreat from one the more efforts one makes to achieve it. What at first seemed just round the corner later begins to seem infinitely far off, impossible of a-chievement.

And yet many years of struggle and failure may be necessary before one comes to a curious psychological fact, which is in reality connected with a very important law indeed. This fact is that although it is extraordinarily difficult to divide one's attention into two, it is much more possible for it to be divided into three: although it is extraordinarily difficult to remember oneself and one's surroundings simultaneously, it may be much more possible to remember oneself and one's surroundings *in the presence of something else.*

As we have seen, no phenomenon is produced by two forces: every phenomenon and every real result requires three forces. The practice of self-remembering or division of attention is connected with the attempt to produce a certain phenomenon, the birth of consciousness in oneself. And when this begins to happen, attention recognises with relief and joy not two but three factors – one's own organism, the subject of experiment; the situation to which this organism is exposed in the moment; and something permanent which stands on a higher level than both and which alone can resolve the relation between the two.

What is this third factor which must be remembered? Each person must find it for himself, and his own form of it – his school, his teacher, his purpose, the principles he has learned, the Sun, some higher power in the universe, God. He must remember that himself and his situation both stand

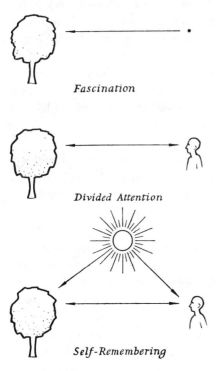

Fascination

Divided Attention

Self-Remembering

Figure 11

in the presence of higher powers, are both bathed in celestial influence. Fascinated, he is wholly absorbed in the tree he notices: with divided attention, he sees both the tree and himself looking at it: remembering, he is aware of tree, himself, and of the Sun shining impartially upon both.

We have spoken of the mineral world, the cellular world, the molecular world and the electronic world. Man's situation, his problems, surroundings, difficulties exist in the material, cellular world – this is passive force: the fine energy of consciousness directed by his attention exists in the molecular world – this is active force: and that which can resolve the eternal struggle between these two worlds can only derive from a yet higher world – the world of the Sun, the electronic world. Like sunlight which unites and inter-penetrates everything, both creating and dissolving individuality, this third factor must be such that in remembrance of it the rememberer is united to his surroundings, he both acquires and loses separate individuality.

If a man can discover such a third factor, *self-remembering* becomes possible for him, and can bring far more even than it promised in the beginning.

Self-remembering must thus always contain three principles, three things to be remembered. And if one is alone and occupied with some inner task, then it is necessary to remember *three worlds in oneself, three places in oneself.*

By this division of attention into three, the fine matter which is the bearer of man's creative force is rightly divided into three streams – one directed to right action in the outer world, one directed towards creating a connection with higher powers, and one retained in oneself. That which is retained in oneself should in course of time crystallise into a permanent vehicle of self-consciousness, that is, into a soul.

At the same time it must be remembered that wherever three forces work together, six orders and six processes are possible. Thus there may be a self-remembering for destruction, a self-remembering for healing, a self-remembering for crime. And beyond all these the only true self-remembering, self-remembering for regeneration. For this, we realise, man must place those hidden and higher powers first, himself and his soul passively at their service, invoking as result that plenitude of life and light to which alone this process yearns.

We can now come to the relation between consciousness and memory.

Ordinary memory is an impulse which travels round the circle of man's life *only in the direction of time*. It arises from a moment of greater consciousness; if there is no consciousness no memory is created. Memory is the trace of potential self-remembering.

A very exact analogy is possible here. In relation to the one-dimensional line of man's bodily life, his essence is two-dimensional; it connects all the points of the line together simultaneously, creating a surface. In relation to the surface of man's essence, soul would be a solid, three-dimensional, for it would not only connect all the different points of his life and all the surface of his essence, but it would join these to quite other possibilities and forces existing *in another dimension*. Let us imagine the circle of man's bodily life to be made of wire, the connecting surface of his essence to be a metal disc, and the potential soul to be a solid wedge, of which essence is as it were an isolated cross-section. The phenomenon of consciousness will now be exactly analogous to heat.

Our ordinary sensation of living is, as it were, a point of slight warmth passing forward round the circle. But suppose a moment of consciousness, say at the age of fifteen. At this point the wire becomes hot. Heat impulses pass along the wire in both directions from this point. But naturally to a perception passing forward along the wire from the point in question, as we are accustomed to move in time, they will always appear to come from *behind*, that is, from the past. The conduction of heat or memory backwards, that is, towards an earlier age, will be unknown to us because of our method of perception. And again, the further we get away from the moment of consciousness, the heated point, the fainter will the impulses appear. Memory, as we all know, will gradually fade.

At the same time, though memory of conscious moments does show a tendency to fade, it is important to understand that this fading does not follow from the passage of time. Our chief illusion about memory is that it decays with time, like clothes or buildings. This is not so. It decays from lack of nourishment. Memory is generated by consciousness, and it must be nourished by consciousness, that is, it must be nourished consciously.

In fact, *memory is a phenomenon not subject to the laws of time.* The man who really begins to understand this will find new worlds opening up before him, and will see practically how to enter and possess those worlds.

Let us examine first how memory is lost, and then, how it can be cultivated and brought to life.

As we have said, the most usual reason for loss of memory is simply negligence and starvation. The ordinary man in ordinary circumstances makes no effort whatsoever to keep memories alive, to feed them, recall them or pay attention to them. Unless they are so pleasant or painful that the emotion itself bites them into his consciousness, naturally they disappear. This is passive loss of memory.

But there is also an active destruction of memory. This lies in replacing memory by imagination, or more simply by lying. For example, I take a walk in the street, where I meet an acquaintance. At first the encounter may be quite clear in my mind – what I said, what he said, how he looked, and so on. But when I get home I recount the incident to my family. In doing so, I make the whole thing rather more amusing and dramatic than it actually was – I make my own remarks a little cleverer, his a little more stupid; I hint something about his habits; maybe I introduce another character, or adapt the conversation to include a joke I heard yesterday.

Afterwards I no longer remember the scene as it was, *but only as I recounted it*. Imagination and lying have destroyed memory.

And if I spend my whole life in this way, then certainly after some years it will be quite impossible for me to distinguish what has actually happened to me from what I wanted to happen, or feared would happen, or from what happened to others or what I merely read about. In this way memory is actively destroyed. The difference lies in the fact that while memory lost by negligence still lies intact, though buried, and with hard work may be recovered, memory destroyed by lying is permanently damaged, if not annihilated altogether.

Yet just as free circulation of blood throughout the body is necessary for physical health and growth, so free circulation of memory throughout the long body of man's life is necessary for health and growth of essence. Where blood-circulation fails, where organs are blocked or constricted against its flow, there disease inevitably strikes. So also in the temporal sequence of life. Those years, months, incidents or relationships which we do not wish to remember begin to fester for lack of understanding. A blockage forms, a 'complex' develops, and without our recognising what is happening, the whole present may become poisoned *by that which we will not remember*.

Several modern psychological systems have recognised this connection between free circulation of memory and psychic health. Some indeed have claimed that the flow of memory may be restored even back into the time before birth. Patients under hypnosis have seemed to describe the sensations of the embryo in the womb. And one reported by Dr. Denys Kelsey even spoke of a state before that: "It was dark, yet filled with colours of indescribable beauty; there was complete silence, yet the place was filled with heavenly music; it was still, yet everything was quivering."

Meanwhile, what has been overlooked by such systems is that loss of memory cannot be corrected by any mechanical method or treatment, but only consciously, by will and understanding.

For *imagination, self-remembering, memory* imply conscious work on the future, the present and the past respectively.

How then can memories be revivified and used? Only by reliving them intentionally and *consciously*. Suppose that I have a particular reason for wanting to recall a meeting with someone – it seems to me that I made a mistake in relation to them, or failed to take advantage of an opportunity which they offered, and it is very important to me to put this right. Carefully, *with attention*, I begin to unroll memory. I remember myself knocking on the door of the room in which they were, feeling the door-handle, entering, sitting down. I remember the position in which they were sitting, the chairs, the furniture, the pictures on the walls, how the light fell on the scene from the window. Then I remember what I said, my voice, how I felt, how the other person reacted, what they said, and so on. Gradually, *if I can hold attention*, all my different senses – of sight, sound, touch, mood – will begin to contribute their separate memories, and little by little the scene will re-enact itself within me *exactly as it was*. All at once, my mistake has re-enacted itself too. I see it quite clearly: *it has become conscious*.

Whether or not I can in the present put things right, or take the opportunity I lost, is a different question. This correction may need very much time, and may not even be possible in this life. But the chief thing is that *consciousness has been put back into the past*. I am more conscious now in relation to the incident, than I was when it actually occurred. In this way, by intentional memory, additional moments of consciousness can always be added to those which occurred naturally in the sequence of time. And to this process of making the past more conscious, there is no limit.

Now if these points of increased consciousness in the circle of life are sufficiently multiplied, we can imagine enough heat being generated to affect man's essence, and even in time the solid of his soul. Though of course the task of heating something of more dimensions from something of less – a disc from a wire, or essence from personality, for instance – must be an immense one. If further, heat were to be transferred from the surface of essence to the solid of the soul, the same disproportion would be apparent.

In fact, such a method of heating is manifestly impractical. And in the same way, the idea of creating consciousness in the soul exclusively *from below*, so to speak, runs counter to all human belief and all human experience. We have to suppose that his efforts to become conscious may sooner or later bring man into contact with a source of heat or consciousness *above*. The fount of consciousness must be looked for in a world of more dimensions.

In a practical way, indeed, it is clear that even the idea of consciousness, penetrating deeply into a man's essence, will make him search for men more conscious than himself, and for 'schools' conducted by such men. Thus his special interest will act magnetically as it were, drawing him to those in whose presence he may actually acquire more consciousness. And if it is a truly *essential* interest it will not give him rest until he finds them.

Further, if a man begins to acquire even the rudiments of a permanent principle of consciousness, or soul, it is certain that this soul, by virtue of its penetration into another dimension, could connect him with some level of the universe where cosmic creative energy is unlimited and can be drawn upon to heighten consciousness to the limit of endurance. Returning to our earlier explanation, we can suppose that the soul might connect a man directly with matter in molecular state, with the infinite world of molecular energy.

Thus in the pursuit of consciousness it must be understood, first, that *man must do everything by himself* – that is, he must penetrate to another level solely by his own efforts: and second, *he can do nothing by himself* – that is, his whole endeavour must be to contact higher sources and levels of energy. For unless he succeeds in so doing, he will get nothing and can get nothing.

In any case, it is now possible to begin to see the effect of different levels or degrees of consciousness. Moments of consciousness in the circle of bodily life, as we have seen, will produce strong memory during the remainder of life, and should theoretically also produce impulses passing *backwards* towards birth. Should, however, the effects of consciousness begin to penetrate essence, much greater changes will take place. Whereas wire cools almost instantaneously, a plate can retain heat for a very much longer time. Instead of being momentary, as it must be on the circle of bodily existence, consciousness which has penetrated into essence already has a certain duration, a certain reliability. It can not be suddenly lost. Moreover, it will radiate heat in all directions, warming the whole mesh of parallel and crossing circles which we know from the interconnection of human lives, are woven into a solid and inextricable mass. Thus the contact or presence of a man with such an essence may actually increase the awareness of those who come within his sphere of radiation or influence.

Should the inner solid become hot, however, that is, should a man have created in him a conscious soul from the accumulated material of consciousness, an enormous change will result. In the first place, a hot solid can retain heat for a very long time indeed. For such a man consciousness will have become permanent, the central fire of his being. Further, it will radiate over an enormously extended area, perhaps a hundred times greater than that warmed by the radiation of essence alone.

We thus have a basis for classifying men according to their degree of consciousness. First, there is the enormous mass of ordinary men in whom consciousness, if it exists at all, only occurs momentarily and by accident in the course of bodily life. Second, there are those for whom the idea of consciousness has penetrated into essence, and thus acquired duration and reliability. And finally, there are a small handful of men, scattered through history and across the world, who have created conscious souls for themselves; for whom self-consciousness is permanent, and who through this consciousness have the power of influencing and enlightening thousands or even millions of other men.

Finally and invisibly may exist men of conscious spirit.

The true history of humanity is the history of the influence of these conscious men.

III   THE PLAY OF HUMAN TYPES

Nine-tenths of the problems of ordinary psychology, and even more of the plots of literature, poetry, drama and legend depend upon the interplay of human types, that is, the interplay of different types of essence. Since the dawn of history, man has never failed to be fascinated by this mystery, which fills his daily life with hope, envy, fear, pain, admiration and longing, and the explanation of which forever eludes him.

All types are clearly necessary in the world, and life would obviously be poorer if not impossible, without any one of them. Yet why are some types obviously incompatible, others irresistibly drawn together? Why do some want only to be more intensely what they are, while others yearn ceaselessly to become their opposites? Why can certain types only understand each other in the presence of a third? And so on, and so on.

All this is unanswerable, unless we begin to study Mankind as a cosmos, and to regard the different types of men as its equally essential but completely different functions – each function with its own innate capacities, potentialities, weaknesses and with an affinity for a different and distinct part of the universe.

Before we do so, however, let us recapitulate what we have now established about the nature of a cosmos in general. A cosmos is a complete creature, made on a universal pattern, and containing within itself all possibilities, including those of self-consciousness and self-transformation. It consists of three parts, each of which receives a different kind of food or sustenance from without; and six main functions which digest, transform, utilise and combine these three foods, creating from them all the energy, matter and understanding of which the cosmos is capable. The six functions and the three foods together give rise to many different internal processes which develop according to the law of musical octaves, the functions standing for the full notes, and the foods entering at the recognized half-tones.

When we studied the Solar System under the aspect of such a nine-pointed circle (chapter 6, II) we saw that its six functions were manifested through the visible planets, while the half-tones were filled by some sort of 'invisible' force or influence. If we take the same circle to represent mankind we can place the different planetary types in corresponding places, and the 'foods' will be the same that nourish an individual man, namely, material food, air, and perceptions of the outside world derived from light.

At the same time, however, we must remember that each of these 'foods' must have an ordinary or unconscious aspect in which it is absorbed by ordinary unconscious man, and a conscious aspect in which it nourishes men who have achieved consciousness. 'Conscious food' is ordinarily unknown to us, but we have to suppose that it is the form in which divinity makes itself available to men and in certain cases succeeds in transforming them from their natural state. Three kinds of 'conscious food' are clearly distinguished in the New Testament under the names 'daily *bread*', 'the *breath* of life', 'the *light* of the world'. Yet it may be more correct to say that the same three kinds of food available to humanity in general *appear* unconscious to unconscious men, but are *seen* as conscious by conscious men.

What concerns us here, however, is the *inner circulation* which connects the different functions, and which in the Solar System we established as a circulation of light, or 'scale of brilliance'. We recognised the Sun as the absolute light, reflected with diminishing brilliance by the Moon, Venus, Mercury, within the Earth's orbit, and then with increasing brilliance again by Saturn, Mars, Jupiter outside the

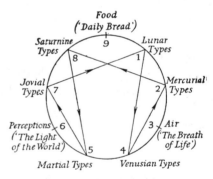

Fig. 12: The Types of Humanity

Earth's orbit. Moon, Venus, Mercury, Saturn, Mars, Jupiter represented a definite order of circulation. If we substitute planetary types for the planets themselves, there should be some similar circulation through lunar, venusian, mercurial, saturnine, martial and jovial men. And, as we saw in the last section, such free circulation would bring health, growth.

Some circulation thus connects all mankind, flows through all the types of which it is composed, *but in a definite order*. This circulation is not a temporal one; it does not develop through time, but criss-crosses time and joins all parts and ages of the life of humanity together. And it bears individual men upon its tide as the bloodstream bears with it the red corpuscles of which it is composed.

Before when we studied types, we studied them as fixed, as static and unchangeable. And studying the glands from which their characteristics derive, we saw how they must, in their static state, inevitably affect each other. We saw how lunar and martial types, like the pancreas and adrenal glands are the natural complement and antithesis of each other, and how martial and mercurial, like adrenal and thyroid, make natural rivals. As men mechanically are, all such reactions can be perfectly relied on.

As we said earlier, the first commandment on the way of development is for man to free himself from pretence and imitation, discover how he reacts, discover the nature of his type, and try to live accordingly. He must learn *to be himself*.

But the circulation of which we speak now refers to something quite different – it refers to the possibility of *movement* for men, the possibility of escape from the limitation of their type and passage to a different function of mankind.

When we think of this in practice, we realise that it does not refer to something which happens within the lifetime of a man. A saturnine boy with his long lanky bones and inner preoccupation does not change into a martial man, short, fiery and 'extrovert'. The body with which a man is born remains more or less what it was, and develops the same characteristics with which it started.

This circulation, then, must refer to some cosmic motion on the scale of all mankind, and in an individual man will appear only as a *tendency*. But this tendency, implanted in him by the cosmic circulation of mankind, will represent for him personally improvement, *the direction of development*. The obstinate lunar type must acquire the warmth and sympathy of the venusian: the lazy venusian must cultivate the quickness and agility of the mercurial: the restless mercurial must learn the breadth and wisdom of the saturnine: the introspective saturnine must achieve the courage and vigour of the martial: the destructive martial must acquire the ease and attraction of the jovial: and the intriguing jovial must relearn the cool instinctive certainty of the lunar – on a higher level.

This does not mean that some types are objectively better than others, that men of the type ahead of mine are in general more advanced than those of my type. The next type is only ahead *for me, on my personal path*. All types are equal, all are necessary, and all enjoy the same opportunity – of movement or of stagnation. What is important is not to be of this type rather than that, but to be sound of one's type, recognisant of others, and uncrystallised in any. Moreover, it is probably more correct to visualise individuals as shifting triads of three successive types with their centre of gravity in the intermediate – lunar-*venusian*-mercurial or saturnine-*martial*-jovial, for example – rather than exclusively of a single type.

In any case, if we recall that on the scale of the Solar System circulation represented a waxing and waning of brilliance, we shall see that this also has a psychological parallel which connects with what has already been said. People, like planets, are also moving, or potentially moving, either towards brilliance or towards invisibility. Everyone, reviewing his acquaintances, will feel that some should express themselves with greater vigour, should 'come out of themselves', shine, grow *more brilliant*; while others on the contrary should become quieter, less demonstrative, less flashy, *more invisible*. In the one case the motion towards brilliance is progress, in the other that towards invisibility. And our strange circulation between types, the figure 142857, shows how this is so.

How much a man unaided by the special work of schools can *actually* move along the path towards the next type is very doubtful. But his *attitude* towards other types, both those he is leaving behind and those towards which he is moving, can vary very much indeed. And this attitude serves as an index of his being, his degree of consciousness.

The most elementary, primitive type of man may feel the reactions of his type to be the only normal ones, and in this case the actions of all other types will appear fundamentally *wrong and perverse*. Or if he is weak and failing as an individual he may on the contrary feel all his own reactions to be wrong, and those of all other types more desirable. Both cases represent the completely subjective man, the man without any tendency to movement, who occupies a fixed point on the line of circulation.

A man of rather more development will notice that he has a natural sympathy for and understanding of certain types, and a natural antipathy for and lack of understanding of others. And he may even in a vague way feel in himself quite different and contradictory reactions at different times. Without knowing why, he will become tired of the qualities of his type occasionally, bored with his own reactions. And he will find sporadically breaking out in him the more mechanical manifestations of the type towards which he is moving. The venusian will develop a taste for aimless movement, the mercurial will indulge in vague speculation, the saturnine will give way to martial rages, and so on.

Such a man has already become less subjective, less fixed. His being has already begun to spread along the line, both before and behind, and he has already some dim understanding that there does exist a scheme of types, although he can not quite grasp it. But his motion, if any, is still mechanical, that is, he moves only towards the weak or facile manifestations of the next type, and he tries to escape only from the more painful or boring aspects of his own type.

The next stage of development, which is rarely reached without special aid and preparation, is that of the man who has fully understood that there exists a scheme of types, in which all are equally necessary and valuable; who has discovered his own type and that towards which he is moving; and who makes conscious efforts to abandon the one and achieve the other.

In such a man the mechanical reactions between type and type will already have become very much modified. He will *accept others as they are.* For he will begin to understand the true role of people who previously appeared to him completely useless and irritating. His attitude to himself will also be quite different. For he will see certain mechanical features of his type as something from which he has to cut himself free, that is, as something which has *to die in him.* And he will see all the highest possibilities and responsibilities of the type ahead as something which has to be intentionally created in him, as something which has *to be born.* He will thus *cease to accept himself as he is.* For he will have engaged in a ceaseless double task, killing the old and generating the new in himself. The former will be extremely painful, the latter immensely arduous. But he will understand that this pain and this effort is exactly what can generate the force *to make him move.*

Such a man has already a certain perception of all parts of the line, and quite new possibilities will begin to open for him, through the fact of his *consciously moving with the cosmic current.* Moreover, cutting himself free from the weak side of his receding type, he will find that he is nevertheless enabled to take with him in essence all the experience and understanding he has gained from it. In moving, he loses nothing but his limitation. The progress of such a man towards a comprehension of the whole thus becomes enormously accelerated. And he may, with luck and help, even in a single lifetime pass through the tasks and accumulate the experience of several different types. His movement is a gathering of experience for the expansion of consciousness.

In the final stage of this movement, from jovial back to lunar type – but now on a higher level – an especially interesting possibility arises. For, as we saw in the chapter on the circulation of light in the Solar System, the Moon's place or point one is also occupied in the next or invisible octave by the planet Neptune. Thus we may perhaps say that true movement for jovial type is not back to lunar but on to a seventh and as yet potential *neptunian* type. If we think of the affinity between Neptune and the pineal gland, and through this with the process of regeneration in general, we shall understand that neptunian type could only mean a quite new kind of man, in whom strivings towards consciousness had borne physical fruit and had actually remoulded his body in accordance with new powers and the effects of their use.

The movement 142857 is in fact the path towards consciousness, towards the creation of a soul. For a soul is precisely that which unites all types, reconciles them, and gives understanding both of the parts and of the whole. At this point of becoming conscious of himself, a man begins to absorb the three foods in their conscious rather than their unconscious aspect. And in doing so, he sees the higher plan behind their consciousness, and begins to participate in it.

We spoke of the motion towards brilliance and the motion towards invisibility. As we see from the figure of circulation, a man who begins to move consciously is drawn at an ever-accelerating pace towards one of these two extremes, and towards the point where both extremes join. The man who is moving consciously towards invisibility is the man who, having abandoned his old self, withdraws more and more from the world, retreats deeper and deeper into his inner understanding, and who learns to achieve, act and accomplish invisibly, without external means. The man who is moving consciously towards brilliance is the man who, having also abandoned his old self, is projected into a role of greater and greater external achievement, greater and greater influence upon men, greater and greater courage, leadership and visible heroism, *in accordance with some higher plan.*

At a certain point, as we saw in the solar system, the two lines cross. The path of invisibility, of utter extinction of individual personality, fuses with the path of brilliance, of pure instrumentality in a cosmic plan. And both men enjoy all, are free from all, understand all, and are all. This point of the intersection of the two lines is symbolised by death. And in all cases that we can imagine, implies death.

XV THE SHAPE OF CIVILIZATION

I FUNCTIONS AND CASTES: CELLS AND MEN

IN THE LAST CHAPTER WE BEGAN TO CONSIDER MANKIND AS A COSMOS, and the different human types as its functions. But to visualize mankind, in all stages of development, in all parts of the world, and in all ages, historic and prehistoric, is very difficult. In practice, the largest unit of human society which we can study in detail, and from many angles simultaneously, is a civilization or culture.

When we were working out the time-scales of different entities we attempted, without much success, to regard a civilization as a living organism. Now we have accumulated enough material about the general 'form' or pattern of organic entities in space and time, to try again.

Our first proposition is that individual men are the *cells* of a civilization. Clearly these cells are of many different kinds. There are farmers and peasants who, like the cells of the digestive organs and juices, have the duty of preparing food for the nourishment of the organism as a whole. There are merchants who like the blood-cells distribute the various products of the organism to all its parts. There are masons, engineers and architects, who build the cities, villages, factories and lines of communication which correspond to the various tissues and organs. There are soldiers and police ready, like the stored products of the adrenal glands, to come to the defence of the whole organism when it finds itself in danger. There are scientists, inventors and thinkers who represent the cells of the cerebral cortex and intellectual machinery; and poets, artists and mystics who correspond to that part of the nervous system which is the conductor of emotional life. Finally there are criminals of all ranks from pickpockets to false prophets who play a similar role to that of the poisons which give rise to illness and disease.

This exact analogy between cells and citizens, between the body and the state was fully worked out by the founder of cellular pathology, the Prussian Rudolf Virchow, in the 1850's. Later, it came to be regarded as too 'picturesque' by the positivist scientists of the end of the century. And a modern scientific compendium,[62] excellent of its kind, says: "Animals and plants as we know them are a community of cells, as the State is a commu-

---

62. 'The World of Science', F. Sherwood Taylor, p. 819.

nity of men, *though the analogy must not be pushed too far.*" But neither here nor elsewhere is it ever explained what 'too far' is, nor *why* the analogy cannot be developed. There is in fact not a single cell in the human body whose function cannot be paralleled in some human occupation or profession. And these functional cells are related to each other and communicate with each other in ways analogous to all those existing between men.

These main functions within the organism of a civilization have been expressed in simplified form in the idea of castes, which has served as the structural ideal of society at different times. Such an idea easily becomes distorted and perverted. But in their origin the medieval castes of priesthood, knighthood, burghers and peasantry, or the corresponding Hindu castes of brahmins, kshatriyas, vaisyas and sudras, were expressions of the true functions of individual men as *cells* in a greater organism.

At its best the idea of castes was never a rigid one. Though heredity played a large part in it, other factors were recognised as over-ruling heredity, and allowance was made for some men to move from one caste to another. In particular, a knight, a burgher or even a serf could enter the priesthood, and thus become incorporated in what was nominally the highest function of society. In twelfth-century Europe as in first-century Rome, it was also possible for a clever serf to buy his freedom and become a burgher, for an ambitious burgher – accepting greater responsibility – to become a patrician or knight. Exclusive castes with impassable barriers between them – as in 18th-century France or 19th-century India – are always indicative of a society grown rigid and ripe for change, as an arthritic body stands in need of heat and exercise.[63]

At different times such caste functions might be carried out by different peoples or races within one civilization, as in India the original Dravidians tended to become sudras and the conquering Aryans brahmins and knights; or as in modern New York Chinese tend to become laundrymen and restaurateurs, and Irish policemen and bus-drivers. This does not alter the main fact that each of the various organic functions must, in a true civilization, be properly carried out by a definite group, with its own ideal, and enjoying a harmonious relation with all the other functional groups. If today this seems impossibly utopian, it is merely an indication of the sickness of our present society.

There is one further implication of this idea. An individual man can, as we know, be ruled by any one of his functions. He can be ruled by his

63. 'The Laws of Manu', an ancient Indian codification of ideas and ideals connected with caste, are well treated in Chapter XI of P. D. Ouspensky's 'A New Model of the Universe'.

digestion and stomach, and live chiefly for eating and drinking. He can be ruled by his motor function, and live chiefly for movement, activity and travel. He can be ruled by his mind and live for theories, research or the pursuit of knowledge. He can be ruled by some strongly emotional desire or aim, and attempt to live his life in accordance with that.

In exactly the same way, civilizations can be ruled by any one of their functional groups. It is possible to think of peasant-ruled states such as Albania; of merchant-ruled states such as 19th-century England; of warrior-ruled states such as Sparta; and of priest-ruled states such as ancient Egypt, the Cluniac monastic empire in the 12th century, and modern Tibet.

While individual men continue to exist under each of the controlling impulses mentioned, in the ordinary way we think of a man as more highly developed if he is ruled by his higher functions, such as reason or the finer emotions. The same applies to civilizations. Though of course we must also recognize that as man can be ruled by a perverse intellect or emotion, so civilizations can be ruled by a degenerate intelligentsia or a corrupt priest-hood. This does not alter the fact that such functions are in their essence of a higher nature, and more suitable for ruling. At the same time we cannot leave out of account that any of the functions may become incurably dis-eased, and the state fall under the control of a criminal proletariat, a crimi-nal High Command, or criminal politicians. In this case it unfortunately corresponds to a man who is ruled, not by a healthy function, but by physi-cal or mental disease.

Theoretically, however, we may say that – although each civilization will have its own special tastes, capacities and understandings – the perfect civilization would be one in which the different functional groups were arranged in an ascending hierarchy according to the fundamental fineness of the energy with which their duties were concerned. As we saw in human physiology, the function of breathing works with finer matter than that of digestion, blood circulation with higher matter than respiration, and the various nervous systems with still more refined energy. By objective mea-surement the functions arrange themselves in this order. So with the functi-onal groups of a civilization. Whether any such objective or organic order of castes has ever historically been achieved is of course a different and very doubtful matter.

We referred to states as ruled by one or another functional group. But this was only to clarify certain principles. States are not in general of very great organic importance. It is the civilization that is the organic being – in the sense in which we speak of Greek civilization, Roman civilization, medieval Christian, Renaissance or Mayan civilization. For a state may or may not approximate to a cosmos. A true civilization is one. A state may or may not depend upon conscious men. A civilization cannot come into being without them.

Professor Toynbee[64] has described nineteen organic civilizations of this kind, all of which had their time of gestation, their birth, development, period of maximum power and influence, and in but a few still existent cases, their decline and death. Most of them, as he points out, are related to one or more of the others as parent and offspring. And although he cannot quite bring himself to describe the creatures of his study as living beings, all his evidence and arguments go to show that in fact they are.

Professor Toynbee's list of full-grown civilizations is as follows: Western, Orthodox, Iranic, Arabic, Hindu, Far Eastern, Hellenic, Syriac, Indic, Sinic, Minoan, Sumeric, Hittite, Babylonic, Egyptiac, Andean, Mexic, Yucatec, and Mayan. He also describes three – the Eskimo, the Polynesian and the Nomad – which like human beings of arrested development, never grew up beyond a certain point but remained pleasantly fixed at the schoolboy age of hunting, fishing and tree-climbing. And he adds two more again, the Irish Christian and the Scandinavian, which were murdered by or sacrificed to other civilizations in the heyday of their youth. The fact that both of these latter had already three or four hundred years' history behind them when they were overcome, gives us some idea of the scale of life of such an organism.

There is one qualification, however, that we may make to Professor Toynbee's list. Some of his civilizations, such as the Western European, which he traces back to the time of Charlemagne (8th century), seem much too long. Later we shall try to show that our Western Civilization has been several times *reborn*, with certain hereditary characteristics, but each time with a new character and a new form. And that which appears to us as one civilization is in fact several successive generations of civilizations, each of which has an organic lifetime as definite and limited as that allotted by nature to man.

How can we regard the time of a civilization? Perhaps we may find some clue if we try to discover how a civilization is conceived and brought to birth.

Men are its cells. In the last chapter we came to the conclusion that there has existed a certain invisible category of men, with *conscious spirits*, by

64. Arnold J. Toynbee: 'A Study of History', passim.

virtue of which they are connected with other dimensions of the universe, and can influence and uplift tens of thousands and even millions of ordinary men. If we study the scale of history, we see that such men are to ordinary men as a sperm cell is to an ordinary tissue-cell; and that they give rise to civilizations, just as a spermatozoon in its conjunction with the ovum gives rise to a new human being. The life of such men represents the conception of a new culture.

This does not of course mean that all men of this level of being found new civilizations, any more than that every sperm-cell generates a man. The time must be right; the conditions and raw material of the surrounding world ready for germination. Nevertheless in principle such men, the microcosm so to speak of their own civilization, have the innate power of originating a new one. And if they do not generate the culture, they heighten its tone, vivify and regenerate it, exactly as does abundant sex energy within the body which produces it.

In most cases, indeed, it is extremely difficult to trace a culture back to one man, just as it has proved practically impossible to study the history of the human embryo earlier than about eight days, when it already contains some hundreds of cells. Moreover, it is a strange principle that the higher the level of the founder, the more historically unseen must he remain. So that of Jesus Christ, the greatest and most glorious of all founders, we have – apart from the Gospels – no contemporary trace whatever.

If one higher man is to a civilization as the reproductive-cell is to human life, then we should expect a similar multiplication of the different phases of the life-cycle proportionately from one organism to the other. In man, gestation, childhood and the full term of life last 10, 100 and 1000 lunar months respectively. Continuing this logarithmic progression, we may propose 100, 1000, and 10,000 lunar months (or roughly 8, 80 and 800 years) as the corresponding phases of a culture. Remembering that the first or period of gestation is the 'invisible' one, passed in the mother's womb in the case of the embryo, and in some hidden incubation – in a monastery, in the desert, in some hidden 'school', or with some teacher in exile – in the case of the founder of a culture, then we see that these periods do appear probable enough.

Eight years will be the period of gestation of certain basic ideas of the new culture. The founder works intensely on his inner circle of disciples or pupils, assimilating them, so to speak, to his own ideas and towards his own level of being. A teaching is formulated, scriptures are written, certain basic discoveries, inventions or codes of law are achieved. Some intensely concentrated memento is created – the laws of Solon for the Greeks, the Gospels for the Early Christians, the Koran for the Arabs – which to the very last days of that culture remains its key and inspiration. The period of gestation of a civilization, it will be noted, is not the lifetime of the founder, but his phase of most intense creation and achievement.

Eighty years will be the period of physical expression of these basic ideas or teachings, and will correspond to those ages of fabulous invention, discovery and creation, which are historically visible at the beginning of each true civilization. This is the lifework of the founder's immediate circle. For one culture we see a blossoming of religion and architecture; for another the spread of order, administration and morals; for a third a sudden wealth of artistic creation and scientific discovery, and so on. While behind each appears, if it can be seen, a certain basic pattern and a certain inner knowledge of an esoteric nature.

This is the childhood of a civilization, the period of the formation of its personality, its golden age, in comparison with which everything that comes after seems strangely wearisome and pedestrian. Later generations look back to it, according to their mood, as men look back to their childhood – either as a time when miracles were possible, or as a time which they have outgrown into the 'wiser' disillusion of old age. The existence of such a period also explains those sudden extraordinary flowerings which in a century or less soar from barbarism to civilization and as quickly disappear.

For example, the Pythagorean culture in Sicily and Southern Italy in the sixth and fifth centuries B. C. raised in those virgin lands the greatest temples and cities of the Greek world, and perfected a whole potential system of science and philosophy – only to be swept away at the peak of its achievement by the rival Roman civilization from the North. In the patrimony of the Western Mediterranean there was not then room for two brother civilizations, and it was the Pythagorean which succumbed.

Finally, there is the period of seven or eight hundred years which will be the total life of the civilization, at the end of which its basic ideas and institutions will 'die'. That is, they will lose all trace of their original meaning and use, though in some cases they may still subsist as mummies or memorials from the past – as do the Gothic cathedrals to this day.

Remembering how the lifetime of man was terminated by an extraordinary conjunction of all the planetary cycles, we must now ask whether the lifetime of a civilization does not also correspond to some great cosmic rhythm. For any period which does not, will be an invented and not an organic one. In fact, we do find exactly such a period. "A period which embraces almost exactly an integral number of days, years, sunspot periods and all the various lunar revolutions," writes Sir Napier Shaw, "would include almost everything external which can be thought of as affecting the earth's atmosphere. Such a period is 372 years . . . one half of a still longer period of 744 years."[65] During this time a civilization undergoes every combination of influences possible, and at the end it has exhausted its potentialities and dies.

In a lifetime of 744 years, however, the elapse of half this period will mark the maximum growth, diffusion, power and influence of the civilization, which will thereafter slowly decay and yield place to a new civilization, of which it is itself most probably the parent. The logarithmic slowing down of time, which we noted in man's life and which means that less and less happens in each successive year, sometimes gives rise to the impression that cultures are shorter than they actually are. The new generation may prove so vigorous that the old becomes invisible: as a king, yielding his throne to his son and living in retirement, becomes invisible, though he is in fact still alive and his influence persists in a limited form. Today, for example, although the Renaissance Civilization is but four centuries old, its outlook and institutions are already half-eclipsed by those of its as yet unnamed successor.

On the other hand, it often happens that history does not notice the birth of a new culture, and may link two or even three generations of cultures, springing one from the other, under one name. Thus the Early Christian, the Monastic Christian, and the Medieval Christian Civilizations are usually regarded as one, although they have three quite distinct and clearly defined moments of birth, three distinct careers, and three deaths. In this way a culture may appear much longer than it actually is.

When one culture springs from another, it appears again to follow the analogy of the begetting of human children, and to emerge some time in the third or fourth century of the parent culture. Usually the latter has already reached a very high level, and the founder of the new is as it were its highest product, who combines in himself all its achievements and understanding. Gautama the Buddha, founder of the Early Buddhist Civilization,

65. Sir Napier Shaw; "Manual of Meteorology", vol. II, p. 318–9. Sir Napier continues: "The lunar-solar cycle of 744 years has been invoked by the Abbé Gabriel. It combines 9202 synodic revolutions, 9946 tropical, 9986 draconitic, 9862 anomalistic, 40 revolutions of the ascending node of the lunar orbit and 67 periods of sunspots."
It is noteworthy that an attempt to establish a time-scale for the rise and fall of civilizations, on the basis of a 'great year' of 360 years, and its double period of 720 years, was made by John Napier, the inventor of logarithms, in the guise of an interpretation of the Apocalypse ('A Plaine Discovery of the Whole Revelation of S. John', London, 1611).

for example, was a Sakya aristocrat who united in himself in the highest possible degree all that the heredity and education of his own time could give: and the same applied to Benedict, who would seem to be the founder of the Monastic Christian culture in the sixth century A. D.

Very often, too, a marriage of elements from two distinct and geographically separated cultures is clearly traceable in the parentage of the new. Thus the Mediaeval Christian culture, although born in the eleventh century from the body of the previous Monastic Christian culture, shows every sign of having been fathered by new knowledge and influence from the brilliant Mohammedan culture flourishing in Spain and the Middle East. But the full development of this idea must await the detailed examples which will be given in the next chapter.

Meanwhile, we may say that the conception of a culture, like the conception of any other living creature, requires that two factors meet in the right conditions and at the right time. First, there must be a fertile and virgin soil, in which either no previous civilization has grown or in which such earlier civilizations have died away, leaving it fallow once more. Except in very rare circumstances, a new culture cannot grow up in the place of an already existing one. It must have free place, fresh soil. At the same time, this soil must show signs of springtime. It must have a natural warmth and vigour of its own, which will germinate whatever is planted in it. It must be rich, healthy and fertile.

All this refers to the passive, the feminine factor in the conception of a culture – to the soil in which it shall be planted. And if we look about the mid-twentieth-century world, we do see – apart from those areas which are obviously the scene of a culture in decline, if not in its death throes – certain soils which do seem to fulfil these conditions. Such a country as Mexico, in which the bones of the ancient Aztec and Maya civilization have long since been washed clean, in which the pseudo-culture borrowed from colonial Spain has died away, and yet where a tremendous and *new* vitality begins to awake, certainly seems ripe for impregnation.

What we cannot calculate or foresee, however, is the *active* element in this begetting of a culture, the masculine germ. For, as we said, this can only come from a very high level of esoteric school, and in the person of an actual and extraordinary man – *a founder of conscious spirit*.

Such impregnation we cannot simulate. We can only wait and watch, assured by history that somewhere and somehow the birth of a new culture *must already be prepared*.

THE SHAPE OF CIVILIZATION

II. THE SOUL OF A CIVILIZATION: THE FOUR WAYS

We took as the *essence* of man the whole stream of his blood from conception to death and all the influences that it bore. And his *soul* as the sum of all the energies that make for consciousness in him, the total of all those moments in which he was really conscious of his own existence and of his relation to the universe around him.

What, first, is the essence of a civilization? In a poetical or artistic way it is not difficult to recognize that each culture has its own characteristic nature, its inner 'essence'. This essence expresses itself in its art, literature, music, manners, customs, interests, ideals, weaknesses, fashions, clothes, postures, gestures, extravagances and so on, all of which must, as it were, be 'seen together' to catch a glimpse of the essence which lies behind; just as all the corresponding attributes of an individual man must be 'seen together' for a clue to his individual essence.

In figures like Uncle Sam, John Bull, La Belle France, and again in paradoxical symbols like the lion and the unicorn, or the eagle and the serpent, men have tried to express the dimly-felt essence of their countries. Still more subtle and elusive will be the essence of the great culture which lies behind them all.

This essence is very difficult to define in any exact way. But quite interesting clues to it are provided by the characteristic monuments of a civilization, its characteristic institutions, and its characteristic way of transmitting its ideas. For instance, the characteristic monuments of the Roman Civilization are its great public works, its roads, aqueducts and amphitheatres; its characteristic institution is its code of law and its system of administration; and its characteristic method of transmitting ideas is by public order, law and literature. For the Mediaeval Christian Civilization the characteristic monument is the cathedral, the characteristic institution ecclesiastical organization, the transmission of ideas by architecture, sculpture and ritual. While Renaissance Culture again is characterized by the university as monument, humanism as an institution, books and naturalistic painting as means of transmitting ideas. All these are expressive of quite different and quite definite essences.

Sometimes, too, a flash of understanding of this idea comes when we notice curious similarities of essence in civilizations widely separated by time and space. There is a striking resemblance in the 'taste' of the times, for example, between the Parthian culture of the first centuries of our era and the early feudal age in Western Europe – both civilizations of hard-riding knights, of chivalry, of courts held in tents, and of a violent emotional people, at one moment passionately devoted to battle and the next to flower-gardens. Or again, between the Roman Empire of the second century and the British Empire of the nineteenth.

The same essence expresses itself in characteristic literature. Think of the essence of the culture behind 'Beowulf' or the 'Chanson de Roland', for example, in contrast to that behind Shakespeare on the one hand or behind Tolstoy's 'War and Peace', on the other. All these works are lasting, they belong to all humanity. At the same time they are perfect expressions of the essence of one particular civilization at one particular age.

Yet we must not be diverted here by difference arising from the *age* of a culture, for its essence is that which connects all its ages, which remains constant throughout its whole existence. In this way the ruling idea of mysticism and the church, although it took different forms and served different purposes, remained constant throughout the Medieval Christian Civilization, just as that of knowledge and education has throughout the civilization deriving from the Renaissance. Essence is what is permanent or inborn in the nature of a culture. In this essence of his race and culture, each man participates directly. It is true that his conscious memory of the past is limited by the generation of his grandparents, from whom as a child he hears tales of the world of fifty years before, and into whose time he can very vividly and personally enter. But beyond his grandparents a man has eight great-grandparents, sixteen great-great-grandparents and so on. Twenty generations or seven centuries back – if we suppose no mixing – he is descended from a million individuals of his own race. An Englishman born in 1950 may be descended from perhaps a quarter of the whole population of England in Chaucer's day. Thus he is heir to the essence of Chaucerian England in a very real way; and if he is a man of observation and sensibility he may find existing in him – like ancient records – traces of different aspects of his race and culture which will astonish him both as a modern man and as an individual.

This explains why all men feel much deeper loyalty to the *ancient* past of their country than to its more recent past. And the more ancient and legendary this past the greater its power to stir them. It is because the further a man looks back into his race, the more completely is he descended from it and the more completely is it represented in him. In his very blood is mirrored, however faintly, *all* the blood of his country's first founders.

Certainly in our time this idea has been stolen by perverted minds and turned to criminal use, like so many other ideas. This does not affect its truth. There can however be no implication of superiority or discrimination here. For all men are descended from an equal number of ancestors, and all equally rich – those of mixed race no less and perhaps more so than those of one, though the former may indeed inherit inner conflicts which the latter do not feel. Thus if we extend our analogy from the human individual to the culture, and say that *its essence is the totality of the blood of that culture*, then we may add that each later man contains in himself quite literally the whole essence of the first days of his culture.

What then is its *soul*? If essence is difficult to define, this is ten times more so. But in some way the soul of a civilization will be the totality of the souls of its children, the sum of all those who throughout its whole span have achieved consciousness. It will be all the human consciousness achieved within that culture. Its traces may perhaps appear to us in those highest scriptures which describe the pattern of the universe and the way to consciousness of it. These may reveal different souls – as the New Testament is different from the Koran and both from the Vedas. But at bottom the soul of a civilization can be made of no other material than the souls of men, and that with which the souls of men connect.

Now this soul of a civilization is fed in three ways – those three traditional ways by which men may become conscious and develop individual souls of their own. These 'ways', and the schools of regeneration which exist to administer them and teach their methods on Earth, depend upon the idea of developing consciousness first in one particular function. By becoming fully conscious in one function, a man finds his way to consciousness of his whole being: by transforming the nature of this one function, he transforms his whole self: by acquiring an instrument to control one function, he acquires a soul.

The first way to consciousness is through the instinctive and motor functions. The second way is through the emotional function. The third is through the intellectual function.

The first way is something akin to what in the west is known as *asceticism*. Though it contains very much more than this word has come to mean, and we use it only for lack of a better. This is the way of achieving consciousness by mastering physical functions, *by overcoming pain*. It is the way of transmuting pain into will. In the East it includes many fakir practices, and in its full form is known as hatha yoga. But whereas the more passive oriental may follow this way by holding his arm above his head, or by sitting on the top of a column for seven years, like Saint Simeon Stilites, in the more active west the mastery of the body usually takes a quite different form.

In modern life, the best examples of men going by the ascetic way are certain explorers or mountain-climbers, men who in attempting to reach the poles or scale Himalayan peaks, endure appalling hardships and force their bodies beyond the limit of endurance, under a compulsion which they can never fully explain. Scott and his companions slowly freezing to death at the South Pole, Irving and Mallory climbing on alone towards the summit of Mount Everest, which they could never reach and from which they could never return, were in fact western fakirs, engaged *in making themselves souls by the first or ascetic way.*

In this way, neither the question of motive nor of understanding enters. The fakir may be earning the only living open to him: the self-torturing anchorite may be trying to forget a girl: the superlative athlete or acrobat may be hungry for publicity. It does not matter. Driving the body consistently past pain and the fear of death is a fact irrespective of motive. He who does so may create a soul. His soul is made by bravery.

The second way depends on a marriage of what are known in the west as *mysticism* and *charity*, though both words are unsatisfactory. It is the way of achieving consciousness by mastering the emotional function, *by overcoming fear.* It is the way of transmuting fear into love. By this way, a man welcomes all situations which ordinarily give rise to fear or distaste, precisely to show that these emotions can be transformed into something quite different, that is, into quite new sensations of ecstasy. He welcomes poverty, celibacy, sickness, absolute obedience to the will of a religious superior, and many other limitations of ordinary pleasure. He sacrifices all small and trivial emotions, in order to acquire one great and transcendental emotion.

Saint Francis of Assisi is perhaps the best western example of a man going by this way, and his embracing of the leper is a classic demonstration of the method of acquiring love by overcoming fear. Others who – like Florence Nightingale – deliberately overcome their natural repugnance in order to serve the sick, the poor, the old or the oppressed, may also be unwitting candidates for this, the second or emotional way to consciousness.

Here, it is clear, motive is of prime importance, though understanding is not. A man who is charitable in order to be well-thought-of, will acquire nothing though his every natural inclination be sacrificed in the process. For by this way it is the emotion not the fact which turns the key. Without positive emotion every visible effort will be but a pretence, hindering rather than helping inner growth: with love the result may be obtained without a man even realizing the difficulty of what he does. His soul is made by goodness.

The third way is what used to be understood by *philosophy*. It is the way of achieving consciousness by mastering the intellectual function, *by overcoming thought*. It is the way of transmuting thought into understanding. By this way a man endeavours to subject the meaningless wanderings of the mind to the pattern of cosmic laws. He tries to think of everything that happens to him, of everyone he meets, not in relation to his personal likes and dislikes, but in relation to great principles. In this way he gradually becomes liberated from a subjective point of view and acquires objective understanding. Not only was this the way of great thinkers of clerical and philosophical schools in the past – of Saint Thomas Aquinas and Isaac Newton, for example – but in our day also it is particularly open to those of scientific mind, *provided they actually try to live all sides of their life by the great laws which they study or discover*.

To succeed in this way, a man must understand what he does and why. He must sacrifice self-deception, prejudice and inconsistency. His soul must be made by wisdom.

We thus see that the three ways – asceticism, charity and philosophy – not only produce separate schools of their own, but may also be followed by independent individuals, having no outward connection with any school at all. And again they may be included as separate 'orders' in some great historical school, such as the Roman Catholic Church. In this case, however, we usually find the ways in one or another combination. Perhaps we may say that the order founded by Saint Francis attempted to combine asceticism with charity, that founded by Saint Ignatius Loyola to combine asceticism with philosophy, that founded by Saint Vincent de Paul to combine philosophy with charity. And perhaps we may also add that the highest point reached by such orders was when, knowingly or not, they tried to combine all three ways in one.

By enabling men to create souls of their own through conscious work on the different functions, by enabling them to create three different kinds of souls, so to speak, these ways do literally *feed* the great soul of their culture. Indeed, they provide the three kinds of nourishment which this great soul requires, exactly as food, air and perceptions, digested by different functions, provide the three kinds of nourishment required by the body.

There is, however, a fourth way, about which much less is ordinarily known. This way consists in mastering instinctive, emotional and intellectual functions *at the same time*; in transmuting pain, fear and thought into their higher counterparts of will, love and understanding *simultaneously*. In this way, a man tries to be conscious in at least three functions at once. And

239

he tries to harmonize the work of these functions, to make them help each other, and serve the same aim. Thus, if he forces his body to carry out some very difficult physical task, he also deliberately works to transform the petty fears and resentments which may arise from it, and further still, he tries to understand what he is doing and why he is doing it, and to relate everything connected with his endeavours to the great natural laws with which he has already made himself familiar. In this way, he has three separate fields of study, each of which explains and reinforces the others.

Thus the consciousness which is developed by the fourth way is more general. It embraces all sides of man, and it is less likely to leave some fundamental weakness or dangerous deficiency unseen. For this reason – unlike the ascetic and mystical ways, which usually require the immediate sacrifice of all that is familiar, and translation to some quite new conditions, like those of a desert or a monastery – the fourth way is carried out in the conditions of ordinary life. The man going by this way has to carry out all his experiments and efforts in his usual surroundings, and all these experiments – apart from the inner results for which he works – must also yield external results which are reasonable and beneficial from an ordinary point of view.

The fourth way towards consciousness is sometimes quicker and sometimes apparently slower than the other ways. But its chief characteristic is that it is more harmonious, and thus more sure. The man who has learned to transform his emotions only in the special atmosphere of a monastery, if suddenly required by fate to struggle for his living in the business world, may find all his methods useless and his work wasted. The ascetic who has acquired will living in a cave and fasting, if suddenly placed in conditions where all kinds of physical pleasures are freely accessible, may find himself overwhelmed by appetites whose existence he did not even suspect. The man who has worked by the fourth way, on the other hand, and who has endeavoured to become conscious in all his functions and in all situations, will not be so easily caught. For him, consciousness will not be dependent on special associations, but will be that which accompanies him always, fasting or drinking wine, alone or in a crowd, labouring or meditating. It will be *that which lights up all that happens.*

There are many strange things about the fourth way. If the ascetic must be brave, the mystic good, and the philosopher wise, he who tries to go by the fourth way must learn to be brave, good and wise at once. And if he fails to aspire to any one of these qualities, his work and development is held up precisely at that point. Thus schools of the fourth way always find themselves working, as it were, upon a knife-edge, and their tendency – whenever immediate influence from higher levels is withdrawn – will always be to slip back into one of the other ways: to content themselves either with austerity or charity or philosophy.

From this it would appear much more difficult to work in the fourth way than in the other three. In one sense it is. He who tries to go by it constantly finds himself losing the thread, which no dogma, method or belief can assure to him. On the other hand, for many people the fourth way represents *the only way open to them*. For no other way will accept them as they are, or show them how to pass through and transmute the interests, loves, longings, weaknesses and habits, which they are quite unable to abandon at one blow.

Schools of the fourth way have existed and exist, just as schools of the three traditional ways existed and exist. But they are much more difficult to detect, because – unlike the others – they cannot be recognized by any one practice, one method, one task, or one name. They are always inventing new methods, new practices, suitable to the time and conditions in which they exist, and when they have achieved one task which was set them they pass on to another, often changing their name and whole appearance in the process.

Thus schools of the fourth way were undoubtedly behind the designing and construction of the great Gothic cathedrals, though they had no special name and adapted themselves to the religious organization of the time. For a time the Cluniacs sheltered them, for a time the Freemasons. In the seventeenth century, similar schools were responsible for much of the new scientific and medical research, sometimes under one name and sometimes under another. In the eighteenth century again, fourth way schools borrowed many of the discoveries of Greek and Egyptian archeology to clothe their ideas and their organization, while some of their leaders – in order to penetrate the luxury-loving and sophisticated circles where they had work to do – might even appear in the guise of fashionable magicians or mesmerists.

For the fourth way endeavours to introduce consciousness into all sides of life, and its form is always connected with that which is most new, with that which prepares the future.

At the same time, by definition, the fourth way – like the other three ways – is primarily concerned with the development of human souls. And its true work, like theirs, is to feed the soul of the culture in which it works. It may thus be said that the stage of development of the soul of any given culture will be the direct result of these four ways, and of the work of the schools which study them.

THE THEORY OF CELESTIAL INFLUENCE

III THE DECLINING ABSOLUTE, OR COMPARATIVE RELIGION

There is indeed a way in which we can compare the souls of civilizations, and the different phases of one civilization. This is according to their view of the universe.

In the earlier part of this present book we tried to establish the general structure of the universe. We had to suppose a philosophical *Absolute*, in which swam, so to speak, infinite numbers of *galaxies*. Similarly within our own galaxy or Milky Way swam innumerable *suns*. Within our solar system swam *planets*. Upon the surface of our planet, the Earth, swam the world of *organic life*. Within this world of organic life swam individual *man*, within man *cells*, within cells *molecules*, within molecules *electrons*.

Now each world or cosmos is incommensurable with the one which contains it. It disappears in the greater one, becomes invisible in relation to it. The higher cosmos contains infinite possibilities for the lower, is god for the lower. In this sense every world may be taken as absolute or as god for the smaller scale of entity. Yet man, by his extraordinarily complex nature, is apparently endowed with the power of apprehending not only the world immediately above him – that is, the world of organic life of which he forms part – but many higher worlds, the Earth, the Sun, the Milky Way, and he can even philosophically suppose an Absolute of absolutes. So that man has many absolutes or gods from which to choose.

If we now consider different civilizations, and even different peoples within the same civilization, we see that in a general way man has set his absolute, that is, his conception of god, now higher and now lower in the universe.

At various times, often at the beginnings of civilizations, attempts have been made to spread the idea of an Absolute of absolutes, an abstract and formless One. But this idea is evidently impossible for ordinary use, for immediately any name or attributes are attached to it, or it is associated with a particular heaven or heavenly body, it has already descended to another level. And since no general worship or study can be carried on without names and images, this level of 'god' is completely out of range of man.

Occasionally we find a galactic absolute, like the Egyptian Khepera, creator of the gods themselves, or like Shiva in a twinkling of whose eye passes the whole life of the Solar System. But such a conception is still much too difficult for ordinary men, and never passes beyond the priesthood or brahmin caste.

Usually, at the very outset of each civilization, along with these abstract ideas, a more possible absolute is set at the level of the Sun. Men can feel the warmth and light of the Sun, understand their utter dependence on it, intellectually study its nature, and emotionally rejoice in it as the source of life, seasons, the beauty of colour, and so on. According to our study, they may even attain its nature. So that often a deification of the Sun gave men a real and living absolute, which could command their worship in a very immediate way. Ra in Egypt, Apollo in Greece, Baal in Syria, Tonatiuh in Mexico, and Indra in India were gods set at such a level.

At other times, often in a later and already rather degenerate stage of civilization, general worship began to shift to the level of the planets, or to the Earth itself. In the late Greek and Roman worlds, in the late Middle Ages, and particularly in many 17th century sects, planetary beings become the highest concept or absolute, and from the idea of the interplay of their influences, or of using or working with these influences in some way, arose the pseudo-science of magic. The prevalence of ideas of magic is nearly always connected with the polytheism inherent in taking the planets as god or absolute.

At a still further stage of degeneration, usually to be seen in the distant descendants of ancient civilizations who now exist as savages, the highest powers are associated with manifestations of nature – thunder, rain, forests, mountains, and so on – that is to say, with the world of organic life, the next above man. This is to place the absolute at a still lower level.

In this way, we have a scheme for the study of comparative religion; and we also see that the development of each civilization is usually accompanied by a degeneration of the idea of the absolute to ever lower and lower levels. On the face of it, this seems absurd, since later men could presumably look backwards and see higher conceptions revealed behind them in history. But a curious trick of human psychology makes the downward transition quite simple. These higher conceptions, seen through the distorting lens of time, appear to more degenerate man as superstition. And applying this name to them he remains entirely satisfied with his own level of understanding.

We spoke of savages who took the world of nature as absolute or god. There is, however, still another stage of degeneration, particularly prevalent in our own age. This is expressed by the acceptance of a *man* as absolute or god. That is, in taking ordinary undeveloped man as the highest being or power in the universe. This is of course quite distinct from the idea of saints, for saints immediately presuppose a god or much higher power for whom the saint acts as intermediary. The deification of a Roman emperor, the worship of a Hitler, absolute obedience to some party government, or on the other hand the idealization of an imaginary figure like the Common Man, *when no higher power is recognized*, are examples of taking man as god or absolute.

Below this lies only the nightmare of superstition – by no means un-known today – when men believe microbes, bacteria and other sub-human organisms to be stronger than man or god, that is, the final power in the universe.

All this is usually indicative of the working of the pathological or criminal process in the body of a civilization. For the characteristic of this process, as we saw much earlier when considering it in the Solar System and in man, is wrong relation between the part and the whole. A general belief in man or microbe as the highest power in the universe means that for the time being mankind has completely lost its right relation with the whole cosmic body. From such a pathological state civilizations rarely recover. And it is then time to reconstruct everything from the beginning, for a quite new civilization to be born.

XVI THE SEQUENCE OF CIVILIZATIONS

I CIVILIZATION'S EARTHLY HOUR

WHEN WE LOOK AT THE SEQUENCE OR DESCENT OF CIVILIZATIONS more objectively, several strange facts emerge. In the first place, we find more or less the same racial stocks becoming incorporated, now into the body of a culture of one character, now into that of a culture based on quite different capacities, ideals and understanding. During most of the last two millenia the actual races of Europe have remained remarkably unchanged, and they continue pure and clearly distinguished among themselves even to this day. And yet this same material, this same agglomeration of cells could be formed into different civilizations of extraordinarily contrasting style.

Certainly the quality of each corresponds to the psycho-physical type and capacity of the race which launches it. One civilization is conceived by Greeks, another by Romans, a third by Frenchmen, and a fourth by Italians again. But very soon all the other races of the European family are imitating with more or less success the example of the leader, and seen on a scale of centuries, the chief endeavour of the whole continent seems to change from thought to labour, to art, to mysticism in a very extraordinary and inexplicable way.

Since the material of the great body of these civilizations is the same, what has changed to produce such different interests, different achievements, and different ideals in succeeding ages? Can we trace any cosmic movement which would appear to correspond with this rate of change?

When we were studying the times of the universe, we came to the conclusion that the time of a solar breath was reminiscent of the period of the precession of the equinoxes, during which the Earth shifts its axis round a complete circle of fixed stars. The effect of this movement is that the Sun's position at the vernal equinox gradually passes through the whole cycle of the zodiac, the original position only being restored after 25,765 years. Thus the signs of the zodiac used as mathematical divisions of the Sun's course no longer correspond to the actual constellations which go by these names, for the latter have, so to speak, *been left behind*. In other words, the radiation of the Sun acts on the Earth in a slowly changing combination with any influence which may be received from the centre of the galaxy.

In an earlier chapter we thought of life on Earth in the analogy of a play on a stage round which the coloured lights of the planets were constantly moving to produce ever-changing emotional effects. But at the same time we thought of the effect being subtly influenced in quite another way by faint music played off-stage which might alter the spectator's whole feeling about the play without his even being aware of it. In our analogy this distant music may be compared to the effect of our changing relation to the zodiac, that is, to the Milky Way. Then if we consider a civilization as one complete performance of the play, it means that each performance will have a quite different musical accompaniment. And this in turn means that the whole emotional effect will be subtly changed, and the same play will appeal to quite different sides of mankind as they are thus evoked.

As we recalled, the axis between the Earth and Sun gradually shifts round the whole zodiac in 25,765 years. This period not only seems equivalent to a solar breath, but, taking the life of Earth as between $1\frac{1}{2}$ and 2 thousand million years, it also exactly represents half a terrestrial day. Thus the time this axis takes to pass through one of the zodiacal signs, that is 2150 years, will correspond to a certain hour in this great day of the Earth; and like an hour of morning, noon or dusk in the ordinary days of men, each cosmic hour will have its own quality, its own possibilities and its own emotional appeal.

Moreover, if we regard this earthly hour of 2150 years as forming an octave, each note of this octave will last just over 300 years. These three centuries seem to correspond to one generation of culture, that is, to the time between the birth of a civilization and the moment when, having reached maturity, it in turn gives birth to the new civilization which will supplant it.

In this way we see that the octave of European civilizations which bridges the last two thousand years, may in some way represent the effect in the world of men of the seven successive notes of a terrestrial hour. And theoretically, a chain of 84 such civilizations might span a single day on the scale of Earth.

Beyond the European cycle we are familiar with, it is certainly difficult to establish anything very definite, though an earlier octave or perhaps even two octaves of civilizations may be discerned in Egypt; and there are traces of other milleniums of culture in America, China, India, and Mesopotamia.

At still further remove, however, it is interesting to consider the many legends of some great terrestrial catastrophe, which is reputed to have destroyed the continent of Atlantis and produced an almost complete break in the chain of human culture. Today, the comparison of astronomical, geological, archaeological and mythical evidence seems to confirm such a catastrophe and to place its date somewhere about 11,000 or 12,000 B. C.[67]

At that remote period, the sun stood at the vernal equinox, not in Pisces or Aries as it has in this last age, but in the sign of Libra. The whole relation of solar and galactic influences must then have been the reverse of what it is today, and it may well be that such disaster was in some way connected with that earthly night, which preceded our present chain of civilizations and separated them utterly from the works of man in an earlier and unrecorded age.

Some modern scholars have tried to explain this break in human history by a cosmic or astronomical cataclysm. The Viennese cosmologist Hans Hoerbiger, developing a theory that large planetary bodies tend to capture smaller ones and at length disintegrate them, has suggested the break up of some satellite previous to our present moon to be the cause. Velikovsky on the other hand claims that the Earth has changed its orbit and magnetism, Venus become transformed from comet to planet, and Mars passed within sparking distance of Earth, all within historical times and with historical results. Such theories are inadmissible in their present form, because they regard the Solar System as a meaningless play of flying balls, in which every traffic accident due to drunken driving is to be expected. If the idea of a living cosmos is accepted, then physical captures and collisions are no more likely between planets in the Solar System than they are between organs in the human body, and for the same reason.

Yet clearly a physical break exists in the story of mankind. We have six thousand years of history, perhaps ten thousand more of legend. Beyond, darkness. Then, far farther back, once again clear traces of men we can recognise and to some extent understand. It is a strange fact that we know more of mankind twenty thousand years ago than ten.

Did man make some great mistake which had to be expunged? Did he merely pass through some terrestrial interval which no more depended on him, than a thunderstorm on a cloud of summer gnats? Were both factors – human fate and cosmic pulsation – equally involved? We do not know. It is only clear that some master-key to the human story is lost.

The further back history goes, the greater the monuments, the more exact the knowledge. The predynastic Sphinx and Great Pyramid are both vaster in concept and more meaningful in detail than all that comes after.

---

67. H. S. Bellamy, 'The Atlantis Myth', particularly p. 113.

In Peru, pre-Inca architecture is more perfect than Inca, and the fabulously ancient ruins of Tiahuanaco, in which stone blocks weighing forty tons are trimmed and dovetailed like plaster, more perfect still. Many of man's strangest achievements have no known origin. As Ignatius Donnelly points out, no animal has been domesticated within human memory: all those which are domestic now were already domesticated at the dawn of history. By whom, and how?

Not only materially, but in grandeur of philosophy, purity of religion, daring of astronomy, subtlety of symbolism, that which we find in most ancient times ranks with anything accomplished since. The charting of constellations by the Chaldeans, the exact measurement of star cycles lasting thousands of years by the Egyptians, the invention of letters, hieroglyphs and writing, the lost concept of deities which create deities – we can hardly imagine greater achievements. None of this is such as could be discovered by accident by ordinary men. All bears the imprint of conscious school.

When we go back ten thousand years more to ancient cave-drawings, we are struck by a great difference. We find the physical daring of the huntsman, the skill of the archer, the pathetic trace of him who prints his palm upon the wall, hunger for meat and sex, fear and love of one's prey. *But no trace of school.* Man is living in a world where the most powerful beings are not gods or stars, but bison and mammoth. And he barely holds his own among them.

Somewhere between Altamira and Egypt, somewhere between 20,000 and 10,000 years ago, schools for the attainment of consciousness seem to have been established upon Earth. Somehow, men attracted the help of higher powers in the universe, were allowed to cooperate consciously in a cosmic scheme. This is the key which is lost. This is what men dimly mean when they look back to Atlantis, a place where all culture was one, all knowledge new, where all subsequent civilizations, languages and religions had their common origin.

We have said that the nature of school is invisible. When schools were first established on Earth, and began the immense task of opening the eyes of half-animal man to the nature of the universe and his possibilities in it, they must have acted openly. Such men could not have responded otherwise. *School has been made invisible since.* For some cosmic reason all traces of its first launching of conscious human effort have been wiped out. And ordinary man has been allowed, perhaps even encouraged, to think that he did everything unaided. This is part of his test, *part of his possibility of reaching independent understanding.*

248

Study of the most ancient cave-drawings teaches us something more. These – apparently the first artistic traces left by man on Earth – date from the so-called Aurignacian Period, about 40,000 years ago. They show us ponderous mammoths, rooted like trees in their immobility, a reindeer-skull with antlers, meandering lines which could be tracks through the forest, heavy hands, the gross torso of a woman without legs. All is heavy, static, patiently rooted as though for ever in the earth. A lunar, lymphatic world – the words come unbidden.

Half of the whole span of time since Aurignacian man elapses before we come to the next or Magdalenian period. In the same or similar caves in France and Spain, notably at Altamira, we find drawings of a completely different character. Here everything is in most violent motion. A bison convulsed in its death-throes, the galloping hooves of a stampeding herd, wiry men running, poised, tensing their bows, letting fly their arrows. Even to look at these drawings communicates action, tension, headlong movement. It is a mercurial, a purely thyroid world.

When we compare these first men whose whole life was rumination, and these second men whose whole life was action, with those of our own day, in whom thought is so evidently dominant, a most interesting idea begins to develop. Could it be that in the history of mankind, different functions were stimulated in the same order and the same way as they are in the life of individual man? In Chapters 10 and 11 we saw how these functions appear to uncoil from a centre, both in his physical anatomy and in his lifetime. Thymus, pancreas, thyroid; parathyroids, adrenals, posterior pituitary; anterior pituitary, gonads, pineal. Like a delayed chain-reaction, each seemed to set off the next and in time be supplanted by it.

Let us suppose the same sequence of stimulation in the life of mankind. Only here, as we saw in studying geology, time has a reverse motion to that of individual man. Instead of slowing down with each passing year, as with him, for the Earth and mankind time becomes fuller and fuller. Earlier periods are longer, later shorter. The logarithmic scale for the stimulation of successive functions must go backwards not forwards.

Let us suppose then, as we shall later try to show, that in the actual present a quite new pressure is being brought to bear on the mental powers of mankind through stimulation of the anterior pituitary. Let us suppose that the period of dominance of the posterior pituitary has lasted a thousand years, and that each previous functional period was twice as long as that which followed. Recasting the individual life-scheme worked out in Chapter 11, we then have a table like the following:

Date	Duration of Age	Gland and Type	Period
60,000 years ago		Thymus–Solar	?
	32,000 years		
30,000 years ago		Pancreas–Lunar	Aurignacian
	16,000 years		Magdalenian
15,000 years ago		Thyroid–Mercurial	(stone)
	8,000 years		Egyptian,
5,000 B.C.		Parathyroid–Venusian	Chaldean,
	4,000 years		Ancient
			Indian
			(copper)
1000 B.C.		Adrenals–Martial	Greco-Roman,
	2,000 years		Iranian
			(iron)
1000 A.D.		Posterior Pituitary–Jovial	European,
			Medieval and
			Renaissance
	1,000 years		(paper)
Present		Anterior Pituitary–Saturnine	Modern
			(electricity)

Evidently it is difficult to embrace in one vision all the traces of man in a certain age in all parts of the world, and come to a clear conclusion about the special functional understanding which he then enjoyed. But the Aurignacian period, as we saw, is strangely lymphatic, the Magdalenian strikingly mercurial. The great slow master-building civilizations of Egypt, Sumer and Ancient India, which were brought to birth about 5000 B.C. with copper tools, do have all the characteristics of poise, solidity and tranquil growth which we associated with the parathyroids and Venus. Again, the invention of iron weapons about 1000 B.C. does seem to usher in a period of passion, turbulence and change which breaks up the fixed forms of the ancient world, and fills Europe, the Middle East and China with martial alarms for two thousand years. And yet again, the last millenium has produced and reconciled a jovial profusion of achievement in all the physico-emotional sides of life in a way the world has never seen before.

Such a table refers to the *growth* of mankind not to its *regeneration:* to its growing up, not to its growing good or wise.

This is not the place to develop the idea in greater detail. But one aspect of it is important. In individual life we found the periods of the pancreas and the thyroid to be prenatal, belonging to gestation. Aurignacian and Magdalenian man, labouring in the dark of womb-like caverns, suggest gestation on another scale. In individual life, somewhere between the moment of the thyroid and the moment of the parathyroid, between quickening and infancy, comes birth into light and air, with all that they imply.

Somewhere between 15,000 and 5,000 B. C., in some place of which we have no trace, was mankind *born*? – born into air, light, culture, the tradition and heritage of conscious evolution? Was esoteric school, established for the first time on Earth in accord with some universal plan, the midwife at this birth? What was the birthright, and who the witnesses? These are among the greatest questions that can be asked, and it is the dim presentiment of them that even to-day lingers about the word 'Atlantis'.

II BIRTH AND REBIRTH OF CULTURES[68]

The ancestral civilization of our Western culture is evidently the Greek. Before that Europe was a forested Eden peopled by scattered tribes living under tribal custom. It had yielded no cities, no literature, no general science or religion. Earlier civilizations – in Egypt, Mesopotamia, India and China – had developed among peoples of quite different race and under quite different climatic conditions, and thus cannot be seen as belonging to this particular line of development.

The identity of the conscious men who, about the beginning of the sixth century B. C., conceived the first true civilization in Europe, we do not know. There is the half-legendary Solon, law-giver, poet, reformer, civilizer, the traditional 'father of his people', and contemporary with him Thales of Miletos, the equally shadowy figure of the first scientist, observer and demonstrator of the laws of nature and the universe. These still only half emerge from the invisible 'period of incubation' of which we have spoken. Perhaps they are no more than figure-heads. For the true founders must have brought the intensely concentrated body of knowledge necessary for such a new beginning from some already highly developed civilization – probably the Egyptian – and it would seem likely that they were men of that alien race.

Indeed, Plato specifically tells us that Solon, his ancestor, was taught by Egyptian priests during his visit to Sais about 590 B. C., and Clement of Alexandria adds that Pythagoras acquired his science from the same source.

68. See Appendix VIII, 'The Cycle of Civilisations'.

In the 'Timaeus' it is further made clear that the school at Sais deliberately revealed knowledge long kept hidden to the visiting Greeks, "for they were great lovers of the Athenians, and said they were in some way related to them." This relationship, esoterically speaking, was that of parents to off-spring.

In any case, it is in the lifetime of their followers that the outlines of the new culture become magnificently apparent. Within eighty years, on the shores of Greece and Southern Italy, where only timber and tile had stood before, rose the most subtle temples ever built by man. To make possible this technical achievement, Pythagoras had already developed the inner laws of harmony and worked out their manifestations for a new architecture and a new music. Anaximander, a pupil of Thales, had invented the basic instruments of a new technology – the gnomon, the clock, the astronomical sphere. Unknown sculptors had woken Egyptian statuary from its age-old immobility, and created the figure of the kouros, the wide-eyed man of the new age. Vase-painters set a symbolic mythology of the relation between men and gods in every home: and the dramatic form of tragedy, created by Thespis, revealed the eternal clash between the wilfulness of man and the higher laws of the universe, at great dramatic festivals where the whole people could in this way 'be purged with pity and terror'.

Yet behind all this diversity we sense one informing source, some hidden centre of vitality which is suggested though never revealed by the strange role of the Eleusinian mysteries.

Within one lifetime a new form was thus established for every aspect and function of the new civilization. Its 'personality' was complete, and it only remained for all the technical and intellectual implications of these new forms to be perfected, elaborated, popularized, and later still to grow stylized, exaggerated and decadent.

It is interesting at this point to observe the working of the laws of scale. We saw how the human organism grows according to a definite curve from a single cell to many billions. So for a civilization. Thus Greek culture, all its potentialities compressed at the beginning of the sixth century into one man or a handful of men, by mid-century had already absorbed some hundreds of the best and most creative individuals, and by the end had 'organized' into a new pattern of life thousands of citizens of Athens, Croton, Syracuse and a half-dozen other centres.

This growth, or incorporation of larger and larger numbers of human 'cells', continued steadily. Through the fifth century, colonies on the Black

Sea, in Sicily and Asia gradually raised the population of the Greek world to hundreds of thousands. In the fourth century, by the instrumentality of a world-conqueror in the person of Alexander the Great, the scale turned to millions.

At the same time, in exact proportion to this 'growth', the intensity of the Hellenization diminishes, and the last millions drawn into the Greek body politic tend rather to obscure its nature – just as layers of fat accumulated by a grown man, though incorporated into his body, may obscure his true nature and possibilities. No doubt they would have accomplished its destruction entirely, had it not been for the more conscious men, like Socrates, Plato, Aristotle and others, who continue to be produced from the centre or highest part of the civilization. These keep the organism alive. Without them, it would become a monstrous automaton or Frankenstein blundering to destruction.

Even so, the time comes when the inner life of the culture is insufficient to hold in check the decay which is always waiting to attack an overripe organism. The conquests fall away, and the Greek world, like an old man, begins to shrink and stoop. When it is but four and a half centuries old, it falls under the sway of the new Roman civilization, and thereafter lives a servile life, teaching or pandering to its young master, until, eight hundred years from its founding, the Greek homeland is overrun by Goths, and the Hellenic civilization finally dies as an independent organism.

But whence has this new Roman civilization emerged? At the beginning of the fourth century B. C., when the Greek civilization had two and a half centuries behind it, there existed at Samos the school of Epicurus, and at Athens the school of Stoics under Zeno. Who passed at this time from these schools to the still barbaric frontier city of Rome, we do not know. But we do know that about this time exactly the same phenomenon of startling growth, of sudden brilliant manifestation in every phase of human activity, occurred in Italy, as had previously occurred in Greece. And we also know that this new Roman civilization, from its very earliest days to its devastation by Huns and Vandals eight hundred years later, was informed by the twin ideals of Epicureanism and Stoicism.

Yet the essence of this Roman culture was quite different from the Greek. Its monuments were not temples but roads and aqueducts; and its instrument of expansion not philosophy but the legions which marched upon these roads. It drew men to itself by the gift, not of art and thought, but of law and order. So that after three centuries of growth, its musculature of

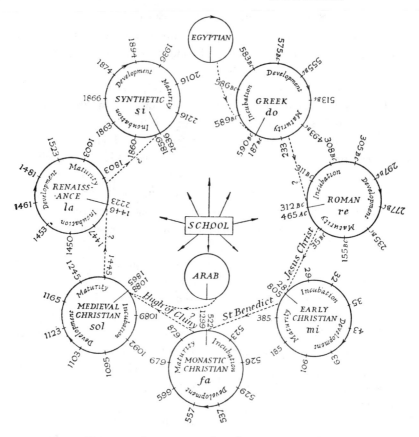

Fig. 13: The Sequence of Civilisations in Europe

Civilization.	Transmission of Ideas.	Monument.
Greek	Drama, music	Temple, theatre
Roman	Code of laws	Roads, aqueducts
Primitive Christian	Preaching	The New Testament
Monastic Christian	Illuminated manuscripts	Monastery, abbey
Medieval Christian	Ritual, sculpture	Cathedral, church
Renaissance	Printed books, painting	University, school
Synthetic	Radio, cinema	Electro-magnetic apparatus

roads and camps served an empire even greater than that earlier unified by the nervous system of Greek philosophy.

Then at this moment of its maturity was conceived into the Roman world a man whom we know historically as Christ, and who, according to the story, in a few years' activity not only laid the foundations of the next civilization, but even established a certain hereditary form or ideal for all generations of succeeding cultures. In this case we have definite literary traces of a single founder, of his immediate circle of twelve disciples, and of the 'Acts of the Apostles' by which in a few decades the new knowledge, ideals and organization were diffused throughout the whole Eastern Mediterranean.

This Early Christian Civilization had its centre of gravity on a more subtle level than either the Greek or the Roman. Its greatest monument was neither road nor temple, but a book, the New Testament; and in its early stages it grew and was united, not by a political or artistic system, but by a metaphysical one of extraordinary refinement. Its centre of gravity, so to speak, lay nearer to its soul than in either of its predecessors.

Yet in this case, too, the material body of the civilization grew according to the same laws, and from the 'seven churches in Asia' of the first century, it in turn reached imperial maturity with the recognition of Christianity as official tenet of the Roman Empire about 320 A.D. Christian civilization embraced the world, declined, degenerated. Eight centuries from its conception, the Papacy, its highest temporal expression, was an object of commercial haggling on the Roman market.

Thus the Early Christian Civilization died. But already in 529, a man who was perhaps its highest product, St. Benedict, had founded at Monte Cassino a monastery where, in a small closed circle, everything was reconstructed, was made over again from the beginning, in a new form, suitable to a new age. It was the birth of the second or Monastic Christian Civilization.

About this new beginning there is something very interesting. With the Greek, Roman, Early Christian civilizations we pass the first three notes of a great historical octave. Here we come to an interval – the Dark Ages – when violence, ignorance and anarchy sweep over Europe like a tide.

Benedict created a form especially adapted to pass this interval. The monastery was a seed-case. Into it were placed the genes of a new culture, which were then sealed up. At the same time, the maxim *'orare et laborare'* allowed each monastery to be self-sufficient, a world in miniature behind the walls which made it half-prison and half-castle. Here all that was of value from the past was kept – Greek and Roman manuscripts copied, Byzantine symbology transferrred to painted miniatures, secrets of music and medicine preserved, the *'opus dei'* or work of regeneration attempted. The physical grandeur of the ancient world was as it were reduced to molecular scale, like memory in the cells of the cerebral cortex, against a time when it might manifest openly once more.

Within two centuries a thousand such monasteries had sprung up in

France. Once again, only a multiplicity of self-sufficient units could hope to pass the chaos.[69] About them conditions grew steadily worse. Saracens from the south, Magyars from the east, Northmen from the Channel, sweep down the river valleys, burning villages and crops, destroying ancient cities. All central authority and security vanishes. "Three men cannot meet two without putting them to death."

But as the centuries pass, the monastic system too grows old and careless. Rules are forgotten, learning discouraged, married lay abbots – living like feudal lords – fill the cloisters with guards and huntsmen. Safety and security, the very conditions which enabled civilization to be preserved, now enervate and undermine it.

By the eleventh century it is time for schools to go out into the world again. The monasteries have been their Ark. Now, like Noah, they must recultivate the earth as the floods recede.

Medieval Christian Civilization is born. As suddenly as ever, an immense wave of hope, energy and effort in a single lifetime transforms the face of France. Its moment of emergence is striking. In 1095, at the sheltered abbey of Cluny in Burgundy, an immense church in a new style is consecrated, forerunner of all the cathedrals of the Middle Ages and the greatest – save Saint Peter's – ever built. Within a generation this extraordinary new image of the universe, perfected in the quiet of the monastery, is being imitated in every city and town of Western Europe. *The work is done not by clerics but by anonymous freemasons.* School has gone out into the world again.

Such are the physical monuments we see, themselves proof of their origin. But in this case we can study in some detail the immense labour – two centuries long – which was necessary to prepare their birth. Cluny, externally a monastery like any other, was founded in 910 when, as the Council of Trosly said, "men destroy one another like the fishes of the sea." A forgotten valley, equally distant from the troubled courts at Paris, Aachen and Pavia, was chosen; and the founding charter threatened with a curse thirty lines long any, even the Pope himself, who should violate its absolute independence. By direct descent the twelve monks who came there brought the tradition of Monte Cassino itself.

The significance of this continuity and this tradition but slowly appears. First the Cluniacs transform their own countryside, improving agriculture, planting vines, stocking the rivers with fish. Soon they are called in to reform other monasteries. Wherever peace is established, new houses spring

69. Compare the role of the rare earths in the table of elements, Chapter 7, I.

up. Within a century they administer a thousand square miles, and deal directly and on equal terms with dukes, kings, the Emperor.

By the year 1000 it is the Cluniacs who have taken the first effective steps against anarchy and violence. Step by step, they secure acceptance of the Truce of God. First, fighting at the weekend is prohibited; no un-armed monk, no man walking with a woman or going to church may be attacked; all may seek sanctuary at the altar. Later, the Truce is extended to half the week, all Holy Festivals; rebellious barons are ceremonially ex-communicated for offending it. But the tradition of violence dies hard. The knight who terrorizes travellers and the countryside from his castle-keep is difficult to persuade. And in 1095 it is again the Cluniacs who, with a shrewdness which is perhaps their undoing, launch the First Crusade that at one blow gives France a kingdom in the east and, employing the incor-rigible plunderers, at last brings peace at home.

Another line of tradition direct from the classical world had been pre-served by the Comacene Masters, heirs of the Roman collegials, who – according to the story – escaped from Diocletian's persecution to establish themselves on an island on Lake Como, whence they influenced architec-ture all over Western Europe from the ninth to eleventh centuries. It seems probable that Abbot Odo of Cluny, on his numerous trips across the Alps to Italy, made direct contact with the Comacenes. For from the tenth century on, Cluny becomes a building centre of first importance, and Co-macene themes appear frequently in its work.

By the eleventh century there are Cluniac centres all over France, save in the areas influenced by connected schools – Chartres with its speciality of medicine, Rheims of music, Mont St. Michel of astronomy. A joint mis-sion from Cluny and Chartres goes to Arabic Spain to study, and sends back the Koran, logarithms, works on astronomy, algebra and alchemy. With the Norman Conquest, it is the Cluniacs who colonize the wild north-east of England. When Sanchez the Great regains Northern Spain from the Moors, it is their help he calls on, and building the immense cathedral of Saint James at Compostella on the Atlantic coast, they organize a thousand miles of pilgrimage route to bring ideas, culture, trade and possibilities to the new-won wilderness.

The Cluniacs, indeed, may be said to *invent* the pilgrimage, creating a network of shrines which for the first time brings intentional movement to a stagnant society. Pilgrimage meant holiday to the serf's grinding la-bour, a wider world opened to the unimaginative. It meant diffusion of skills, arts, agricultural improvements. Few could return from Canterbury,

Compostella or Rome without new impressions, new ideas, and even perhaps an intimation of that great inner work which lay behind them.

All this immense task was but *preparation* for that new culture, which
finally blossomed in Western Europe in the twelfth and thirteenth centuries. As it blossomed it passed from Cluniac hands. The *'iussu et imperio
Hugonis'*, the order and empire of the Abbot Hugh, which at its peak included 15,000 establishments stretching from Portugal to Poland, and ad-
ministered lands as great as most European kingdoms, grew overripe, was
plundered, disintegrated. The world which it had brought to birth became
racked by monstrous persecution, dogmatic quarrel, the Inquisition.
Thought became frozen by superstition and scholasticism. As always, that
which at the beginning had stood for all that was new and hopeful, itself tried to stamp out change. Latent pressure grew. And nine hundred
years from its foundation, the mobs of the French Revolution wrecked
the great Abbey of Cluny so thoroughly that hardly a trace of its mag-
nificence remains.

But yet again, within this aging culture, a new one had already been
conceived. At the very moment when the fires of the Spanish Inquisition
showed to what depths the medieval idea could fall, a new light appeared in
Italy. As before, an unnoticed corner, away from the warring and unwieldy
empires, was birthplace. But in keeping with the new age, not abbots nor
priests, but a family of rich bankers, made possible the conditions.

Cosimo Medici found himself chief citizen of Florence at a time when his
small city was becoming focus both of mounting opposition to Papal Rome,
and of passionate devotion to classical antiquity, whose statues, temples and
manuscripts – after a thousand years' indifference – were now being un-
earthed. These naked figures, smooth columns and clear minds seemed –
by contrast with the superstition, elaboration and ritual of the later Middle
Ages – to open a window on paradise. Cosimo collected about him the best
of the findings, and a pleiad of young artists who were fired by them – Do-
natello, Ghiberti, della Robbia, Lippi. He gathered Greek and Latin manuscripts, opened the first public library in Europe, and by 1440 was accepted
as first patron of what was already called 'The New Learning'.

A strange thing then occurred. In 1438 the Emperor John Paleologus of
Constantinople, with a train of scholars, artists and churchmen, came to the
west in a last endeavour to enlist help against the Turks. A joint council
with the Pope and the Western Church was arranged at Ferrara. As it was
about to open, Cosimo Medici persuaded Emperor, Pope and the whole
assembly to adjourn to Florence at his personal expense. No western aid

was forthcoming, and the Emperor returned empty-handed to Constantinople to face the inevitable tragedy alone.

But behind the scenes something very important had happened. Schoolmen in the Emperor's suite seem to have been looking for a refuge for their tradition. Cosimo, with some intimation of the role of Florence and the need of his time, seems to have been looking for school. Or perhaps he belonged to school already, and recognized his peers. An understanding was reached. Fourteen years later Constantinople fell, as it had to. But all that was important had already been transferred to Florence.

We are told that the idea of his famous Platonic Academy was suggested to Cosimo by the Greek scholar Plethon. What took place in it we cannot know. We only hear of weekend gatherings at the Villa Careggi or at Fiesole. We look at paintings by Botticelli or Dosso Dossi in which the models, as though self-remembering, seem consciously to act the idea to be conveyed. And in Benozzo Gozzoli's fresco of the cavalcade of the Wise Men which winds round the chapel of the Medici Palace, we seem to see its group self-portrait. All who took part – Greek priests, artists like Fra Angelico and Gozzoli himself, the new philosophers like Pico Mirandola and Marsilio Ficino – pilgrimage through Tuscan hills and woods towards the Nativity upon the altar. The Old King is the Patriarch of Constantinople, the Young King the boy Lorenzo de Medici, and the Second King who rides over against the Nativity, both heralding and echoing it, the Emperor Paleologus. It is the record of a group in school.

From this group went out Politian and Mirandola to launch a literary renaissance, Botticelli and Verocchio to create an artistic one, Reuchlin to sow the seeds of the Reformation in Germany, Linacre to found the College of Physicians in London. To it belonged Leon Battista Alberti, father of Renaissance architecture, whose inspiration was the divine proportion and Pythagorean system of numbers, here taught by Ficino. Lorenzo, its nominal head, discovered and brought up the boy Michelangelo, selected young Leonardo da Vinci to work in Milan. Upon the art, technique, literature, ideals and freedom it engendered, Western culture has existed into living memory.

So culture is born from culture, each fathered by seed from some alien but esoteric source – the Mediaeval by new knowledge from the Arab world; the Renaissance by savants driven west at the fall of Byzantium; the new civilization of our own day by release of ancient wisdom from India and Tibet.

For those concerned, the birth of a new civilization must over and over again in history have meant that *everything had to be reconstructed, every-*

thing had to be made over again from the beginning, in a new form, suitable to a new age. Looking back from our standpoint over the whole descent of history, we can see that each new beginning was in reality but a tremendous effort to continue. There was no beginning, but only a continuation of the life of humanity. To those who had to begin, to engender a new phase of human development, this beginning was life or death. But from the point of view of the stars nothing was altered, because humanity and all its potentialities remain the same.

III   THE AGE OF THE CONQUEST OF TIME

The more we study this cycle of past civilizations, the more urgently we are faced by the questions: What is *our* civilization? What are its characteristics? How can it develop? Are we assisting at a new birth or only at an obvious death?

These questions are very difficult to answer. For seen closely, decay very often looks like progress, and progress like decay; just as a spring day and an autumn day may for a moment be indistinguishable.

Yet if we look back, we see that we do indeed live in a different world from that which existed a hundred years ago – different in ideals, expression, understanding, interests, possibilities, and in every other way. And if we take a generation of culture as between 300 and 400 years, and the birth of the Renaissance civilization as about 1450 A. D., then again it becomes clear that a new age *should* already have dawned for us.

But when did it begin? How is it recognizable? By what signs can we distinguish the growing new from the declining old?

The chief feature of this new culture, which may one day come to be called 'The Age of the Conquest of Time', was not at first apparent. Just as the Renaissance, that age of the conquest of space, began not with the discovery of America, but with the invention of perspective drawing, which first enabled men accurately to project three spacial dimensions within two, so this new epoch was ushered in by mechanical and philosophical novelties whose real significance lay hidden in the future.

Certainly, 'the conquest of time' is an anomaly, just as the 'conquest of space' was. Nobody conquers either time or space. They represent, and always will represent, two different projections of our universe, the plan and elevation, as it were. And it is as impossible to 'conquer' either, as it is to 'conquer' the surface of a table or an apple. Yet such surfaces can be studied, explored, penetrated, and their configuration permanently altered, as when one feels, pinches and finally takes a bite out of the apple. And in this period, whose conception lay somewhere round the year 1865, men did indeed learn to explore time, understand time, and enter into a different relation to time from that which they had enjoyed before.

Out of the innumerable inventions of this period we need take only three to demonstrate this trend. In 1872 Edward Muybridge anticipated the moving-picture by breaking up motion into constituent units with coordinated cameras which recorded the successive positions of racing horses. Hidden in this invention lay the possibility of putting these 'units' of motion together again *in different ways*, that is, of reproducing events either faster or slower than they actually occur, or in reverse. In one blow a technique was shown of breaking the illusion with which men had lived for thousands of years – that of a *time flowing in one direction at a uniform speed.*

Four years later Alexander Graham Bell invented the microphone. And again, within this apparently simple invention lay the possibility of a single man addressing not hundreds, but millions of men simultaneously, of projecting his voice and presence all over the world, *without the mediation of time.* Previously, human communication beyond earshot had been based on time. If a man wished to address large numbers of other men, he had to speak to a crowd in one place, then travel to a second place, speak there, move to a third place, and so on. Even if he wrote a book, the book had to be printed and copies conveyed to the places or countries where the readers lived. And all this meant *time*.

A third invention, that of the phonograph by Edison in 1877, had the reverse effect. Before, sound-waves vanished almost instantaneously with their production. There was no way of preserving them beyond the time they took to reverberate or echo, a half-minute or so at most. Now, suddenly, sound could be preserved in the same way as visual images had for centuries been preserved. A speech delivered today could be exactly reproduced in ten or a hundred years. Time was suddenly introduced as a dimension into phenomena where there had been no room for it before.

There is in fact one definite condition of this change of man's relation to time, and this condition began to be discovered in the sixties of the nineteenth century. Mechanical motion implies time; whereas electro-magnetic motion, in relation to human perception, is instantaneous. A wheelbarrow, for instance, can only exist in one place at one moment; the same light, on the other hand, can exist in many places simultaneously. Since the beginning of the world men had been surrounded by phenomena of these two orders. But up to the nineteenth century they had remained entirely distinct. The motion of a physical body could only be carried out mechanically, and took time. The motion of a sensual impression, which depends on electro-magnetic vibrations, was instantaneous and unpreservable.

The seed inventions of the Time-Age arose from the gradual discovery that mechanical motion and electro-magnetic motion were interchangeable. By changing electro-magnetic waves into mechanical motion, as in the cinema or phonograph, time was introduced where it had not entered before. By replacing mechanical motion by electro-magnetic impulses, as in the radio or telephone, phenomena were made instantaneous, which previously could only be accomplished by the aid of time.

Even in medicine the replacement of natural drugs acting on the organs by synthetic ones acting on cells, or by short-wave treatment acting on molecules, was an attempt to speed up the process of healing by transferring it to the faster time of a lower cosmos. All this implied a new interchangeability between dimensions.

The bible of these new possibilities was 'A Treatise on Electricity and Magnetism', published by Clerk Maxwell in 1865. And the translation of its laws into actuality took exactly one generation. In 1895 came the cinema, radio-telegraphy, and the discovery of radium, that curious offspring of the world of minerals and the world of light. Ten years more, and Einstein with his theory of relativity, was endeavouring, with incomplete success, to paint a picture of the fantastic universe which was beginning to unfold before men's ununderstanding eyes. While by 1950 the actual instruments of time-penetration – the cinema, the radio, television, the tape-recorder, penicillin – were available as playthings to all those who in the previous age would have possessed books or pictures.

Meanwhile, the strain put upon the old order by these changes in the value of time, and by the sense of universality which arose from it, could not be confined to the world of science. It was soon clear that they must also operate in the political sphere, and there too bring about similar changes and engender men of similar temper. The small elastic princedom, expanding and contracting with the alliances of its ruling family, could hardly hope to survive such pressure. Something larger, more rigid, and more aware of its own unity was necessary.

A tendency towards the federation of smaller units into larger ones had already been at work for more than a hundred years previously. This tendency now showed itself in a passionate preoccupation with frontiers, in which both the great nations (in a desire to consolidate their gains), and the small ones (in the fear of losing their identity) equally participated. So that the earlier idea of 'Great Britain' was now taken over by 'United Italy', 'All the Russias', 'Greater Germany', and so on. The greater nation was in fact the furthest that human prejudice could go at that moment towards that universal brotherhood, which the technical advances of the day implied.

The apparent contradiction between this growing sense of nationality and the general tendency to diffusion is only the result of a pause in this tendency becoming visible. In the middle ages, a man belonged to the unit of his 'manor', his town, or his religious order, and men in neighbouring towns were as much foreigners as were later those of neighbouring countries. In the 18th century a man born in England was more 'Cornish' or 'Kentish' than 'English' – it was the county which represented the unit, rather than the nation, which did not and could not in practice act as a whole, except symbolically through its leaders or its token army. But by 1865 the nation had in fact become the social unit, and men with reason thought of themselves as English, French or Germans. Although nations had long existed, this represented a great stretching of human imagination.

Actually, there is much to suggest that the natural unit to which a man feels organic allegiance, his 'homeland', is measured by a day's journey. It is that which he can see between sunup and sundown. Even into the early nineteenth century this was a region not more than fifty miles across. Then suddenly, with the coming of railways, a day's journey was no longer fifty but five or eight hundred miles. And it is striking that in Europe the nations which began to crystallize about 1865, and towards which their inhabitants began to feel much new and passionate patriotism, were for the most part of this scale of size. Just as, in the mid-twentieth century, the habit of thinking by continents and sub-continents was forced upon men by the day's span of the aeroplane.

In fact, the increasing self-consciousness of nations which developed so markedly from 1860 on has another aspect. It provides a parallel on another scale with the increasing self-consciousness which for cosmic reasons was evidently expected from the individual also, and which we must later study in detail.

As always, the new concept of the state crystallized round dramatic individuals. Just as King Arthur, Charlemagne, el Cid, had personified the first England, the first France, and the first Spain, so now quite suddenly new national heroes arose or were invented to personify their rebirth. These heroes represented 'unity', 'reform', 'democracy'. They represented the struggle against caste, against the aristocratic principle, which – whether it worked or not – was now forced into the villainous role, since the 'people', in accord with the new tendency to diffusion, assumed the noble one. So that the same heroes who in the older, more mature and stable countries appeared as writers and philosophers, in the younger and emergent ones now rose as political rebels and unifiers.

In the United States, the poor farm-boy Lincoln was to symbolize the defeat of the old aristocratic South; in Mexico, the Indian Juarez the defeat of the European conqueror; in Italy, the Genoese sailor Garibaldi the defeat of the political power of religion. All these represented also the new unification of their countries, and all three were to be transformed by popular imagination into superhuman figures, far greater and grander than in life – the new national heroes.

Both the physicists who now tried to see everything in terms of vibrations, and the politicians who tried to consolidate larger and larger areas within their respective frontiers, thus represented a deep tendency towards synthesis, towards unification. The International Red Cross of 1864, the International Postal Union of 1875, and the First Workers' International of 1864, were other expressions of the same impulse to override frontiers, to reconcile the far and the near, which followed spontaneously from the overcoming of certain hitherto rigid barriers of time.

All these, however, had been anticipated in a very curious way. About the same time that the scientists had been making their startling discoveries, but completely independent of them, an extraordinary pleiad of poets and writers had arisen in the great countries of the west who, in their own way, were also reconstructing the whole past, future, and manifold present of modern man.

In the year 1870, Victor Hugo was 68, Hans Andersen 65, Tennyson 61, Whitman 51, Tolstoy and Ibsen 42, and Nietzsche 26. And all were in the full flood of creation. The presence of this group of poetic prophets in the west at one moment is of itself extraordinary. All were deeply religious, but in a new free manner, unconfined to any doctrine. All possessed a breadth and grasp, an immensity of view of time and space, which the discoveries of the new age for the first time made possible. And all in a very special way resumed and incarnated the spirit of their particular countries, reconstructing, as it were, the heritage of each for survival in the age to come.

In the Gothic flowering such men would have been abbots or churchmen, in the Renaissance painters and philosophers. Now they appeared primarily as writers, but as writers who, like Hugo and Tolstoy, could on occasion enter and act in the external world of politics and social reform, and who there appeared as of greater and not less stature than the professional politicians and statesmen.

One task of these men, in its effect on time, was curiously parallel to that of the scientists already mentioned. For it was to reshape the past of their own countries, and to make that past *acceptable from a new point of view*. A striking example is Victor Hugo's 'Notre Dame de Paris'. For in this book he not only evokes medieval Paris with uncanny reality, but he puts back into that Paris a humanitarian point of view *which did not exist there*. And he does this in such a way that the picture of medieval Paris is permanently altered — for all later men it becomes a compound of actuality and of Hugo's reconstruction, and they can never undo his work.

In the same way, Andersen reconstructed and permanently fixed a picture of pre-Christian Scandinavia, Tennyson reconstructed and permanently fixed a picture of Arthurian England, Tolstoy reconstructed and permanently fixed a picture of Napoleonic Russia, and Whitman reconstructed and permanently fixed a picture of Lincoln's America. In each case the reconstruction was so grand, so all-embracing, and it corresponded so truly to certain attitudes of the new age that it was almost instantly accepted in preference to other memory.

All these men, in one aspect, played the strange role of improving the past, that is, of making it acceptable to the present and the future, which belongs to all founders of an age. This extraordinary work, which every man who cultivates memory is forced to do in relation to his own life, they performed in relation to their countries. For this task of reconstructing the past is the first and essential step towards any real change in the future; as Karl Marx also realized when he prepared the way for bolshevism by reconstructing history on the basis of 'economic motive' and 'class struggle'.

But Hugo, Andersen and Whitman worked upon time in the reverse way to Marx. Instead of eliminating the ideals which actually existed and ruled in the past, and replacing them with the lowest human motives of greed and violence, as he did, they attempted to put back into the past higher ideals than had actually prevailed there, or at any rate ideals more comprehensible to the new age. Thus their attempt, whether successful or not, was to regenerate the past, whereas that of Marx, again whether successful or not, could only serve to degenerate it.

The same men also helped to reconstruct the general approach to human ideals and to religion itself. The very inventions which removed time from human communication and neutralized space, made it inevitable that certain fixed religious forms and understandings, which had very well served a certain racial type or group living on its own, would be subjected to impossible strains when brought face to face with other forms, also perfectly satisfactory to the races which practised them, but which side by side could only appear contradictory. Such a broadening could not come from within the churches or from the guardians of particular religious ways themselves, for their task was clearly to preserve the purity of their rites. And when such attempts were made, they usually led to such a weakening of religious practice that nothing but some feeble form of social benevolence remained.

These new poetic prophets, however, were more free, and exactly by their lack of attachment to one form were enabled to release through the world a strong fresh wind of tolerance and larger understanding. If no time, then was there not Christianity before Christ? If no space, may not the gods of East and West be one? It seemed that all that was true had to be gathered together into one whole, and shown to be *complementary* rather than hostile. Such a new universal view of religion and of God is expressed by Whitman in 'Chanting the Square Deific' (1871), by Victor Hugo in 'Religions et Religion' (1880), by Tolstoy in 'What I believe In' (1884).

This embracing and reconciling of different forms and messages, *without destroying their individuality*, the parallel of what was made possible in the physical realm by the use of electro-magnetic waves, is very characteristic of the new line of religious thought which begins to develop in the 60s and 70s. And what Hugo and Whitman did for religion in a broad and poetic way, scholars and mystics independently developed in their own fashion.

It was in 1876 that the German Oriental scholar, Max Müller, launched in Oxford his programme for a translation of the 'Sacred Books of the East' which were to include the key writings of Hinduism, Buddhism, Zoroastrianism, of Islam and of China. A year earlier a Russian woman, Madame Blavatsky, had founded the Theosophical Society, which was a first attempt at a new synthetic or basic religion, that should demonstrate the fundamental unity of all previous religious forms. While the one great contemporary religious figure in the East, Ramakrishna, between 1865 and 1875 practised one after the other not only all the rites of different Hindu sects, but also those of Islam and Christianity, with the aim of reaching by these different paths the same transcendental goal.

As a result of a generation of this new 'universal' view of mysticism and religion, Dr. R. M. Bucke was able in 1901 to attempt an objective 'psychology' of higher or 'cosmic consciousness', as he called it, irrespective of race, creed or epoch.

The whole of the new culture thus seemed to be based on the quite new possibility of transcending the divisions of space by escaping from one-dimensional time. This attempt, however, took two quite different lines. The scientists, physicists and designers concentrated on the possibility of a *mechanical* escape from time; while the poets, writers and mystics studied the possibility of a *conscious* escape. What continued to lack was a bridge between the two points of view.

Looking back on the genesis of previous civilizations, where all aspects and applications of the new knowledge seem to spring from a single source – whether the Eleusinian mysteries in the sixth century B. C., or the Cluniac order in the 11th A. D. – we ask ourselves whether, somewhere and among some people, these two apparently contradictory sides of nineteenth century culture were not in fact united in a higher understanding? Did there somewhere exist a hidden school of regeneration from which all radiated?

The extraordinary speed of diffusion of ideas in the 19th century, the new possibilities of travel which in a few months could scatter the pupils of such a school across the whole world, makes it difficult to say. Certainly, the very characteristics of this age seem to imply that new ideas may spring to life in many places simultaneously, without direct communication.

At the same time, it is strange how many of the key-works which accompanied its birth and which have the peculiar quality of direct school knowledge, seem to derive from Rome.

Goethe's 'Faust' was completely reconstructed after the famous 'Italian Journey' of 1796, to which he had looked forward so longingly, and in his old age he ascribes its success to the fact that "it permanently preserves *the period of development of a human soul.*" From the same period in Rome dates his 'Theory of Colours', which claimed that *light* is the highest form of energy we know, and that *colours* are but modifications or corruptions of pure light. Identically the same idea is expressed poetically by Shelley in 1821, *immediately after his return from Rome:*

> Life, like a dome of many-coloured glass,
> Stains the white radiance of Eternity . . .

This is particularly striking when we remember that exactly at this time Rome was the scene of the birth of the German school of pre-Raphaelite painters, whose work was based on a new understanding of colour connected with the idea of different perception and the change of being required to attain it. In 1848 the English Pre-Raphaelite Brotherhood sprang from the same group. And though it is difficult to trace the French Impressionists to this source, except possibly through Manet's visit to Rome in the late '50s, it is notable that from the beginning their aim was precisely to paint *light* by the contrasted use of pure instead of mixed colours. The artist had to become conscious of and reproduce *his own impressions resulting from light*, for it is through these that each man lives and is acquainted with reality.

By the 1860s, Clerk Maxwell's analogy between the octaves of colour and sound, between pitch and hue, loudness and shade, finally brought the painter's study of light into direct relation with the new knowledge of electricity and magnetism, and showed its obedience to the same laws which rule countless other phenomena previously regarded as unconnected.

This new theory of light and of vibrations was used by another of the Rome group, Charles-Sebastian Cornelius, to reconcile the phenomena of the material and spiritual worlds in such books as '*On The Reciprocal Influence of the Body and Soul*' (1871). While about the same period the implications of this same understanding in the realm of *time* also began to be released. Ibsen's 'Peer Gynt', which hints at this and so many other esoteric truths in dramatic form, was written during his stay at Frascati near Rome in 1867, as was Nietzsche's 'Eternal Recurrence' during his Italian journey of 1881. This latter book, which for the first time connects the idea of recurrence (implicit in the electro-magnetic theory of vibrations) with the questions of consciousness and of man's development, was deeply to influence first Hinton and later Ouspensky, whose explanation of the three dimensions of time paved the way for a final reconciliation between the new knowledge of modern science and the ancient ideas of eternity and regeneration.

Exactly what kind of a school existed in Rome between 1800 and 1880, from which so many creative ideas of the new age could emanate, we cannot know. Yet in all its traces we find the same understanding – *light* as the one creative and unifying force of the universe, the *octave* as the modification of pure light into form and colour, and *time, recurrence,* and the *fulfilment of all possibilities* as the three stages of man's ascent to the nature of light.

So that if it be asked what is characteristic of the new age, and how may it be distinguished from the old, we can now answer: That which separates and divides belongs to the past. That which reconciles and unites belongs to the future. And the way towards unity lies through escape from time.

XVII THE CYCLES OF GROWTH AND WAR

I PHYSIOGNOMY: THE MIRROR OF MERCURY

BEFORE WE GO ON TO STUDY THE PLANETARY CYCLES, THAT IS, THE varying effect of individual planets on man in time, it becomes necessary to study in greater detail the mechanism through which such influence may work.

We have already begun to see the general plan of a cosmos, and we have seen how – all cosmoses being built on this same general plan – each part of a smaller cosmos reflects and reacts to the corresponding part of a larger one. We have seen the cosmos of the Solar System reflected in the cosmos of the World of Nature, and both reflected in turn in the cosmos of mankind and of individual Man.

When we consider the possible effects of individual planets on man, we have first to realize that each of them is itself a cosmos or potential cosmos, just as the Earth is a cosmos. And further, that the instrument in which each is reflected must follow the same pattern, just as a radio receiving-set is a replica in miniature and in reverse of the transmitting apparatus.

In the chapter on 'Man as Microcosm' we came to the conclusion, after discovering such a replica of the solar system in the human body, that the individual planets should control the individual endocrine glands, and through them the individual functions of man. For example, the planet Mercury seemed to bear an affinity to the thyroid gland, through which it might control the whole *function of movement*.

This function of movement works through the voluntary muscular system of the body, that is, through all muscles that can be moved intentionally by mental will, through their co-ordination, speed of reaction, power of learning new movements, and so on, and so on. This complete system in turn is reflected on a reduced scale in the muscles of the head and face, in which the whole mental, emotional and physical life of the individual is constantly reflected *as movement*.

All cosmoses, as we already saw, are divided into three parts and possess six or potentially seven functions. In the same way the head, as mirror of the whole body, is also divided into three parts:

(a) upper part of head, including brain, mirror of the head itself, as seat of the intellect:

(b) middle part of head, including cerebellum, mirror of the chest, as seat of the emotions:

(c) lower part of head, mirror of the belly, as seat of the physical functions.

At the same time the head also contains muscles and nervous controls reflecting all seven functions which serve the body. But since it is the *movement and expression* of the face, rather than the inner anatomy of the head, which now concern us, we prefer to note the octave of external orifices and organs by which food, air and perceptions are received into the organism, and matters elaborated in the body emitted:

The four ordinary groups of orifices in the head are:

(1) the mouth, which receives food and drink, emits speech:

(2) the nose, which receives air and scent, emits carbon dioxide:

(3) the ears, which receive sound, emit ?:

(4) the eyes, which receive light-impressions, emit emotional signals.

Further, the whole head and the orifices referred to are covered by:

(5) the skin, which receives touch and temperature impressions, emits physical warmth and magnetism.

In addition, old physiology noted two potential and invisible orifices in the head, undeveloped in ordinary man, but which if developed would serve to receive and emit two different kinds of superphysical influence:

(6) an orifice between the eyebrows:

(7) an orifice in the crown of the head.

The disposition of these orifices in the head indicates their chief service. Thus the mouth, situated in the lower part of the head, serves the belly and physical functions. The nostrils, standing on the boundary between the middle and lower parts of the head, serve both chest and belly, both emotional and physical functions. The eyes, on the boundary between upper and middle parts of the head, serve both head and chest, intellectual and emotional functions. The skin, covering the whole head, serves all functions. While the orifice between the eyebrows would serve the head itself; and that in the crown, standing on the boundary between the head and the non-physical world above, would serve as final exit to a different state of existence altogether.

In studying physiognomy, that is, the external signs of the psychology of ordinary man, we have to omit the last two orifices, being invisible. Physiognomy therefore consists principally in study of the relation between the three parts of the head; and in study of the shape, size and relative movements of the mouth, nose, eyes and ears, together with the corresponding effects of these movements upon the skin in the form of lines and wrinkles. Physiognomy is the study of the being of individual man reflected in the *movement* of his face, and in the traces left there by habitual expressions in the past.

In the face all functions – digestion, respiration, metabolism, thought, physical emotion, sex – find themselves translated into movement, into expression. And, as is well known in endocrinology, the subtlety and vivacity of this consequent play of expression is directly connected with the balanced working of the thyroid gland. Feverish, wild, uncontrolled grimacing implies overaction of this gland: a wooden unresponsive face its deficiency. The face is thus the instrument of movement, the mirror of Mercury.

If we examine more closely this mirror or instrument of the moving function controlled by the thyroid gland, we see more and more evidences of its cosmic pattern. For example, the external forms of mouth, nose, eyes and ears are in their turn divided into three parts in which the intellectual, emotional and physical aspects of the corresponding functions are reflected. In the eyes, the shape and motion of the top lid particularly reflects the state of intellectual function, the eye itself the state of emotional function, and the lower lid the state of instinctive function. Similarly in the ears, the configuration of the upper part of the shell is connected with 'intellectual perception, of the entrance to the auditory canal with emotional perception, and of the lobe with instinctive perception. And again in the nose, exaggeration of the upper part represents predominance of intellect, of the middle part of emotion, and of the lower bulb and nostrils instinct: so that a straight nose, always regarded as a sign of beauty, in fact represents perfect balance between these three sides. Although it is not apparent to the sight, and therefore does not concern our immediate study, it is interesting to note that the skin is similarly divided into three different layers, with similar significance.

In principle three states are possible for any orifice – normal relaxed state, dilated state, and contracted state: and the three chief positions of mouth, nose, eyes and ears are based on this principle. The eyes and lids may be in their normal relaxed shape, they may be wide and dilated, or they may be narrow and contracted. Similarly with the mouth and nostrils; and although in the case of the ears the amount of dilation and contraction is almost unnoticeable in men compared with animals, nevertheless corresponding muscular and physiological states may be observed.

Again in principle, a dilated state of the orifices of perception represents a desire to take in more from the outside world, while a contracted state represents a desire to take in less or at least to control and limit that which is taken in. Further, the dilation of one orifice, say the eyes, and the contraction of another, say the mouth, represent the desire to take in food for one function but to reject food for another, or to give out the product of one function but to repress the expression of another. From this springs the possibility of discrimination in man, and the infinite variety of expression which arises from different dilation and contraction of the mouth, nose, eyes and ears.

Greater subtlety is introduced by varying contractions in the different parts of each organ, representing its intellectual, emotional and instinctive aspects.

For instance, in the eye, the upper lid may be arched representing intellectual awareness, or it may droop representing intellectual somnolence: the lower lid may be tensed, representing instinctive well-being and control, or it may sag, representing instinctive weariness and exhaustion: the eye itself may be brilliant, representing emotional stimulation, or dull representing emotional indifference. Indeed, the iris in turn constitutes an exact mirror of the whole organism and its different organs, whose individual health may be clearly diagnosed in this way.[70]

These differing states of upper and lower lids and of the eye itself may combine in an almost unlimited number of expressions, each of which provides an exact index of the state of the individual concerned. Moreover, each person will have a usual or habitual expression of the eyes, which will be the resultant of the relative states of his intellectual, emotional and instinctive functions over many years. In this connection the Oriental artistic canon may be noted, which requires that ordinary men be drawn with both upper and lower lids curved, gods with upper lids arched and lower straight, and demons the reverse.

Again, besides being dilated or contracted, the eyes may look to the left or right, or up or down: and the mouth, besides being shut or open, may curve upwards or curve downwards. In general, motion upwards may be taken to represent aspiration or pleasure, motion downwards dejection or sadness, and motion to one side or another distraction without any particular emotional flavour.

At this point, it is necessary to introduce a further principle inherent in the study of physiognomy, namely, that all manifestations of man may be divided into two kinds – those deriving from his essence, that is, the physical qualities, capacities and tendencies with which he was born; and those

70. Modern iriscopy was worked out by the Hungarian Von Peczeley, and developed by Nils Liljequist, Angel Bidaurrazaga and others.

deriving from his personality, that is, all that he has since learned, acquired, pretended and superimposed upon his essence. In physiognomy, the right half of the face is supposed to be the mirror of personality, and the left of essence; as are the right and left hands in palmistry. As too the heart, main-spring of the essential organism, is housed in the left-hand side of the chest.

Besides all the other motions of mouth, nose, eyes and ears referred to above, we therefore find as well that the right eye reflecting the state of personality may differ from the left eye reflecting essence; and similarly the left nostril from the right. While the 'wry smile', in which the upward curving of the right half of the mouth by personality contradicts the down-ward curve of the left half produced by the real feelings of essence, is proverbial. The two unknown and invisible orifices, situated in the centre line of the head, would if developed refer to the man as a whole or to the complete unification of essence and personality.

All the expressions of the human face we thus see to be governed by six main principles:

(1) The threefold division of the head, reflecting the intellectual, emotional and instinctive parts of the whole organism:

(2) The sevenfold division of the orifices and organs of perception, corresponding with the seven human functions:

(3) The threefold division of each organ representing the intellectual, emotional and instinctive parts of the corresponding function:

(4) Dilation, relaxation and contraction of each organ representing acceptance, balance or rejection in the corresponding function:

(5) Motion upwards, sideways and downwards of each organ representing aspiration, distraction and dejection in the corresponding function:

(6) The twofold division of the face, and thus of all the orifices and organs of perception, corresponding with the essence and personality of the individual concerned.

All possible expressions available to the human face, from the most devilish to the most ecstatic, are produced by the interaction of these six principles, and may be analysed with their aid. And if it be objected that the classification is arbitrary and unproven then we must emphasize once again that it – like all other indications in the present book – is given *as a basis for observation*. Plausible or unplausible, proven or unproven, all theory will remain theory for the reader until he has *established or refuted it for himself on the basis of his own personal observation and experience*. For neither belief nor disbelief, conviction nor scepticism, can ever substitute for this, the only way in which the thesis of a book can affect real life and actual men.

The chief purpose of this analysis of the external instrument of one particular function is to show that such instruments are designed to reflect in miniature all the motions and laws of a higher controlling cosmos. Exactly how such instruments respond to the influence of their heavenly archetypes it is difficult to say except in a general way. But just as, discovering in one place the mechanism of a radio-controlled aeroplane and in another place the exactly corresponding mechanism of its ground control, we should deduce that the one was designed to respond to the other, so we deduce the functional mechanism of man to be designed to respond to the functional mechanism of the Solar System.

There is one way, in fact, in which a good case might be made out for such control and such response. If we could prove that the stimulation and inertia of such instruments, among mankind as a whole, were to follow the same cycle as do the corresponding planets in relation to the earth, then this would be, if not proof, at least a very clear sign of connection.

In the case of a relation between the moving function controlled by the thyroid gland and the cycle of Mercury, we are hampered by the shortness of the latter's cycle and by its extremely erratic term. It is obviously quite impossible in practice to discover whether mankind on the whole grows more active, more mobile, more expressive, every three months or so, or not. Too many other factors confuse such short-term observation.

To attempt to show a connection between human functions and the planets we must therefore move on to cycles of longer duration.

II VENUS AND FERTILITY

Our first problem when trying to study the effect of planetary cycles on the life of humanity, is connected with our failure to recognize similar phenomena when translated to different scales. It is a commonplace that men regard surgery or assault committed by an individual in one light, but surgery or assault committed by nations under the name of war in a quite different light. The scale changed, the phenomenon appears to our perception to be different in *its nature*.

So that we have first to recognize very well the play of each function in individual men, and the effect of a planetary stimulation of this function in one case: and then by an effort of the imagination we have to picture how the effects of such stimulation would appear when multiplied a millionfold, that is, when suddenly changed from an individual foible to a universal *fashion*, backed by all the authority of morals, political expediency, and religious sanction.

Very often the effect of this change of scale is to make the phenomenon seem to change into its opposite. For in the first case, stimulation will look like an expression of what we call individual 'choice', 'freedom of conscience', 'liberty', 'personal happiness' and so on, while in the second exactly the same thing may by sheer weight of mass example take on the guise of 'duty', 'fate', 'custom' or some other limitation of individual action. In fact, both cases will represent the same influence or law at work, the different interpretations arising from man's illusory belief that he is doing, choosing, and arranging his life, independently of the world in which he lives. Very much of the suffering of human life arises from the conflict in the individual between such compulsions on personal and on national or racial scales; and this conflict provides almost the basic theme of classical Greek tragedy.

Another difficulty of studying these cycles in action lies in the fact that they mutually affect each other, and one cycle can never quite be taken out of the general pattern, any more than in a symphony the performance of the flute can or should be separated from the general orchestration.[71] We noticed in studying functions in the individual organism how the manifestations of sex, for example, could combine with other functions – with passionate action, with sensuality, with intellect, and so on – to produce quite different results. Similarly for the rhythms affecting the whole of humanity.

Let us, however, begin with the simplest and least complex rhythm. Suppose the stimulation of the parathyroid glands by the planet Venus to encourage tissue-building in the organisms concerned. When such an influence is at its height and shines impartially on the whole Earth, that is, on men, animals, fish, birds and plants, inducing in all the same or comparable metabolism, we shall have the 'fat years' of legend. When the same influence wanes, 'lean years' will follow.

Plumpness, however, is also connected with fertility, or at least with the rate of survival of offspring, so that probably such 'fat years' will also witness an increase in fecundity on a biological level. Thus the 'fatness' will apply not only to individual bodies, but also to the growth of communities – whether of men, animals, fish or caterpillars.

In the case of man, whose life is ten times longer than the 8-year cycle of Venus, the effects of changes in fecundity according to the latter's cycle

---

71. See Appendix IX, 'Planetary Periods and Cycles of Human Activity'.

are smoothed out and hardly reflect in the total population. But with creatures whose life is as short or shorter than this cycle, numbers should, if our thesis is correct, vary in some direct proportion to this synodic period. If we refer to work recently done on the study of biological cycles we find interesting confirmation of this. Elton in particular found a clear four-year rhythm in the number, migrations and epidemics of lemmings, mice, squirrels and the foxes that prey on them in regions as far separated as Norway, Newfoundland and Canada. The full venusian periodicity of eight years was clearly established by Moore in the yield of chief crops in the Middle Western states of America; and in consequence is found particularly reflected in cotton-prices.

Looking for further biological rhythms on a large scale, however, we next encounter a very curious cycle of $9^2/_3$ years, which is perhaps the most marked of all. The rhythms of many short-lived pests, such as the tent-caterpillar which attacks fruit-trees, and the chinch-bug which attacks cereals, can be established very exactly, and both of these have been found to follow a $9^2/_3$ year rhythm for long periods, the latter for more than a century. The same cycle is seen in the catch of salmon in New Brunswick, and in the trapping of fur-bearing animals such as the Canadian lynx, marten, fisher, mink and muskrat.[72]

An interesting and fairly successful attempt has been made to connect this rhythm in biological potency and fecundity with an exactly similar rhythm which has been traced in atmospheric ozone. An increase in ozone is well known to have a highly stimulating effect on the sex and tone of all living creatures, including man. This connexion is particularly interesting from our point of view because it shows clearly the interrelation of different scales – changes in the world of organic life following directly upon changes in atmospheric conditions which belong to the next higher world, that is, the world of Earth. While changes in the composition of the atmosphere can in turn be shown to result from variations in electrical and magnetic radiation received from *outside* the Earth, that is, to depend upon changes in the astronomical world.

Put in another way, electronic radiation from the heavenly bodies produces molecular change in the Earth's atmosphere, while such molecular change in the atmosphere in turn produces cellular change in the organic bodies dwelling therein. In this way we can see the practical influence of celestial phenomena upon creatures living on the Earth's surface, and bridge the

---

72. Ellsworth Huntington, 'Mainsprings of Civilization', pp. 462–3 and 488–507.

apparently insuperable gap between the movement of a planet and the individual impulses of a man, a salmon or a lynx.

Only, what is the connexion, if any, between this curious period of 9 $^2/_3$ years, and the venusian cycles of 585 days and eight years? We should be entirely at a loss did we not recall the principle established above, namely, that the planetary rhythms never act singly, but always in combination with other rhythms, producing in their different conjunctions the unending variety of nature.

For on consideration it is evident that increase in fecundity is not traceable to stimulation of the parathyroid or glands of tissue-building alone, but is also dependent on certain passionate urges connected with stimulation of the adrenals. Adrenal impulses by themselves, without the favourable conditions of 'fatness', tend to be sterile; while 'fatness' without the stimulation to mating resulting from adrenal activity, again fails to lead to prolific reproduction. So that if, as we supposed, the parathyroids are under the influence of Venus and the adrenals under the influence of Mars, we should expect conditions favouring fecundity to be produced when the maximum effect of these two planets coincided.

The observed fecundity cycle of $9^2/_3$ years expresses just such a double conjunction. For at 3510 days the completion of six periods of Venus exactly coincides with the completion of four and a half periods of Mars. The two influences 'shine together', so to speak, with the results which have been described and which we would expect.

Huntington makes a further illuminating remark upon this cycle. "As we go from mammals, insects and fish to trees and crops, the $9^2/_3$ year cycle becomes less distinct. If we go in the other direction from animals to human health (heart diseases) it also grows less distinct. This suggests that the conditions which give rise to the cycle have a particularly direct effect upon animal vigour."

In other words, the cycles referring to the parathyroids and adrenals, the glands of growth and passion, do refer to the essentially *animal* constitution, whether found embryonically in insects, typically in animals, or combined with higher functions in man. This cycle cannot be well seen in the vegetable world, because it is there obscured by the stronger rhythm of still lower functions. It is also unclear in man, exactly because in him the impulse to fatten and procreate is modified by reason, foresight, loyalty and aspiration which derive from higher rhythms governing mind and emotion. In this way man differs from the animals, and in such mitigation of the rhythms of Venus and Mars lies the beginning of his individual choice.

Every state of matter is under its own inevitable laws: but that which is so incorporated may owe allegiance to a superior level and thus enjoy the right of appeal to a higher court. A wooden statue is subject to the danger of burning which applies to all wood; but the form of the saint which is incorporated in it may be remembered, revered and recarved quite independently of the perishable qualities of wood. So man in his cellular body is subject to the Venusian cycles which govern the growth and flux of cells. But his special possibility as man lies precisely in his chance of appeal to a permanence beyond cycles, a level beyond planetary influence. This permanence resides in consciousness, this level lies in the possibility of supercellular life.

Indeed, there is something deeply repugnant to man in the idea that he fattens and propagates by the same laws and cycles as do fish or foxes. And even though it be so proven, precisely because he is man, he is forced to ask: If such is the mechanical action of this influence, how would it seem if received consciously? What can men make of the Venusian cycle, which animals cannot?

Immediately he asks such a question the whole picture changes. And the very influence which made him a helpless piece of flesh among all other flesh, now enables him to understand and consciously feel one with other life. If Venus inescapably influences him as a cellular creature, it also enables him to feel what all other cellular creatures feel, and by consciously realizing her influence on himself, to become aware of its effect on them also. If men were not in one aspect made as plants and animals are made, plants and animals would be forever strange and incomprehensible to them. Because man is plantlike and animal in one part of himself, he enjoys the possibility of acting as intelligence and conscience for the whole World af Nature.

The more he realizes the wonder and beauty of that world, the higher will he value this opportunity.

III MARS AND WAR

Mars is so traditionally the god of war that it is difficult to come to a consideration of his cycle without having this significance already in mind. And the apparent effect of Mars upon the adrenal glands, of which the medulla controls impulses of fear and flight, and the cortex those of rage and pugnacity, bears out this thesis. By the very existence of different types of men there must always be differences, disputes, quarrels. But when the adrenals or glands of passion are stimulated such differences are far more likely to become translated into violent and uncontrolled action. Obviously a tendency to panic on the one hand and rage on the other, induced in millions of people simultaneously, will produce conditions very favourable to the outbreak of war.

Thus the first thing which it is necessary to understand about war is that *all* men are responsible for it, *all* men are guilty of the passionate reactions against others which, enormously multiplied and harnessed in a definite direction, make war possible. The motion of a certain gland produces 'passion' in man, and in his ordinary state of subjectiveness and illusion, this passion finds its outlet *against others*. This is man's ordinary state of being. And without a definite change of level of being, without a definite abandonment of a certain illusory sense of 'I', no men – however cultured, however 'liberal' – are exempt from this guilt.

'Passion' is a constant factor in human life. All that changes is the cause which provokes passion or the means which it employs. Some 'martial' types can indeed grow passionate and quarrel over anything at all, and at certain times in the past when this type was in the ascendant, special concepts like 'slighted honour' or 'outraged decency' had to be invented to justify the complete irrationality of their actions. Dean Swift lampooned this tendency once and for all in his wars between Big-Endians and Little-Endians, which wracked Lilliput over the vexed question as to which end a breakfast egg should be opened.

At the same time it is necessary to realize that *all* types grow passionate and quarrel. Instinctive types will quarrel and fight over food or women, emotional types over religion or 'justice', while intellectual types who pride themselves on their 'broadmindedness' in relation to sex or religion, will quarrel and fight with equal bitterness over rival scientific theories or over some entirely subjective conception of 'taste' in art or literature.

There is in fact only one way out of this impasse. This comes about only with a complete revision of a man's whole attitude both to himself and to others. Only when he begins to understand men's place in the universe, and their inevitable actions under different influences; only when he fully realizes that neither he nor anyone else *does* anything but what they must do in the light of their being and their type; only *when a certain fundamental illusion of his personality has actually died*, will he become free of fighting and quarrelling. For only then will his passionate nature cease to be directed against others, and will enable him instead to conquer himself, to accomplish the impossible, and to fight, not with other men, but with matter and mechanicalness. Such a transformation of the role of passionate impulse is rarely possible except with the aid of school.

Martial tendencies are transmuted by becoming invisible. Mechanical passion is the most obvious of all planetary characteristics. But when passion is swallowed, digested and made invisible, it is precisely that which moves mountains and achieves miracles. The end of war would be just such a miracle.

The passionate reactions against others which make war inevitable are thus the responsibility and the guilt of all men. It is the greatest possible illusion to believe a particular class, or interest, or country, or religion to be responsible for war. This idea is indeed the chief cause of new wars. And in its wilful propagation by all factions against their opponents we see the corruptive process of criminality ally itself to the terrible but natural process of destruction. Even the fact that wars are occasionally instigated by real criminals cannot justify such lying. For passionate reactions are, on the contrary, a definite hallmark of man's ordinary state of being. And it can even be said that 'peace', in the political sense, is merely the result of millions of passionate reactions neutralizing each other by their very triviality and subjectiveness.

Having fully understood this general guilt of mankind, however, having fully understood that all men are responsible for war, it is next necessary to understand that *no one is responsible*. From another point of view war can be seen as a purely cosmic phenomenon, produced by celestial influence on a scale where men's reasons and men's feelings have no significance whatsoever. A certain planet, at a certain stage in its cycle, creates a general tension on the surface of the Earth, as a result of which men – *in their ordinary state of being* – have no choice but to fight.

This does not mean that the influence itself implies war, any more than turning on an electric current implies that light-bulbs shall fuse. If men enjoyed a different level of being, that is, if they could use a sudden increase in inner tension to produce changes in themselves, instead of automatically relieving it against others, then the martial cycle would have quite a different significance. But as men now are, they can bear very little increase in pressure without violence, and in certain parts of the United States, for example, strikes and race riots as inevitably accompany the electric storms of July as do thunder and lightning. So too with the influence of Mars.

If the history of the last two centuries, for example, be searched for a correspondence between the incidence of war and the fifteen-year cycle characteristic of this planet, the evidence does seem to support such a connection. Every fifteenth year, with extraordinary regularity, finds a number of the nations of Europe involved in wars between themselves, or in warlike adventures and disasters in other parts of the world.[73] While the intermediate periods, if not exactly peaceful, nevertheless seem to bring the nearest approximations to peace possible in the present state of humanity and widespread lipservice to peaceful ideals and aspirations. Perhaps the clearest indication of this cycle is that its peaks mark a general fashion of belligerent patriotism, while in its troughs even politicians tend to adopt a conciliatory and international attitude.

The clarity of this cycle is probably due to the fact that it is accentuated by another planetary rhythm which bears an octave relationship to it. The cycle of Saturn, as we saw, has a duration of 30 years, and the anterior pituitary gland, controlled by Saturn, is in one aspect connected with the impulse and power to dominate, to master, both oneself and others. It is the gland connected with the exercise of will. In view of the average level of being among masses of humanity, the general stimulation of this gland will inevitably produce a desire to master – not oneself, which is difficult and painful – but somebody else.

In combination with the passionate urges produced by adrenal stimulation, this brings a state of mind particularly provocative of war. Thus if the synodic period of Mars produces a tendency to war every fifteen years, the superimposed period of Saturn may be expected to exaggerate this tendency every thirty years, that is, at alternate peaks.

Further, at every third peak, or forty-five years, this martial inclination will coincide with a peak in the nine-year rhythm of the asteroids and will thus be heightened in a different way by general economic and psychological depression, together with its attendant wave of crime.

It is this fact that the influence of Mars is always found in combination with some other influence, that makes it so difficult to assess the real nature of war itself. We can only say for certain that there must be many different kinds of war, according to the nature of the synchronizing influence – there will be wars of domination and conquest when Mars combines with Saturn, wars of panic and cruelty at its conjunction with the asteroids, wars resulting from growth of population under Venus, and even Holy Wars when the martial cycle is modified by Neptune.

What is the common factor of all these wars? It is surely *destruction*. All

73. See Appendix X, 'The Cycle of War'.

wars, even the most noble, the most holy, *destroy* – lives, property, even societies and civilizations. An outbreak of war can never do anything but destroy, and all that can be added is that at some periods it is evidently required by Nature that certain things should be destroyed. Only man in general appears to destroy *much more* than need be destroyed. The destruction in 1944 of the monastery of Monte Cassino with all that it implied may be taken as a case in point. All civilizations are ultimately destroyed by war, or so weakened by it that they fall victim to disasters which they might otherwise overcome.

Having said so much, it must be emphasized again that the process of destruction in itself is necessary to Nature and cannot be avoided. It is quite different from the process of crime or corruption, which can never under any circumstances lead to good or useful results. Only in war destruction is nearly always combined with crime.

This distinction makes it possible to understand why the nature of war has baffled men throughout the ages, and it explains the evident unreality, for ordinary men, of a purely pacifist position. For the pacifist can never explain how it is that, although war seems absolutely futile and undesirable, nevertheless some of the strongest and noblest men take part in it, and often act then with much greater courage, loyalty, devotion and self-sacrifice than they do at any other time.

Looking back into other ages, we sometimes find very high ideals upheld by a warrior class or knighthood. And in certain special conditions, the art of war could even provide the form for an esoteric school, as it did for the Knights Templars and for archery schools in Persia and India. If war itself belonged to the criminal process this would be quite impossible, for all taking part in it would become defiled. And one of the first conditions of all esoteric work is that it *must not be touched by crime*.

War then is an expression of the destructive process working through mankind. By the introduction of fear, hatred and cruelty man renders it criminal. This distinction is very well expressed in the Hindu Gospel, 'Bhagavad Gita', where the knight Arjuna, finding himself on the battlefield and assigned by duty to mortal combat with his own kin, begs his divine guide Krishna to be excused the ordeal. Krishna replies: "Realize that pleasure and pain, gain and loss, victory and defeat, are all one and the same: then go into battle. Do this and you cannot commit any sin".[74]

74. 'The Bhagavad Gita', trs. by Swami Prabhavananda and Christopher Isherwood, p. 44.

THE CYCLES OF GROWTH AND WAR

Arjuna's revulsion represents the highest possible emotion of civilized man in relation to war. Yet an even loftier attitude is indicated to him. Thus war, like sex, provides one of the final tests of man's being, and by his attitude towards it and his action in it each individual demonstrates, with mathematical exactness, *what he is*.

At the same time, although the causes of war which lie in the heavens and man's nature have not changed since Arjuna's time, its scale most evidently has. One factor has altered completely, at once outmoding all previous ideas and explanations. This factor is the amount of energy placed in the hands of unregenerate man.

By means of club, bow and arrow, sword or spear, men could only be killed laboriously and one by one. And it was precisely this *labour* of killing, rather than human scruples, which for thousands of years kept war within certain bounds. With Greek fire and the first cannon ten men could be killed at a time, with the bombs of the First World War a hundred, with those of the Second World War a thousand, and with the atomic bombs of today a hundred thousand. Both the hard work and the personal element have now been taken out of killing, as they have out of so many other sides of human life.

Man thus finds himself quite unexpectedly faced with the question of human survival, when he thought he was dealing with a question of individual morals. And, in accord with the extraordinary speeding up of time which we noticed in so many other aspects, he seems suddenly to have but decades to solve a problem which he was quite prepared to put off for centuries.

Studying the vast mechanics of the universe, and the slow span of human history, it becomes increasingly difficult to attribute man's mastery of almost infinite energy to his own cleverness or indeed to anything originating in himself. The two things are quite disproportionate, as would be the idea of a monkey inventing a bicycle. If a monkey rides a bicycle, it is only because it has been put into its paws by a man. If man enjoys the use of atomic energy, it is surely because it has been put into his hands by some higher power.

But man's destructiveness must certainly be well known to and calculable by such higher power. The desperate danger of his enjoyment of unlimited energy is understood even by himself, let alone by any superior being. The penalty is obvious – what then is the possible prize? For we can hardly imagine a universe so devilish that danger goes unaccompanied by equivalent opportunity.

Is it that by mortal danger man is being forced on to some great decision and some great jump in conscious development, which he could never have faced except in emergency?

We do not know. But the idea is difficult to avoid.

XVIII THE CYCLES OF CRIME, HEALING
AND CONQUEST

I THE ASTEROIDS, ECONOMICS AND CRIME

A PPLYING THE SAME PRINCIPLES WHICH WE STUDIED IN THE CASES
of Mars and Venus, we should expect the motion of Mercury, acting upon the thyroids, to produce waves of universal restlessness
or movement. But as we noted earlier, the orbit of Mercury is so eccentric,
and its period so short, that any cycle it may induce is far too erratic for
serious study.

What is strange is that enquiry does introduce us to such a cycle of
activity – but apparently connected with an astronomical rhythm of an
entirely different order. This cycle is one of nine years, which all statisticians
are at pains to distinguish from the 9 $^2/_3$ year biological rhythm which
has already been discussed.

This nine-year rhythm controls prices and the stock market, the recurrence of financial crises, building activity (18 years), and many other factors
reflecting the curious waves of optimism and pessimism, initiative and depression, which mark all economic and industrial phenomena. Such a cycle
is most pronounced in industrialized societies. It appears very strongly in
large cities, and is particularly characteristic of the United States – other
cycles, of eleven years, for example, being more dominant in Europe.

Translated from statistical into emotional language, this 9-year cycle
evidently represents a fluctuation in that strange hidden force which appears to move the hurrying crowds of any great city now this way, now
that, at one tempo in the morning, at another in the evening, and to fill
these same crowds at one season with strange excitement and at another
with listlessness and indifference. Any observer in the streets of New York
or London will have noticed, almost with horror, the extraordinary impression of being *sucked* somewhere, given by urban masses as they move, and
the apparent indifference of this invisible suction to any considerations of
human happiness or human profit. Men flow into the subway as grains of
wheat flow into the mill, drawn down by some power which keeps them
ever on the move, hurrying in fact not to the office but to the grave.

What god or devil could induce such restlessness? Searching in the
heavens for a 9-year rhythm, we find one in a very unexpected place.

According to the harmonic rule now known as Bode's law a planet should
exist between Mars and Jupiter at a distance of 260 million miles from the

sun. No trace of such a heavenly body was discovered, however, until 1801, when the first of a series of miniature planets was located in this area. Since then over 1200 have been recorded, varying from 250 to a few miles in diameter. Ninety-five per cent of these asteroids are disposed in a band between 205 and 300 million miles from the sun, the average distance being almost exactly equal to that supposed by the rule in question. According to Kepler's third law, the orbital period of a body at this distance from the sun is about 1700 days, which is in fact the average periodicity of the asteroids. A planetary mass revolving at this speed should make a lesser conjunction with earth and sun every 468 days, while its full synodic cycle would be exactly nine years.

Let us recall the octave of true synodic periodicity which was established in chapter 6:

	Jupiter x 2 Venus & Mercury x 3	Ast-er-oids x 3	Mars x 2 Saturn x 1	Venus and Mercury x 4	Jupiter x 3 Aster-oids x 4	Venus and Mer-cury x 5	Mars x 3 Aster-oids x 5	Jupiter x 4 Venus & Mercury x 6
Years	24	27	30	32	36	40	45	48
Notes	*do*	*re*	*mi*	*fa*	*sol*	*la*	*si*	*do*

The periodicity of the asteroidal mass thus strikes the notes *re*, *sol* and *si*. The note *re*, however, is struck by the asteroids alone, and would therefore seem to be most characteristic of them. In the next octave this note will be represented by 54 years, in the next by 108, and so on. Thus in order to study the influence of the asteroids on human life we should look for phenomena of a periodicity not only of nine, but also of 27, 54 and 108 years.

Characteristics of the 9-year cycle have already been described. A much stronger rhythm of more or less the same character, however, is observed every 54 years; American wholesale prices, for example, reaching very striking peaks in 1813, 1865 and 1919, dates which incidentally coincide with the end of the 1812, the Civil and the Great Wars. The same periodicity is also seen in iron and coal production, and in industrial wages.

Kondratieff and other observers go further and claim that such 54-year cycles are marked by radical changes in the whole economic structure – the period of 1788-1842 covering the industrial revolution in the United States and England, 1842-1896 the age of coal, steam and railways, 1896-1950 that of chemistry, electricity and the internal combustion engine, with the coming period potentially marked by a new economic structure and a new source of energy. Others again have tried to associate this rhythm with the incidence of wars, though this phenomenon probably depends more upon the conjunction of asteroidal and martial cycles already considered.

At bottom, all the above cycles in multiples of nine years seem connected with a certain nervous stimulation or exhaustion among large masses of city-dwelling people. Attempts have been made to connect this in turn with the electric potential of the air, which has been remarked to show a 9 or 18-year rhythm at a city observatory (Kew), though no such cycle was noticeable at a rural station (Eskdalemuir).[75]

In this connection it is interesting to speculate what kind of influence the motion of countless asteroids might be expected to set up, and what effect such influence could produce in the magnetic field of the Earth. Consider in the first place the physical nature of this throng of particles of varying sizes, pursuing at different speeds hundreds of separate and highly eccentric orbits. Then remember the discordant or confused impression given by the independent conversations of a thousand people during an interval at the theatre compared with the harmonious impression created by the same number taking part in choral singing under a single conductor. Such is the physical relation between the asteroidal mass and individual planets.

In some way the nature of the asteroids thus appears to represent the influence of multiplicity in the concert of the Solar System, to symbolize the independence or insurrection of component units against the whole. In such a sense pathological conditions are caused by the independent action or inertia of separate organs or cells of the body; while rebellions and revolutions represent such a condition in the body politic. Such 'individualism', in which each pursues his own ambition, unmindful either of the whole or of that which drives him, is notoriously characteristic of modern industrial economics and particularly of the life of large cities.

All this seems to hint in some way at a maleficent, disturbing or restless influence. For even from the economic aspect, this cycle is rightly described as a cycle of depressions, that is, a cycle of general fear and panic. Such fear, as we saw in our study of psycho-physical processes, represents a definite psychological poison. And it in turn gives rise to the waves of suicide, murder, embezzlement and other crime which are also found to follow a nine-year cycle and to correspond with the troughs of economic depression.

75. Ellsworth Huntington: 'Mainsprings of Civilization', pp. 477–484.

In the light of this, we recall with interest that a certain note in the octaves of organic compounds we found to be characteristic of poisons, that is, of the matters of disease. In every world, by the triple nature of creation, all six processes must operate, and even the planetary world cannot be exempt. Moreover, the different notes of any octave appear to correspond in some way to these different processes or to the matters concerned in them. We should thus expect the various planets, on their own level, to be also associated in some way with the operation of these processes. We have already seen how the influence of Venus appears connected with the process of growth, and that of Mars with destruction.

It is thus difficult to avoid the conclusion that the cycle and influence of the asteroids is particularly associated with the process which for want of a better description we have called corruption or crime.

This strange affinity between the asteroids and corruption in turn recalls age-old legends of crime on an angelic or planetary level — the rebellion of Satan, the fall of Lucifer. Such stories are always introduced in context with the well-known planetary figures or demiurges – Mercury, Venus, Mars, Jupiter, Saturn – which under one name or another occur in Babylonian, Greek, Roman, Arabic, Aztec and Medieval cosmology. The asteroids are never mentioned by name, but in every case we are told of a 'fallen angel'. "How art thou fallen from Heaven, O Lucifer, star of the morning!" (Isaiah xiv)

In chapter IX of the Book of Revelations this legend is elaborated in mystical-mythical language. Strange visions are described referring to each of the seven planetary angels. It is the vision of the fifth angel which particularly interests us, since the asteroids do in fact fill the fifth place in the planetary sequence – after Mercury, Venus, Earth and Mars. When this angel sounded, we are told, a star was seen to fall from heaven into 'the bottomless pit', from which arose clouds of smoke which darkened the sun. Out of this smoke came a swarm of 'locusts', with streaming 'hair' and 'breastplates of iron', the sound of whose wings was like countless chariots rushing into battle. The 'king' of these 'locusts', or the angel of the bottomless pit, was Apollyon, later to become Satan.

A further vision describes "a woman clothed with the sun and the moon under her feet, and upon her head a crown of twelve stars" (a personification of the descending scale of worlds from the twelve zodiacal signs of the Milky Way through our Sun down to the moon), who is about to give birth – presumably to a new satellite. Satan or 'the dragon' waits, however, to devour the infant; and as a result of this danger there is war in heaven

288

between Michael and his angels (the Sun and major planets) and Satan and his demons. The latter are defeated, "neither was their place found any more in heaven . . . And the great dragon was cast out, that old serpent, called the Devil, and Satan, which deceived the whole world: he was cast into the Earth, and his angels were cast out with him."

In the seventeenth century these various legends were synthesized by Milton in his 'Paradise Lost', in which the fall of Lucifer from Heaven was connected with 'pride', independence, or rebellion against a cosmic order. Throughout this and all other such references runs the idea that Lucifer is the spirit of multiplicity, chaos, of disorder among a mass of disorganized individuals. He is the 'prince of demons', whose name is 'legion'.

At the beginning of the 19th century, the astronomer Olbers, who discovered the second asteroid, strangely echoed these legends by suggesting that the newly-found bodies were fragments of a once-existing planet which had exploded into innumerable particles. It was further supposed that the diminutive total volume of these fragments (approximately that of the moon), might be explained by the fact that·much of the material of the lost planet had been drawn into the orbits of the Earth, Mars, or Jupiter, either as falling meteors or to form satellites to these other planets. The tiny formless moons of Mars are indeed difficult to explain in any other way.

This theory of Olbers recalls and fits in with the idea, outlined in chapter 16, that at a remote period some tremendous cosmic tension may have been set up which represented 'night' for the Earth, producing the cataclysm which engulfed Atlantis and making an almost complete break in human history. For a similar tension might in certain circumstances have caused the 'explosion' of a faulty planet, with all the consequences described.

In this way, the legend of the fall of Lucifer, 'star of the morning', the war of the other planets against him, his being cast out of his place down to Earth, and his final relegation to a new role as prince of a legion of demons or 'flying locusts' – finds itself transcribed into astronomical language.

Moreover, the influence of these 'demons' or asteroids upon the earth is now found to fluctuate by a nine-year cycle, which in fact corresponds to the waves of depression, suicide, murder and insanity observable among men.

II. JUPITER, OR THE HARMONICS OF MOONS

The most striking thing about the planet Jupiter from an astronomical point of view, is the complexity of the system of satellites which it supports. Jupiter has twelve known moons, four of which are easily visible through field-glasses and are of the same order of size as the Earth's own moon. This planet stands midway between the Sun and the Earth in size, having a volume one-thousandth that of the former and 1300 times that of the lattter. Moreover, the whole relation of Jupiter to the Sun appears to follow a definite and significant ratio.

The system of Jupiter, in number of satellites, their size, distance, speeds of revolution and so on, seems to present to us an exact model of the Solar System. At any rate the approximation is so close that it is impossible not to believe that the two are constructed or have grown according to the same laws. The orbits and periods of Jupiter's moons, for instance, are found to have a constant relation to the orbits and periods of the planets of the Solar System, though naturally with different factors for orbital distance and for orbital time.

Taking the jovial satellites Io, Europa, Ganymede and Callisto (I, II, III, IV) to correspond to Mercury, Venus, Earth and Mars, distances in the Solar System are found to average about 140 times those in Jupiter's system, while periods average 51 times longer. [76] These figures approximately fall into the sequence connecting relative time and relative distance which we established in chapter 2, and show that the principle expressed in Kepler's third law[77] not only applies to satellites within a single system, but also to the relation between one system and another. Moreover, it confirms that Jupiter, like the Sun, is a complete living entity or cosmos.

There are a number of implications of the highly developed state of Jupiter's system and its almost complete reflection in miniature of the solar one. In the first place, the influence or radiation produced by such a system must be an extremely subtle one, incorporating a large number of different frequencies in a harmonic relation. Whereas the planet Venus has only two movements (rotation and revolution), and thus sets up only two kinds of frequency, the system of Jupiter includes fifteen or twenty different movements, that is, fifteen or twenty different harmonics. Jupiter, in other words, must produce an extraordinary wealth of overtones which would put it in the same relation to Venus as a cello to a penny whistle.

Moreover, the fact that Jupiter's system is a scale-model of the whole Solar System brings other implications. We supposed the structure of man to be an image of that of the Solar System, and the endocrine glands

76. See Appendix XI: 'Relation of Solar and Jovial Systems'.

77. "The squares of the periods in which the planets describe their orbits are proportional to the cubes of their mean distances from the Sun."

in him to correspond to the various planets and to react to their several influences. Jupiter by its place in the Solar System appears to emit a 'note' or frequency which activates the posterior pituitary gland and produces in it a corresponding rhythm. But by the same laws Jupiter's moons will produce faint harmonics which affect *all the other glands*. Although each of these other glands will be chiefly controlled by the influence of its 'own' planet, it will also in a very much less pronounced way react to the influence of the corresponding moon of Jupiter, since each of these emits a frequency harmonically related to a certain planet but nearly six octaves higher.

This calculation gives us quite a new idea about the significance of a planet's satellites in relation to man. If each planet controls one of his functions, the number of that planet's moons controls the interaction of that particular function with others, its power of harmonizing with others. In this way we see that the functions corresponding to Mercury and Venus, which have no moons, are as it were 'crude' functions, lacking the harmonics which will enable them to 'blend' with others. Mars has two moons, though very small and embryonic. This means that the adrenal or passionate function has harmonics relating it, but very faintly, to two other functions. It also means that with the remaining functions – such as abstract thought – the passionate function cannot blend, and it must always clash with them.

Only Jupiter and Saturn have a complete system of moons, producing harmonics corresponding to all the other functions; and thus the pituitary gland, in both its parts, bears a quite special relation to all other functions and to the organism as a whole.

The power of blending with or producing echoes in all other functions, which the pituitary, by virtue of its planet's overtones, possesses, has rather a different meaning in its two halves. It were more simple to say that it takes on a masculine significance in the anterior lobe, and a feminine significance in the posterior. Thus it endows the anterior lobe with the function of overseeing, directing and 'controlling' all other functions – dominating them, so to speak. While it endows the posterior lobe with the function of tending all these other functions, smoothing out discords between them, healing them, and in general of 'mothering' the organism. Just as Saturn and Jupiter act as 'father' and 'mother' to their respective systems of satellites, so the anterior and posterior lobes of the pituitary gland act as 'father' and 'mother' to all the glands and functions of the body.

If Jupiter promotes a healing and harmonising function in the individual, its cycle, affecting millions of people, should be reflected in a universal fluctuation in the gentler and more humanitarian instincts of man. Traces of its 12-year rhythm may thus be sought for in medicine, in works of charity, in attention to social services, and in general in the more humane aspects of human life.

In order to be able to search more effectively for such a rhythm, however, we should do well to study the nature of this healing activity more closely. As we said earlier, healing, fundamentally, is that which restores to health things touched by the corruptive or criminal process. In fact, since almost everything and everybody we know is so tainted, the 'original sin' of mankind in the course of ages having penetrated into every corner of our world, *everything stands in need of healing in one way or another.*

In order to take part in the process of regeneration, a being must be normal. The abnormal and the subnormal cannot regenerate, cannot be reborn. A rotten seed and an imperfect seed cannot sprout. Thus healing is not only restoration to normality, but also preparation for regeneration. It is the cosmic antidote to corruption.

When we studied the rhythm of the corruptive process in relation to humanity, we saw that it expressed itself in two ways – in periods of lassitude and despair known to economists as 'depressions', and in periods of violence expressed as riot and rebellion. This is interesting, for this process works through two main classes of human emotions – violent or malicious emotions, and hopeless or despairing emotions. Carried to their extreme, the first lead to murder, the second to suicide – both representing the destruction of all possibilities, the first for another, the second for oneself.

In a general sense, therefore, healing – as far as mankind goes – means neutralizing the traces of malicious and despairing emotions. It means preventing murder and suicide, restoring lost possibilities.

Further, if we think of the objective results of these two complementary activities, we see that while crime naturally leaves behind it an atmosphere of suspicion, hate and fear, healing just as inevitably and naturally leaves behind it an atmosphere of love and gratitude. If we think of the immense amount of love and gratitude evoked by the example of Florence Nightingale or Louis Pasteur in healing bodies, of Saint Vincent de Paul in healing a social condition, of Bernardo Las Casas in healing the wrong done by one people to another, of Joan of Arc in healing a nation, then we shall understand that this activity not only achieves the immediate result of restored health, but it also gives rise to great quantities of the emotional raw material necessary for the process of regeneration to begin.

In certain abject conditions of poverty and degradation, in certain conditions of deep-rooted disease, in madness, and under hypnotism, regeneration is impossible. These conditions must first be healed. Then regeneration can begin.

Men are thus right in recognizing instinctively that healing is the highest activity, *save one*, in which human beings can take part.

III SATURN AND CONQUEST

The synodic cycle of Saturn is of 30 years' duration. We have already seen how this period is a higher octave of the martial cycle, and that it superimposes upon that cycle the otherwise inexplicable urge to *dominate* which suddenly possesses one nation or another, and lends to the wars on which they then embark a strange and very special character.

In individual psychology this 'masterfulness' is a recognized characteristic of anterior pituitary types. And probably there are certain nations whose typical stock approximates to such a type. From the seventeenth to the nineteenth centuries the British appear to have had special tendencies in this direction. But apparently the very racial stock itself gradually modifies, for from the turn of the century this tendency gradually seems to die out of the British race, who become first content with the *status quo* and then even self-deprecatory in their international role.

Instead, from the middle of the nineteenth century to the middle of the twentieth this urge to dominate appears to pass to the German peoples who in 1870, 1914 and 1939 embark on a series of ever more carefully planned wars which could have no other design than eventual world conquest. Today similar tendencies, though not necessarily using the means of war, seem to manifest in the United States and Russia.

Apparently, when a certain combination of influences reaches its maximum, this urge to dominate, temporarily expressed in one nation or another, reaches explosive pitch. The incredible expansion of the Greeks under Alexander in 332–326 B. C., of the Tartars under Jenghis Khan in 1215–1223, of the Spaniards in Mexico under Cortes in 1520-1525, of the French in Europe under Napoleon in 1805-12, of the Germans under Hitler in 1938-43, and of the Japanese in Asia in the same years, are clear examples. These cases are warlike. But the impulse is not necessarily so; and though less dramatic, the commercial expansion of the Venetians in the 14th century and of the Dutch in the 17th expresses the same unconfinable force.

Such adventures are completely inexplicable by any logical reasons, and in some cases, such as the Spanish one, where a vast empire was acquired in two years by less than 400 men, they seem to verge on the miraculous. The urge to dominate, accentuated by certain cosmic cycles and by the racial types of the conquerors and conquered, becomes for the time being irresistible.

This apparently miraculous quality of certain conquests, which is evidently the result of cosmic conditions, naturally endows the men who ride on the crest of such waves – the Alexanders, Napoleons and Hitlers – with the appearance of either gods or devils. And in fact such leaders may be either very noble, or very wicked, or neither the one nor the other. There are examples of world-conquerors in each class. But in all cases it is very important to understand that *they do not do what they appear to do*. In fact they do nothing. Planetary cycles do everything, and the cycle of Saturn perhaps most of all. The conquerors are simply men with a certain natural capacity for rhetoric or strategy, who in a curious way typify their racial character, and above all who are endowed with a very special sense of timing – or as it is more often expressed, 'a sense of history'. They learn to listen to planetary influence through the temper of the people.

This 'cycle of domination' is one aspect of Saturn's waxing and waning influence on the anterior pituitary gland in millions of men. But it represents only one side of the work of this organ. For as we saw earlier the anterior pituitary is also the gland which, working strongly, gives the power of synthetic thought, that is, of coordinating the knowledge acquired through all the other functions, and in consequence of making inventions or discoveries. For invention is, after all, only the perception of new connexions between items of knowledge – theoretical and practical – which have not previously been put together in that way.

We should therefore expect the maximum phase of the cycle of Saturn not only to bring an urge to conquest, but also to have some special effect on human knowledge and invention. And in fact we are faced by the curious and frequently remarked fact that in certain periods of aggressive war, science and invention take extraordinary leaps ahead at a speed quite disproportionate to their progress in peacetime. The revolutionary advance in medicine and aviation made during the first World War, and the still more revolutionary development of engineering, physics, electronics, bacteriology, and practically every branch of human knowledge during the second World War exactly thirty years later, have been repeatedly pointed out.

The observation is quite correct. But the deduction that war *stimulates* invention or *induces* a thirst for knowledge is probably unjustified. Pituitary stimulation is the primary cause: conquest and invention the equal and secondary effects. This gland is the seat of discovery, and the inventiveness of nations – even expressed as prosaically as in the figures of patents taken out – is indeed found to vary by a cycle of thirty years, that is, according to the synodic period of Saturn. However, the more we understand of this saturnine influence – with its stimulation to conquest, both physical and mental, as well as to invention and to intellectual understanding – the more it seems not only a recurrent one, but also in a very special way the dominant influence of our present age.

We already saw how different civilizations seemed based on the dominance or special development of a single function. And according to our thesis, this is the same as saying that each culture finds itself under the special influence of one planet – that which controls the function then in the ascendant.

If we think of the last, the Renaissance culture, for example, we immediately picture its flamboyance, display, colour and many-sidedness. In striking contrast to the cool inward-turning of the Monastic Christian culture, the Renaissance was characterized by gregariousness and enterprise, by a vast mixing and melting, a tendency to embrace and tolerate all sides of life. And it was accompanied by a very special development of medicine and the art of healing. These qualities, in an individual, we should call jovial, and we should associate them with the stimulation of the posterior pituitary gland. The Renaissance, we may hazard, was a culture *under Jupiter*.

Passing to our own culture, whose origin we attempted to trace in Chapter 16, we are struck by quite other characteristics. Certainly, invention – from the steam-engine to the atomic bomb – has deluged it with good and evil gifts at a rate unparalleled in history. But if we think of the *total effect* of these inventions, we realize that it has chiefly been to place an extraordinary strain on the *intellect* of mankind. Such a strain would have been unimaginable in the Middle Ages. In those days, as to-day in remote parts of Mexico or India, a peasant received no impressions from outside his valley or his village. Objects or stories from different backgrounds brought no associations, *they had no meaning*. What a man knew about the weather, his neighbours, the crops, he knew very deeply, in all parts of himself. But about distant things he knew nothing, and he was required to know nothing.

Suddenly, with the telegraph and popular education, and their corollary the newspaper, all men were required not only to know of the existence of

China or Alaska, but even to worry daily over the fate of their inhabitants, to follow wars, famines and plagues in such remote parts of the Earth, and in general to take as their own the troubles of the whole world. Later, the radio and television ensured that those who had escaped such responsibility hitherto should do so no longer.

Apart from this intellectual pressure from the present, men were also required to know and worry about wars and revolutions in the distant past, about the fall of ancient civilizations, about the disintegration of remote stars, and even about the fate of the whole universe.

All these became questions which *occupied men's minds*. Further, all men had not only to conquer heat and cold, the soil, food and vegetation, as they had done for all history, but in addition they had to conquer extraordinarily intricate machines, dealing with forces whose existence their grandfathers did not even suspect. All these machines, all these foreign countries, all history, all the universe they were required – in however rudimentary a way – *to understand*. An immense and quite new strain – or an immense and quite new stimulus – was evidently being brought to bear on the intellectual understanding of mankind as a whole. If in previous ages there had been no rest for men's muscles, now there was no rest for their minds. And the chief focus of all this stimulation, in any single man, was the *anterior pituitary gland*. Thus in a very real way, the present culture may be said to be especially *under Saturn*.

Now if the procession of celestial influence does require that the intellectual understanding of man be now especially stimulated, many features of our present civilization become more comprehensible. For we see that its weaknesses, failings and crimes are also predominantly intellectual, that is, they arise from *minds* which are unable to adapt themselves to this new stimulus – just as the weaknesses, failings and crimes of the Middle Ages were predominantly emotional, that is, they arose from *hearts* which were unable to respond to the tension then required of them.

Every celestial stimulation which is brought to bear upon man is thus his opportunity and his danger. It opens new possibilities for him, but it also brings a new test of his being. In the Middle Ages, the auto-da-fe, religious persecution, and the fantasies of witchcraft were the result of men of weak being being exposed to a universal and cosmic stimulation of the heart. The prevalence of mental madness, of scientific superstition, of inane triviality in thought and amusement, which characterises our age, is the result of men of weak being being exposed to a universal and cosmic stimulation of the mind.

THE CYCLES OF CRIME, HEALING AND CONQUEST

All this is the negative result of such stimulation, which may be observed upon every side. What we must study, however, are the positive possibilities of such stimulation, available to men of strong being. For these, and these alone, are able to atone for all the rest. Our age, like all other ages, must have its own 'models', its own special vision of higher man. Who are these men? Who are the heroes of our time? What kind of men are looked up to for a way out of the chaos?

When we try to answer this, we see that many heroes of past ages would be hard put to maintain their stature now. For our needs are no longer simple ones. The warrior hero – Roland or Sir Galahad – might feel curiously lost today, and even the saintly hero like Francis would have to carry his achievement into many other sides of life to fulfil men's expectations.

The figures who rise indisputably into the forefront of our age may fall short of these in passion and one-pointedness, but they are more all–round men. In an anterior pituitary age they typify that quality of the anterior pituitary which must master, coordinate and give meaning to all other functions.

Winston Churchill, journalist, soldier, statesman, historian, artist, sitting as lightly in a great historical role as in the adopted one of bricklayer; Albert Schweitzer, as quietly sure in philosophy as in playing Bach on the organ or creating a hospital in the Congo; Fridtjof Nansen, now struggling with a dog-team to reach the pole, now to relieve a famine, now to organize a passport system for stateless refugees; Jan Christian Smuts, architect of an army, a country, a League of Nations; Sir Wilfred Grenfell, redeemer of the fate of Labrador; or on the other hand a man like Piotr Demianovich Ouspensky, who could be called mathematician, mystic or traveller precisely because his real work was unmeasured and invisible – these are the true heroes of our time.

As in all periods, such heroes may be over-estimated or under-estimated. Some may be made over from what they were into what men need; others may teach men to need what they have made themselves. It does not matter. The hero of our time is the man who can reconcile all sides of life in one all-embracing view; who can understand, act, organize and make compassion manifest. Perhaps the archetype of such a man has not yet appeared, and all these are but his forerunners. In any case, they have helped to create conditions in which a man of to-day can find his conscience. Such is the work of heroes. And it is the work of the fourth way consciously and invisibly to produce them.

Thus from a study of the various planetary cycles in relation to observed cycles in the different fields of human activity, we come to the conclusion that the planets not only rule the various glands or functions in individual human beings, but that for the whole of mankind they also rule the six different varieties of cosmic process which we have encountered on so many scales.

The cycle of Venus appears to rule the growth and multiplication of mankind. The asteroidal cycle rules man's crime and his disease. Mars rules destruction in the human world, Jupiter its healing, and Saturn its knowledge and invention. While connected with the long slow cycle of Neptune, yet to be considered, is the process of regeneration, both as regards individual man and as regards mankind.

The shifting lights of planetary influence produce through history an ever-changing interplay of these six processes, and these six alone. For there are no others, and it is impossible that anything should happen which is not produced by one or other or several of them in combination. These processes in action make all of human history, all of human life – both what we see and what we do not see.

Moreover, they are harmonized and unified among themselves by the seventh cycle, which blends them into a single whole and creates from their counterpoint *another cosmos*. This is the cycle of sex, ruled by the planet Uranus.

XIX THE CYCLE OF SEX

I FASHION: THE MASCULINE AND FEMININE PHASES OF URANUS

STUDY OF THE LONG CYCLE AFFECTING SEX IS OF SPECIAL INTEREST because it helps us to understand better the general manner of working of all such cycles. For very obviously sex is always present as a dominating principle in man, and in all countries and in every age it is the moving force in the greater part of his occupation and pursuits.

Despite this, it takes very different forms, clothes itself in many different fashions. It is now overt and unashamed, now very hidden and disguised. Moreover, these phases alternate, and their period being half the full cycle of Uranus, which is 84 years, we have the eternal spectacle of staid grandparents shocked by wayward children, or modest maidens blushing at ribald gaffers. It always was like this, and it always must be.

The attitude of an age towards sex is very clearly indicated by its literature, poetry, art, and above all by its dress. Innumerable examples of a complete reversal of attitude towards sex and women in forty years or so can be gathered in this way. Such a period separates the etherealized women of Pinturicchio, unnoticeable behind their cascades of velvet and brocade, from the sensuous promiscuity of Bronzino's 'Venus, Cupid, Folly and Time' and the fashionable nudity of the school of Fontainebleau. Forty years again separates this from the austere angels and virgins of Greco; while a further forty brings us back to the fleshly nakedness of Rubens.

These examples refer to the sexuality of women; but this is evidently only half the picture. And it is interesting to note that in the intermediate periods, when women are represented as pale, modest and voluminously dressed in neutral shades, men are seen to blossom into gay colours and fantastic clothes or at least to pose before the artist in vigorous and excessively virile attitudes.

Contemporary with the anaemic women of Pinturicchio, an almost comical sexuality invests the lower half of masculine attire. In the age of Greco's sack-clothed angels, the gentlemen of Elizabethan England go dressed in gold, ruby and sapphire blue, enhanced with ruffles, slashings, embroidered hose and elaborate jewelry. The coronation of George IV in 1821, falling just two years after a masculine peak, was marked by such gorgeous and fantastic recostuming that it established the ritual dress of British pageantry in permanence. Periods when women undress appear to alternate with periods when men dress up. For these are indeed the fundamental tendencies of sexual display, as they apply to the different sexes.

From all this it seems more correct to regard the 84-year cycle of Uranus not so much as an alternation between overt and hidden sexuality, but rather between a feminine age and a masculine one.[78]

If we now turn to a study of the planet Uranus itself, we find a very curious astronomical parallel to this state of affairs. Unlike all the other planets, whose axes lie more or less at right angles to the plane of the Solar System, and which thus present chiefly their equators to the Sun and to their fellows, the axis of Uranus lies almost flat upon the plane of its orbit. This means that, alone of all the planets, it presents its two poles in turn directly to the Sun and to the Earth. Every eighty-four years its positive pole, illuminated by the full solar brilliance, shines vertically upon the Earth while its negative pole lies hidden and in darkness: in the intermediate periods it is the negative pole which so directly reflects the Sun's light towards us, and the positive which lies obscured in the direction of outer space.

If the positive and negative poles of planets have some cosmic affinity for masculinity and femininity in general, then we can understand why Uranus – by reason of its unique movement – is the planet which governs the sex function in man, and further, why the alternating stimulation of the two sexes on Earth follows the eighty-four year rhythm which we clearly see in history.

Both sexes are always present and always of exactly equal strength, as are any two poles; but among humankind, as with the poles of Uranus, the light of fashion shines first upon the one and then upon the other, leaving at each phase the partner invisible and eclipsed. Today femininity is spotlighted; in forty-two years masculinity will be at its zenith; and in eighty-four femininity again. While in the intermediate years – as when the two poles of Uranus share the Sun's light – the two sexes must shine for a short while with equal brilliance.

We have taken our illustrations from fashion, because this is the clearest mirror of the sexual ideas of a people or a period. Costume is, as it were, the natural artistic expression of sex. And the dress of every age, and indeed of every individual, is an exact signature of his sexuality, his feelings and ideas about sex. In this way everyone, without exception, publicly expresses his sexual self.

At the same time, the idea of alternating masculine and feminine periods

78 See Appendix XII, 'The Cycle of Sex'.

can be equally well demonstrated in any field of human endeavour. The Elizabethan age of masculine display is also that of the sea-dogs, whose strange piratic life represents a very definite aspect of virility. Such adventurers certainly exist in every age, but in this one they were in a certain way accepted, fashionable, a social and sexual ideal.

Again, the two periods may be seen as alternations of struggle and langour in relation to sex. In the masculine periods, the whole idea of sex will be hedged round with questions of honour, rivalry, morals; it will be seen as the great prize, to be guarded and fought for; it will be that which is most of all hard to get. In the feminine periods, on the contrary, it will be full of ease and invitation; it will be not the prize but the gift, the one earthly joy in which all may find comfort and refreshment. In the one case it is typified by the 'Roman de la Rose', to which only the purest and best can attain by trial: in the other by Bosch's Fountain of Delights, in which all may bathe and be vivified. These two great visions were created, the first a little before a masculine peak (1225), the second a little before a feminine one (1510), and they symbolize the two complementary ideals of sex in a very vivid way.

As we saw earlier, sex can combine with every other function to produce endless varieties of human expression. And in the same way these two phases of the sexual cycle of Uranus may coincide with any of the other planetary cycles to yield every conceivable idea and attitude in this relation.

Sometimes sexual cycles will coincide with cycles of war or crime, with resultant waves of rape and sadism. On the other hand, in some countries where the racial type is already of a sensuous caste – as in India or Malay – sexual cycles could combine creatively with 'spiritual' ones. In this case sex becomes a 'mystery', symbolic of the creative power of the universe, and a 'way' to mystical experiences and union with god. Though the idea is strange to the more intellectual and less sensuous racial types of the West, actual physical union could then be used as a true sacrament, and the intense energies so released be deliberately harnessed for the enhancement of consciousness.

We find clear traces of such a teaching in the sculpture of the Kushan civilization of the 2nd century in Southern India; while again in the Shivaite temples of the 8th century the mystical pleasures of a superphysical world are represented in the figures of sensuous young girls for the enjoyment of whom the worshipper, as a little mannikin, distantly yearns. At other times again – among the Persian sufis, for example – a more emotionalized aspect of sex has served both as intimation and allegory of man's highest possibility.

Such developments seem possible only at the feminine phase of the cycle of Uranus, and then only among peoples of a sensuous physical type. In any case, these possibilities evidently imply great understanding, a very special emotionality, and the absolute purification of sex from the faintest admixture of shame or violence. Apart from the secret knowledge of higher physiology required for such 'ways', even these outward conditions are very rare among occidentals, against a background of western education and social custom.

Despite this, many individuals, by lucky accident as it were, achieve their highest level of consciousness in sex: and through sex acquire their first intimation of its potential development.

II THE PSYCHOLOGY OF SEX

One of the strange things about the 84-year cycle of sex ruled by Uranus is its almost exact correspondence with the average duration of human life. This means that a long -lived man, or more significantly, any given generation, dies in a similar sexual 'atmosphere' to that in which it was born. In a later chapter, when we try to penetrate the mystery of love and death, or death and conception, we shall understand that this fact may have a very special meaning.

The same fact also implies that at the prime of life, when a man's or woman's understanding of sex is fullest and deepest, he or she lives in the *opposite* sexual atmosphere to that of his birth, that is to say, in an atmosphere of maximum stimulation. This explains the rarely admitted fact that sexual feeling is often stronger and richer at forty than it is at thirty.

In the meantime, the study of various sexual fashions in the past can be of little more than academic or erotic interest for ordinary people, who have no choice but to live in the sexual atmosphere of their own age, and adapt their individual understanding of sex to that as best they can.

For them the chief thing to be understood about sex is that it should be *the highest creative function*, resulting in the harmonizing of all other functions – whether in the creation of children in the physical image of their parents, in the creation of the arts, or simply in the creation of the individual's true role in life. Unfortunately, in many people, far from harmonizing other functions, sex obstructs them, interferes with them, prevents them carrying out their proper task.

It must be remembered that sexual energy is the finest energy normally produced and conducted through the human body. This means that it is also the most volatile, the most difficult to store or keep under control. Like a supply of high octane petrol, its presence represents both a source of immense power and potentiality, and also a constant danger of catastrophic explosion. At any moment it may leak into the mechanism of other functions, and like such petrol leaking into a heating system or into a storeroom, suddenly give rise to flareup fires which in a few seconds can destroy long-accumulated stocks of other materials and even damage the basic structure of the building.

Usually, however, these violent and destructive manifestations of sexual energy are directly or indirectly traceable to a negative attitude towards sex in general – that is, to suspicion of it, fear of it, or to a cynical, brutal or obscene sense of sex. For such negative attitudes prevent sex from finding its proper and natural expression and force its energy into channels and functions *for which it is far too strong.*

This may result in violent, pointless and clumsy activity, often leading to physical accident and destruction. Or in bursts of passionate anger; or in bitter and wounding repartee; or in feverish imagination; or in violent denunciations of others, or the imposition of impossible tasks and disciplines upon them. All these and countless other unpleasant aspects of human behaviour result from sexual energy being forced into systems appropriate to the much coarser energies required for thought, action or instinct. Passing through these systems, sexual energy resembles electric current passing through a wire too small to carry it – the wire first becomes hot, and in the end may fuse altogether.

Those who emotionally understand the idea of sex as the force which harmonizes all other functions, and who manage to live their life in accordance with this understanding, although they obviously cannot be entirely free of the unpleasant manifestations described above, will never be dominated by them in the same way. In any case they will never justify such violence, or pretend that it can have any useful function, for they will realize its origin and its nature.

Sex can become a destructive instead of an integrating element in man's life in two ways – it may play too large a part, or too small a part.

Huntington paints a striking picture of social conditions in a tropical district of Central America where young men spend all their time either scheming how to possess a certain woman or resting after the success of such schemes. Obviously in such a state no civilization, no culture, nor even material improvement is possible.

On the other hand, large numbers of people in highly civilized cities in fact spend just as much time dreaming, not even about a desired woman or a desired man, but about sex in general or about sex in connexion with some imaginary figure from the stage or screen. And they do not realize that such dreams use up the fine matter of true sex even faster than actual indulgence.

Moreover, such imagination produces a kind of psycho-sexual impotence, so that when faced by the actual sexual demands of life – which never correspond to this imagination – they find themselves at a loss, unable to respond to them in any normal way.

The sexual sense is an extraordinarily subtle one, working by virtue of its fine energy at a very high speed. Most of its manifestations take place on a molecular level, where impulses are transmitted thousands of times faster than they are by the mind. The effects of scent, which also take place on a molecular level and thus have a close affinity for the sexual function and power over it, can teach us very much about this extraordinary speed and subtlety of sex. A perfume, for instance, can diffuse through all the volume of a large room in an immeasurably short time, that is, it can at once encompass everything within that room from all sides simultaneously.

Similar capacities belong to the proper functioning of sex. The idea of love at first sight, if it actually occurs, is based on the fact that in certain cases the sex function can perceive everything that can be known about a person in a single instant. This is connected with its speed of working and the nature of the molecular state of matter with which it operates.

For such perceptions the logical or imaginative mind is far too slow. It cannot possibly follow, control or encourage the working of the sex function. It can only inhibit its action, interfere with it. And this almost invariably results when the mind occupies itself too much with sex, either in imagining about it or in reasoning about it. True sex cannot be improved by imagination or by reason, and it is very often destroyed by them and rendered sterile by them.

We have already mentioned the effect of imagination in this connection. But it is necessary to understand that the introduction of too much 'reason' or 'will' into sexual affairs has exactly the same effect. Evidently a man must have sufficient self-control to keep his sexual expression within bounds, and not spend this fine energy too much or too promiscuously, or there will be none left for other creative activity. On the other hand, so volatile is the nature of sex energy that the man who decides to 'control' it, to exercise his 'will' over it, to 'sublimate' it or something similar, very soon finds that he has no time left for anything else.

The struggle to keep sex 'in its place' without expression is like an attempt to keep a scent in one small corner of a room. It is quite impossible. So that the man who prides himself on being most self-controlled often spends far more thought, time, energy and ingenuity on sex than anyone else. He can never get sex out of his mind, and he is thus never able to consider any other side of life impartially. Every question, even the most trivial or academic, decides itself in him on the basis of the sexual opportunity it will offer or avoid. In this way his whole life becomes poisoned, and he sacrifices even ordinary opportunities and possibilities. Such a man is the most abject slave of sex; and with neither profit nor pleasure.

The key to the understanding of sex is the knowledge that sexual energy is the finest and subtlest naturally produced in the human organism. Thus sexual energy can be turned to any purpose, can express itself on any level. It contains the potentiality of the highest forms of creation, and it also contains the possibility of destroying a man, and wrecking him, physically, morally and emotionally. It can combine with his most bestial side, with criminal impulses of cruelty, hatred and fear; or it can combine with his most refined aspirations and keenest sensibilities. And in either case it will immensely heighten the tendency to which it becomes attached.

In a very mysterious way, sexual energy contains within itself on a molecular level the universal signature or cosmic pattern. This cosmic pattern can become clothed with flesh, in the form of physical children begotten from the sexual energy of the parents. But it can also be transmuted into some artistic or literary expression of this cosmic pattern, or of whatever aspect of it may appeal to the artist. Sexual energy contains the image of all truth: from it each man derives as much of the truth as he is able.

This fact that sexual energy contains within it a complete cosmic image, and particularly the complete cosmic image of the individual from whom it springs, has another side. When in the sexual act a man or woman give up, are parted from their sexual energy, it means that they are in a strange way giving up, being parted from themselves. The sexual act is a strange foreshadowing of death, when the man or woman is parted – not only from his seed – but from his whole physical body, of which that seed is the microscopic signature.

Many analogies – both physical and psychological – suggest that sexual ecstasy, in which opposites are reconciled, in which the sense of union is in proportion to the sense of annihilation, and in which one seems both to lose oneself and find oneself at once, may be a true foretaste of what may be expected in death. And as a man, parting from his seed in the sexual act, in

305

the instant reveals and experiences his whole being, falls into oblivion, is seized with despair or transported with ecstasy, so may a man parting from his body in death be so revealed and rewarded – not for an hour but for a lifetime.

At the same time, in sexual union man and woman themselves unknowingly create a cosmic image of the whole. The separate halves, divorced since the dawn of life, become for a moment one perfect creature, its eyes looking to earth and sky at once, the rhythm of its two hearts united, breathing its own breath, fulfilling its own yearnings, and completing its own incompleteness – a new creature purged of evil and of self, and filled with a single ecstasy, the image of a cosmos in its perfection.

Thus for every individual sex brings a foretaste of death, and a foretaste of perfect life. In the words of the parable, it is his 'talent' given him by nature, and from which he can make anything which his being desires. In this way sex provides a universal test or examination of every human being, and by his use of it he determines his future possibilities.

III SEX AS THE QUEST FOR PERFECTION

We thought of sex as the function which, rightly working, harmonizes all other functions in the individual. That is, it can produce accord between all the different functions and processes and realize from them the highest potentiality of the available material.

But this harmonizing capacity has another aspect. By its nature *the sex function seeks perfection.* It not only seeks to create harmony between the other functions in its own organism; but it also seeks to complete each of these functions, to supply what is missing in them, to make up any deficiencies, and thus to create a perfect whole. This perfect whole will be made by finding another being who can supply exactly what its own organism lacks, function by function, and which combined with it, will constitute the complete or perfect man. Sex then is literally the faculty by which, as Plato expresses it, "souls seek the other half from which they were severed at creation."

In the chapter on chemical elements we saw how these elements were attracted together or tended to combine, according as the number of electrons in their top shell were complementary. The perfect shell being constituted of a definite number of electrons, sodium with one outstanding electron rushed irresistibly to embrace chlorine with one missing. On the other hand nothing could make sodium with its extra electron combine with other alkalis similarly composed. This was the principle of the marriage of the elements, and the basis of all chemistry.

Exactly the same principle applies to the attraction and marriage of men and women. Only in this case, the search for a complement occurs *in every* function, and the sense of attraction, indifference or repulsion between a man and a woman is, as it were, the result of a highly complicated calculation of the factor of reciprocity existing in each function and of the average or total of all these factors together. Fortunately, this abstruse calculation does not have to be done in the logical mind, but in the sexual function where a correct result may be given in a second or even less.

It will be recalled from the chapter on man as microcosm how the different glands and their dependent systems and functions work in pairs, one controlling a male and the other a female characteristic. The most obvious example can be seen in the pituitary, where the anterior lobe is connected with reason, will, the power to coordinate and dominate, both one's own organism and one's surroundings; and the posterior lobe with the inner workings of the body, the power of the organism to tend and heal, both itself and others. Evidently the anterior lobe affects masculine, and the posterior feminine or, as the endocrinologists express it, 'maternal' instincts. These two parts together form a single organ.

In the same way the thyroids and parathyroids, or the glands of motion and growth, and the cortex and medulla of the adrenals, inducing respectively fight and flight, represent male and female counterparts. This union of two sexual elements in each of the main glands of the body is well represented in the imagery of Tibetan tantricism, where each 'god' or 'power' may be pictured in union with his shakti or female counterpart.

Now every man and every woman will in each function have one or other of these two aspects dominating – in infinitely varying proportions. And in each function he or she will instinctively search for a member of the opposite sex who has a complementary proportion. Moreover, he may find a partner who is exactly reciprocal in one function, though not at all in others. From this arises all the infinite complication of human sexual relations – the 'platonic friendships', the purely physical liaisons, the *amitié amoureuse*, and so on. It also explains why men and women may quite rightly feel no contradiction in several relations with the opposite sex, and yet find it quite impossible to justify this feeling in face of convention or criticism.

The same causes lie behind the eternal plot in which A loves B, but B, unresponding, loves C. Certainly a man whose centre of gravity lies in one function, may find a woman who is his complement in that, and who thus arouses his keenest excitement. But she, although truly his companion in that function, may have her own centre of gravity in quite a different function where he can give her nothing and where her instinctive needs are met by somebody else.

Again, the working of these natural correspondences is still further complicated and confused by the quite imaginary sexual pictures which may exist in a man's mind – both of himself and of a desirable partner. These pictures, modelled on heroes or heroines in books, plays or on the screen, and influenced by considerations of 'smartness' and fashion, render those who believe in them particularly sensitive to the pseudo-sexuality of exaggerated make-up, provocative dress, suggestive talk and so on. This in turn leads to pornography, which does not at all correspond to the essential nature of the organism, and can only frustrate its true desires at every point.

Nevertheless, the sexual instinct of each individual must continue to search for a member of the opposite sex who can provide its complement in every function simultaneously. And attraction will be felt with increasing intensity as the woman (or man) encountered approaches this ideal. A woman who is his complement or nearly his complement in all functions must always arouse in a man an inexhaustible sense of fascination and mystery, and must ever stand for him as an *ideal*, that is, as that by which he himself is made whole and perfect.

When men and women first hear this idea, they immediately begin to dream about such an ideal partner, about imaginary ecstasies of completion, and about their misfortune in having an actual partner who falls so far short of this ideal.

This is a very great mistake. For in real life such intense attractions, if by chance they are encountered, as often as not bring disaster and tragedy rather than fulfilment. Or even if they do bring some short period of intense ecstasy and understanding, this perfect complement may still be quite unsuitable as a life-partner. For she will occupy a man's attention too much, prevent him from thinking seriously about anything else, or taking other possibilities and duties at their true value. The being of most men and women is not strong enough to deal with the problems arising from finding one's perfect complement.

Moreover, such dreams very effectively prevent the dreamer from recognizing the actual man or woman who is his complement, even should he encounter them. For so dreaming he will be asleep, and *asleep he cannot even recognize what he most desires.*

The relations between the sexes can indeed only be understood on the basis of planetary types. And planetary types can only be recognized *if one is awake.*

Three of these types – the lunar, the venusian, and the jovial – are predominantly feminine in their nature, and the general ideal of feminine beauty and perfection eternally shifts between them. Diana represents the ideal of lunar woman; Aphrodite of venusian woman; Juno of jovial woman. While in a complementary way, the popular masculine ideal moves from one to other of the three male types – the mercurial, the martial, and the saturnine.

Once again, it is art which gives us many clues about these types and the natural sexual attraction between them. For the artist tends always to paint men of his own type, and women of the type which most intensely attract him. And the successful artist unwittingly expresses the ideal types of his age, for precisely in the recognition of this lies his success. In this way, art very often reveals the fundamental laws of type much more clearly than life, where pure types are rare and the affinity between types is confused by imagination, convention, fear, pretence and material interest.

Wandering through picture galleries, we very soon notice that most artists not only always paint the same types, but that they always paint the same type of man in combination with the same type of woman. For instance, we see that Dürer and El Greco paint tall, bony, ascetic *saturnine* men, with meek, round, pale *lunar* women; that Veronese and Rubens paint fierce ruddy *martial* men with flamboyant *junoesque* women; that Correggio, Fragonard and Boucher paint lithe *mercurial* youths with langorous *venusian* goddessess. And this is not accidental, for these combinations of types are indeed natural and fundamental ones.

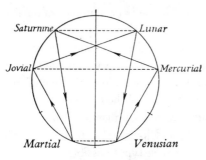

Fig 14 : *The Round of Types*

In life, however, the situation is not so simple. For, as we know, people of either sex may belong to any of the six types; and there can be mercurial or martial women who are still very much women, and lunar or jovial men, who are still very much men. At the same time, in these cases the sense of sex is not so clearly defined, not so exclusive, as it were. And if we take Moon as the midmost point of femininity and Saturn as that of masculinity, we can understand why most tendencies to homosexuality are found on the one hand among lunar men and on the other among saturnine women.

Nevertheless, the circle of types which we worked out when studying human psychology and which we then saw to reflect a cosmic pattern, can throw a great deal of light on this question of attraction of opposites. For if we fold this circle down the middle, it is clear that the types do dispose themselves – both diagrammatically and actually – into three such pairs. The saturnine is opposite to the lunar; the jovial is opposite to the mercurial; and the martial is opposite to the venusian. These represent the combinations of maximum attraction. Such pairs gravitate naturally together, whether in sexual love, in friendship, or simply in physical proximity. For some, the impulse to this pairing may be irresistible: others, unconsciously fearing the disruptive power of such attraction, may carefully avoid their opposites all their lives. For, as we said earlier, such combinations are not necessarily the most satisfactory or the most lasting.

Very often, if strong feeling exists, there will be a quality of transience, of the precariousness of love. And this may even bring with it a passion and desperation which can shake individual lives to their foundations. Under such stress a man or woman may suddenly throw away all that life has given them for a momentary satisfaction, knowing in advance that they can hope for nothing lasting or permanent from it. In such combinations there is often a sense of the tragic, the illegitimate. Weak characters, characters without roots, can be destroyed by them. And yet, for people of set and narrow lives, the very suddenness and violence of the passion may break through convention and open the way for new possibilities which could come to them in no other way.

Yet another very right and very rich relation between types of men and women exists, and one which – like the attraction of opposites – also derives from a cosmic pattern. When studying the psychology of types we noted that everyone may be regarded as *in movement* between one type and the next. That is, as moving – however slowly – along the line of inner circulation between types, which we then established. Lunar, as we saw, tends to move to venusian, venusian to mercurial, mercurial to saturnine, saturnine to martial, martial to jovial, and jovial back to lunar. In this order, and in no other, is movement between types possible.

If we regard this inner movement as representing higher possibilities for men, as the *direction of progress* for mankind as a whole; and if we understand marriage and sexual relations as cosmic means to this end, then many things will become clear. For men and women, by loving and learning to understand each other, *in right combination,* do lead each other along this path of human progress. The mercurial man, loving and enjoying the venusian woman for her warmth and sympathy, can yet lead her out of her sloth and give her a taste of the quickness, lightness, agility and application which she lacks. And in the same way the jovial woman, loving and admiring the courage of the martial man, can begin to tame his violence and lead him towards understanding and tolerance.

Studying men and women in real life in the light of this sequence, we see that the most enduring and permanent partnerships arise when one party – the 'leader', so to speak – is a full stage ahead of the other. Thus Venus may lead the Moon, Mercury lead Venus, Saturn lead Mercury, Mars lead Saturn, Jupiter lead Mars, and the Moon lead Jupiter. For in such combinations, if both equally manage to move towards the next type, both will remain just as mutually attracted and complementary as before. And only if one becomes fixed and left behind, will they cease to enjoy and help each other.

Certainly other sexual combinations of types are possible, and may even bring ecstasy and great understanding. But few will have the permanence and quality of enduring creativeness which belong to the union of those who naturally follow one another. For this may be said to produce growth, where others produce explosion.

Between yet other types sexual relations are truly illegitimate. They are illegitimate because no sexual feeling exists at all; and if attempted they can only outrage the sexual nature of those concerned, and leave deep psychic wounds very difficult to heal. For sex is a function in which *pretence* is very dangerous. And most abnormalities are the result of pretending that sexual attraction does not exist where by type it must, or that it does exist where by type it cannot.

On the other hand, through sex – where it is pure and unperverted – it is given to men and women to understand the greatest laws of the universe directly and, as it were, by birthright. By this force, if they respect it, they are enabled to discriminate between what is right for them and what is wrong for them. By this force, if they let it teach them, they may be led along the path of human development through all types towards perfection. By this force, if they keep all that is negative away from it, it is granted to them to taste for short moments and in one connexion those sensations of ecstasy and union, which are of the nature of higher consciousness.

By pure sex, the ordinary man may gain in a moment what the ascetic denies himself for years to achieve, what the saint prays for a lifetime to feel.

But this only on condition that he approaches it already free from fear, from violence, and from greed. And on condition also that he does not afterwards deny what he learns in sex, but on the contrary allows the understanding attained in sex to pass into all other sides of his life, mellowing, harmonizing and enriching them also.

To man woman must be that which reminds him whence he came. To woman man must be that which reminds her whither she must go. Together they must remind each other of the beginning and the end, of the whole and of perfection.

XX THE CYCLE OF REGENERATION

I FAVOURABLE PERIODS

ON SEPTEMBER 23, 1846, THE OUTER PLANET NEPTUNE WAS DIS-
covered nearly three thousand million miles from the Sun at a
point previously indicated by mathematical deductions. This planet was later found to be of a size midway between those of the inner planets and of giant Saturn and Jupiter. But it appeared to be extremely rarified, to generate its own inner heat, and above all to possess an atmosphere
of pure methane.

Now if we remember the idea that the atmospheres are those parts of
the planets by which they transform and retransmit the sun's light, this fact
becomes very interesting. For of all the major gases so far traced in planetary atmospheres, methane is the finest, the least dense. Whereas the carbon
dioxide of Mars and Venus has a molecular weight of 44, the oxygen (O_2)
and nitrogen (N_2) of the Earth 32 and 28 respectively, and the ammonia of
Jupiter 17, the figure for methane is only 16. Thus Neptune possesses the
most 'delicate' transforming mechanism in the Solar System. And we may
expect its influence to correspond.

From the diagram of the human body, in which we found that the various
endocrine glands lay on a spiral radiating from the heart in an order corresponding to that of the planets, we noted that the 'outermost' gland was
the pineal, situated in the centre of the brain. As far as we could see, this gland
does not work in ordinary man, or at any rate performs only a small part
of its possible functions. And since the glands are arranged in order of
ascending intensity of energy, this seemed to be because man does not
ordinarily dispose of energy of sufficient intensity to set working this outermost and most far-reaching gland. Other clues suggested that its working
would in fact be connected with the regeneration of man's whole being and
the opening in him of new powers and perceptions.

If there exists some connexion or influence from Neptune governing the
pineal gland and its potential function we could hardly trace it in relation
to individual man, because of the length of this planet's cycle. But for
mankind as a whole there should be some visible effect of the waxing and
waning of this influence. The cycle of Neptune is about 165 years. Though
Neptune is so far away that its influence is almost constant, nevertheless
there must be within this cycle a time when this influence is at its strongest

or perhaps in most favourable conjunction with other forces in the universe, such as those from the galactic centre; and another time when it is at its weakest.

What would be the effect on mankind of the most favourable moment of this influence? One would expect to find in general a deeper interest than usual in the *idea* of regeneration, a more widespread *search* among mankind for a new way, a new life, an escape into the unknown. And one would also expect that more men or perhaps we should say some men would *actually succeed* in becoming regenerated, in being transformed or transfigured into new beings. About these, however, it is difficult to tell, because very often – though not always – by their very transfiguration they disappear out of the ordinary course of history and are no more seen.

Certain traces of their existence may be left, however. Once they have succeeded in becoming regenerated or transformed their work will be in organizing 'schools of regeneration', whose inner work must remain unseen. But such schools may also have engaged in some external expression of their work, such as the building of temples, the writing of scriptures, the conduct of scientific research, and so on. And it is by these by-products, so to speak, that we may get a clue to the times when most or *some conscious men existed*.

Probably schools always exist, in some form or another. But in unfavourable times they may exist in a very hidden and concentrated form, as the life of a plant remains hidden and concentrated in the seed during the winter. At most favourable times, on the other hand, though the inner school will still be hidden and concentrated, its preparatory schools and its external work or effect may reach large proportions and even fundamentally affect the course of visible history. At such times, some of the men who have in themselves succeeded in achieving the aim of the school may even appear as famous figures, in the guise of priests, saints, architects, painters and so on.

Apart from this, there will be large numbers of imitation schools, arising spontaneously from the general interest in regeneration, but having no conscious men connected with them and so having to content themselves with the study of old literature, the invention of counterfeit methods, and in general with talk about the idea of regeneration. Curiously enough, it is often these which give us our best clue to the existence of favourable periods. Self-perfection is, so to speak, a fashionable idea.

In fact, true schools are only distinguished by their fruits – they actually produce the conscious men whom imitation schools describe. But since these men cannot be seen or studied in later years, and at best are themselves described by their contemporaries, it is in retrospect almost impossible to distinguish the true from the imitation, first from secondhand. As time goes on, what men were and what they hoped or were believed to be fuses into a single picture, which we have no choice but to study whole. For noble talk is but a later by-product of noble being and the latter must bear the inevitable burden of the former.

What true schools are like, how they are organized, what are their rules and methods, how suitable pupils or raw material are drawn out of the general run of life, we do not know. Evidently one of their chief requirements is secrecy and anonymity, just as a dark, hidden and enclosed point in the soil is necessary for the germination of a seed. For even where we can guess the actual existence of a school – as in the Eleusinian mysteries at certain times, or in the groups of Cathedral-builders – all those connected with it remain unknown to us as individuals.[79] As in the case of the germination of a seed, this is quite understandable. The regeneration or germination of men can only begin in an undisturbed and favourable medium, concealed from external interference.

In fact almost all our very slender information about 'schools of regeneration' and their original knowledge comes to us from seceding pupils, or through some exceptional circumstance which some pupils interpreted as releasing them from their vows. Much of our knowledge of the Orphic mysteries, for example, comes from those like Clement of Alexandria and Athenagoras, who forsook elementary grades of those mysteries for Christianity and then used their partial information to denounce them.

Another curious case concerns the school conducted at Alexandria in the 3rd century by the mysterious Ammonius the Sackbearer. Apparently one of the rules of the school was that nothing should be written down, and Ammonius' chief pupils, Herrenius, Origen the Christian and Plotinus had accepted this condition. Herrenius, however, broke his vow, upon which both Origen and Plotinus felt it incumbent upon them to correct a false impression. In fact, nothing now remains of Herrenius' writing, but Plotinus is our chief source for indications of the inner teaching of the true Neo-platonic schools.

Sometimes it appears that certain schools release knowledge intentionally through some outsider, or through some professional scientist or writer who is sympathetic. For example, one of the best expositions of the secret cosmo-

79. The names revealed by recent research on cathedral-building seem to be simply those of foremen-craftsmen.

logical theories of the 17th century Rosicrucians is by an English doctor, Robert Fludd. Fludd is by nature a self-opinionated bombast: but having rhetorically expounded this cosmological theory and violently abused his more empirical opponent, John Kepler, he lets fall a curious remark:

"But do you really believe that it is impossible for a man by means of divine virtue *to create a new universe* called a Microcosm? If this is your opinion you are entirely mistaken . . . But let not the cobbler leave his last. In *that* I confess myself to know nothing, for I am content with my investigation of nature".

Fludd is referring to the possibility of *creating a new man*, of regeneration; and he admits that he does not belong to the 'school of regeneration', but has only been given some of its cosmological theory. Elsewhere he describes how he was shown *certain experiments* by men "who, without doubt, are a thousand times to be preferred both to Fludd and Kepler in the mysteries of philosophy, and in their deep and true knowledge of cosmic harmony".[80]

Such accidental revelations of special knowledge of 'schools of regeneration' through freed pupils or 'experts' invited from the outside, is in a sense the luck of those who follow in history, like ourselves. If it were not for this we should know nothing at all of schools or their knowledge except through the highly enciphered language of certain 'scriptures' left by them, or through the symbolism of certain special sculptures or buildings.

As it is, these revelations can only refer to certain theoretical knowledge about the universe and man's physiology. They could never convey the *methods* and *practice* of such schools, even if the writer wished to reveal them.

In trying to relate the unfolding and renewed construction of 'schools of regeneration' to the cycle of Neptune, our first difficulty is to know where to start. Certain general tendencies are clear, but the exact year of maximum development is difficult to find. Probably the clearest examples in historic times concern the consolidation of the Gothic Cathedral schools about 1125, and the most overt moment of the Rosicrucian alchemical school about 1620, after which year the school in question 'went underground' and is no more referred to in literature.

If we take 165-year periods from these two points, we have marked the years 30 B. C., 135 A. D., 300, 465, 630, 795, 960, 1125, 1290, 1455, 1620 and 1785. In these years, incidentally, Neptune is found in the centre-point of Libra, that is, it lies in the direction of the galactic centre, whatever significance this conjunction may have.[81]

80. Robert Fludd: 'De Monochordum Mundi', Frankfurt 1623.
81. See Appendix XIII, 'The Cycle of Regeneration'.

While this is not the place to examine in detail the development of esoteric movements in relation to history, many of the above dates do recall the emergence of some quite new influence of this kind. The year 135 A. D. marks a striking renaissance of Buddhism, which at that time suddenly burst from the region of its birth and surged north-east into China and west into Afghanistan. About 300 A. D. the development of anchorite life in the Egyptian desert provided an unexpected loophole of escape from the doomed and bankrupt Roman world, and the beginning of a new aspect of Christianity. A cycle later, St. Benedict created at Monte Cassino a pattern for the whole monastic system of the West; while in 630 Mahomet had completed preparations leading to the spread of Islam from India to the Atlantic. Yet another cycle, and Padma Sambhava was introducing into Tibet that influence which was to render it the chief home of esoteric knowledge right down to our own time.

About the effects of those schools which at the beginning of the 12th century designed the Gothic Cathedrals and remodeled mediaeval society and custom from top to bottom, we have perhaps most material of all. Everywhere we see their influence; in architecture, music, art, in the ritual of the church, in the spread of political peace, in the right organization of castes and guilds, even in a popular wisdom of legends and proverbs. Upon the stability so created Europe continued to exist into living memory. Hardly any other esoteric current in history created such profound and lasting effect.

Yet at the same time we must remember that all these are in fact *only effects*, perhaps even quite remote effects, of the real work of such schools. The men who actually produced these changes in external life and history, and whose existence we can verify, were probably not in schools at all. They may have been influenced or guided by school-men, or they may merely have imitated others who already had this influence at second-hand.

In any case, we may be practically sure that those who formed the inner circles of such schools were as invisible in their own time as they remain to us. For the real and *only* work of such men is to regenerate other men, that is, to help a few suitable men to create conscious souls. This is a very special and intense work, which can only be carried on in conditions insulated, so to speak, from the harsh and disruptive influences of life. For although the men produced by these schools must become sufficiently strong to return into life and begin to influence it, there may be stages in their development when they are much more vulnerable than ordinary men, and when the whole work can be nullified by influences which the latter, protected by their shells of habit and indifference, may not even notice.

The material wealth of modern society is the product of machines, the existence of which depends in turn on the comparatively small but highly skilled industry for making tools to make machines. In just the same way, all true civilizing effects are indirectly produced by conscious men. But they in turn depend on the existence of schools *to create conscious men.* And these we never see. Such is the connexion between the visible improvement produced by civilizing influences in history, and the invisible work of schools of regeneration.

How far back such invisible work penetrates we cannot know. But we may find a clue in the recognized principles of academic teaching. Suppose fifty 'good' men in ordinary life can be prepared in right understanding by one man for whom the pursuit of consciousness has become a permanent feature of essence. And suppose fifty men of the latter level to be instructed by one man of conscious soul. What level of man would now be necessary to conduct a school of fifty conscious men?

Again we can give no answer. But we can see from this principle that the greatest 'golden age' might indeed be created by no more than fifty conscious men, who in their turn might depend on the presence in the world at that time of one single man of an unknown but even higher level. In such historical roles as Christ, Buddha, Mahomet, we appear to see at least the *trace* of such latter men.

From the point of view of ordinary men the characteristic of favourable periods will be that in them it is easier to respond to higher influences. Seen from above, however, the chief point about such periods may be that certain cosmic conditions then permit the entrance into the world of one man of normally inconceivable development, and that all the rest depends on him. In fact, both these ideas are equally true and equally important.

At the same time, it must be remembered that favourable or unfavourable periods in themselves *make no difference* to ordinary men. It never occurs to us to imagine that a gnat which lives on a sunny day in June is a *better* gnat than one which lives on a cloudy day in September. He is only luckier. The difference is simply that in June the sun is made relatively visible to gnats; just as at the time of the dramatic festivals of the Eleusinian mysteries or the pilgrimages arranged by the cathedral-builders, truth was made relatively visible to ordinary men.

These paradoxical ideas are well expressed in a story which comes down to us from the time of the Egyptian hermits, exactly one of the favourable periods mentioned above. One anchorite received a vision. He seemed to be beside a broad sea, from the near shore of which, as he watched, a monk rose up and flying with powerful wings soared straight to a distant and almost invisible shore. As the hermit wondered at this, a second monk arose, but with much weaker wings, so that he could keep but little above the waves, and only after heavy labour and much danger came at last to the other side. While he still looked, however, a third monk rose up, but with such feeble flight that he fell again and again into the sea, only managing with the greatest effort to escape from drowning. Yet in the end, against all probability, this monk also reached the distant shore.

After much pondering, the hermit went to his superior and recounted his vision. The superior gave this interpretation. "The first monk you saw was he who aspires to fly to heaven in our own time – it is relatively easy: the second monk represents those who attempt the task in the time after us – it will be much more difficult: the third monk is one who tries to come to heaven in the very distant future, when it will be almost impossible. Rejoice that you live in our time: but do not forget this – the third monk's effort is worth all the rest."

II THE WORK OF SCHOOLS

Little as we know about schools of regeneration, one aspect of their work cannot be omitted.

We said that their object must be to help a few suitable men to create conscious souls. From one point of view, the success or even partial success of this work would mean that such pupils would acquire many new powers as compared with ordinary men. For example, we described them as becoming aware of their own nature, and of their true relation to the surrounding universe. From this they would begin to understand what they could do, and what they could not do. They would thus be enabled to concentrate all their force on possible objectives, and would be spared the ordinary man's expenditure of great labour and effort on impossible tasks which by the laws of nature can never be accomplished.

Thus all ordinary men spend a vast amount of physical and emotional energy in an endeavour to alter the people about them. They are always requiring their friends, enemies, partners or acquaintances to behave otherwise than their type dictates. They require intellectual people to respect their feelings, emotional people to accept their theories; they require slow types to be quick, impatient types to be patient, gypsies to be diligent, and warriors to be mild. This is all fruitless endeavour.

One of the first things a man who becomes more conscious of himself and his surroundings will learn is that he cannot alter anybody: he can only alter his own point of view. And paradoxically, this understanding, if it really penetrates into him, immediately endows him with quite new powers and quite new freedom. By virtue of it he is at an immense advantage in the world. All his forces are liberated for the attainment of what he really can achieve.

This refers to the subjective acquisition of new powers through being freed from certain common illusions. But beyond this, increased consciousness may also bring objective powers, connected with the working of a new function through a hitherto unused nervous system, as discussed in earlier chapters. Such a power is true telepathy, that is, the power of placing definite thoughts in the minds of others, at will. The question of these objective or true powers does not fall within the scope of the present book. We can only say that their development is possible, and must form part of the work of all true schools.

We have seen how even the elimination of certain illusions gives a man an enormous advantage. The moment he ceases to think that he can alter others, and begins to realize that *each man's weakness can be absolutely relied on*, one of two questions may arise in him – either, how can he take personal advantage of his new knowledge of others? or, how can he help them? And the very fact that he now sees more clearly, means that he can do either with far greater success than before.

Which of these questions arises is a fundamental test of the man's *being*. Moreover the two possibilities make clear to us a very essential distinction, which must be clearly understood. *Powers* have nothing to do with *being*.

We already saw that lucky gnats are not necessarily better gnats. In the same way, a strong man is not necessarily a good man. These two qualities are incommensurable, because the first refers to powers and the second to being. Thus a strong man may either use his strength to labour for others, or to force others to labour for him, or again he may be too lazy to use his power at all. These three courses refer to different states of being.

Exactly the same problem arises in a very much more acute form in connection with the acquisition of new powers through increased consciousness. For although a strong man may meet a stronger man in any town he comes to, a more conscious man may travel very far through the world without meeting anyone else in a similar position. He may thus appear for some time to be free from *force majeure*. At the same time, his new powers may be such that, from the point of view of humanity as a whole, they simply *cannot be permitted* in unprepared men. Imagine, for instance, the terrible effects of the power of telepathy – that is, of being able deliberately to place thoughts in other people's minds – if exercised by a cruel or fearful man, or even by a man still subject to ordinary curiosity, ambition or malice.

It is for these reasons that in all genuine schools work for increased consciousness must be exactly paralleled by work for the improvement and purification of being. This work is chiefly concerned with *the way a man regards himself*. And for some people it may be the most difficult part of school-work to understand and bear.

At the same time this precautionary work on being is only necessary for a certain while. It is very important during the period when a man already understands more than he can understand in ordinary life, but does not yet understand enough to see the full implications of his new knowledge. During this time, school discipline may appear to be very strict and harsh; for it is now that the learner may destroy both himself and others through partial knowledge. Later when he understands *enough*, that is, when he sees all the principles involved, and the inevitable results of misuse of new powers, certain wrong courses will become quite impossible for him. Thus the chief danger is that he stops on the way of development, or rests content with a slight improvement in consciousness. And this in turn may be expressed as a failure in being.

Now it becomes possible to see better what is and what is not altered by the cycle of regeneration ruled by the planet Neptune. In favourable periods of this cycle, such as those already mentioned, the acquisition of new *powers* connected with increase of consciousness may become slightly easier. The problem of *being*, on the other hand, always remains exactly the same, and work on being is never easier or more difficult than at any other time.

Moreover, while increase in consciousness may be only possible with the help of schools of regeneration, the problem of improvement of being is one that faces all men everywhere by the very fact of their birth into the world. It provides a test for every living individual, and unless this test is successfully passed, the question of schools and their possibilities does not even arise.

Earlier on, we referred to the idea that on the way of true development, *something old must die in a man, and something new must be born in him*. Now we can discuss this idea further, for in fact all the work of schools is connected with one or other of these processes, and with these alone.

Thus although the secondary aim of a school may be to spread a true understanding of natural laws and of man's nature and possibilities among large numbers, its primary aim in relation to those more intimately attached to it, must be first, to help them destroy their old personalities, and second, to help them acquire conscious souls. And obviously, all those submitting to school discipline must – as far as they personally are concerned – fully understand and concur in both these aims.

It is very necessary to realize that these are two separate processes, not necessarily following one from another. In a very general way, what has been described about the improvement of being may be said to refer to the first process, while direct work for the development of new powers leads towards the second. In any case, quite different school methods and exercises are involved in the two processes, though they may and should go on together. If they do not, it may happen that the old personality is destroyed without a soul being acquired, resulting in some form of possession by another or in insanity. Or it may happen that a soul is acquired without the old personality being destroyed, in which case the latter, with all its weaknesses, cruelties, lusts and ambitions, becomes permanent and is endowed with extraordinary powers of carrying out its irrational impulses. Fortunately, both these cases are very rare, though they may exist as tendencies to be corrected within a general work of development.

The most exoteric work of a school is thus the spread of understanding. This side of its work may affect hundreds or even thousands of people.

The next part of the work of a school is the gradual breaking down of the old personality among its more intimate pupils. This work also may touch in stronger or weaker degree quite a large number. And in an individual the process may go on for years, or even for all that remains of a lifetime.

This process may be compared with the drying-out of nuts in preparation for shelling. When a walnut, for example, is green, it is impossible to remove the shell without seriously damaging the kernel. Shell and kernel then form an inseparable whole. After a suitable drying-out process, however, the shell becomes brittle and separated from the kernel, at which stage a comparatively light tap will split it, revealing the kernel in its perfection.

All those entering a school from the outside may be regarded as 'green': while those who honestly expose themselves to school influence, after a certain number of years begin to approach the state when essence and old personality have become loosened from each other, and a comparatively light blow is sufficient to separate them. This loosening of personality from essence is one of the chief purposes of school discipline. Different methods, ranging from violent reproof to an example of complete humility, may be used by the teacher, according to his nature, to produce the same result.

While this effect is being produced in the pupil by school influence, his own inner work is that of self-purification. Put in another way, this means that he strives to eliminate from his organism everything that he does not want to keep permanently. Such things will include disharmonious physical states and bodily sickness: harmful emotions and uncontrollable attachments and longings: malicious, fearful and self-centred thoughts. Physical purification is not absolutely essential, but if it is ignored, the suffering of the learner at a later stage is greatly increased, and a tremendous strain is put upon his will in order to overcome physical inertia and pain. One of the effects of physical purification is to eliminate unnecessary suffering.

During this period of preparation, the pupil has also to learn how to make himself do difficult things and how to carry out certain painful or repetitive exercises, which will later be necessary to fix a certain state in him. He should not carry them too far at this stage, because he does not want to fix anything. At the same time, he must master them so that they will be quite familiar at the moment when he needs to use them intensively.

All this preparation leads to the point where it is time for the old personality to die or to be killed. This death depends upon many things and it may come about in many ways. It may be the deed of a teacher, either gradual or in one terrible assault. It may perhaps be induced by some overwhelming pressure from life, which the pupil has voluntarily accepted or invoked. Hardship and sacrifice, spread over many years of preparation, may have reduced personality to a powerless wraith. Pain, prison, starvation, torture, abandonment or ruin – swallowed and not rebelled against – may equally destroy it. As in the analogy of the nut, if dessication is complete, any blow can split the shell which will fall away of its own accord.

What is left has no position, no money, no family, no acquaintances, no ambition, no power of acting for itself. Many of these things may return to the pupil later in a different way. But at this moment – whether in school, in prison, or on the battlefield – he finds himself without anything and without any past. It is as though his body were placed naked on a desert island where it had no previous connections of any kind. For a little while he is as a new born child.

Quite separate from the death of the old personality, though it may take place at the same time, is the conception of a conscious soul in him. This process appears to be analogous to the conception of a physical body. The essence of the pupil plays as it were the female part, and into this a seed from the source of consciousness must be set.

These two processes – the killing of the old personality and the planting of a soul – may perhaps be better understood from the analogy of the grafting of a cutting of a cultivated fruit-tree on to the stock of a wild one. First the wild tree is cut down to the ground, leaving only its roots and bole intact. One or two incisions are then made in the bole, and into these are set cuttings from the cultivated tree. Soon sap begins to flow from the wild root into the cutting, and in time a new tree grows, bearing the desired fruit, but fed by the strength and roots of the old tree.

Once the soul has 'taken' in the pupil's essence, the time comes for all to be fixed. And once again, this fixing may appear voluntary or involuntary – it may be a trial deliberately sought, or an unavoidable one borne with understanding.

Perhaps the pupil feels in himself an irresistible call to go away alone, in conditions of special difficulty, without food or drink. Maybe he has received some great ecstasy or enlightenment, and something tells him that that for which he has not paid he cannot hope to keep. Or perhaps a man, not even knowing himself a pupil but come to this same point by another way, is struck down by an agonizing illness which he must summon all his strength to bear.

Alone in his retreat or alone with his agony, he is thrown upon his own resources. Suggestions may be conveyed to him by his teacher, if he has one, by inspiration if he has not. But the way he carries them out, the methods he uses, and the conclusions he comes to, all derive from his own essence.

Now he has to put into practice as intensively as he can all that he previously learned. In general, pain and repetition are fixative agents, and the exercises or experiences of which we speak use one or other or both principles to fix the soul in him and to set in it certain general attitudes, beliefs and principles. Nor does it matter if this pain arise from the fakir's holding up his arm, the explorer's defiance of heat and cold, the stricken man's wound or illness. The repetition may equally consist in a Russian pilgrim's endless repeating of a prayer, a prisoner's endless enduring of his routine. What is important is the *attitude* which accompanies them. For these experiences may indeed fix permanently in a man a certain attitude towards God, towards his fellow-men, towards his duty. And if they are sufficiently intense, such attitudes will remain with him for the rest of his life.

It is at this time that the effect of preparation and purification is seen. For not only the general attitudes aroused in him by the situation and his suffering will become fixed, but also any casual thoughts, longings, regrets, fears and ambitions still left over from his personality. For example, his anticipation of what he most desires to do when he emerges, he is freed, or he recovers will become set in him as a permanent tendency. If during the fixing experience, he thus finds arising in him regrets, longings or imaginations apart from the understanding he wishes to fix, he must seriously consider whether he is willing to live with such thoughts or feelings for the rest of his life. This idea will give him strength to keep his mind one-pointed.

At this time the value of physical purification also appears. If this has been neglected, abstinence and fixation may involve much suffering. It is true that if the pupil is strong enough, the overcoming of this suffering will give him enormous emotional energy. On the other hand it may prove too great a distraction, and leave him marked with certain fears that he is unable to set aside. But if physical purification has been carried some way in advance, this time of fixing need not to be too difficult. The hardship will not be what it seems to be. In any case, *there will be nothing beyond his power to bear.*

At the same time, men are right in their natural aversion from the pain and hardship which cause crystallisation, and in their efforts to avoid them. For who is yet ready to have all that he finds within him fixed? And even if he is, let him remember that fixing without understanding is like baking without yeast – something almost impossible of later correction.

For during fixation is set the future course of the man's life and work. All his natural capacities, his acquired interests, everything that he has really learned and mastered, his own understanding, even his own true pleasures contribute to this. All this must come together and combine with the general attitudes and beliefs which he is fixing to show his line of work in the future, and perhaps even some of the external events and stages which will be connected with it.

When his trial is over, the pupil should know without question and permanently what he is, what he believes, and what he must do. It does not mean that these ideas become fixed in a narrow way; it means that certain basic ideals and attitudes are established in him which he can never go back on, and upon which his understanding may grow infinitely in the future.

The four processes which have been described – the loosening of the personality and preliminary purification; the death of personality; the implanting of a soul; and the fixing of this soul and the attitudes and understanding characteristic of it - may be more simply represented by the figure of preparing and dyeing wool. First, the wool must be washed and cleaned, the impurities and fats removed. This corresponds to preparation and purification. Second, it must be bleached. This corresponds to the killing of the old nature. Third, it must be dyed to the required colour. This corresponds to the implanting of a soul. Fourth, the dye must be fixed. This corresponds to the period of trial. When all these processes are complete, the wool is ready to be woven into some material and to receive upon it designs or embroideries according to the requirements of a higher intelligence.

As far as we know at present, the destruction of the old personality and the imparting of conscious souls constitute the whole work of schools.

III SCHOOL AS A COSMOS

That which distinguishes a true school of regeneration from all other kinds of human society is the fact that it endeavours to simulate and, in successful cases, *actually creates a cosmos*.

The reason for this is clear. As we have seen, a cosmos and only a cosmos contains all six cosmic processes, including that of regeneration. In order to become regenerate, a man must participate in the process of regeneration in a higher cosmos. But this process, in naturally existing cosmoses, such as the Earth or the World of Nature, is far too slow from the point of view of individual man. With a lifetime of 80 years, it does not help him much to participate in regeneration on the scale of tens or even hundreds of thousands of years. There is only one way out. An artificial cosmos must be created, which will exhibit the same processes and permit the same possibilities – *but very much faster*. This work is the work of a school.

Little by little the different aspects of a cosmos have been revealed - its circle of life developing logarithmically in time; its informing triangle at the points of which three kinds of 'food' or inspiration from higher cosmoses enter and sustain it; the inner circulation which unites its different functions. All these motions cross and recross, and at their points of crossing definite phenomena are created – 'batteries' or 'organs' which are alternately charged and discharged according to the motions which pass through them. At one certain crossing within the cosmos, regeneration – that is, the escape of an individual 'cell' from a lower to a higher circulation – is possible.

All this must be perfectly known and understood by the leaders of schools. They must understand not only the whole plan of a cosmos, but also the inner meaning of all its motions and parts in the world of men. And they must organize a kind of living ritual, lasting decades or centuries, and in which tens, hundreds or even thousands of men actually perform the movements required of them. If we think of the games of living chess that were sometimes played at the time of the Renaissance, and if we imagine them carried out, not in a single stadium on a particular day, but all over the world for scores of years, and if we further imagine the human pieces *actually changing their very being and nature* when moved from one square to another, then we shall have a faint idea of what is meant.[82]

One of the studies traditionally connected with esoteric work is that of acting and the theatre. There are many aspects of this. As he observes himself in a new way, that is, from the point of view of consciousness, the student very early begins to realize that everything *happens to him*. Whereas before it seemed to him that he was arranging his life, either well or badly, now he sees that his life happens to him, his behaviour happens to him, his friends happen to him, his quarrels and loves all happen to him. His life and everybody else's life seem full of involuntary reaction, unconscious and unwished for conduct which happens to people, just as the colour of their eyes or the shape of their nose happens to them.

At this stage the idea of 'acting' becomes connected with conscious intentional conduct as opposed to conduct that happens. 'Acting' means behaving in a way that one has decided in advance for a reason one has decided in advance. It means deliberately choosing and expressing one feeling out of many contradictory ones that may arise. It means deliberately holding some positive posture in order not to fall into a familiar but unconscious one. Indeed, as the student soon sees, intentional 'acting' in this sense means 'acting' what one wants to become – 'acting' as though one were responsible, in spite of irresponsible impulses, 'acting' from sincere feelings which one's mechanical impulse is to hide, and so on.

Yet though what the pupil may learn from such experiments is unlimited, he is not the chief reason for them. They are the first preparations for a great drama, which – somewhere and at some time – will have to be performed. This drama represents *the perfection of a cosmos*.

Now it is clear why all ordinary societies for the moral or cultural improvement of men, all ordinary religious practices and philosophical methods, differ from true schools of regeneration. Men in ordinary life know nothing about the constitution of a cosmos, or that such a thing exists, and even if they were to be shown its theoretical plan, they could never see its detailed application in the realm of human psychology, or persuade all the different types required *to move with understanding, each to his own goal*. This is only

82. This idea is touched upon in the author's 'The Theory of Eternal Life', chapter 12, and in a sketch 'The Christian Mystery'.

possible to a man who has reached a completely different level of consciousness, a level of consciousness in which he can actually see the working of cosmoses in the world around him. In fact, a true or complete school can only be initiated by a man of conscious spirit.

One of the most difficult things to understand about the working of the cosmos of school is the nature of the informing triangle which connects it with higher cosmoses and endows it with all possibilities. The first point of this triangle, the beginning and the end, the place in ordinary man where the first impulse originates and where the final process of regeneration culminates, we may call 'higher school'. This means school on a higher level than the one being created, school where the regeneration of higher beings than ordinary man is being conducted. From higher school must derive the necessary plan, the necessary knowledge, and the necessary force, in their abstract form.

The second point of the triangle, where breath enters in man, is the visible 'teacher', who appears in the world, gathers men round him, and breathes the 'breath of life' into principles too abstract for them otherwise to understand. At this point stand Christ, Buddha and in higher or lower degree, all the great teachers of humanity.

It is the third point of the triangle which is most difficult for the logical mind to understand. This is the point where perceptions of light enter man, and as a result the possibility of understanding as well as feeling begins. Here lies 'the knowledge of good and evil'. And one of its strangest aspects is that this point also implies disagreement, division, hostility. By blood and breath men understand each other, on a certain level. By perceptions and the different interpretation which each type places upon them men misunderstand each other. The contrast between the peacefulness of primitive 'instinctive' man, and the quarrelsomeness of civilized 'mental' man shows very well the conflicting nature of these two successive stages. Thereafter men can understand each other again only *on a very much higher level*, when a new function begins to awaken.

In school this point 6 is the mechanism by which instinctive 'belief' must be broken, in order to make possible a higher 'understanding'. All normal men, confronted by a Christ, believe. But how can they be made to understand his work? To achieve this, an artificial opposition or hostility must be created. As when a match is struck, intense *friction* is necessary in order to produce light. The school thus has *to oppose its own first expression*. This is the 'second shock'.

A very interesting hint of this role is expressed in the New Testament by the figure of Saint Paul, who begins by 'persecuting' the first Christians, and later 'persecutes' Christ's own teaching, giving his inner precepts an exterior and organizational form which at once both distorts them and makes them accessible. The implied struggle between Plato and Socrates, or their Sufi counterparts Jellal-edin Rumi and Shems-edin, suggests the same thing. The first teacher is too far from ordinary men, who can love him but cannot understand him. A mediator must also be provided by school who will explain the teacher to the world, who will *throw light on him*. This mediator will lay the foundations of an organization. And to those who knew and loved the first teacher, *it will seem that he is destroying the latter's work*.

If we wish, then, to put names to the three sides of the triangle, we can call the first side 'Outflow from Higher School', the second 'Struggle with Resistance' or 'Persecution', and the third 'Return to Higher School'. This triangle will then represent the three aspects of direct communication with the original impulse.

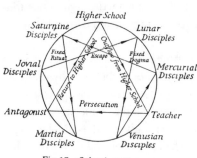

Fig. 15 . *School as Cosmos*

The circle, as in all other cosmoses we have studied, will represent the 'life' of the school in the world, its development in time. Thus the first third, or gestation, will represent the hidden appearance of the ideas of the school in the world, the first few years of the teacher's intimate instruction of his own circle. Then at a certain point, where the circle touches the triangle again, the teacher will throw off his disguise, and appear openly as the representative of higher school. He will seem 'transfigured'.

From this moment, his own group will 'know', doubt will no longer be possible for them. But simultaneously with this, some violent opposition will suddenly arise, both *from the outside world and from another aspect of the school*. The period of 'persecution' will begin. And precisely the fire of this persecution will wring out of the teacher's influence all the meaning, all the understanding, all the implications, on great and small scales, which it contains. Such a struggle, as we see from the logarithmic scale, may continue for several generations.

At the same time, this necessary tension also implies danger for the school experiment. Precisely here may criminality enter and spoil all. The greater the tension between two aspects of school the higher the possible understanding and achievement. But suddenly this tension may prove too much for the being of those concerned, and the whole mechanism fuse.

An interesting example is found in the great twelfth century flowering. For a while, tension between the more masculine monastic expression of esotericism in northern France and the more feminine and sensuous expression of the Catharists in the Midi produces a richness and completeness in mediaeval culture which has rarely been equalled. The tension mounts: then quite suddenly connects with tides of political rivalry and personal violence which have been lying in abeyance. With appalling cruelty, one pole of the tension is wiped out by the Albigensian Crusade – a crime from which the mediaeval experiment never quite recovers.

We said that the cosmos of school, like every other cosmos, must contain all six processes. It must thus contain crime. Only this crime is not produced by it. It is the crime always and inevitably existing in the world and hearts of men. A certain definite amount of this crime, it is the task of every school experiment to take in and neutralize. Just as for a man, the highest possibility depends upon him taking in and neutralizing pain and corruption within himself.

Inner school knows that the process of crime is neutralized, not by opposition or the process of *destruction*, as is usually believed, but only by the quite different process of *regeneration*. As long as this secret knowledge is in control, the experiment triumphs. But sooner or later, someone connected with the school falls into temptation. Patience gives out – and he meets crime, not with regeneration, but first with destruction and then with other crime. In this way, a part of the experiment must always fail. The proportion between this failure and this triumph is the great unknown, the cosmic gamble in every school experiment.

At a second point, however, where the circle again touches the triangle, the figure who has come to personify 'persecution' will also throw off his disguise, will also appear openly as the representative of higher school, will also seem 'transfigured'. Thereafter, the work of the two figures will become fused, the inner and outer forms will be reconciled, and a single 'church' or 'tradition' will stand created. The third third of the circle, developing ever more slowly through many centuries and ever more widely among men, will represent the influence and work of this 'church', this 'tradition'. Until at last the form of this particular school comes to an end, and its experience and achievement is recalled into the higher school from which it sprang.

THE CYCLE OF REGENERATION

We now see that the cosmos of a school follows the same time-scale as the cosmos of a civilization. And we at last understand that they are in fact one and the same, since it is only the hidden presence of a school which makes a civilization really self-evolving and thus really a cosmos. 'Civilization' indicates the outer form, 'school' the inner meaning.

From this we also see what 'favourable periods' mean – they mean periods near the points where the informing triangle of influence from higher school actually touches the circle of time. And simultaneously we see that no points are in reality more favourable than others, for the possibility of change for individual man lies not along the circle of time at all, but along the figure of inner circulation which crosses time in all directions, and begins at every point.

The meaning of this figure of internal circulation in relation to school has already been touched on in the chapter on 'Human Psychology'. As in humanity, the 'functions' of school are symbolized by the different types of men, and this circulation thus becomes a conscious speeding up of the interchange between types and a conscious development of balanced 'super-types'. In this aspect, as in its total work, the school represents a controlled experiment, aimed at enormously increasing the general process of regeneration of the universe, within definite limits and conditions.

Thus the figure of circulation must never be regarded as a continuous movement on one level. In school it is a rising or spiral movement, each change being not only to a different type but to that type *on a higher level* than the one abandoned, accompanied with greater understanding, greater consciousness, and greater perception of the whole.

Unlike the figure of the circle, this motion does not proceed in time, but is a 'flow' composed of the movement of all men of all types who come under the influence of the particular school in all ages. Nevertheless, it will be necessary for the teacher to establish the form of the movement by choosing among his disciples representatives of the six distinct types and helping them to accomplish, each for himself, an actual movement to the next stage. The change from the belligerent, impatient Simon Peter who strikes off the soldier's ear in the Garden of Gethsemane to the wise, understanding, all-embracing, 'jovial' Peter of the Acts of the Apostles is an example of such a 'move'.

It will be noticed that the path of this inner circulation makes many 'crossings' - it crosses itself, twice outside and once inside the triangle; and it crosses the triangle itself, twelve times. Each of these crossings has a definite meaning. In the cosmos of man's body, as has been said, its crossings of the triangle are represented by certain 'batteries', or organs which store the energy of consciousness in a very concentrated form and both collect it from and feed it into the bloodstream. The crossings *outside* the triangle represent certain fixed forms, like hair or bones, which although an integral part of the organism, do not include the possibility of consciousness available to the rest. The crossing *inside* the triangle, as explained in the chapter on 'Human Psychology', represents the point where radiance and invisibility coincide, where two different nervous systems cross, and thus where individual cells can finally 'escape' or become regenerate.

In the 'performance' of this figure arranged by the leader of the school, not only have the individual movements of types to be achieved, but corresponding phenomena have to be produced at the crossings. At the twelve crossroads with the triangle definite 'monuments' or 'memorials' have to be created, from which for ever after all men concerned with the school will be able to draw different kinds of inspiration, each according to his type, and which will serve as signposts showing each how he must proceed.

These twelve 'batteries' are symbolized in the drama of Christ by the twelve apostles, who establish a series of permanent ideals, to one of which each particular man at the particular point in his movement can aspire or make appeal. Gradually, these 'batteries' are supplemented by concrete expressions of the work of the school in lasting form – on the outgoing side of the triangle by the four Gospels, on the lower side by conflicting 'creeds' and 'dogmas', on the returning side by great cathedrals, rituals and works of art.

In some cases, the creation of a necessary 'battery' will be through the instrumentality of a particular individual chosen by the leader, as a condition, so to speak, of his move. It will, at a certain point, be his 'task' – like Saint John's Gospel or Saint Peter's establishment of apostolic succession. As time goes on, further expressions will continue to be added to each of the different batteries – as various 'orders', 'reformations' and even 'heresies' continued to be added to the Christian tradition.

These twelve batteries thus represent the devices by which the flow of individual types, continuing through the ages, can both feed and draw upon the original creative impulse deriving from higher school.

The crossings outside the triangle manifest in school in a very curious way. They are represented by the fixed bodies of opinion, which have accumulated round one or another external aspect of school, who spend all their time defending this particular aspect, attacking all other aspects, and who have become completely dissociated from the informing triangle which alone gives meaning to the whole. These are they whom Paul pictures declaiming: "I am of Paul; and I of Apollos; and I of Cephas; and I of Christ" – those for whom the group is more important than the work. And in later times they become, on the one hand, 'primitive Christians' who ridicule all forms of ritual and church as hypocritical, and on the other 'professional ecclesiastics', concerned only with perpetuating a particular dogma or a particular organization. Among these two fixed bodies, outside the triangle, there can never be either understanding or consciousness, and the best that can be said for them is that, like the skeleton, they serve to give form and rigidity to the whole.

About the crossing within the triangle little can be said, save that, for all individuals who come in contact with the school in all its ages, this point represents the point of escape, death and rebirth, the actual possibility of regeneration. In the presence of this point, and the actual penetration of the possibilities contained in it, the whole purpose of the school resides.

Thus we see the tremendous trace of school in the past. But the world goes on, principles remain the same. Schools as great exist and must be created, in the present or the future, wherever man shall be found.

XXI MAN IN ETERNITY

I DEATH

IN THE LOGARITHMIC SCALE OF MAN'S LIFE, WE CAME LEVEL WITH the ninth milestone, and then stopped. The ninth milestone is death. In the circle the ninth milestone is also zero or the beginning, conception. Death and conception are one. This is the mystery of love and death. At every milestone a more intense energy entered. At the first milestone the energy for digestion, at the second for motion, at the fourth the energy for building the body, at the fifth the energy for thought, at the seventh the energy for passionate action, at the eighth the energy for sex, creation and self-mastery.

At the ninth an energy of such intensity enters that for ordinary man it is absolute and final, as fire is absolute and final for a piece of wood. His individuality completely vanishes in it. He is destroyed, and it appears to him as death.

But there exists the possibility that this energy, which comes to ordinary man only to destroy him, for other beings could have quite a different meaning. The energy of the candle-flame exists for a moth only to destroy it, but the flame enables man to see. It is *too strong* for the moth, but this very strength gives man a new perception.

The energy of death is the energy which unites all things, merges all things in one, just as all wooden objects put into a fire are united in the same heat and the same ash. Ordinary man has not enough consciousness to withstand this energy, so he cannot *know* what such unification means.

What does he know about death? All that we can ordinarily describe are purely physical signs – the immediate cessation of breathing and heartbeat, the gradual loss of bodily heat in 15 or 20 hours, the wave of rigidity which slowly passes from the jaw to the feet and disappears in the same way, and the onset of putrefaction in two or three days.

All this only tells us of the disappearance of an individual body out of the line of historical time. It tells us nothing about what happens to the essence of the man, to his individuality. Nor does it tell us what happens to his consciousness, if he has acquired any. And it throws no light on what unification in death could mean.

Where does a man's essence go at death? What is the mystery of death and conception being one? No ordinary knowledge, no ordinary experience, and certainly no ordinary 'spiritualism' give us any hint at all.

Yet we have found a clue to death. From our scale of times, we can establish that with each breath a man takes, the molecules in his body 'die' and are replaced by new. With each breath, he possesses *a quite new molecular body*. And in a barely perceptible pulse of attention, 'himself' – all he knows, understands, remembers, all his habits, likes, dislikes, all that he calls 'I' – has fallen asleep and woken again to find everything as before.

Similarly each night, while 'he' sleeps, the cells of his body die and are replaced by new. In the morning he possesses *a new cellular body*. Yet when he wakes his new body has the exact form, constitution and health of the old, and into it awakes exactly the same self as inhabited the other.

In this way man is continually dying and continually being reborn. Yet himself, his individuality, remains the same. For those parts which die are recreated *as they were before*. Only an infinitesimal change, sufficient after tens of thousands of repetitions to produce the difference between youth and old age, occurs with each rebirth.

What causes this continuity? It is the relation of cosmoses, and the relation of dimensions. The time of the cell is made up, not of generations of molecules, but of their *recurrence*, that is, of their fifth dimension. The time of man is made up, not of generations of cells, but of their recurrence, their eternity.

With every breath, man's molecular body dies and is reborn. He falls asleep for a moment. And in that moment each molecule recurs, is reborn the same. Reborn to the identical point in the identical cell it occupied before, at the identical instant of its death, of identical material, and inheriting all the effects it previously produced upon its surroundings – it cannot be other than the same. If it were not so, the cell could not continue.

With every night, man's cellular body dies and is reborn. He falls asleep. In that sleep each cell recurs, is reborn the same. Reborn to the identical point in the human body it occupied before, at the identical instant of its death, of identical material, and inheriting all the effects it previously produced upon its surroundings – it cannot be other than the same. If it were not so, the human body could not continue.

With every life, man's human body dies and is reborn. He falls asleep. In that sleep this body recurs, is reborn the same. Reborn to the identical point in the world of mankind it occupied before, at the identical instant of its death, of identical material, and inheriting all the effects it previously produced upon its surroundings – it cannot be other than the same. If it were not so, mankind could not continue.

We have let the analogy run its course. What is the meaning of this strange and terrible result? It can only mean that each ending life leaves a residue of effects – upon nature, environment, other men and women – which become the automatic causes of a life to come. The impress left by this body's deeds is the exact mould of the next body's form. This impress is the trace of man's being. The trace is the image of its cause, and the cause of its next image. Being and its effects are one.

In the moment of death, the pattern of these effects, transformed by this cosmic lightning into a single sign, is struck through time upon the waiting embryo. This is the secret of what happens to man's essence at death. *It causes the same body to be born again, in the same place, of the same parents, at the same time.*

Such a possibility cannot belong to ordinary time, that is, to man's fourth dimension. It can only belong to his fifth dimension, his recurrence, his eternity.

Death and conception are one in *eternity*. Each man's life lies in time, but the sum of his lives lies in eternity. The point at which one life joins the next is the point at which time joins eternity. At that point the effects of his life pass out of one time into another time. What was creates what will be. And all that man calls 'himself' must fall asleep to wake again to the same body, the same surroundings, the same problems that he left before – unaware that it was ever otherwise.

Because we cannot penetrate directly to lower worlds, we do not guess what blinding disintegration, explosion and ecstatic fusion the oxygen of our breath brings to the molecules of blood. But for ourselves we realize that this shock which separates the end of one life from the beginning of the next, which severs essence from the corpse and launches it back into the seed, is the most tremendous which a human being is called upon to face. In fact, it is too strong for ordinary man, who has *no choice* but to forget and fall asleep.

Earlier we compared birth and the end of childhood to the two critical points at which steam changed to water and water to ice. The moment of death and conception could then be likened to a point at which, in a single flash, the ice passed back through all the other stages, split into oxygen and hydrogen, and in the same instant condensed as steam again. But to split the molecule into its separate atoms, and bring these atoms together again, not only heat, but an intense electric shock would be required. The energy of death appears to have some similar effect on the whole being of man, splitting it into its component parts of body, essence, personality and life, and in the same moment rejoining that which survives in a different way.

The instant at which all the unfulfilled causes set up in the past life are torn from the corpse by death is the same terrible instant of impregnation when the genes or signature of the body that will be rush together into their new pattern. This is that.

The old body decays and returns to earth. The magnetic field that was its life flies to the moon. Personality, a reflection in any case, vanishes with the object which reflected it. And essence, now a quintessence of accumulated causes, passes instantaneously across time to launch the body of another life.

But ordinary man has no conscious soul to accompany it. So he cannot *know* what death is, nor the unification of death. Causes pass from one life to another, unaccompanied by consciousness. If man had a conscious soul, then death would have a different meaning for him.

II RECURRENCE

Man usually pictures his journey to the end of time as the Middle Ages pictured a journey to the end of the world. It was believed, the Earth being flat, that at a certain point one must come to the edge and fall off forever into the unknown. Only when a brave man held a single course and, after great hardships and strange adventures, sailed back to the same scenes from which he had set out, did they learn that the Earth was round and his course a circle.

Now we learn that time too is round, and that our voyage through it must bring us inexorably to the same years we left behind. This is difficult and dangerous knowledge. When men learned the Earth was round, their sense of the known widened, but their sense of the unknown weakened. This is the temptation of new knowledge. The known, however strange, can never be more than zero to the infinite unknown. Only with this saving sense can men use strong ideas.

For instance, we said that the *effects* of one life become the *causes* of the next. The same causes give rise to the same effects, and the same effects to the same causes again. This is recurrence. But now we can add that one of the very few *different effects* that can work directly in man's life is that produced by his attitude towards new knowledge.

To prepare ourselves to think about recurrence it becomes very necessary to understand that the incidents and events which happen to us in a continuous stream from birth to death arise in very different ways. The causes of these events lie at different distances from us, so to speak. And it is important for us, in relation to any given incident, to begin to recognize how near or how far back the cause lies.

For instance, there is one class of events whose cause lies in the incident itself, lies in the present. I am walking along the street in a normal way. Quite suddenly a man rushes out of a shop, collides with me, pushing me into the gutter, and disappears in the crowd. I never see the man again, and the incident closes there. Such events, which are led up to by nothing in the past, and whose cause lies within the moment itself, we call *accidents*.

Another class of events which happen to us are the result of a general tendency or a series of accumulated causes in the past. Every day I drive my car along a certain road faster than the speed limit. For thirty-five days nothing happens. On the thirty-sixth I am arrested and fined. This arrest cannot be said to be caused only by the actual drive on which it occurred: it is clearly the result of all thirty-six offences put together, for if it had not happened on that day it would certainly have done so a few days later. Such events, the results of a typical and continued tendency, and whose causes lie in time, are similar to what in the east is called 'karma'. They are the product of temporal *cause and effect*.

For a third class of events, although they are obviously of the deepest and most intimate importance to a man, no cause can be found within his present life. I am born in a certain year on a certain day, at a certain place, and of certain parents. Quite evidently nothing I have done or could do in this life can affect this, for it all happened before I began to create causes. As far as I am concerned, such events are my *fate*, and we may perhaps say that their causes must lie, not in time, but in recurrence or eternity, that is, in some previous life or lives.

Theoretically, a fourth class of events is also possible for a man. In this case, the cause lies neither in the present, nor in the past, nor even in recurrence. And only if we begin to understand the almost inescapable hold which his fate has over every side of a man's life, shall we realise that from his point of view such events will be *miracles*.

In this way it becomes clear that if a man wants to study the possibility of recurrence personally, he has particularly to study his own fate, and to begin to distinguish the kind of events which belong to this fate.

Now if one life is a recurrence of that which went before, what we thought of as the circle of human life is in fact a spiral. The destiny or totality of a human being now appears not as a circle existing in time, the long body of a man, but as a spiral existing in eternity, the coiled sequence of his long bodies. His greater form repeats the spiral of the moon's motion about the Earth, the Earth's motion about the Sun, the Sun's motion about the galactic centre. One life coils out of the last, past the insulator of death, as one day coils out of the last past the insulator of sleep.

This is the eternal recurrence which Ouspensky penetrated, and of which Nietzsche wrote: "Desire to live again, for that will be your lot in any case." The circle of one life lies parallel to the circle of that before and the circle of that after, forming as it were a repeated image of it in every detail. The day of a man's birth in this life lies next to the day of his birth in the last life and in the next; the day of his marriage lies next to those other days of his marriage then; the day of his death is paralleled by the days of all his other deaths. And every sight, sound and motion that filled those days before must fill them again, and again.

When a man first hears this idea, he asks: "How can I know? Why cannot I remember?" In the ordinary way he cannot know, and cannot remember. He cannot remember other lives for the same reason that he cannot remember most of his present one – *because he is not conscious of his existence in it*.

His form of perception, as we saw much earlier, is a faintly warm or aware spot, passing slowly forward always in the same direction – not only round the circle of life, but round and round the spiral of many lives. Its warmth or awareness is barely enough to affect the 'present' of seconds or minutes and to extend even more hazily over days and weeks. Further than this, before and behind the moving spot, is cold and unremembered save for a few bright moments, for the most part irrelevant and unconnected.

In the chapter on 'Human Psychology' we studied what must be the significance of consciousness and memory in relation to the circle of life; how moments of increased consciousness were like points of suddenly intensified heat, which must transmit impulses forward towards the receding moment of perception which it reaches as memory. This ordinary memory corresponds to the phenomenon of conduction of heat along the wire of life.

How could one conceive memory of another life becoming possible? It goes without saying that the greater the consciousness, the further along the line of time will memory penetrate. But when consciousness rises beyond a certain intensity – or when the heated point rises above a certain temperature – a quite new possibility enters. We will suppose the successive spirals in our model not actually touching, but separated by a small space. Thus a point in the fifteenth year will lie exactly below but slightly separated from the similar point in the next recurrence.

Should now this point in the fifteenth year become, say, white-hot, it will begin to heat the corresponding points in the spirals above and below – but this time *by radiation*. The transmission of heat by radiation is under quite different laws from its transmission by conduction, and for this *a very much greater heat* will of course be necessary. Nevertheless, in this way we can conceive a moment of consciousness so intense that memory is created in another life.

In fact, there is a faculty in us which knows our fate, that is, which preserves memory from previous recurrences. Examples are infinite, though of course they must remain unproven till the event. Stendhal wrote to his most intimate friend: "I consider there is nothing ridiculous about dying in the street, provided one does not do it on purpose." Almost exactly a year later he did die in the street – presumably not on purpose.

Such a faculty has nothing whatever to do with ordinary negative imagination, and indeed appears only to work in its absence or in those who have definitely sacrificed negative imagination concerning themselves, as Stendhal shows that he has in the same letter. "I did not ask the doctor the name of this illness," he wrote, "in order not to put gloomy thoughts into my head". Thus the faculty of knowing one's fate can perhaps only unfold in them who already have a certain impartiality towards it. Memory awakens in those who have found a conviction which will enable them to look beyond memory.

In any case, we may say that increase of consciousness in man's present life must mean increase of consciousness in all directions, that is, not only into the past and future of time, but also into the past and future of eternity.

Having come to an image of the many lives of man in the spiral of recurrence, we can try to represent to ourselves the connection of different individuals in recurrence. Let us suppose that a husband in the prime of life and his wife, a girl, conceive a child. We have in one life three circles intersecting, one at the eighth milestone, one at the seventh, and the third, that of their offspring, at the ninth. This relationship will always be fixed for men on ordinary levels, and it is inconceivable that the relative ages of husband, wife and child should change, however many lives one could imagine. Since this day of their conjunction will be the same for each, it must also be the same for all together.

In recurrence we shall have three interwoven spirals, which all cross at the same relative point on each spiral. From this construction it is seen that the lives of all individuals are equal and complete, no matter if the husband live to 100, the wife to 50, and their child only to 10. As soon as we approach recurrence, we leave behind altogether the measurement of time by years, which as we already saw in the decelerating scale of one life-cycle, has only a relative meaning even there.

But we must also remember that this intersection of different life-spirals is only one way of looking at it. For individuals meet also on different levels of energy – by purely physical contact, by community of thought, by sensuality and physical attraction, and by the highest love, reverence or pure sex. Still more important, all these reactions may be blindly undergone, or *consciously experienced*. Perhaps *this* can change, and if it could, then everything would both appear the same and yet be utterly different.

As we have seen, recurrence is simply *one way of realising the fifth dimension*. Seen in this way, the fifth dimension looks like an infinite reliving of the fourth dimension, which is man's known life. But can we be aware of this fifth dimension in other ways?

The fourth dimension is measured by the extension of time from conception to death, by days, months and years as a line without thickness. But we know very well that our sensation of these days and moments is not always as a line without thickness. Whole days do indeed pass with complete 'flatness'. But then comes an instant when time seems suddenly to expand sideways. The moment has a strange *intensity*, or *depth*, and this intensity is connected with unknown vistas opening up at right angles to the path of time, on either side of time, so to speak. An hour which yesterday was a duration between high walls which revealed nothing and suggested nothing is today the same duration, but through an immense landscape, stretching to distant mountains and under a huge expanse of sky. This variation in the intensity or depth of the moment must be another way of perceiving the fifth dimension.

And again, we have to recognise that this intensity depends precisely on our degree of consciousness, that increasing consciousness alone brings the means of penetrating into the fifth dimension: that the man, woman and child are connected together not only by age and by functions, but beyond all this, transcending and transmuting these limitations, *by their degree of consciousness*.

If we now try to represent the interconnection not of three, but of the hundreds of different lives which touch each individual between birth and death, and their interconnection not at one moment but at recurring moments or continuous periods, we shall reach an unimaginable figure of recurrences.

It is unimaginable, because again the dimension has changed. For it is clear that if we extend this interconnection of spirals to include all men existing on earth, there is produced a figure so intricate that it is in fact a solid. The total of all the recurrence-spirals of all human beings produces the solid of humanity, in the same way that the recurrence of all cells produces the solid of a man.

Of this solid we can even have a certain vague apprehension. It will be, as it were, a sort of solid tapestry, composed of billions of threads, which in spite of their inconceivably elaborate weaving, appear all to lie in the same direction which is eternity. We can even suppose each of these threads to have a different nature or colour, according to the level of energy which dominates its totality of lives. And we might find that in large areas or periods of humanity, a certain nature or colour dominates the whole design – the red of purely physical existence, the yellow of intellectual activity, or the green of moving skill and sensation.

Remembering the existence of men with conscious souls, and with conscious spirits, we shall also suppose threads of a different materiality which stand out from the fabric in a quite exceptional way, which impart life to the rest, and about which the whole design of the solid body of humanity is formed.

For those threads are threads only in our metaphor. In fact they are *alive* and their total mass is alive. They are the cells and capillaries and nerves of a body, the Adam Kadmon of the Kabala, Mankind.

III BEYOND RECURRENCE

A man's life, his extension in the plane of history, so to speak, constitutes his own 'time', and in the ordinary way he can know nothing outside this time by direct experience. This is his *fourth dimension.*

The idea of an eternal recurrence of this life, an infinite repetition of the same historical duration, introduces us to a second dimension of time, that is, to man's *fifth dimension.*

Theoretically, such a dimension implies an absolutely exact and inexorable re-enactment of life in every detail, like the image of a face reflected backwards and forwards between two mirrors. For if we suppose that *anything* – even the smallest word or gesture – could be different in a repeated life, then we immediately posit still another dimension, as the smallest deviation in a straight line immediately implies a plane, or as even a minute change of expression in one of the reflected images would mean a miracle.

If we suppose that in another life a man could hear something he did not hear before, meet someone he did not meet before, or visit some place he did not know before, then we have to admit the possibility of movement – however slight – in a third dimension of time, that is, in man's *sixth dimension*. As we saw in the second chapter, the sixth dimension of any cosmos is that in which all its possibilities are realised. And if even *one* new possibility is realised that was not realised before, this already means the beginning of movement in the sixth dimension.

Thus the first principle to be realized is that of repetition, that is, that the same habits and tendencies must recreate the same circumstances and situations over and over again, in a hundred lives as surely as they do in one, and each time more inevitably than before. But the second principle that must be equally understood is that nothing can remain the same for ever, and that exactly by sheer weight of repetition things must eventually change. A vehicle which moves over the same lines sufficiently often, must sooner or later either wear out its tracks and come to a standstill, or acquire a new method of progression and rise in the air. The very principle of repetition itself implies that things must become better or worse, that is, they must eventually move in the sixth dimension.

We have then to admit that the idea of a recurrence of lives – though absolutely necessary – is very incomplete. Beyond this must exist for a man a dimension in which all is possible. And it is in *this* dimension that must be placed the possibilities of heaven and hell, of illumination and damnation, and all the other conceptions of *completely new states*, unrealized before, which have occupied men's minds since the beginning of thought. If such concepts correspond to any reality at all, that reality must exist in the sixth dimension.

The great mistake that men have made is to suppose change before they even guess the terrible and tremendous truth of recurrence, that is, to try to imagine the sixth dimension without the fifth. This fundamental error has vitiated all ordinary ideas of heaven and hell, and made men think of such states as mere extensions of their physical conditions and their personal lives. It is as impossible to think of omnipotence, omnipresence and immortality, qualities of the sixth dimension, without understanding the impotence, insignificance and inevitability of man's fate in the fifth dimension, as it is to think of the fulness of a sphere without first understanding the flatness of a plane.

Moreover, only deep realization of all the horror and futility of an eternal repetition of ordinary life can generate in man sufficient emotional force to undertake the tremendous task of penetrating consciously into that unknown and unimaginable dimension which lies beyond.

How is such penetration possible? Where do we touch this dimension of all possibilities? Since the beginning of time men have known intuitively that it is at the moment of death. No man in whom conscience is still alive has to be told that here he comes to the threshold of completely new and inconceivable states. The very impossibility of imagining himself or his perceptions or feelings without the physical body which houses and gives rise to them is proof of it. And traditionally man has always attributed to this unknown state both the most magnificent and the most terrible fates which lay within his power to imagine. In other words, he placed there *new possibilities*, incommensurable with all his experience in this present life.

Yet we already reached the conclusion that the moment of death and conception is one, and at that instant man passes into the beginning of a new life which is no more than a simultaneous repetition of the old. If this is so, then his movement at death is in the fifth dimension, the dimension of eternal recurrence. Where then is our gate to the sixth dimension? What has become of heaven and hell?

A strange idea now comes to us in connection with the logarithmic scale of life, which we turned back upon itself to form a circle. *That scale had no beginning*. Like all logarithmic scales, it began not at zero but at one. And at earlier stages on it, beyond one, must lie one-tenth, one-hundredth, one-thousandth, to infinity. In other words, the same scale must have continued from *somewhere else*, outside the circle of physical life, and thus even *outside the spiral of its repetition*.

Returning towards birth and beyond towards conception, we found each unit of time filled with more compressed experience, more intensity of growth. At conception the speed of processes was no longer measurable by the time of organic bodies, but by the time of a single cell, which in an earlier chapter we saw to be many thousands of times faster than the time of adult man. Faster than this, processes are too explosive for cellular structure.

The circle thus represents the limit of man's existence in cellular form, the duration of his organic or physical body. In this sense, death marks his exit from the world of cellular matter, and conception his entrance into it. From one point of view the door of his entrance is but the other side of the door of his exit. But is there after all *another door* at the same threshold? And where could it lead?

The answer can only be, *into a faster state of matter*. If the logarithmic

344

scale continues to recede at ever-increasing speed towards its unknown source, then we have to imagine, even before conception, individuality attached, not to cellular matter, but to matter in molecular or, beyond that again, in electronic state. We have to imagine the signature of man, his pattern or fundamental nature, impressed first upon a vehicle resembling air, and second upon a vehicle resembling light. That is to say, we have to imagine the individuality of man attached to a soul without a body, and even to spirit without a soul.[83]

Admittedly we cannot imagine any such thing. Our ideas and imagination, conditioned by the perceptions of the physical sense-organs, are not subtle enough for this task. For in the ordinary way, all our functions – even those that deal in very fine, rare and pervasive matter – are so securely locked into the physical organism, that all their perceptions are received and interpreted in terms of our cellular matter, and its pleasure, pain or well-being. Only in special conditions, such as long fasting or the rare air of very high mountains, do the different functions become a little loosened one from another, and we begin to catch a glimpse of what some of them might mean if freed from their heavy ballast of flesh and its attendant processes of digestion.

What, for example, would the function of logical thought be like, without a material body checking results in the material world? What would be the meaning of emotional function, apart from a cellular body, or sex function apart from the possibility of physical union? What indeed – since all bodies must be made on the same pattern – would be the nature of the seven functions of a molecular body, or the seven functions of an electronic one? What would be the anatomy and psychology of the soul, or of the spirit?

Certainly, we have very little material for such speculation. Yet preparation for states after death or states before birth exactly implies such a task in intentional imagination. And if we attempt it we do dimly begin to understand that were human individuality attached to molecular or electronic bodies, such bodies would enjoy all kinds of powers, properties and possibilities, which from the point of view of cellular bodies are inconceivable and miraculous.

Molecular bodies, like gases, could embrace and pervade other bodies; could take any form; would be undecaying and indestructible. At their speed a whole lifetime of experience could be contained in a few weeks. Electronic bodies could travel with the speed of light, like light occupy

83. This argument is continued further in 'The Theory of Eternal Life.'

vast tracts of space simultaneously, like radio-waves produce objective phe-nomena at a distance without visible means, and above all they would participate in that state where all matter in the Solar System is of the same nature and interchangeable. At electronic speed a human lifetime of experi-ence would be compassed not by years, months or days, but *within minutes*.

We can then conceive, beyond man's circle of life in the cellular world, another and incommensurable circle of life in the molecular world, and yet another and again incommensurable circle of life in the electronic world; each complete in itself, each leading into the others, and all touching at one point - the simultaneous moment of death and conception, where all is foreordained yet all is possible.

At the beginning we saw how the spatial measures of man's body could represent time or fourth dimension for the cell, eternity or fifth dimen-sion for the molecule, and absolute or sixth dimension for the electron. Now we perceive that the reverse is also true. The disintegration of this cellular body of man into the molecular world at death represents his advent into eternity or recurrence; while the disintegration of his mole-cular body into the electronic world would mean his entrance into the sixth dimension, his merging with an absolute.

This principle – of successive existence in different states of matter – we must accept as a completely mechanical feature of the universe. In it there is nothing moral, nothing desirable or undesirable, nothing dependent in the least degree on individual merit or defect. For the great masses of ordinary men such transition, if it is a fact, is no more significant than the change of a given quantum of energy from coal and heat to mechanical motion and electricity. And were the signature of such men released at death into the electronic world, this need be no different from the release of millions of tunes and words into this same world by radio at every hour of the day and night.

Death and transformation are man's unchosen and unchangeable fate. All that he can choose and change is consciousness. But to change this is to change all. For now at last we begin to discern the one immense difference between men on Earth. Their common possession of a physical body, with a head, two arms, and two legs, may in this world tempt us to discount the difference between conscious and unconscious man. In the sense that food goes in and words come out from both their mouths, Christ and the criminal are equal. It is only the disintegration of this deceptive body, and the passage of what remains into other states of matter, that reveals to us the vast gulf between sleeping man and him who has created a permanent and indestructible principle of consciousness.

The one is a mechanical impulse endlessly reproducing itself; the other a human spirit inheriting all possibilities and tasks which the universe contains. And the great work is to build a bridge between them, which either shall pass across. For how otherwise shall creation become conscious of its origin, and all its infinite promise be fulfilled?

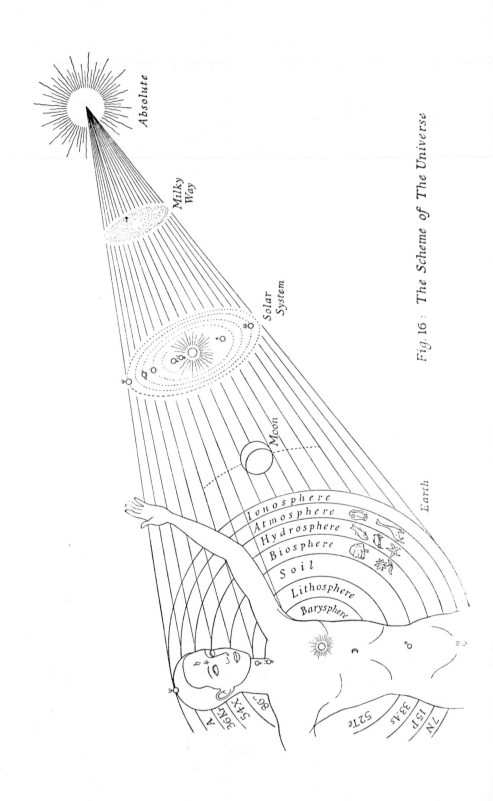

Fig. 16 : The Scheme of The Universe

APPENDICES

THE LOGICAL AND SUPER-LOGICAL MINDS
IN SCIENTIFIC ILLUMINATION

(see Introduction)

(*a*) Sir Arthur Eddington on the limitations of the logical mind:

"Let us suppose that an ichthyologist is exploring the life of the ocean. He casts a net into the water and brings up a fishy assortment. Surveying his catch he proceeds in the usual manner of a scientist to systematise what it reveals. He arrives at two generalisations.

(1) No sea-creature is less than two inches long.

(2) All sea-creatures have gills.

"These are both true of his catch, and he assumes tentatively that they will remain true however often he repeats it.

"In applying this analogy, the catch stands for the body of knowledge which constitutes physical science, and the net for the sensory and intellectual equipment which we use in obtaining it. The casting of the net corresponds to observation: for knowledge which has not been or could not be obtained by observation is not admitted into physical science.

"An onlooker may object that the first generalisation is wrong. 'There are plenty of sea-creatures under two inches long, only your net is not adapted to catch them.' The ichthyologist dismisses the objection contemptuously, 'Anything uncatchable by net is *ipso facto* outside the scope of ichthyological knowledge, and is not part of the kingdom of fishes which has been defined as the theme of ichthyological knowledge. In other words, what my net can't catch isn't fish!' Or – to translate the analogy – 'If you are not simply guessing, you are claiming a knowledge of the physical universe discovered in some other way than by the methods of physical science and admittedly unverifiable by such methods. You are a metaphysician! Bah!'

". . .When the ichthyologist rejected the onlooker's suggestion of an objective kingdom of fishes as too metaphysical, and explained that his purpose was to discover laws (i. e. generalisations) which were true for catchable fish, I expect the onlooker went away muttering: "I bet he does not get very far with his ichthyology of catchable fish. I wonder what his theory of the reproduction of catchable fish will be like. It is all very well to dismiss baby fishes as metaphysical speculation; but they seem to me to come into the problem.' " *"The Philosophy of Physical Science."* (pp. 16 – 17, 62)

(*b*) The German chemist, Kekulé, and the discovery of the idea of the benzene ring:

"But it did not go well (the writing of his chemical text-book); my spirit was occupied with other things. I turned the chair to the fireplace and sank into half-sleep. The atoms flitted before my eyes. Long rows variously, closely unite; all in movement; wriggling and turning like snakes. And see, what was that? One of the snakes seized its own tail and the image whirled scornfully before my eyes. As though from a flash of lightning I awoke. I occupied the rest of the night in working out the consequences of the hypothesis . . . Let us learn to dream, gentlemen."

Quoted: *"The Art of Scientific Investigation"*, W. L. W. Beveridge, p .66

(*c*) The mathematician, Gauss, on the solving of an arithmetical theorem:

· "Finally, two days ago, I succeeded, not on account of my painful efforts, but by the grace of God. Like a sudden flash of lightning, the riddle happened to be solved. I myself cannot say what was the conducting thread which connected what I previously knew with what made my success possible."

Quoted: *"Man is a Microcosm"*, J. A. V. Butler, p. 147.

(*d*) The French mathematician, H. Poincaré, on the solution of the problem of fuchsian functions:

"Just at this time, I left Caen, where I was living, to go on a geologic course under the auspices of the School of Mines. The incidents of the travel made me forget my mathematical work. Having reached Coutances, we entered an omnibus to go to some place or other. At the moment when I put my foot on the step, the idea came to me without anything in my former thoughts seeming to have paved the way for it, that the transformations I had used were identical with those of non-Euclidean geometry. I did not verify this idea; I should not have had time, as, upon taking my seat in the omnibus, I went on with a conversation already commenced – but I felt a perfect certainty. On my return to Caen, for conscience's sake, I verified the result at my leisure."

H. Poincaré: *"The Foundations of Science."*

(*e*) The astronomer Kepler on the discovery of his third law:

"What I prophesied twenty-two years ago, as soon as I discovered the five solids among the heavenly orbits . . . what sixteen years ago I urged as a thing to be sought, that for which I settled in Prague, for which I have devoted the best part of my life to astronomical contemplations, at length I have brought to light, and have recognised its truth beyond my most sanguine expectations. Not indeed in the manner which I imagined (that is not the least part of my delight), but in another very different yet most perfect and excellent way. It is now eighteen months since I got the first glimpse of light, three months since the dawn, very few days since the unveiled sun – most marvellous to gaze on – burst upon me . . . If you forgive me, I rejoice: If you are angry I can bear it. The die is cast, the book is written. It may well wait a century for a reader, as God has waited six thousand years for an observer."

Kepler: *"Harmonicis Mundi"*, Book V.

(*f*) Francis Bacon on the discovery of laws:

"Men are rather beholden generally to chance, or anything else, than to logic, for the invention of arts and sciences . . . The present system of logic rather assists in confirming and rendering inveterate the errors founded on vulgar notions, than in searching after truth, and is therefore more hurtful than useful."

Quoted: *"The Art of Scientific Investigation"*, W. L. W. Beveridge, p. 81.

Schiller on the discovery of laws:

"It is not too much to say that the more deference men of science have paid to logic, the worse it has been for the scientific value of their reasoning . . . Fortunately for the world, however, the great men of science have usually been kept in salutary ignorance of the logical tradition."

Quoted: *ibid*, p. 82.

Max Planck on the discovery of laws:

"Again and again the imaginary plan on which one attempts to build up order breaks down and then we must try another. Imaginative vision and faith in ultimate success are indispensable. The pure rationalist has no place here."

Quoted: *ibid*, p. 55.

Albert Einstein on the discovery of laws:

"There is no logical way to the discovery of these elemental laws. There is only the way of intuition, which is helped by a feeling for the order lying behind appearance."

Quoted: ibid, p. 56.

(g) A modern commentator on scientific method:

"There are, I believe, two different levels of 'simplicity', and between them there is a region of 'complexity'. There is the lower kind of simplicity which we find when we isolate one fragment of Nature from the rest, and ignore all awkward facts that refuse to fit into the scheme which applies to the fragment. There is, or there well may be, a higher kind of simplicity, where we have recognised the fundamental structure of Nature as a whole, and have seen how the structure of special regions of Nature is just a special case of these fundamental relations. But, in order to pass from the lower to the higher kind of simplicity, we must traverse an intermediate stage of confusion and complexity, in which we confront the lower simplicity with awkward facts which it has ignored . . . The final stage, that of finding the simple plan on which all this complexity is constructed, can only be accomplished by men who combine the *insight of the genius* with *technical mathematical ability* of the higher order . . . We still await the man who will show us in detail how the world of physics and the world of sensible appearance are united into the one whole of Nature."

C. D. Broad: "Scientific Thought", p. 547.

APPENDIX TWO

TABLE OF TIMES AND COSMOSES

(see Chapter 2)

Cosmos	Moment of Recognition	Breath	Minute	Hour	Day	Week	Month	Year	Lifetime
Electron	–	–	–	–	–	–	–	–	$1/1500$ s.
Molecule x 28,000	–	–	$1/90$ s.	–	$1/1500$ s.	$1/200$ s.	$1/50$ s.	$1/4$ s.	18 sec.
Blood-Cell x 4,800	–	$1/1500$ s.	$1/90$ s.	$2/3$ s.	18 sec.	$1^3/4$ m.	7 min.	$1^1/2$ hr.	6 days
Man x 28,000	$1/30$ s.	3 sec.	1 min.	1 hr.	1 day	7 days	29 days	1 year	76 y.
Nature x 365	$1/4$ hour	1 day	18 days	$3^1/4$ y.	76 y.	537 y.	2150 y.	25,800 y.	$2^1/4$ mn.y.
Earth x 7,800	$3^1/2$ days	1 year	18 years	1075 y.	25,800 y.	187,000 y.	750,000 y.	$9^1/2$ mn.y.	750 mn.y.
Sun x 100,000	75 years	7000 y.	135,000 y.	8 mn.y.	200 mn.y.	–	–	–	5.6^{12} y.
Milky Way	$7^1/2$ mn.y.	700 mn.y.	13,500 mn.y.	–	–	–			5.6^{17} y.

353

APPENDICES

APPENDIX THREE

THE THEORY OF OCTAVES

(see Chapter 6)

Extracts from 'Grand Memento Encyclopedique Larousse', Paris 1937.

"The seven sounds in the order: *do, re, mi, fa, sol, la, si, do*, serve as basis of *musical* or *tonal progression* in the whole of music. The range of sounds produced by voice or musical instruments . . . is represented by linking several times over the seven notes of this musical progression . . . The sequence of sounds is called *ascending* when the development is from below upward, and *descending* when the development is from above downwards . . . .

"The steps of this progression are unequally separated from each other. They are separated either by a *semitone* or by a *tone*. The semitone is the smallest distance between two following steps: there is a semitone between *mi* and *fa*, *si* and *do*. The *tone* is the largest distance between two following steps: there is a tone between *do* and *re*, *re* and *mi*, *fa* and *sol*, *sol* and *la*, *la* and *si*." II, p. 938.

"To determine the frequency of all the sounds constituting an *harmonic scale* (octave) it suffices to fix the frequency of one of them . . . These sounds, ranged by increasing sharpness and separated by the simple intervals of an harmonic scale, bear the names of 'notes':

Names of notes	do	re	mi	fa	sol	la	si	do
Intervals of the notes in relation to *do*	1	$9/8$	$5/4$	$4/3$	$3/2$	$5/3$	$15/8$	2

"The eighth note, at the octave of the *tonic* or first note, has a frequency double that of the tonic: it bears the same name and serves as starting point, that is, tonic, for a new scale, whose notes bear similar names to those of the preceding octave and are respectively separated by an octave from the similarly-named notes of that octave."

II, p. 413, para. 588.

APPENDIX FOUR

APPENDIX FOUR

PLANETARY TABLES

(see Chapters 3 and 6)

(a) *The Solar System as Transformer* - comparative theoretical tensions of planetary coils.

Planet	Coils in 84 years	Volts	Amperes
Neptune	.5	1	10,000
Uranus	1	2	5,000
Saturn	2.75	5.5	1,820
Jupiter	7	14	770
Mars	43.5	87	115
Earth	84	168	60
Venus	137.5	275	36
Mercury	343.5	687	14.5

(b) *The Solar System as Transformer* - tensions theoretically corrected for cross-sectional area and conductivity.

Planet	Section million squ. kil.	Metal	Conductivity°	Section x Conductivity	S x C x equalizing factor (6.6)	Amperes (see (a))
Neptune	2.14	Silver	60	128.4	8474	10,000.
Uranus	1.86	Gold	41	76.2	5029	5,000
Saturn	11.43	Antimony	2.5	28.6	1888	1,820
Jupiter	15.95	Bismuth	.77	12.3	812	770
Mars	.03	Copper	56	1.7	112	115
Earth	.13	Iron	7.2	.9	59	60
Venus	.12	Strontium	4	.5	33	36
Mercury	.02	Brass	9	.2	13	14.5

° Reciprocals of resistance factor: "Tables of Physical and Chemical Constants". Kaye and Laby. p. 85.

(c) *Distance of Planets from the Earth* - (millions of kilometres)

Planet	Minimum Distance	Maximum Distance	Coefficient of variation
Neptune	4,350	4,660	1 : 1.07
Uranus	2,880	3,160	1 : 1.1
Saturn	1,180	1,650	1 : 1.4
Jupiter	585	966	1 : 1.7
Mars	45	401	1 : 8.9
Venus	28	260	1 : 6.8
Mercury	78	222	1 : 2.8

APPENDICES

(d) *Planets' Speed in Relation to the Earth*

Planet	Orbital Speed (kils. per second)	Maximum angle	Maximum Speed in relation to Earth (kils. per second)
Neptune	5.3	2.5	.16
Uranus	6.5	4	.24
Saturn	9.6	6	.52
Jupiter	13	11	1.6
Mars	30	40	13.3
Venus	36	90	36
Mercury	48	90	48

(e) *Estimated Strength of Magnetic Fields of the Planets in the Earth's Atmosphere*
(Mass x orbital speed x reciprocal of the square of the distance)

Sun		62,000 amps.°	
Moon (at equinoxes)		5,300 amps.°	
Jupiter	max: 1,300 amps.		min: 500 amps.
Venus	1,200		50
Mars	125		3
Saturn	75		8
Mercury	40		5
Uranus	1.3		1
Neptune	.5		.5

°Sydney Chapman: "The Earth's Magnetism."

APPENDIX V TABLE OF THE ELEMENTS

	do Neptune	si Uranus			la Saturn	Metals — Magnetic							sol Jupiter			fa Mars	- Venus	mi Mercury	re Moon
	Inert Gases	Alk. Met.	Alk. Earths	Earths						Magnetic						Quadriv.	Triv.	Bivalent	Halogens
																Metaloids			
op Neptune					1 H 1														
si Uranus	2 He 4	3 Li 7			4 Be										5 B 11	6 C 12	7 N 14	8 O 16	9 F 19
la Saturn	10 Ne 20	11 Na 23			12 Mg 24										13 A 27	14 Si 28	15 P 31	16 S 32	17 Cl 35.5
sol Jupiter	18 A 40	19 K 39	20 Ca 40	21 Se 45		22 Ti 48	23 V 51	24 Cr 52	25 Mn 55	26 Fe 56	27 Co 59	28 Ni 59	29 Cu 64	30 Zn 65.5	31 Ga 70	32 Ge 72.5	33 As 75	34 Se 79	35 Br 80
fa Mars / Venus	36 Kr 84	37 Rb 85.5	38 Sr 88	39 Y 89		40 Zr 91	41 Nb 93	42 Mo 96	43 Ma	44 Ru 102	45 Rh 103	46 Pd 107	47 Ag 108	48 Cd 112.5	49 In 115	50 Sn 119	51 Sb 122	52 Te 128	53 I 127
mi Mercury	54 X 131	55 Cs 133	56 Ba 137	Rare Earths		72 Ct 179	73 Ta 181	74 W 184	75 Re 186	76 Os 191.5	77 Ir 193	78 Pt 195	79 Au 197	80 Hg 200	81 Tl 204	82 Pb 207	83 Bi 209	84 Po 210	85 ?
re Moon	86 Em 222	87 ?	88 Ra 226	89 Ac 227 (Rare Earths)		90 Th 232	91 Pa 231	92 U 238	93 Np	94 Pu	95 Am	96 Cm							

APPENDIX SIX

TABLE OF HUMAN FUNCTIONS

(see Chapter 10)

Note	Planet	Gland	Function	System	Category of Energy	Speed	Key Element	Deriving from
do	Sun	Thymus	Growth	?	VIII	3 mm per day-1 cm per hour	?	Entoderm
re	Moon	Pancreas	Digestion, assimilation of food	Lymphatic	VII	1 cm per hour-1 m per hour	?	
mi	Mercury	Thyroid	Respiration, combustion of air	Pulmonary	VI	1 m per hour-1 cm per sec.	24-30 Cr-Zn	
—	Venus	Para-thyroids	Blood-circulation, tissue-building	Arterial and Connective tissue	V	3 cm per sec.-3 m per sec.	20 Ca	
fa	Mars	Adrenals	Exterior motion, fight and flight	Cerebro-spinal and voluntary muscle	IV	3 m per sec.-300 m per sec.	19 K	Mesoderm
sol	Jupiter	Posterior Pituitary	Inner reflexes, physical sensation	Sympathetic and involuntary muscle	III	300 m per sec.-30 km per sec.	11 Na	
la	Saturn	Anterior Pituitary	Mind and reason, bone structure	Cerebral cortex and skeletal	II	30 km per sec.-3000 km per sec.	9 F(?)	Ectoderm
si	Uranus	Gonads	Reproduction, creation, higher emotion	Genital, Vagus	I	3000 km per sec.-300,000 km per sec.	1 H	
do	Neptune	Pineal	?	?	0	300,000 km per sec.-		

APPENDIX SEVEN

TABLE OF ORGANIC COMPOUNDS

(see Chapters 7 and 12)

The molecular weights of certain organic and inorganic substances in relation to a scale of descending octaves.

do			
—	narcotics:	agents of magic	
si	certain vitamins:	agents of reproduction (regeneration)	
la	certain poisons:	anaesthetic agents (degeneration)	
sol	amino-acids, etc:	agents of growth	
fa	dyes:	agents of colour (destruction)	
—	narcotics:	agents of magic	
mi	natural drugs:	agents of healing	
re	sugars:	agents of digestion	

1st octave SI

do	12	carbon 12
—	13	
si	14	nitrogen 14
la	15	acetone 15
sol	16	oxygen 16, methane 16, ammonia 17
fa	18	water 18
—	19	
mi	20	heavy water 20, neon 20
re	$22^1/_2$	

2nd octave LA

do	24	
—	26	acetylene 26
si	28	ethylene 28, carbon monoxide 28
la	30	formaldehyde 30, ethane 30
sol	32	methyl alcohol 32, hydrogen peroxide 34
fa	36	
—	38	
mi	40	
re	45	cyanic acid 43, nitrous oxide 44, carbon dioxide 44, formic acid 45

3rd octave SOL

do	48	ozone 48
—	52	
si	56	
la	60	urea 60, acetic acid 60, isopropyl alcohol 60
sol	64	nitric acid 63
fa	72	propionic acid 72
		ether 74, glycine (aminoacetic acid) 75
—	76	carbolic acid 76
		benzene 78
mi	80	
re	90	tryptophane 88, butyric acid (butter) 88, alanine (egg) 89, lactic acid (milk) 90, glycerine 92, homogentistic acid 93
do	96	aniline 93, phosgene 99

	—	104	valerianic acid 102, aspirin 104
			creosol (antiseptic) 108
	si	112	histamine 111, creatinine 111, caproic acid 116
			amyl nitrate 117
	la	120	chloroform 119, coniine 121, cystene 121
4th octave FA			niacine 123
	sol	128	chromane 130, leucine 130, lysine 132, creatine 131, salicylic acid 138, para-aminobenzoic acid 137
	fa	144	
			anethol 148
	—	152	camphor 152, vanillin 152, eucalyptol 154, menthol 156
			mustard gas 159
	mi	160	nicotine 162, glycogen 162, cellulose 162, thymol 165
			sulfanilamide 172, carbonic acid 174
	re	180	ascorbic acid (vitamin C) 176, fructose 180, galactose 180
	do	192	ephedrine 183, adrenalin 186, caffeine 194
			meconic acid 200
	—	208	opianic acid 210, mezcaline 211, sulfaguanidine 214
	si	224	amytol 226, nitroglycerine 227, picric acid 229
			phenobarbitol 232
	la	240	
5th octave MI	sol	256	sulfathiazol 255, estrone 270, belladonine 271
			vitamin A 286, testosterone 288
	fa	288	alizarin orange 285, alizarin yellow 288, malachite green 288
			atropine 289, curarine 298
	—	304	cocaine 303, morphine 303, hyoscine 303, thebaine 311
			progesterone 314, codeine 317
	mi	320	tannic acid 322, quinine 324, strychnine 334, vitamin B1 337
			laudanine 343, penicillin sodium 356
	re	360	cortisone 360, maltose 360, milk-sugar 360, lactoflavin (vitamin B2) 364, heroin 369, riboflavin 376
	do	384	cholesterol (vitamin D) 385, ergosterol 396
			iodoform 393
	—	416	narcotine 413
	si	448	vitamin E 450, vitamin K 450, glycocholic acid (bile salt) 465
	la	480	
6th octave RE	sol	512	aureomycin 508, taurocholic acid (bile salt) 515
			carotene 536
	fa	576	xanthophyll 568, bilirubin 573, streptomycin 581
			haematin 592
	—	608	
			thyroxin 629
	mi	640	aconite 643
	re	720	digitalin 718
	do	768	

APPENDIX EIGHT

APPENDIX EIGHT

THE CYCLE OF CIVILIZATIONS

(See Chapter 16)

These tables should be studied with the chart of civilizations given in chapter 16. Influences producing the conception and growth of the civilizations, and those leading to their disintegration are included without distinction.

(do) Greek Civilization
(BC 590 – AD 187)

Incubation

590 BC	Solon archon of Athens: his reforms, code of laws, poetry.
640–562	Thales of Miletos: science and cosmology.
580	Code of Pittakos at Mytilene.

Development

ca 570	François vase.
561–527	The Golden Age of Pisistratus.
ca 535	First Tragic Festival at Athens.
ca 550	Anaximander of Miletos: technical instruments; founds colony of Apollonia.
ca 530	Pythagoras: foundation of Pythagorean colony at Croton.
530–480	Doric temples at Paestum, Agrigento, Selinunte.
ca 510	Organization of free peasant class in Athens.
ca 510	Heracleitos of Ephesos: 'Concerning the Universe'.
ca 510	End of archaic sculpture: beginning of Ionic style.

Maturity

494–479	Medic Wars: Marathon, Thermopylae, Salamis: fortification of Athens and building of the Piraeus.
ca 490–460	fl. Aeschylus: ca 470–410 Sophocles: ca 450–405 Euripides.
468–457	Temple of Zeus at Olympia: 447–438 The Parthenon, Phidias.
470–399	Socrates: 427–348 Plato.
ca 440	Age of Pericles: colonization in Southern Italy, Sicily, Black Sea.
ca 400	Beginning of Corinthian style.
ca 385–322	Aristotle, teacher of Alexander the Great.
323	Maximum diffusion of Greek culture under Alexander.
283	Ptolemy Soter develops Alexandria as Greek city.
146	Greece falls under Roman domination.
260 AD	Greece overrun by the Goths.

(re) Roman Civilization
(BC 312 – AD 465)

Incubation

312–304 BC	End of Samnite War: Roman rule over Campania and Apulia.
312	Appius Claudius censor: opening of the Appian Way to Capua, first Roman road: earliest aqueduct.

APPENDICES

322   Stoic school at Athens under Zeno, 306 school of Epicurus at Samos: formative influences of Roman culture.

Development

280–275   Pyrrhic War: unification of Italy.
264–241   First Punic War: conquest of Sicily.
ca 300–240   Development of military machine, the legion.
284–204   Livius Andronicus: translator of Greek classics.

Maturity

219–201   Second Punic War: conquest of Spain.
ca 220–190   fl. Plautus: ca 160 Terence.
ca 200   Introduction of Oriental religions to Rome.
168   Conquest of Macedonia, 146 Greece and Tunisia, 133 Asia Minor: 146 Destruction of Carthage.
87   All Italians made Roman citizens.
74–63   Conquest of Syria and Palestine by Pompey: 58–51 of Gaul by Caesar.
70–13   Cicero: 71–19 Virgil: 59–17 AD Livy: 2–66 AD Seneca.
31 BC   Conquest of Egypt.
29 BC–14 AD   Augustan Age: rebuilding of Rome: Pax Romana.
41–54 AD   Conquest of Britain: the senate opened to Gauls.
ca 100   Maximum expansion of Roman Empire under Trajan.
100–300   Provincial Emperors from Spain, Illyria, Syria.
211   Roman citizenship made universal.
270–300   Revolts in Gaul, Africa, Greece, Syria, Egypt.
410   Sack of Rome by Alaric.
453   Ravaging of Italy by Attila.
476   Imperial ensigns sent to Constantinople by Odeacer the Vandal: end of Western Empire.

(mi) Early Christian Civilization
(AD 28 – 805)

Incubation

28–33 ?   Supposed teaching of Christ.

Development

ca 35–60   'The Acts of the Apostles': travels of St. Paul: foundation of churches at Antioch, Ephesus and Rome.
ca 100   The Gospels and the Apocalypse of St. John of Patmos.
ca 100   Establishment of 'the seven churches in Asia' and the authority of bishops.

Maturity

ca 150–200   Establishment of Churches at Alexandria, Carthage and Lyons.
ca 200–220   Tertullian of Carthage attacks heresies.
ca 200–258   Persecution of Christians by Imperial Rome.
ca 230–250   Origen of Alexandria combines Christian and Hellenic philosophy.
285   Beginning of monastic life in Egyptian desert: first pilgrimages to the Holy Places.
ca 300–400   Cult of martyrs developed.

320	Christianity made official religion of Roman Empire by Constantine.
314	Synod of Arles, 325 Council of Nicaea.
ca 350	Athanasian creed.
ca 400	Beginning of Western monasticism: Tours, Lerins.
ca 390–430	St. Augustine: 'The City of God': his struggle with the Manichaeans.
ca 480–500	Conversion of the Franks under Clovis.
ca 500	Schism between Western Church at Rome and Eastern Church at Constantinople.
640	Destruction of the Library at Alexandria by the Arabs.
800–850	Lowest level of the Papacy.

(*fa*) *Monastic Christian Civilization*
(AD 522 – 1299)

Incubation

ca 520	fl. St. Benedict, Dionysius the Areopagite, Boethius, Priscian.
523	Boethius: 'The Consolation of Philosophy'.
ca 526	Building of pilgrimage shrines at Jerusalem by Justinian: development of school of mosaic work.
529	St. Benedict founds the Monastery of Monte Cassino.

Development

532–537	Building of Santa Sophia at Constantinople.
547	Building of St. Vitalus at Ravenna: mosaic work.
529–534	Code, Digest and Institutes of Justinian.
533–554	Pacification of the Mediterranean: recovery of North Africa from the Vandals, Italy from the Ostrogoths, Spain from the Visigoths.
563	St. Columba at Iona, converts the Scots: from 600, in Ireland.
589	Conversion of the Visigoths.
590–604	Pope Gregory the Great: 596, sends Augustine to Britain. First monk to become pope: his 'Dialogues' link between classical and mediæval teaching: his school of music at Rome establishes Gregorian chant.

Maturity

627–635	Christianization of England by Augustine.
656–682	First Benedictine monasteries in England:Peterborough, Wearmouth, Jarrow.
732	Defeat of the Arabs at Poitiers by Charles Martel.
741–768	Spread of monasticism in France under Pepin the Pious.
768–814	Christian empire of Charlemagne: court school under Alcuin.
754–800	Christianization of Germany by St. Boniface: 800, of Scandinavia: 864, of Moravia and Bohemia.
917	Foundation of the Abbey of Cluny: 926–942 Odo abbot, 948–994 Maieul, 994–1049 Odilo.
ca 1100	Maximum extent of Cluniac empire in Europe under Abbot Hugh.
1215	Albigensian crusade against heretics: 1228, establishment of the Inquisition.
1250–1300	Decadence of monasticism, and control by secular powers.
1306	Holy Roman Empire separates from Rome.
1309	The Pope held captive at Avignon.

APPENDICES

(sol) *Mediæval Christian Civilization*
(AD 1088 – 1865)

Incubation

1089–1130	Abbey Church of Cluny rebuilt under Hugh: maximum extent of Cluniac influence.
ca 1090–1110	School at Chartres under Ivo: at Mont St. Michel: at Canterbury under Anselm.
1073–1085	Cluniac pope, Gregory VII: 1088–1099 Urban II.
ca 1090	Building of cathedrals at Pisa, Mainz, Winchester, St. Albans.
ca 1070–1110	Normanization of England and Sicily.
1095	First crusade rids France of warlike elements.

Development

1100	Norman kingdom set up in Palestine.
ca 1110–1140	Adelard of Bath in Near East: research mission from Chartres in Spain: translation of the Koran, logarithmic tables, alchemical works.
1122–1152	Suger, Abbot of St. Denis, leading French statesman under Louis VI and VII.
1118	Order of Knights Templars founded.
1134–1150	Western façade of Chartres cathedral: scientific and classical studies established there by Thierry.
1148	Norman conquest of Tunis and Tripoli.

Maturity

ca 1165–1200	Notre Dame de Paris, Sens, choir of Canterbury, Chichester, campanile of Pisa.
ca 1215	St. Francis of Assisi, Walter von der Vogelweide, Nibelungenlied.
1167–1243	Universities of Oxford 1167, Padua 1222, Naples 1224, Toulouse 1229, Salamanca 1243.
1200–1240	Cathedrals of Lincoln, Chartres, Rheims, Amiens, Mainz, Laon, Wells, Peterborough, Ripon, Bamberg, Burgos, Toledo.
1200–1225	Peak of Venetian power: Venetian-Oriental trade: German-Russian trade: St. Gotthard Pass: Lubeck a free city.
ca 1260	fl. Cimabue, Roger Bacon: ca 1300 Dante, Albert the Great, Thomas Aquinas, Chaucer.
1347–1351	The Black Death in Europe.
1378	The Great Schism: two popes at Rome and Fondi.
ca 1480–1500	Spanish Inquisition under Torquemada.
1520	Luther launches the Reformation.
1530–1540	Independence of the Anglican Church: dissolution of the English monasteries.
1789	French Revolution: 1793 dispossession of the church in France and 'abolition of Christianity': destruction of abbey of Cluny.
ca 1830	Gothic revival in England.
1867	Karl Marx – 'religion the opiate of the masses'.
1870–1880	Abolition of Catholic orders and congregations in Germany, of monasteries and theological faculties in Rome; expulsion of Catholic orders from France, of Papal Nuncios from Belgium and Switzerland.

APPENDIX EIGHT

(1a) Renaissance Civilization
(AD 1446–2223)

Incubation

1439	Visit of Emperor John Paleologus to Florence.
1440	Invention of printing by Gutenberg.
1453–1456	Printing of the Gutenberg Bible at Mainz.
1440	First public library formed by Cosimo Medici.
1450	Formation of the Vatican Library by Nicolas V.
ca 1440–1460	Platonic Academy at Florence.
ca 1440–1460	Schools of painting and architecture in Italy: Botticelli at Florence, Mantegna at Padua, the Bellinis at Venice, Alberti at Rome.
1453	Capture of Constantinople by the Turks drives scientist and artist refugees to Italy.

Development

1450–1480	Universities of Cambridge (Queens) 1447, Glasgow 1451, Freiburg 1457, Oxford (Magdalen) 1458, Basle 1459, Ingolstadt 1472, Buda 1475, Mainz and Tübingen 1477, Copenhagen 1479.
1463	Completion of the Doge's Palace at Venice: 1489, of the Sistine Chapel at Rome: 1506, foundation stone of St. Peters' Rome: 1520, of Medici Chapel, Florence.
ca 1500–1520	fl. Michelangelo, Leonardo, Raphael, Dürer.
1509	Establishment of the Aldine Press at Venice.
1487–1500	Voyages to Cape of Good Hope by Diaz 1487, San Salvador by Columbus 1492, Labrador by Cabot 1498, Calcutta by Vasco da Gama 1498, Venezuela by Vespucci 1499, Brazil by Cabral 1500, round the world by Magellan 1519-1522.
1519–1521	Conquest of Mexico by Cortes, 1532–1534 of Peru by Pizarro.
ca 1520	fl. Erasmus, Sir Thomas More, Machiavelli, Ariosto.

Maturity

ca 1530–1560	Beginnings of modern medicine by Paracelsus, astronomy by Copernicus, anatomy by Vesalius, zoology by Gessner.
ca 1590–1620	Elizabethan Renaissance in England: Spenser, Shakespeare, Bacon, Marlowe, Donne.
ca 1600	fl. Cervantes, Montaigne, Galileo, El Greco: 1620 Boehme, Spinoza, Rembrandt.
ca 1600–1630	Discovery of terrestrial magnetism by Gilbert 1600, laws of gravitation by Galileo 1602, laws of planetary motion by Kepler 1603, logarithms by Napier 1614, laws of refraction by Snellius 1616, circulation of the blood by Harvey 1628.
1661	Foundation of modern chemistry by Boyle, modern microscopy by Leeuwenhoek.
1675	Discovery of speed of light by Ole Roemer.
1700–1780	First encyclopædias, Chambers 1727, Diderot's 1751–80, Britannica 1771.
ca 1800	Beginnings of modern music: fl. Beethoven, Haydn, Mozart.
1810–1835	First public scientific societies, museums, picture galleries.

1874	Universal education in England.
ca 1890	Popularization of newspapers, public libraries.

(*si*) *Contemporary Civilization*
(AD 1859 – 2636)

Incubation

1859 — Darwin, 'Origin of Species': J. S. Mill, 'On Liberty': 1862 Victor Hugo, 'Les Miserables': 1865 Clerk Maxwell, 'Treatise on Electricity and Magnetism': Tolstoy, 'War and Peace': 1866 Dostoievsky, 'Crime and Punishment': 1867 Ibsen, 'Peer Gynt': 1863 Salon des Refusés.

1865 — Principles of heredity established by Mendel, antiseptic surgery by Lister.

1861 — Emancipation of serfs in Russia: 1862 State socialism advocated by Lasalle: 1864 International Workers Association: 1867 Karl Marx 'Das Kapital'.

1859 — Suez Canal begun: first oil-well discovered in U. S.: first electric-light plant in New York: discovery of spectroanalysis: 1861 construction of telephone by Reiss, 1866 of dynamo by Siemens, of transatlantic cable: 1867 invention of dynamite, the typewriter, the collotype process.

ca 1866 — Madame Blavatsky in New York: Mary Baker Eddy founds Christian Science: 1860–85, Shri Ramakrishna teaching in India.

1865 — Unification of the United States after the Civil War, of Mexico after French intervention.

Development

1868 — Bakunin's 'Alliance Internationale': 1869 German Social Democratic Party: 1871 Trades Unions legalized in England.

1870 — Franco-Prussian War.

1871 — First Impressionist Exhibition in Paris.

1874 — International Red Cross: 1875 International Postal Union.

1872 — Wundt, 'Principles of Physiological Psychology': 1895 Freud, Psycho-analysis.

1875 — Foundation of the Theosophical Society by Madame Blavatsky: 1876, Max Müller's programme for translation of the Sacred Books of the East.

1876 — Invention of telephone by Bell, 1877 phonograph by Edison, 1878 repeating-rifle by Männlicher, microphone by Hughes, 1879 electric bulb by Edison: 1883 first automobile factories.

1883 — Nietzsche, 'Zarathustra': 1889 Shaw, 'Fabian Essays': 1898 Tolstoy, 'Resurrection'.

1881 — Canadian Pacific Railway Co. formed: Panama Canal begun: 1884 St. Gotthard Tunnel: 1889 Eiffel Tower: 1891–1901 Trans-Siberian Railway: 1894 Trans-Andean Railway: 1895 electric submarine.

1895 — Discovery of the cinema, wireless, x-rays; 1897 of helium, 1898 of radium.

1903 — Formation of Bolshevist Party in Russia under Lenin and Trotsky.

1902 — Lorentz' electron theory: 1900 Max Planck's quantum theory: 1905 Einstein's theory of relativity.

1908 — Early aeroplane flights by Wright brothers, airship flights by Zeppelin and Santos Dumont.

1914–1918	First World War.
1910	Mexican Revolution: 1917 Russian Revolution.
ca 1915	Popularisation of the cinema.
ca 1920	Popularisation of the automobile.
ca 1925	Popularisation of radio.
ca 1935	Popularisation of air transport.

Maturity

1939–1945	Second World War.
1944	The splitting of the atom: 1945 first atomic bombs.

APPENDIX NINE

PLANETARY CYCLES AND HUMAN ACTIVITY

(see Chapter 17)

In the left-hand column are given both cycles of observed periodicity in various human and biological phenomena with the names of observers, and also cycles of phenomena referred to in the present book. The right-hand column shows the relation of such cycles to the synodic periods of the planets, and multiples of them, which are given in days. Major synodic periods or half-periods, i.e. of planet, earth, sun and zodiac, are italicised.

Observed Cycles	*Planetary Cycles*
41 month cycle	*days*
Prices, industrial production, sales (Beveridge, Hoskins, Dewey). Whooping-cough (King).	1170 Mars x $1^1/_2$ (opposition) 1170 Venus x 2 1170 Mercury x 10 1170 Jupiter and Saturn x 3
4 year cycle	
Number, migration, epidemics of lemmings, mice, squirrels, foxes (Elton).	1462 *Venus x $2^1/_2$* 1462 Moon x 50
6 years 5 months	
One-twelfth of human lifetime	2340 Mars x 3 2340 Venus x 4 2340 Asteroids x 5 2340 Jupiter and Saturn x 6
7.5 year cycle	
Barometric pressure (Clayton), tree-rings, lake-deposits, rock-laminae (Gillette).	2730 *Mars x $3^1/_2$* 2730 Saturn x $7^1/_4$
8 year cycle	
Cotton-prices (Dewey)	2925 *Venus x 5* 2925 Mercury x 25 2925 Moon x 100

Observed Cycles	*Planetary Cycles*

9 year cycle

Prices, stock-market, suicides
(see chapter 18)

3276 *Asteroids x* 7

9 years 8 months

Salmon catch (Canada), tent-caterpil-
lars (N. J.), chinch-bugs (Shelford and
Flint), lynx-skins (Canada), ozone
(London and Paris).
One-eighth of human life.

3510 Mars x $4^1/_2$
3510 Venus x 6
3510 Jupiter and Saturn x 9
3510 Mercury x 30

11.2 year cycle

Weather, sunspots, etc

4095 Venus x 7

12 years 10 months

One-sixth of human life

4680 Mars x 6
4680 Venus x 8
4680 Asteroids x 10
4680 Jupiter and Saturn x 12
4680 Mercury x 40

15 year Cycle

Wars (see chapter 17)

5460 *Mars x* 7
5460 *Saturn x* $14^1/_2$

18 year cycle

Real estate, building (Dewey and Dakin), electric potential (Kew)

6552 *Asteroids x* 14

22.4 year cycle

Temperature in S. Dakota, level of
African lakes, sunspots, Nile-floods,
tree-rings (Clayton)

8190 *Mars x* 10 $^1/_2$
8190 Venus x 14
8190 Jupiter and Saturn x 21
8190 Mercury x 70

36 year cycle

European weather (Bruckner)

13104 *Asteroids x* 28
13134 Jupiter x 33

54.5 year cycle

US price-level, English wheat prices, se-
curities, coal production, industrial periods (Kondratieff)

19890 Venus x 34
19656 *Asteroids x* 42
19900 Jupiter x 50
19890 Mercury x 170

APPENDIX TEN

Observed Cycles	Planetary Cycles

77 year cycle
Human lifetime (see chapter 11)

28,080 Mars x 36
28,080 Venus x 48
28,080 Asteroids x 60
28,080 Jupiter and Saturn x 72
28,080 Mercury x 240
28,080 Moon x 960
28,094 Uranus x 76

84 year cycle
Sex (see chapter 19)

30,646 *Jupiter x 77*
30,627 *Uranus x 83*

165 year cycle
Regeneration (see chapter 20)

APPENDIX TEN

THE CYCLE OF WAR

(see Chapter 17)

The dates above the sections are those between which the planet Mars passed from 15° Libra to 15° Gemini. The historical events are based on Steinberg's 'Historical Tables' and Langer's 'Encyclopaedia of World History', and for the most part refer to wars originating in Europe. As the earlier peaks fall earlier and earlier in the summer, there is a tendency for outbreaks to become shifted to the previous year, probably for seasonal reasons of weather and harvest.

Striking exceptions to the cycle are the American Civil War (1861–5), the Polish Revolution (1863–4), the French Expedition to Mexico (1863–4), the Seven Weeks' War (1866), the Ethiopian War (1934–6), the Spanish Civil War (1936–9), the War in China (1937–9). In fact, war is continuous, and these peaks seem only to represent its moments of maximum tension.

July 3, 1794 – May 26, 1795

Feb. – Mar. 1793	France declares war on Britain, Holland and Spain.
1793–4	General fighting throughout Europe.
March 1794	Kosciusko's rising in Poland.
1793–4	Reign of Terror in France.
Sept. 1795	British occupy Cape of Good Hope.

July 10, 1809 – June 2, 1810

May–June 1808	Spanish insurrection against France.
Aug. 1808 – Nov. 1809	Anglo–French War in Spain.
Aug. 1807 – Sept. 1809.	Russo–Finnish War, Danish–Swedish War.
Feb. – Oct. 1809	Austro–French War.
July – Dec. 1809	British expedition to Walcheren.
1810	Mexican War of Independence.

APPENDICES

July 18, 1824 – June 10, 1825

April 1823	War between France and Spain.
May 1824 – Feb. 1826	Burmese War.
1825	Wars of Independence of Brazil, Bolivia, Uruguay.
Dec. 1825	Revolt in Russian Army.

July 25, 1839 – June 17, 1840

Oct. 1838	First Afghan War.
Nov. 1838	France declares war on Mexico.
Dec. 1838	Boer–Zulu War in Natal.
July 1839	Opium War in China.
1839	Turkish–Egyptian War.

August 4, 1854 – June 25, 1855

June 1854	Austria occupies Danubian principalities.
March 1854 – Sept. 1855	Crimean War.
Feb. – Mar. 1855	Taiping Rebellion in China.

August 13, 1869 – July 3, 1870

July – Sept. 1870	Franco – Prussian War.

August 21, 1884 – July 10, 1885

Oct. 1884	Beginning of War in Sudan: Jan. 1885, siege of Khartoum.
Aug. 1884 – Feb. 1885	German occupation of African colonies.
March 1885	Anglo-Russian tension in Far East reaches maximum.
Sept. 1885	Revolution in Roumelia and Serbo-Bulgarian War.

Aug. 30, 1899 – July 19, 1900

1898	Spanish-American War in Cuba.
Oct. 1899	Outbreak of Boer War.
Jan. 1900	Acute Anglo-German naval tension.
May 1900	Boxer Rising in China.
Sept. 1900	Annexation of Transvaal by Britain and Manchuria by Russia.

Sept. 7, 1914 – July 28, 1915

Aug. 1914	General declarations of war: Sept. Battle of the Marne.
1914 – 5	General fighting on Eastern and Western Fronts, and in Near East.

Sept. 14, 1929 – Aug. 5, 1930

Jan. 1930	Outbreak of Bolivian-Paraguayan War in the Chaco.
Sept. – Oct. 1930	Revolutions in the Argentine and Brazil.

Sept. 16, 1944 – Aug. 15, 1945

July 1944	Invasion of Normandy by the Allies.
Oct. 1944	Invasion of the Philippines by the U. S.
1944 – 5	General fighting in Western Europe and the Pacific.
August 1945	Atom bombs on Japan.

APPENDIX ELEVEN

RELATION BETWEEN THE JOVIAL AND SOLAR SYSTEMS

(see Chapter 18)

SOLAR SYSTEM

Satellite	Distance		Speed	Sidereal	Diameter
	Real	*Bodes Law*	*mn. kils.*	*period*	*thousand*
	million kils.		*per day*	*years. days*	*kils.*
(o) ?	—	—	—	—	—
(1) Mercury	58	60	4.64	.88	4.7
(2) Venus	108	105	2.96	.225	12.4
(3) Earth	150	150	2.56	1.	12.7
(4) Mars	228	240	1.44	1.322	6.9
(5) Asteroids	416	420	—	—	—
(6) Jupiter	778	780	1.12	11.315	142
(7) Saturn	1427	1500	.83	29.167	120
(8) Uranus	2868	2880	.61	84.7	51
(9) Neptune	4494	—	.46	164.280	55
(10) Pluto	5850	5870	.40	247.248	8

JOVIAL SYSTEM

				days. hours	
(5)	.181	—	2.64	.12	—
(1) Io	.419	.420	1.60	1.18	3.8
(2) Europa	.667	.600	1.31	3.13	3.4
(3) Ganymede	1.064	1.020	.96	7.4	5.8
(4) Callisto	1.871	1.680	.70	16.16	4.0
?	—	3.120	—	—	—
?	—	6.000	—	—	—
(6)	11.356	11.760	.29	251.	—
(7)	11.852			260.	—
(8)	23.920	23.280	.21	739.	—
(9)	25.337			745.	—

COMPARISON

	Sun	Jupiter	Factor
Rotation period	29.5 days	10 hours	x 70
Diameter	1,391,000 kils.	142,000 kils.	x 10
Density	.25 Earth	.25 Earth	same
Mass	331,950 Earth	315 Earth	x 1000
Distance of satellites	average		x 141
Period of satellites	average		x 50
Speed of satellites	average		x 2.5

APPENDICES

Appendix Twelve

THE CYCLE OF SEX

(see Chapter 19)

The years suggested as representing the feminine and masculine phases of Uranus are those in which the planet presents its north and south poles respectively to the Earth and the Sun. The former occurs when Uranus is at 15° Gemini and the latter at 15° Sagittarius.

Feminine Phase	Masculine Phase
1945	1987
1861	1903
1777	1819
1693	1735
1609	1651
1525	1567
1441	1483
1357	1399
1273	1315
1189	1231
1105	1147

Appendix Thirteen

THE CYCLE OF REGENERATION

(see Chapter 20)

The dates above the sections are those in which Neptune stands at 15° Libra, that is, every 165 years. It is by no means claimed that all the societies mentioned were in fact schools of regeneration, for such periods are equally marked by imitations, both sincere and fraudulent, and in most cases we have no means of distinguishing the true from the false. Nor are the historical figures named necessarily the product of schools, though they are representative of a deep interest in the idea. The purpose of the table is only to show how a general inclination to the idea of regeneration reaches a maximum according to a definite cycle.

30 BC

1 – 35 AD	Supposed lifetime of Christ.
ca 1 AD	Essenes in Palestine: Therapeutae in Egypt.
50 BC – 50 AD	Development of the Kabala: the Zohar of Simon-ben-Joachai.
40 BC – 40 AD	Union of Platonism and the Kabala by Philo of Alexandria.
ca 1 – 90 AD	Lifetime of Apollonius of Tyana.

135 AD

ca 80 – 130	Carrying of Buddhism from India to China.
ca 80 – 120	Spread of Buddhism in NW India and Afghanistan under Kanishka.
ca 70 – 100	The editing of the Gospels.
ca 95 – 100	The Apocalypse of St. John of Patmos.

300 AD

244 – 305	Development of Neoplatonism by Plotinus and Porphyry: Hermetic writings.
270 – 277	Foundation of Manichaeism, Gnostic sect, by Mane in Persia.
285	Beginning of Christian pilgrimages: of monastic life in Egyptian desert.
311	Circumcellians founded by Donatus, Bishop of Carthage.
311	The Emperor Constantine tolerates, and 320, makes Christianity official.

465 AD

432 – 461	St. Patrick's evangelisation of Ireland.
ca 480 – 500	Spread of Christianity among the Franks under Clovis.
ca 500	Neoplatonic writings of Dionysius the Areopagite.

630 AD

ca 600 – 615	Irish monks under St. Columba.
622	Mahomet flees from Mecca to Medina (Hegira): 632 dies.
627 – 635	Christianisation of Northumbria, East Anglia and Wessex by St. Augustine of Canterbury.

795 AD

747 – 797	Buddhist teaching of Padma Sambhava in Tibet.
760	Kailasa temple at Ellora: Buddhist revival.
790	Greatest period of Mayan temple building: Palenque, Chichen Itza.
ca 750 – 800	Christianisation of Germany by St. Boniface: 822 Hrabanus Maurus Archbishop of Fulda.
ca 790 – 804	Charlemagne's court school under Alcuin.
813	Foundation of Abbey of Cluny.

960 AD

931	Papal charter of independence for Cluny: 924 – 942 Odo abbot, 954 – 994 Maieul.
959 – 978	St. Dunstan Archbishop of Canterbury under Edward the Martyr, King of England.
989	The Truce of God in France.
987	Mayan New Empire and Renaissance: Kukulcan.

1125 AD

1089 – 1130	Abbey Church of Cluny rebuilt: 1122 Peter the Venerable abbot.
1097 – 1105	St. Anselm at Rome and Cluny: 1115 St. Bernard founds the Cistercian order: 1122–1152 Abbot Suger of St. Denis leading French statesman.
1115	Chancellor Bernard reorganises cathedral school at Chartres: cathedral schools of music at Rheims, of astronomy at Mont St. Michel.
1118	Foundation of the Knights Templars in Palestine by Hugh des Payens and Godfrey de St. Omer.
ca 1125	Arrival of Catharists from the East in Toulouse and Orvieto.
ca 1100 – 1135	Teaching of Milarepa in Tibet. 1145 Building of Angkor Vat.
ca 1100 – 1150	Greatest period of temple-building in India: Khajraho, Puri, Konarak.

APPENDICES

1290 AD

1273	Death of Jellaledin Rumi in Turkey: founding of Mevlevi Dervish order.
1270	Thomas Aquinas, 'Summum Bonum': 1292 Dante, 'La Vita Nuova'.
ca 1290	Apostolic Cathari under Colcino in Italy.
ca 1290	Schools of troubadours in Southern France: Peter Cardinal.
ca 1290	Catholic alchemists: Albert the Great, Roger Bacon, Raymond Lully.
ca 1290	German and English mystics: Meister Eckhart, Matilda of Magdeburg, Duns Scotus.

1455 AD

ca 1440 – 1460	Cosimo Medici's Platonic Academy in Florence.
1455	Death of Fra Angelico: 1471 of Thomas a Kempis.
ca 1450 – 1500	Schools of painting in Italy.
1442 – 1458	John of Cologne builds towers of Burgos cathedral: Milan cathedral in progress.
1446	Bursfelde congregation of German Benedictine monasteries.
1450	Bohemian and Moravian Communion of Brethren formed.

1620 AD

ca 1590 – 1605	Age of Akbar in India, his attempt to synthesise Oriental and Western religions.
ca 1600	Foundation of Society of Rosicrucians: 1615–20 publication of original Rosicrucian literature.
1620 – 1630	Medical and physical discoveries by Rosicrucian doctors: Michael Meyer physician-in-ordinary to the Emperor Rudolph, Harvey–circulation of the blood, Gilbert – magnetism, Kepler – planetary laws.
1616	St. Francis de Sales, 'Traité de l'Amour de Dieu': Jacob Boehme, 'Mysterium Magnum', etc: 1620 Francis Bacon, 'Novum Organum', 1627, 'New Atlantis'.
ca 1630	Descartes, Pascal, the Jansenists.

1785 AD

1760 – 1785	Foundation of Swedenborgian rites.
1736 – 1790	Wesleyan revival movement in England at maximum.
1760	Illuminati of Avignon: 1766 Illuminated Theosophists of Paris: 1783 Order of the Universal Aurora: Cagliostro, Mesmer, St. Germain.
1754	Foundation of Martinism by Martinez Paschalis: 1768 – 1788 in Paris and Lyons: ca 1780 extended to Germany and Russia by Claude de St. Martin and Prince Repnin.
1780	Order of Asiatic Brethren founded by Baron Ecker.
ca 1785	fl. Goethe, Kant, Hegel, Beethoven.

APPENDIX FOURTEEN

APPENDIX FOURTEEN

BIBLIOGRAPHY

of books chiefly consulted, quoted or enjoyed (non-fiction)

Bainbridge and Menzies (ed. H. Hartridge). Essentials of Physiology. London 1929.

Bellamy, H. S. The Atlantis Myth. London 1948.

Berman, Louis. The Glands Regulating Personality. New York 1929.

Best and Taylor. The Physiological Basis of Medical Practice (5th ed.) London 1950.

Bok and Bok. The Milky Way. Philadelphia 1946.

Bonestall and others. The Conquest of Space. New York 1949.

Bragg, Sir William. Electricity. London 1936.

Branfield, Wilfred. Continuous Creation. London 1950.

Bucke, R. M. Cosmic Consciousness. New York 1923.

Butler, J. A. V. Man is a Microcosm. London 1950.

Calder, Ritchie. Profile of Science. London 1950.

Carson, Rachel L. The Sea Around Us. New York 1951.

Chapman, Sydney. The Earth's Magnetism. London 1951.

Davey and Dakin. Cycles, the Science of Prediction. New York 1947.

da Vinci, Leonardo. Movement of the Heart and Blood. London 1952.

Doig, Peter. A Concise History of Astronomy. London 1950.

Donnelly, Ignatius (ed. Egerton Sykes). Atlantis: The Antediluvian World. N.Y. 1949.

Durant, Will. The Renaissance. New York 1953.

Eddington, Sir Arthur. The Philosophy of Physical Science. Cambridge 1939.

Eisler, Robert. The Royal Art of Astrology. London 1946.

Fletcher, Sir Banister. A History of Architecture (15th ed). London 1950.

Flinders Petrie, W. M. The Revolutions of Civilisation. London 1912.

Fludd, Robert. Utriusque Cosmi Historia. Frankfurt 1617.

        De Naturae Simia. Frankfurt 1618.

        De Monochordum Mundi. Frankfurt 1623.

Gombrich, E. H. The Story of Art. London 1950.

Gray's Anatomy. (ed. Johnston and Whillis). (29th ed.) London 1946.

Gray, Ronald D. Goethe the Alchemist. Cambridge 1952.

Hinton, C. H. The Fourth Dimension. London 1906.

Hodgman, Charles D. (ed.) Handbook of Chemistry and Physics (31st ed). Cleveland 1949.

Hottenroth, Friedrich. Le Costume chez les peuples anciens et modernes. Paris n. d.

Hoyle, Fred. The Nature of the Universe. Oxford 1950.

Huntington, Ellsworth. The Mainsprings of Civilisation. New York 1945.

Jamieson, E. B. Illustrations of Regional Anatomy. Edinburgh 1947.

Jeans, Sir James. Through Space and Time. Cambridge 1934.

Jung, C. G. Psychology and Alchemy. London 1953.

Kahn, Fritz. Psychological Types. London 1949. Man in Structure and Function (2 vols.) New York 1943.

Kaye and Laby. Tables of Physical and Chemical Constants. London 1948.

Kenton, Edna. The Book of Earths. New York 1928.

Kuiper, Gerard P. (ed.) The Atmospheres of the Earth and Planets. Chicago 1949.

Kyan, John Howard. On the Elements of Light. London 1838.

Langer, William L. (ed.) Encyclopædia of World History. Boston 1948.

Laubenfels, M. W. de. The Pageant of Life Science. New York 1949.

Larousse. Grand Memento Encyclopédique (2 vols. ed. Paul Augé). Paris 1937.
        Medicale Illustré (ed. Drs. Galtier-Boussiere and Burnier). Paris 1924.
Lee, Oliver Justin. Measuring our Universe. New York 1950.
Leicht, Hermann. History of the World's Art. London 1952.
Lemaitre, Georges. The Primeval Atom. New York 1950.
Lewinsohn, Richard. Histoire des Animaux, Paris 1953.
Life's Picture History of Western Man. New York 1951.
Lockyer, Norman. The Dawn of Astronomy. London 1894.
Martindale and Westcott. The Extra Pharmacopoeia. London 1932.
Metalnikov, S. Immortalité et Rajeunissement. Paris 1924.
        La Lutte contre la Mort. Paris 1937.
Moreux, Abbé Th. Le Ciel et l'Univers. Paris 1928.
Mottram, V. H. The Physical Basis of Personality. London 1949.
Nicoll, Maurice. Living Time. London 1952.
Ouspensky, P. D. Tertium Organum. New York 1931.
        A New Model of the Universe. London 1934.
        In Search of the Miraculous. New York 1949.
        The Psychology of Man's Possible Evolution. New York 1952.
Pettigrew, J. Bell. Design in Nature (3 vols). London 1908.
Poincaré, Henri. Science and Method. London n. d.
Polynov. B. B. The Cycle of Weathering. London 1937.
Radio Handbook, The Amateur. London 1940.
Rudaux, Lucien. Sur les Autres Mondes. Paris 1937.
Saint-Martin, Louis-Claude de. Tableau Naturel. Paris 1901.
Scientific American. passim.
Shaw, Sir Napier. Manual of Meteorology. Cambridge 1928.
Sherwood Taylor, F. Science Past and Present. London 1949.
        The World of Science (2nd ed). London 1950.
        The Alchemists. London 1951.
Singer, Charles. A Short History of Science. London 1943.
Sparks, John B. The Histomap of Evolution. Chicago n. d.
Spencer Jones, Sir Harold. General Astronomy. London 1946.
Steinberg, S. H. Historical Tables. London 1939.
Thompson, C. J. S. The Lure and Romance of Alchemy. London 1932.
Thompson, Sir D'Arcy Wentworth. On Growth and Form. Cambridge 1942.
Toynbee, Arnold J. (ed. D. C. Somervell). A Study of History. New York 1947.
Van Nostrand's Scientific Encyclopædia (2nd ed). New York 1947.
Van Sickle, C. E. A. Political and Cultural History of the Ancient World (2 vols). New York 1947–8.
Various authors. Golden Ages of Great Cities. London 1952.
Vernadsky, W. La Biosphere. Paris 1929.
        La Geochimie. Paris 1931.
Vesalius, The Illustrations to his Works (ed. Saunders and O'Malley). Cleveland 1950.
Vinogradoff, I. Theory of Cosmic Reason. St. Petersburg 1905.
Weizsäcker, C. F. v. The World View of Physics. London 1952.
Whitaker's Almanack. London 1953.
Whyte, Lancelot Law. The Next Development in Man. New York 1950.
    (ed.)   Aspects of Form. London 1951.
World Almanac. New York 1953.
Young, Col. G. F. The Medici. New York 1930.

INDEX

INDEX

INDEX

Change 223, 278; and planetary influence 85 ; others, desire to 318 ; impossibility of 319; inevitability of 342.
Charity 237s.
Chemical marriage 305.
Chemistry, organic 103s; synthetic 184.
Childhood 156, 162; of a culture 231.
Chivalry 235.
Chlorophyll 97, 105, 123.
'Choice' and 'duty' 274.
Christian Science 195.
Christianity 254s, 265.
Christians, primitive 332.
Chromosphere 64s.
Chromosome 107.
Church 329.
Cinema 260 1.
Circle 328.
Circulation of light 88s, 221; through time 173; of memory 217; of types 222s.
City crowds 284, 286.
Civilisation 226s; functions of 227; the perfect 228; rebirth of 229; time-scale of 230; childhood of 231; lifetime of 232; soil for new 233; essence of 234s; soul of 236s; collapse of 243; and scale 251; our own 259s; and school 330.
Classical world, rediscovery of 257.
Class struggle 263.
Closed circle 254.
Clothes 124, 361.
Cluniacs 240, 255s, 266.
Coal, deposits in arctic 74; age of 285.
Coil-structure of universe 41, 45.
Collegials, Roman 256.
Colour, three factors in 49; blindness 163; agents of 185; theory of 266.
Comacene masters 256.
Common Man, as god 243.
'Complex' 217.
Compromise 174.
Conception 144, 155, 161, 171, 335, 343; of a civilisation 168, 230, 233.
Concepts 124, 131, 162.
Conquerors and conquest 292s.
Conscience 200, destruction of 191.
Consciousness, higher xii, xviii, 18, 76, 200, 266, 340; and light 36, 39, 200, of part and whole 39s; and cellular matter 72, 169; manlike 125, 169, without intelligence 136; and nervous systems 153; and perceptions 178; and memory 215s; transfer into past 218; different degrees 219, 340; balanced 239 beyond cycles 277; and sex 301; and powers 319.
Constellations, charting of 247.
Constipation 188.
Constitution, of cosmoses 39.
Control 290, 303.
Cooking 124, 178.
Copper age 249.
Corona, solar 64.
Coronation of George IV 298.
Corruption, process of 55, 76, 188s, 193, 199, 243, 281, 291, agents of 185.
Cosmic repulsion 4; rays 13.
Cosmos, three-dimensional for itself 5; definition of 17, 220, 325; seen in seven ways 20; man as 86; earth and nature as 126; combination of laws of three and seven in 138; vision of 165; of mankind 226; sexual image of 305; artificial 325; perfection of 326.
Council of Churches 258.
Cow, lymph production of 138.
Creation of universe 3.
Creative function 301.
Creeds 331.
Crime 190s, 286, 329 artificial; 191; social 191.

INDEX

INDEX

INDEX

Form, and magnetism 44; and planets 52s, 290; death of 72; in vegetable kingdom 123.
Founders, of cultures 230, 233, 250.
Freemasons 240, 255.
Friction 200, 327.
Four states of matter 57s.
Functions, languages for different xii; potential xiii, xv, 125, 145, 150, 164, 207, 228, 312; and perception of laws 26; and planets 47, 290; and elements 98; of earth 125; sevenfold arrangement 137; 'voltage' and 'amperage' 138; origin in embryo 139; table of 140; grading of 140, 176, 312; cycle of 151; excretions of 180; and energy 176; wrong 189, 213, 302; and poisons 190; and attention 199; of a culture 227s; made conscious 236; in history 248s; reflected in face 270; necessity for recognition of 273; crude and subtle 290 ; complementary 306; and physical body 344.
Future, what belongs to 267.

Galactic phenomena 101.
Galaxies 3, 4s, 9, 241s; universal sphere of 2; distance of 3s; form of 4.
Gas, interstellar 73.
Gases, rare 94, 129.
Gearing, between moon and sun 114.
Gemini, constellation of 11.
Genes 107.
Geological periods 129s, 167.
Geology 99; octaves in 129.
Germicides 194.
Gestation 156; of a culture 230.
Ghosts 118.
Giant, imagination of 198.
Gnat, perceptions of 132.
God 72, 74, 199, 214, 241s.
Gods, choice of 241.
Golden age 231.
Gonads 149.
Goods, money, man 50, 52.
Gospels xiii, 231, 236, 254.
Gratitude 291.
Greek culture 250s; tragedy 251, 274.
Growth, process of 53, 171s, 276-7; in sun 69, 72; and thymus 146; matters of 173, 184; slowing down 173; of mankind 248s.

Habit 112.
Habitation of the earth 127.
Halogens 98, 129.
Happenings 326.
Hardening agents 185.
Harmonics 290.
Harmonising role of sex 301, 305.
Hatha Yoga 236.
Head, structure of 268.
Healing, process of 56, 192s, 291, 306; psychic 117; substances of 185; necessity of 291.
Heart 150, 272; built-in pump 111; origin of human organism 139; weaknesses of 295.
Heaven 128; and hell 342.
Heavy water 187.
Hellenization 252.
Herbal medicine 185, 194.
Heredity 144, 163, 172.
Heroes, national 263; of our time 296.
Hierarchy, of school 317.
Hieroglyphs, invention of 247.
High Command 228.
Hindu chronology 28f.
Hinduism, Shiva, Parvati, Vishnu 49.
History, result of six processes 297; esoteric movements in 316.
Hæmophilism 163.

INDEX

INDEX

Knowledge, release of 314; of good and evil 327; new 336.
Koran 231, 236, 256.
Kushan civilisation 300.

Language xiis, 99; and functions xii; scientific xiv.
Law, Bode's 35, 285; of diffusion 127; Kepler's Third 23, 289.
Laws xiv; relating time and space 23; seen on different scales 45; and training of thought 238; for different states of matter 277.
Lead, atom of 92.
'Learning, the New' 257.
Lenses, planets seen as 46.
Lichens, on Mars 61.
Life, on subhuman level 106s; matter, form 53s, 171s
Lifetime 20, 24, 28, 30; cycle of experience 31.
Lifting effect, of moon 115.
Light, movement of 11; and consciousness 36, 39, 187; characteristic of suns 44, 67, 101; speed of 57, 99; matter into 62; and hydrogen 68s; waves 70; eternal and omnipresent 71; diffusion of 72, 101; and death 72; food for man 73; circulation of 86s, 221; intervention of 187; attempt to paint 267; and new age 267; vehicle like 344.
Line, plane and solid 5, 16, 20.
Linear space and duration 24.
Liquid phenomena 102.
Liquids and moon 109s.
Liver 147, 151, 161, 197.
Lives, all same length 34.
Lizard 197.
Local star system 14; ecliptic of 16.
Logarithmic scale, of life 156, 333, 343; of culture 230, 232; of earth 248.
Logarithms 256.
Loss of dimension 5.
Love 238, 291, 306, 309; at first sight 303.
Lunar age 248.
Lying 191s, 216.
Lymph 111; and moon 111; age of 248.

Madness 292, 321.
Magdalenian period 248.
Magic, and planets 242; agents of 187.
Magnetic fields, caused by electric current 42; strength of planetary 43, 81, 286; of sun-spots 67; variation of planetary 81.
Magnetic body 117; fixing of 118; at death 121.
Magnetism, speed of 44, 101, 121; and form 44; characteristic of planets 43, 77, 143; of sun 67; and moon 114s, 121; historical study 115; animal, planetary, terrestrial 116; and bloodstream 117.
Mahayugas 28f.
Mahogany, and moon clause 110.
Mammals 129.
Man, seven aspects 21 ; as nature, earth see him 21; units of time 26; contains all times 31 ; states of matter in 58; three foods 73; as cosmos 86; realm of 124; difference from animals 124; and universe 124; and ionosphere 128; age of 130; average and perfect 146; time of 155, 169; higher 197, 219, 230, 313, 316-7, 330, archetypal 203; his essence 205; imagination about himself 205, 207; of conscious spirit 219, 230, 233, 317, 327, 341; as god 243; his background 261; his illusion of doing 274; conscience of nature 277; modern 296; sexuality of 298; how he sees himself 320.
Mankind, cosmos 226; break in history of 246; solid of 341.
Manlike, what is? 124.
Mars, surface-speed and vegetation 61; and adrenals 163.
Martial tendencies, transmutation of 279.
Mass, of organs 90; astronomical 90; of moon and earth 109.
Mastery 280, 292.
Maternal instincts 290, 306.
Matter, speeds of 58; and spirit 92, 98; characteristic of different processes 173.

INDEX

Maturity 156.
Maya culture 233.
Measurability 99.
Mechanicalness, and moon 112.
Medicine 193s, 261, 291; medieval 193; modern 194, 261; and Chartres 256.
Medieval Christian culture 233, 255s; medicine 193; life 316.
Medium, in which worlds exist 16; of life 129.
Memorials 331.
Memory 215s; word- 152; not subject to time 216; loss of 216; destruction of 216; and negligence 217; revival of 217; of other lives 338-9.
Men, cells of civilisation 226s.
Mental function 181, 189.
Mercury, non-rotating 59; within zodiacal light 65; restless effect 82; and thyroid 161; and movement 268.
Mercurial age 248.
Mesmerism 117.
Mesmerists 240.
Mesoderm 139.
Metabolism 181; of animals 134; and parathyroids 148, 162.
Metallic change, speed of 102.
Metals, and composition of planets 42; octave of 85; rare 92; precious 96s; realm of 123; affinity for planets 142.
Meteorology 99.
Microbes, as gods 243.
Microcosm, creation of 315, 325.
Microphone 260.
Microscopic worlds 7.
Milky Way 4s, 8, 73, 78, 101; size of 10; centre of 11; units of time 28; age of 29s; as god 242; changing relation to 245.
Mind, logical xvi; higher xvi.
Mineral state of matter 58, 60, 98, 122; phenomena 103; realm 123, 128.
Miracles 337.
Model of the universe xis.
Modern civilisation 259s; origin of 266s.
Modification of the Absolute 1.
Molecular state of matter 57, 60s, 69, 72, 98, 170, 187, 194, 202, 209, 214, 275, 343-4; weights 105, 183s; motion, discovery of 194; body 200, 334, 344.
Molecule, units of time 26; and cell 105.
Monasteries 254s.
Monastic Christian culture 233, 254, 294.
Money, man, goods 50, 52.
Monkeys 130.
Monochord, cosmic 63.
Monuments, prehistoric 246.
Moon 108s; non-rotating 59; possibilities on 59; Greek legends 108; relative mass 109; distance 109; and tides 106; and liquids 110s; power over movement 111; escape from power of 113; and magnetism 115s; as earth's offspring 118s; temperature 118; unchanging 118; possibility of rotation 119; as unborn planet 120; and pancreas 147, 161.
Motive 237s.
Motor function 177.
Mountain-climbers 237.
Mountains 344.
Mouth 269.
Movement, in a new direction 20; and lymph 111; voluntary and involuntary 111; aimless 112; of types 222, 309, 326, 330; and time 260; mechanical and electromagnetic 261; and Mercury 268.
Murder 191, 291.
Muscular phenomena 102, 268; system 135.
Music 99; notation 78, 85, 96, 105, 176, 285; of the spheres 79; and Rheims 256.
Mysticism 237.

Names, for the same thing 99.
Narcotics 186.

Nation, the great 262.
Nature 122s; seven aspects 21; units of time 27; realms 122, 126s; as cosmos 126; as higher function of earth 126; in man 137; as god 242; man conscience of 277.
Nebulae, see Galaxies.
Neptune, cycle of 87, 312s; discovery of 312.
Nerve plexuses 141; and planetary influence 144.
Nervous system, elements for 97; speed of 102, 141, 153; phenomena 102; higher 124, 208, 319; threefold control 137, 152.
New Testament, see Gospels.
Nitrogen, as catalyst 104.
Nomad culture 229.
Nose 269.
Nucleus and satellites 108.
Nudity 298.
Nylon 184.

Obscuring layer 9.
Observation, necessity for 272.
Octaves, planetary 79, 285; meaning of 80s; of elements 95s ; between molecule and cell 107; cubing of 129; in geologic time 129; of digestion 176; of molecular weights 183; of cultures 245; modification of light 267; of orifices in the head 269.
Opacity and radiance 200.
Opinions, fixed 331.
Opportunity, great 282.
Opus dei 255.
Orbits, planetary 81.
Order, of forces 52s; of glandular secretion 151.
Orders, Roman Catholic Church 142.
Organs, and functions 47; of nature 47; as receiving-sets 83; free 134; healing of 194; intelligence of 195; of a cosmos 325.
Organic growth, invisible 87; chemistry 103s; compounds 105; liquids, and moon 110.
Organic life, on planets 61; octave of 85; elements of 97.
Orifices in head 269s.
Origin, of culture and religion 247.
Orphic mysteries 314.
Osmosis 102, 111.
Ovum, and solar system 91, 172; development of impregnated 171.
Oxygen, basis of organic matter 106; as shock 176.

Pacifism 281.
Pain 323; overcoming 236, 239.
Painting 234; Renaissance 258; pre-Raphaelite 267; Impressionist 267.
Palmistry 272.
Pancreas 139, 147, 161.
Papacy 254, 257.
Paper age 249.
Parthian culture 235.
Parasympathetic nervous system 137, 152.
Parathyroids 139, 148, 162, 274, 276, 306.
Passion 148, 163, 278.
Past, present and future 8; for cell 8, 19; of Milky Way 11; regeneration of 218, 264; man's participation in 235; what belongs to 267.
Peace 279.
Penicillin 261.
'People, the' 263.
Perceptions, actual as guide 21, 87; faster 25; moments of 31; minimum 32; of solar system 34; higher of the solar system 38; digestion of 178, 208.
Perfection, sex and 311.
Periodicity, of planets 77s.
Periods, of elements 95s, 127.
Peristalsis, speed of 102.
Persecution 328.
Persona 205.

INDEX

Races, and type 203; and castes 227; and cultures 244.
Radiance, of planets 77, 89, 160; and opacity 201.
Radiation, influence of 1; of galactic centre 13; of higher worlds 16; and quantum theory 70.
Radio 261, 295.
Radio-active elements 97, 127.
Radium 261.
Rancour 210.
Rebirth, of civilisations 229, 232, 259; of man 322, 335; of molecules and cells 334.
Recognition 33.
Reconstruction xxi, 259.
Recurrence 267, 334, 336s.
Red-shift 82f.
Reform 263.
Refinement, process of 55, 175s.
Regeneration, process of 56, 175, 197s, 202, 291, 312s, 329; agents of 185; of experience 199, 64; speed of 325.
Regrets 189.
Relativity, theory of 261.
Relationship, between worlds 7, 14; sense of 124; world of 201, 211; sexual 306, 309; husband, wife, child 339.
Religion 99 ; comparative 241; degeneration of 242; a new 265; broadening of 265; oriental in west 265.
Renaissance civilisation 232, 234, 249, 257s, 294.
Repetition 22s, 323, 338, 341, 346; of history 86.
Research, and fourth way 240.
Resonance 158.
Respiration, elements for 97; system 138.
Responsibility 108.
Revolution, French 257.
Rheumatic crystals 185, 188.
Ritual of school 325.
Roads, Roman 252.
Roman civilisation 231, 234, 252s; Empire 235; Catholic Church 143, 238; Emperor, as god 243.
Rotation, about vital centre 26; of planets 42, 160; and magnetism 43; possibility for moon 119.

Sagittarius, constellation 11.
Sankhya, three gunas 49.
Saros 114.
Satellites 108, 160, 289.
Saturn 71, 80s, 355.
Scale, effect of changed 273-4.
Scandinavian civilisation 229.
School, esoteric xi, 218, 230, 236, 238, 247, 279, 281, 313s; of fourth way 240; methods and tasks 240, 321; invisibility of 247; origin of 250; at Sais 250; Stoic 252; Epicurean 252, at Renaissance 258; at Rome 267; of archery 281; hidden 313; imitation 313; Neoplatonic 314; Rosicrucian 315; cathedral-builders 315; hierarchy 317; discipline 320; work of 325; an artificial cosmos 325; great performance of 326, 331; higher 327; neutralises crime 329; and civilisation 330.
Science, and killing 282.
Sciences, classification of xx.
Scientific theories, origin of xvi.
Scriptures 230, 315.
Sea-dogs 300.
Search xi, 313.
Seasons, shape of 166.
Secondary period 129.
Secrecy 314.
Self-consciousness 207, 210; of nations 262.
Self-development, of cosmoses 39.
Self-hypnosis 196.
Self-pity 210.
Self-preservation, and adrenals 148.
Self-purification 322, 324.

INDEX

Self-recognition, moment of 33.
Self-remembering xx, 179, 202, 207, 209s; new idea 212, 338; requirements of 213.
Sensations, memory of 218.
Separateness, in three dimensions 22.
Separation 59, 199s, 344.
Seven, and unity 89.
Sex, cell a cosmos 17; cell, life of 29; fluids, and moon 110; speed of 141, 303; and creation 149, 163, 177, 365, 301, combines with other functions 149, 300; substances 185, 210; and regeneration 199, 298 ; and atmospheric conditions 275; and dress 298; alternation of 299; as prize or gift 300; and higher consciousness 300; as harmonising element 301, 305; negative attitude towards 302; and scent 303; irrepressible 304; act 305; attraction and repulsion 306-7; and types 308; violence of 309; 'leader' in 310; illegitimate 310; and pretence 310.
Shock 327.
Signature, human 335.
Sirius 14s, 27, 73.
Six processes 53s, 104, 153; and planets 287, 297.
Six, dimensional world, 76, 342; movements of the face 272.
Sizes of creatures 24.
Skeletal system 138.
Skin 269.
Skin effect, electrical 115.
Social unit, growth of 262.
Society, rigid 227.
Solar plexus 139.
Solar System 7, 11; and blood-cell 7; orbit of 10; relation to other cosmoses 14; time, space, motion in 23; long body 35; as catherine wheel 35; rotation of 37; seen in its own time 38; forward speed 38; size 38; as transformer 14; growth of 69, and ovum 91; movement of 101; accidents in 246; and jovial system 289.
Solid, of light 90; of humanity 341.
Soul 103, 145, 201, 207, 225, 234, 241, 344; and other dimensions 219; of culture 236; birth of 209, 215, 237, 266, 316, 318, 322.
Sound, characteristic of earth 44; speed of 44, 58, 100, 101; for insects 132; waves, reproduction of 260.
Space, conquest of 259.
Speed, of living 25; of magnetic influence 44; of light 44, 57; of planets 82; of diffusion 99s and endocrine glands 140; of nervous impulses 153; of emotions 169.
Speeding up, of earth's time 130, 282.
Sphinx xii, 246.
Spinal column 124.
Spiral, motion of nebulae 4; of natural forms 139; of functions 139; 213, of lives 337, 343.
Spirit 103, 201, 344, 346.
Stars, distance of 12, 14.
States 226, 228.
Stealing 191.
Stone age 248s.
Strength, chief 113.
Suffering 322.
Suicide 291.
Sumerian culture 249.
Sun 63s; of our sun 14s; seven aspects 21; all man's possibilities in 21; units of time 28; age of 29, 69; earth, planets 51s; interior 63 ; surface and composition 64; temperature 65; spots 66, 101; magnetism 67; generation of energy 68s; relation to Milky Way and Absolute 73; relation to man 74; six-dimensional world 76; music for 80; as god 242.
Supergalactic phenomena 101.
Supersolar energy 100.
Supersonic motion 101.
Superstition 242, 257.
Surface-speed, of planets 61.
Sweating 189.
Symbols xiii; national 234.
Sympathetic nervous system 137, 152.
Sympathy 117.

INDEX

INDEX

INDEX OF PROPER NAMES

INDEX OF PROPER NAMES